PEARSON

ALWAYS LEARNING

W9-AUK-581

College Algebra

Fourth Edition

University of Texas at Arlington

Patricia P. Ellington
Department of Mathematics
University of Texas at Arlington

Pearson Learning Solutions, 501 Boylston Street, Suite 900, Boston, MA 02116
A Pearson Education Company
www.pearsoned.com

Printed in the United States of America

1 2 3 4 5 6 7 8 9 10 V031 17 16 15 14 13 12

000200010271660111

EEB

ISBN 10: 1-256-69424-X
ISBN 13: 978-1-256-69424-3

College Algebra

Geometry-Algebra Review

Triangle
> **Pythagorean Theorem:** $a^2 + b^2 = c^2$
> **Area:** $A = 1/2\, bh$

Square
> **Area:** $A = s^2$ **Perimeter:** $P = 4s$

Rectangle
> **Area:** $A = LW$ **Perimeter:** $P = 2L + 2W$

Parallelogram
> **Area:** $A = bh$

Rhombus
> **Perimeter:** $P = 4a$

Circle $(x-h)^2 + (y-k)^2 = r^2$ **with center (h,k) and r = radius**
> **Area:** $A = \pi r^2$ **Circumference:** $C = 2\pi r$ **or** $C = \pi d$
> **Diameter:** $D = 2r$

Midpoint $\left(\dfrac{x_1 + x_2}{2}, \dfrac{y_1 + y_2}{2} \right)$

Distance Formula: $d = \sqrt{(x_1 - x_2)^2 + (y_1 - y_2)^2}$

Variation
> Direct: $y = kx\,(k \neq 0)$
>
> Inverse: $y = \dfrac{k}{x}\,(k \neq 0)$
>
> Joint: $y = kxz\,(k \neq 0)$

Interval Notation
> $(a,b) = \{x \mid a < x < b\}$
>
> $[a, \infty) = \{x \mid x \geq a\}$

The <u>union</u> of two intervals is used to show that elements can be an element of either of two intervals. $(a,b) \bigcup (c,d)$

The <u>intersection</u> of two intervals is used to show that elements are common to both intervals. $(a,b) \bigcap (c,d)$

Equation Solving Tools

if $a = b \Rightarrow a + c = b + c$

if $a = b \Rightarrow ac = bc$

if $x^2 = k \Rightarrow x = \sqrt{k}$ or $x = -\sqrt{k}$

Subsets of Real Numbers

Natural numbers $= \{1, 2, 3, \ldots\}$

Whole numbers $= \{0, 1, 2, 3, \ldots\}$

Integers $= \{\ldots, -3, -2, -1, 0, 1, 2, 3, \ldots\}$

Rational $= \{\frac{a}{b} \mid a$ and b are integers with $b \neq 0\}$

Irrational $= \{x \mid x$ is not rational$\}$

Properties of Real Numbers

(with real numbers a, b, and c)

Commutative: $a + b = b + a;\quad a * b = b * a$

Associative: $(a + b) + c = a + (b + c);\quad (ab)c = a(bc)$

Distributive: $a(b + c) = ab + ac;\quad a(b - c) = ab - ac$

Identity: $a + 0 = a;\quad a * 1 = a$

Inverse: $a + (-a) = 0;\quad \dfrac{1}{a} * a = 1 \,(a \neq 0)$

Multiplication property of zero: $a * 0 = 0$

Absolute Value

$$|a| = \begin{cases} a & for\ a \geq 0 \\ -a & for\ a < 0 \end{cases}$$

Order of Operations

1. Evaluate within group symbols
2. Exponential expressions
3. Multiplication and division
4. Addition and subtraction

Exponent Rules

$a^{p+r} = a^p * a^r$ $\qquad\qquad \dfrac{a^p}{a^r} = a^{p-r}$

$(a^p)^r = a^{pr}$ $\qquad\qquad (ab)^r = a^r b^r$

$a^{-r} = \dfrac{1}{a^r}$ $\qquad\qquad \dfrac{1}{a^{-r}} = a^r$

$\left(\dfrac{a}{b}\right)^r = \dfrac{a^r}{b^r}$ $\qquad\qquad \left(\dfrac{a}{b}\right)^{-r} = \left(\dfrac{b}{a}\right)^r$

$$a^0 = 1 \qquad\qquad a^{-1} = \frac{1}{a}$$

Roots and Radicals

$$a^{1/n} = \sqrt[n]{a} \qquad\qquad a^{m/n} = (\sqrt[n]{a})^m = \sqrt[n]{a^m}$$

$$\sqrt[n]{ab} = \sqrt[n]{a} * \sqrt[n]{b} \qquad\qquad \sqrt[n]{\frac{a}{b}} = \frac{\sqrt[n]{a}}{\sqrt[n]{b}}$$

Factoring

$$a^2 + 2ab + b^2 = (a+b)^2$$
$$a^2 - 2ab + b^2 = (a-b)^2$$
$$a^2 - b^2 = (a+b)(a-b)$$
$$a^3 - b^3 = (a-b)(a^2 + ab + b^2)$$
$$a^3 + b^3 = (a+b)(a^2 - ab + b^2)$$
$$ax + bx + ay + by = x(a+b) + y(a+b) = (x+y)(a+b)$$

Rational Expressions

$$\frac{a}{b} + \frac{c}{b} = \frac{a+c}{b} \qquad\qquad \frac{a}{b} - \frac{c}{b} = \frac{a-c}{b}$$

$$\frac{ac}{bc} = \frac{a}{b} \qquad\qquad \frac{a}{b} + \frac{c}{d} = \frac{ad+bc}{bd}$$

$$\frac{a}{b} * \frac{c}{d} = \frac{ac}{bd} \qquad\qquad \frac{a}{b} \div \frac{c}{d} = \frac{a}{b} * \frac{d}{c}$$

If $\dfrac{a}{b} = \dfrac{c}{d}$ then $ad = bc$.

CHAPTER 1

Functions, Graphs and Math Models

Section 1.1 Functions

Functions

A function can be described as a relationship between an input number and an output number. Functions are commonplace in everyday life and show up in a variety of forms. A function can be represented as a set of ordered pairs, a graph, an equation or a table (which can be reduced to ordered pairs).

If we define some **relationship** using ordered pairs, we are showing a correspondence between the first and second coordinates of the ordered pairs. We can graph the ordered pairs and also see the relationship. An equation can be used to represent the correspondence.

An example of a function in equation form is

$$y = 5x$$

In this example y is a function of x because y is defined by values of x.

We call x the **independent variable** and y the **dependent variable**. Each time we replace x with a number we will find a unique value for y.

The various input values that we assign to x is called the **domain** of our function, and the possible resulting values of y is called the **range**.

For each member of the domain (often called elements) there is only one member of the range that corresponds to the given domain member.

Another way of describing a function is to say that **for each member of the domain (our input choices) there is a unique resulting member from the range (our output results).**

Function:

A function is a correspondence between one set, the domain, and a second set, the range, that assigns to each element of the domain only one element of the range (and every range value has a domain value).

Example 1: Which of the given correspondences is a function:

10

a. $2 \rightarrow 4$ $-8 \rightarrow 64$ $0 \rightarrow 0$
    $-2 \rightarrow 4$ $8 \rightarrow 64$

b. Christmas $\rightarrow$ December 25
    April Fools $\rightarrow$ April 1
    New Years Day $\rightarrow$ January 1
    Independence Day $\rightarrow$ July 4
    Thanksgiving $\rightarrow$ November 24
    Thanksgiving $\rightarrow$ November 28

c. Domain: Correspondence   Range
    real numbers   squared numbers   a subset of the
                                                  real numbers

d. Domain: Correspondence   Range
    all city names in US   in what state   all states in US

Solution:

a. This correspondence is a function because each number of the domain corresponds to only one number of the range. It is okay for two different members of the domain to correspond to the same range member.

b. This correspondence is not a function because Thanksgiving does not correspond to a unique element in the range.

c. This correspondence is a function because each real number has only one squared value.

d. This correspondence is not a function because a city name can be located in more than one state.

If a correspondence between two sets is not a function, it can be an example of a **relation**.

Relation:

> A **relation** is a correspondence between a first set, the **domain**, and a second set, the **range**, so that each member of the domain corresponds to **at least one** member of the range. (Domain members can correspond to several range members).

Notice: In Example 1 all of the correspondences are relations, but not all of them are functions.

Example 2: Which of the given relations is a function? Define the domain and range.

    a. (6, 3), (6, 4), (5, 8)
    b. (1, 2), (2, 3), (3, 4)
    c. (4, 2), (16, − 4), (5, 2)

Solution:

    a. Not a function because two different ordered pairs have the same first
        Coordinate (x-value) and different second coordinates (y-values).
        Domain: set of first coordinates: 6 and 5
        Range: set of second coordinates: 3, 4 and 8

    b. Is a function since no ordered pairs have the same first coordinate.
        Domain: set of first coordinates: 1, 2 and 3
        Range: set of second coordinates: 2, 3 and 4

    c. Is a function since no ordered pairs have the same first coordinate. Note that
        two different first coordinates may correspond to the same second coordinate.
        Domain: set of first coordinates: 4, 16 and 5
        Range: set of second coordinates: 2 and − 4

Functional Notation: We often see functions represented by equations. We perform calculations to determine the range value that corresponds with a given domain value.

If we are given the equation: $y = x^2 - 5x + 4$, we can input values for x (domain values) into the given equation and get values for y (range values).

    For $x = 1$ $y = (1)^2 - 5(1) + 4$ or $y = 0$

    For $x = 2$ $y = (2)^2 - 5(2) + 4$ or $y = -2$

    For $x = -1$ $y = (-1)^2 - 5(-1) + 4$ or $y = 10$

Using functional notation we will call the function f and we will use x to represent our input values and our output values we call $f(x)$. Most often functions have names of f, g or h. The term $f(x)$ is stated as "f of x" or "the value of f at x" or "f at x".

Changing to functional notation, the equation above would be described as:

    $f(x) = x^2 - 5x + 4$

Our results would be:

$$f(1) = (1)^2 - 5(1) + 4 \qquad \text{thus } f(1) = 0$$

$$f(2) = (2)^2 - 5(2) + 4 \qquad \text{thus } f(2) = -2$$

$$f(-1) = (-1)^2 - 5(-1) + 4 \qquad \text{thus } f(-1) = 10$$

Example 3: If $f(x) = 2x^2 - 2x + 4$, find each of the following:

    a. $f(-2)$ b. $f(0)$

    c $f(3b)$ d. $f(s + 2)$

Solution: Think of $f(x) = 2x^2 - 2x + 4$ as:

$$f(?) = 2(?)^2 - 2(?) + 4$$

We can replace the ? with any number we want.

    a. $f(-2) = 2(-2)^2 - 2(-2) + 4$ or $f(-2) = 16$

    b. $f(0) = 2(0)^2 - 2(0) + 4$ or $f(0) = 4$

    c. $f(3b) = 2(3b)^2 - 2(3b) + 4 = 2(9b^2) - 6b + 4 = 18b^2 - 6b + 4$

    d. $f(s + 2) = 2(s+2)^2 - 2(s+2) + 4$
                          $= 2(s^2 + 4s + 4) - 2s - 4 + 4$
                          $= 2s^2 + 8s + 8 - 2s$
                          $= 2s^2 + 6s + 8$

Example 3 can be solved using a graphing calculator. See Chapter 6, Example 1.

Graphs of Functions:

We can graph a function just like we graph equations. We find ordered pairs as $(x, f(x))$ and plot these points and then sketch the graph.

Example 4: Graph the following.
    a. $f(x) = x^2 - 4$
    b. $f(x) = x^3 - 3x$

Solution:

a. $f(x) = x^2 - 4$

Using points $(x, f(x))$, we will plot points and sketch the graph.

x	$f(x)$	$(x, f(x))$
-3	5	$(-3, 5)$
-2	0	$(-2, 0)$
-1	-3	$(-1, -3)$
0	-4	$(0, -4)$
1	-3	$(1, -3)$
2	0	$(2, 0)$
3	5	$(3, 5)$

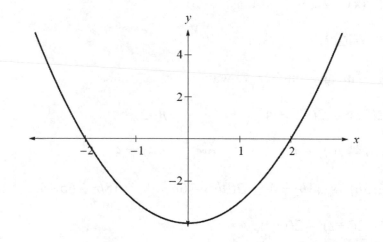

b. $f(x) = x^3 - 3x$: Make a table like above and plot the points:

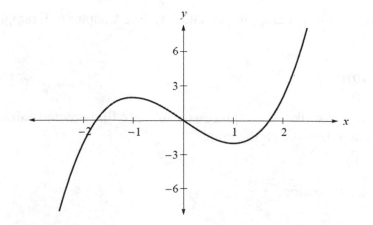

We can use a graphing calculator to check our graphs.

14

We can also find the value of a function by reading its graph.

To read a graph, locate an input value on the *x*-axis and then move up or down vertically to the graph, and then read the value of the graph at that point on the *y*-axis. Look at the last graph of $f(x) = x^3 - 3x$.

To find $f(-2)$ we can locate $x = -2$, move down to the function graph and then read the *y* value on the *y*-axis. We find that $f(-2) = -2$.

When we discussed the definition of a function we noted that each member in the domain can point to only one value in the range. Thus, each *x*-value can have only one *y*-value. If any *x*-values point to two *y*-values, we do not have a function. Note that two points with the same *x* coordinate would be vertically above/below each other. Keep this in mind as we study the vertical line test.

The Vertical-Line Test: This test can be used to determine if a relation is a function. The graph of a set of points is the graph of a function if every vertical line intersects the graph in, at most, one point.

The best way to use the vertical-line test is to try to find any vertical line that will cross the graph more than once. If none exists, then the graph represents a function. The definition states that every vertical line intersects the graph of a function in at most one point.

Example 5: Which of the graphs below is the graph of a function?

a.

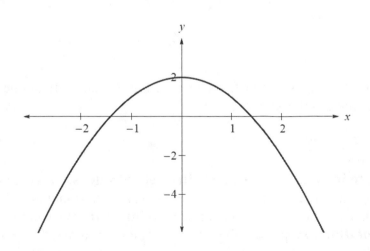

15

b.

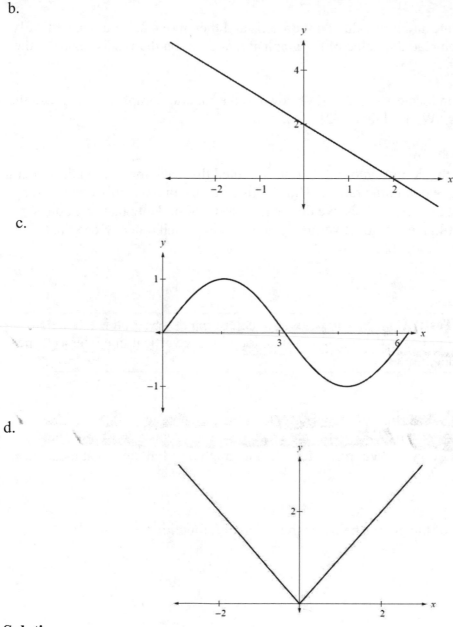

c.

d.

Solutions:

All graphs are graphs of functions because there is no vertical line that can be drawn that crosses the graph more than once.

Interval Notation:

Solutions to inequalities are most often <u>sets</u> of values. If we think about the solution set for the inequality $x > 4$, we see that the set would include all real numbers greater than 4. This solution set is an example if an **interval**. We can use a notation called **interval notation** to represent the interval. The interval for this example would be $(4, \infty)$. The symbol ∞ is not a real number, and the symbol represents infinity which helps us show that our interval includes all real numbers greater than 4. The interval

$(4, \infty)$ is an example of an **open interval**, since the endpoint, 4, is not part of the interval. Parentheses are used to describe open intervals, and square brackets are used to show that an endpoint is part of an interval.

Type of Interval	Set	Interval notation
Open	$x < a$	$(-\infty, a)$
Open	$x > b$	(b, ∞)
Open	$a < x < b$	(a, b)
Half open	$a < x \le b$	$(a, b]$
Half open	$a \le x < b$	$[a, b)$
Half open	$x \ge b$	$[b, \infty)$
Closed	$a \le x \le b$	$[a, b]$

You will encounter interval notation in many types of algebra problems.

Domain of a Function:

The domain of a function is the set of all numbers that can be input into the function, which will result in output results of real numbers. If a number is substituted into the function, and the result is not defined, then that number is not a part of the domain.

In many cases, we can simply remember that the **domain is the set of x-values** and the **range is the set of y-values.** These can be specific numbers, intervals, or the set of all real numbers.

Example 6: For each of the given functions find the function value and then determine if the value is in the domain:

a. $f(x) = \dfrac{1}{x - 4}$ find $f(2)$ and $f(4)$

b. $f(x) = \sqrt{x} - 14$ find $f(9)$ and $f(-4)$

Solution:

a. $f(2) = \dfrac{1}{-2} = -\dfrac{1}{2}$ this is a real number and so 2 is in the domain of f.

$f(4) = \dfrac{1}{0}$ this is not a real number since you cannot divide by zero so 4 is not in the domain of f.

b. $f(9) = \sqrt{x} - 14 = 3 - 14 = -11$ this result is a real number, and so 9 is in the domain of f.

$f(-4) = \sqrt{-4} - 14$ the result is not defined because we cannot take the square root of a negative number, so -4 is not in the domain of f.

17

Example 7. Find the domain of the following functions and write the answer using interval notation:

a. $f(x) = \dfrac{1}{x-2}$ notice that this is a fraction, so look for values that would make the denominator become zero

b. $f(x) = \dfrac{x^2-9}{x^2-4}$ this is a fraction, so what values give a denominator of zero?

c. $f(x) = x^2 - 4$

Solution:

   a. Since 2 will result in a denominator of zero, 2 cannot be in the domain. The domain is all real numbers except 2 and can be written as $(-\infty, 2) \cup (2, \infty)$. Use the union symbol to combine the 2 intervals into 1 answer.

   b. Since this is a fraction, we must look for values that make the denominator zero. Factoring the denominator gives $(x+2)(x-2)$. To find the values, set the factors equal to zero and solve. $x^2 - 4$ would be zero if x is 2 or -2. These two numbers are not in the domain of f.
The domain is $(-\infty, -2) \cup (-2, 2) \cup (2, \infty)$.

   c. This contains no fraction and no square root, so we can use any real number $(-\infty, \infty)$ and the function will be defined. Thus, the domain is all real numbers.

Finding the Domain and Range using a Graph:

We know that the domain is the set of all values that can be input into the function. These are x-values, and x-values are found along the x-axis of the graph.

The range is the set of all values that can be the output of the function. These are y-values and are found along the y-axis of the graph.

When we look at the graph of a function we can often determine the domain and range.

Example 8: Graph the given functions and see if you can determine the domain and range.

a. $f(x) = \dfrac{1}{x-3}$ b. $f(x) = x^3$ c. $f(x) = x^2 + 1$

18

Solutions

a.

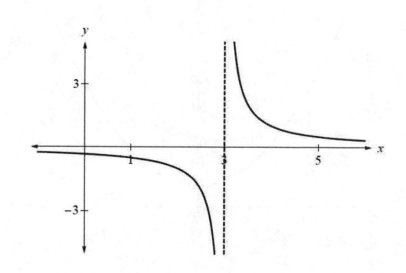

Domain = $(-\infty, 3) \cup (3, \infty)$
Range = $(-\infty, 0) \cup (0, \infty)$

b.

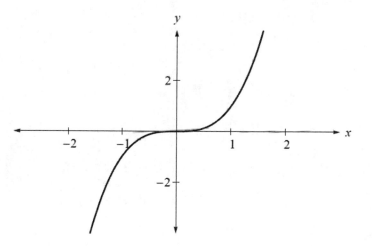

Domain = all real numbers $(-\infty, \infty)$
Range = all real numbers $(-\infty, \infty)$

c.

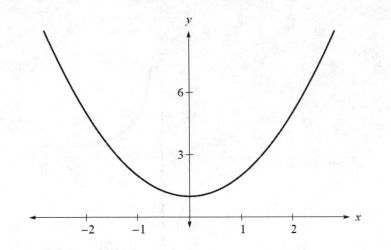

Domain = all real numbers $(-\infty, \infty)$
Range = $[1, \infty)$

Section 1.1 Exercises

In Exercises 1 − 12, is the correspondence a function?

1. $a \rightarrow p$
   $b \rightarrow s$
   $c \rightarrow t$

2. $p \rightarrow z$
   $r \rightarrow y$
   $s \rightarrow x$

3. $-4 \rightarrow 16$
   $-3 \rightarrow 9$
   $4 \rightarrow 16$

4. $3 \rightarrow 5$
   $2 \rightarrow 6$
   $1 \rightarrow 7$
   $1 \rightarrow 8$

5. $t \rightarrow A$
   $r \rightarrow C$
   $p \rightarrow E$
   $m \rightarrow C$

6. $p \rightarrow m$
   $q \rightarrow m$
   $r \rightarrow m$
   $s \rightarrow n$

Domain	Correspondence	Range
7. Set of seats in an arena	Each seat's row and number	A set of numbers and letters
8. Set of houses in one block	Each house's address number	A set of numbers
9. A set of family members	Each person's age	A set of numbers
10. A set of members of a basketball team	Each person's height	A set of numbers
11. A set of solid color cars in a garage	Each car's color	A set of colors
12. A set of class members	GPA of each student	A set of numbers

13. A graph of a function is shown. Find the indicated function values. $f(1), f(3),$ and $f(4)$.

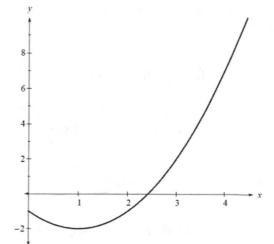

14. Find the indicated function values $g(-2)$, $g(0)$, and $g(4)$.

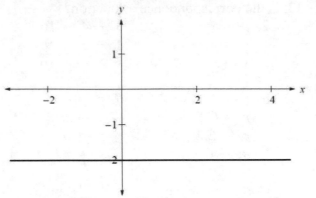

15   Find the indicated function values $t(-2)$, $t(0)$, and $t(1)$.

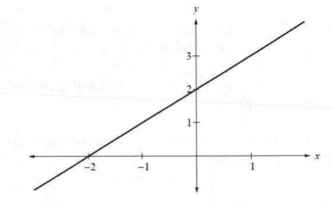

16. Given: $g(x) = 2x^2 + 3x - 4$, find each of the following:
    a) $g(0)$ b) $g(3)$ c) $g(-2)$ d) $g(-t)$

17. Given: $f(x) = x^2 + 3x$, find each of the following:
    a) $f(0)$ b) $f(-1)$ c) $f(5)$ d) $f(3m)$

18. Given: $h(x) = 2x^3$, find each of the following:
    a) $h(-2)$ b) $h(1)$ c) $h(p)$ d) $h(-y)$

19. Given: $s(x) = \dfrac{x+2}{x-1}$ find each of the following:

    a) $s(-2)$ b) $s(0)$ c) $s(1)$ d) $s\left(\frac{1}{3}\right)$

20. Given: $f(x) = \dfrac{x-3}{x}$ find each of the following:

    a) $f(3)$ b) $f(y+2)$ c) $f(0)$ d) $f(m^2)$

21. Given: $h(x) = |x| + 2$ find each of the following.
    a) $h(-2)$ b) $h(-3)$ c) $h(p)$ d) $h(0)$

22. Given: $f(x) = x^3 - x^2$ find each of the following:
    a) $f(-1)$ b) $f(-2)$ c) $f(3y)$ d) $f(\tfrac{1}{2})$

23. Given: $d(x) = 2x^2 + 3x - 4$ find each of the following:
    a) $d(2)$ b) $d(-1)$ c) $d(2m)$ d) $d(0)$

Find the domain of the given functions for problems $24 - 37$.

24. $f(x) = 5x + 2$

25. $f(x) = 2|4x - 3|$

26. $f(x) = 3 + \dfrac{4}{x}$

27. $f(x) = 0$

28. $f(x) = \dfrac{5.0}{3 - x}$

29. $f(x) = \dfrac{x + 8}{x^2}$

30. $f(x) = \dfrac{x^2 - 4}{x^2 - 9}$

31. $f(x) = x^3 + x^2$

32. $f(x) = \sqrt{4 - x}$

33. $f(x) = \dfrac{1}{3}|x|$

34. $f(x) = x^2 + 3$

35. $f(z) = \dfrac{\sqrt{x + 2}}{2x}$

36. $f(x) = \dfrac{x^2 - 3x + 2}{x^2 + x - 6}$

37. $f(x) = \sqrt{x^2 + 1}$

Sections 1.2 Linear Functions, Lines and Slope

Linear Functions:

A linear function is a function whose equation is a straight line.

A linear function is a function that can be transformed into:

$$f(x) = mx + b$$

(handwritten: slope, Y)

where x is any real number and m and b are constants.

A **constant function** is a function in the form $f(x) = mx + b$ where m equals zero. Thus a **constant function takes the form $f(x) = b$**.

The identity function is a function in the form $f(x) = mx + b$ where $m = 1$ and $b = 0$. The **identity function is written as $f(x) = x$.**

The graph of the identity function $f(x) = x$: *(handwritten: Y = X)*

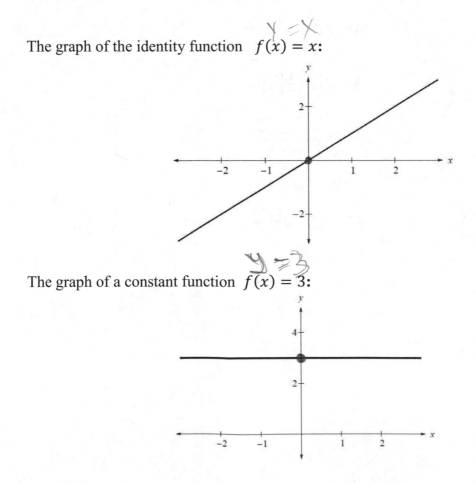

The graph of a constant function $f(x) = 3$: *(handwritten: y = 3)*

Horizontal Lines

1. Horizontal lines are parallel to the *x*-axis.
2. These lines are defined by an equation in the form: $y = b$.

Horizontal lines are functions and may be written as $f(x) = b$.

Vertical Lines

1. Vertical lines are parallel to the *y*-axis.
2. These lines are defined by an equation in the form: $x = a$.

Vertical lines are NOT functions.

Slope and Linear Functions:

When we discuss the slope of a line we are talking about the steepness of the line. Slope can be defined as a fraction. The numerator is the vertical change, called the rise of a line, and the denominator is the corresponding horizontal change, the run of a line.

Slope

The slope m of a line containing the distinct points $P_1(x_1, y_1)$ and $P_2(x_2, y_2)$ is given by:

$$m = \frac{change\ in\ y}{change\ in\ x}$$

$$= \frac{rise}{run}$$

$$= \frac{y_2 - y_1}{x_2 - x_1}$$

Example 1: Graph the function $f(x) = -\frac{5}{2}x + 4$ and find its slope.

Solution: The function is a linear function because it is given in linear form. We know that the graph is a straight line, and we only need two points to be able to draw the graph.

25

We can pick two different values for x, then get the corresponding y-value, and thus we have two points on the line.

$$f(0) = -\frac{5}{2}(0) + 4 = 4 \qquad \rightarrow \qquad \text{Point } (0,4)$$

$$f(2) = -\frac{5}{2}(2) + 4 = -1 \qquad \rightarrow \qquad \text{Point } (2, -1)$$

$$m = \frac{y_2 - y_1}{x_2 - x_1} = \frac{-1 - 4}{2 - 0} \rightarrow m = \frac{-5}{2} = -\frac{5}{2}$$

Graph the line using the two points and count the rise over run:

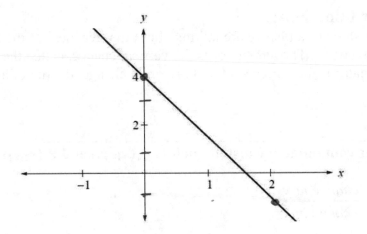

We could have chosen other points, and the slope would have been the same. Pick two more points and see if you find the same slope for the given function.

Notice that we calculated the slope to be $\frac{-5}{2}$ and that is the value of m in the equation:

$$m = -\frac{5}{2} \qquad \text{and} \qquad f(x) = -\frac{5}{2}x + 4.$$

Slope in a Linear Function

The function given by $f(x) = mx + b$
    has a slope of m.

General Rules for the Slope of a Line

General rules for the slope of a line:

   Vertical line → slope is undefined or has "no slope"

   Horizontal line → slope is zero

   A line that slants upward from left to right → positive slope

   A line that slants down from left to right→ negative slope

   The steeper a line is, the larger the absolute value of the slope will be

Remember that a slope of zero is not at all the same as "no slope". When we say "no slope" we mean that the slope cannot be calculated and is undefined.

Applications of Slope:

We find the use of slope in many real-world applications.

When driving in the mountains the steepness (or slope) of a road in the mountains are given in highway signs as grade so that drivers are aware of the rise or fall of the road and can reduce their gears if necessary. Signs that say 5% grade are stating that the road ahead will rise or fall 5 feet vertically for every 100 feet. Highway standards require that interstate or state highways have maximum limits for road grades.

A treadmill uses the same concept of steepness or slope. The walker on a treadmill will raise the slant of the treadmill in order to increase his heart rate and aerobic levels. Most treadmills have a grade (slope) of 0 which means the treadmill is flat and a grade up to 8 or 10 which is rather steep.

Access ramps for wheelchair use must adhere to standards of grade or slope. Laws state that the maximum steepness of these ramps cannot exceed 1 foot rise for every 12 feet of horizontal run. The slope defined by "rise over run" would be $\frac{1}{12}$.

Example 3: Sketch a line through point $P(0, -3)$ that has a slope of $\frac{4}{3}$.

Solution: An easy way to work this problem is to start by graphing the point $(0, -3)$ then we can obtain a second point by using the slope.

Move to the right using the denominator of m since that is the horizontal change.

Next we will either move up or down using the numerator:

If m is positive, we will move up.
If m is negative we will move down.

In this example we will move right 3 and up 4.

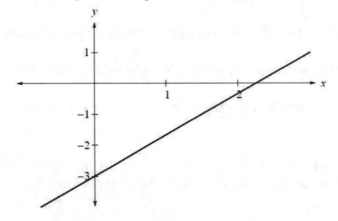

Example 4: Sketch a line when given the following:

a) through the point P(1, $\frac{7}{2}$) that has a slope of $m = 0$

b) through the point P(2, 3) with a slope that is undefined

Solution: Start with the given point and mark this point on the graph.

a) Since the slope is zero, we know that this will be a horizontal line. So, we draw a horizontal line at the given point.

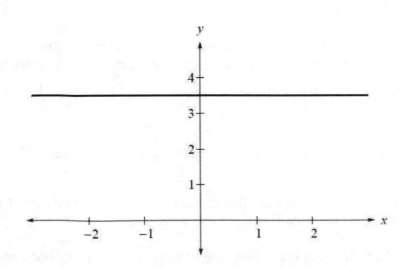

b) Since the slope is undefined, we know that the line will be a vertical line. Draw a vertical line at the given point.

c)

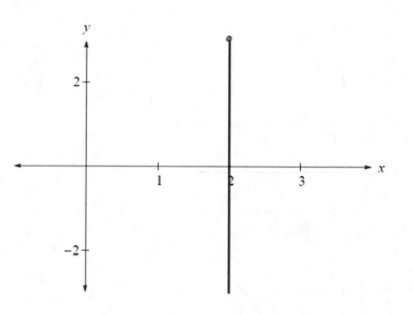

To Find Slope

The method you use to find the slope of a linear equation depends on what information you are given.

Given a graph → count rise over run

Given 2 points → use formula $m = \dfrac{y_2 - y_1}{x_2 - x_1}$

Given an equation → put into $y = mx+b$ form and then m = slope

Section 1.2 Exercises

Find the slope of the lines shown on the given graphs.
1.

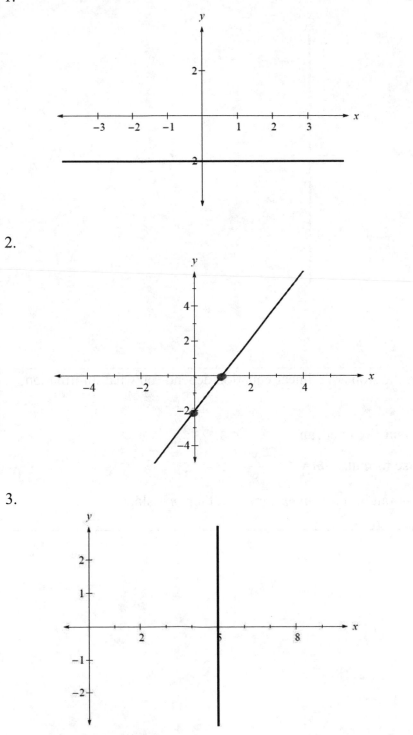

2.

3.

4.

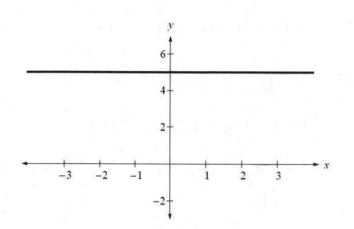

5.

6.

In problems 7 – 19 find the slope of the line when given 2 points.

7. (4, 1) and (-3, 2)

8. (-2, 5) and (-4,-5)

9. (-2,-1) and (-5,-9)

10. (0.4, 0.3) and (0.7, 0.4)

11. ($\frac{1}{3}$,$-\frac{1}{8}$) ; ($\frac{2}{3}$,$-\frac{7}{8}$)

12. (5.12, 3.14) and (0, 0)

13. (2, 6) and (3, 6)

14. (1,-4) and (1, 4)

15. (-2,-3) and (-1, 1)

16. (0, 0) and (1, 1)

17. (-9,-4) and (-9, 4)

18. (0, 0) and (-3,-4)

19. (4.5, 0) and (3.7, 1.3)

Graph the equation and find the slope for problems 20 - 31.

20. $y = -3x + 2$

21. $y = \frac{3}{2}x - 5$

22. $y = 4$

23. $x = 4$

24. $x + 2y = 8$

25. $2y - 4x = 6$

26. $y = 1.5x - 2$

27. $y = -\frac{1}{3}x + 3$

28. $x = -4$

29. $y = -\frac{2}{3}$

30. $2x - y = 4$

31. $x + \frac{1}{2}y = 3$

Section 1.3 Linear Equations

Slope-Intercept Form of an Equation:

The slope-intercept form of an equation is $y = mx + b$ with:
  slope = m
  y-intercept of (0, b)

The graph is a line.
Notice: slope is a number and does not contain a variable.

If we rewrite the equation of a line so that it is in slope-intercept form, we see that the slope m is the coefficient of x.

Example 1: What is the slope and y-intercept of the line with the equation:

$$y = \frac{2}{3}x + 14$$

Solution: Since the equation is in the form $y = mx + b$, we need only look at the equation and find the slope and y-intercept.

The coefficient of x is $\frac{2}{3}$ which is the slope.

The number 14 is the b term and gives us the y-intercept.

Since the y-intercept is the place where the graph crosses the y-axis, the value of x at this point is zero.

$$m = \frac{2}{3} \qquad y\text{-intercept} = (0, 14)$$

A linear equation is any equation whose graph is a straight line.

To find the slope of a line, we solve the equation for y. The equation is now in slope-intercept form, which is:

$$y = mx + b$$

the slope is m and the y-intercept is (0, b).

33

Example 2: What is the slope and *y*-intercept of the line with the equation?

$$4x - 2y = 5$$

Solution: Since we are given an equation, the method we can use to find the slope is to rewrite the equation in slope-intercept form. We do this by solving the given equation for *y*.

$4x - 2y = 5$	given equation
$-2y = -4x + 5$	subtract $4x$ from both sides
$y = 2x - 5/2$	divide both sides of the equation by -2

Reading the changed equation for *m* and *b*

the slope is 2   and   the *y*-intercept is $(0, -\frac{5}{2})$.

We can write the equation of a line if we know the slope and *y*-intercept.

Example 3: Find the equation of a line given a slope of $\frac{3}{4}$ and *y*-intercept of $(0, 6)$.

Solution: We will use the slope-intercept form to write the equation.

Use $\frac{3}{4}$ as *m* and 6 as *b*.

$$y = mx + b$$
$$y = \frac{3}{4}x + 6$$

Example 4: Find the equation of a line with slope of $-\frac{1}{3}$ containing the point $(-6, 3)$.

Solution: Notice that this problem did not give the *y*-intercept. Use the slope-intercept form to find the equation, and then we will use the slope and point to find the *y*-intercept:

$y = mx + b$ Slope-intercept form of equation

$y = -\frac{1}{3}x + b$ Next, use the given point for *x* and *y* to find *b*.

$3 = (-\frac{1}{3})(-6) + b$ Now we solve for *b*.

$3 = 2 + b$
$b = 1$

The equation of the line is $y = -\frac{1}{3}x + 1$.

We can also graph linear equations if we know the slope and y-intercept.

Example 5: Graph the equation:

$$y = \frac{2}{3}x - 2$$

Solution: Since the equation is in slope-intercept form, we know that the slope is $\frac{2}{3}$ and the y-intercept is $(0, -2)$.

First plot the y-intercept.

Next use the slope, and remember that slope is $\dfrac{rise}{run}$.

Our denominator tells how many units to move horizontally to the right from the y-intercept, and then count up or down the number of units in the numerator.

If the slope is positive, count up; and if the slope is negative, count down.

Beginning at the y-intercept $(0, -2)$, count right 3 and up 2 to a second point.

The new point is $(3, 0)$.

Now draw the line between $(0, -2)$ and $(3, 0)$.

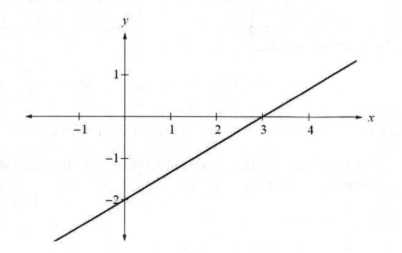

Point-Slope Equation of a Line:

The point-slope equation of a line is most often used to find the equation of a line (or write the equation of a line).

Point-Slope Equation: An equation for the line through the point (x_1, y_1) with slope m is:

$$y - y_1 = m(x - x_1)$$

This equation is very important because it can be used to WRITE EQUATIONS OF LINES.

If we know the slope of a line and one point that the line passes through, we can write the equation of the line using the point-slope equation.

Example 6: What is the equation of a line passing through the points (1, 2) and (2, 6)?

Solution: When asked for the equation of a line, we find it using the point-slope equation. We begin by finding the slope using the slope formulas given 2 points.

$$m = \frac{y_2 - y_1}{x_2 - x_1} = \frac{6-2}{2-1} = 4$$

Now use the point-slope equation with $m = 4$ and one of the points. Use (x, y) as the other point:

$$y - y_1 = 4(x - x_1)$$
$$y - 2 = 4(x - 1)$$
$$y - 2 = 4x - 4$$
$$y = 4x - 2$$

Parallel Lines:

Parallel Lines:

Non-vertical lines are parallel, if and only, if they have the same slopes but different y-intercepts.

Vertical lines are parallel.

36

Parallel lines do not ever intersect as they have identical slopes, but different y-intercepts.
Lines such as $x = 2$ and $x = 5$ are both vertical lines and thus are parallel.

Two non-vertical lines that have the same slope but different y-intercepts are parallel also. For example:

$y = 3x + 4$ and $y = 3x + 7$ are two lines that have the same slope of 3.

These lines have different y-intercepts. These two lines are parallel lines.

Example 7: Write the equation of a line that is parallel to the graph of the line $2y - 4x = 8$ and contains the point (3, 2).

Solution: In order to write the equation of a line, use the point-slope equation

$$y - y_1 = m(x - x_1).$$

To use this equation, we need to have a slope for our new line and a point on our line.

We have the given point, but we do not have the slope. However, we can find it.

If we find the slope of the given line, we will find the slope of the new line. Since our line is parallel to the given line, our new line will have the same slope.

First transform the equation of the given line into slope-intercept form to get the slope. Solve for y:

$$2y - 4x = 8$$
$$2y = 4x + 8$$
$$y = 2x + 4$$

The slope of this line is 2 and we will use the slope of 2 with the point (3, 2).

$$y - y_1 = m(x - x_1)$$

$$y - 2 = 2(x - 3)$$

$$y - 2 = 2x - 6$$

$$y = 2x - 4$$

Perpendicular Lines:

> **Perpendicular Lines:**
>
> Two lines are perpendicular if one is a horizontal line $y = a$ and the other is a vertical line $x = b$.
>
> Two lines with slope m_1 and m_2 are perpendicular, if and only if,
>
> $m_1 m_2 = -1$
>
> The graph of two perpendicular lines will intersect at right angles.
>
> **A horizontal line is perpendicular to a vertical line.**

From this definition we see that perpendicular lines have **slopes that are opposite reciprocals**. If one line has a slope of 2 and a second line has a slope of $-\frac{1}{2}$ then the lines are perpendicular lines since $(2)\left(-\frac{1}{2}\right) = -1$.

Example 8: Determine whether the following pairs of lines are parallel, perpendicular, or neither:

a) $y + 3 = 6x$ and $2y - 12x = 4$ 　　　　b) $y + 1 = 2x$ and $2y + x = 3$
c) $y + 2x = 4$ and $2x = 5 + 2y$

Solution: Determine if the lines are perpendicular, parallel, or neither by looking at the slopes of each set of lines

a) The slope-intercept form of the two equations are: $y = 6x - 3$ and $y = 6x + 2$. Both lines have slope of 6 with different y-intercepts. These two lines are parallel.

b) The slope-intercept forms of these equations are: $y = 2x - 1$ and $y = -\frac{1}{2}x + \frac{3}{2}$. One line has slope of 2, and the other has slope of $-\frac{1}{2}$. The product of these two slopes is -1, and these lines are perpendicular.

c) The slope-intercept forms of these equations are: $y = -2x + 4$ and $y = x - \frac{5}{2}$. The lines have slopes of -2 and 1. The lines do not have the same slope and the product of the two slopes is not equal to -1. These lines are neither parallel nor perpendicular.

Example 9: Write the equation of a line that is perpendicular to the graph of the line $3y - x = 9$ and contains the point (4, 1).

Solution: In order to write the equation of a line, use the point-slope equation $y - y_1 = m(x - x_1)$.

To use this equation, we will need the slope of our line and a point on our line. We have the given point, but we do not have the slope.

Find the slope of the line that is given, and since our line is perpendicular to the given line, we take the opposite reciprocal of the given line's slope and use the result for our new line. First transform the equation into slope-intercept form to find the slope.

Solve the equation $3y - x = 9$ for y:

$$3y = x + 9 \qquad \text{Add } x \text{ to both sides}$$

$$y = \frac{1}{3}x + 3 \qquad \text{Divide both sides by 3}$$

The equation is in the slope-intercept form $y = mx + b$, and the slope is the coefficient of x. The slope of the given line is $\frac{1}{3}$.

Our slope will be the opposite reciprocal which is -3 and our point is (4,1).

$$y - y_1 = m(x - x_1)$$
$$y - 1 = -3(x - 4)$$
$$y - 1 = -3x + 12$$
$$y = -3x + 13$$

Line/Slope Information:

To find slope:	$m = \dfrac{y_2 - y_1}{x_2 - x_1}$	Use if given 2 points.
	$m = \dfrac{rise}{run}$	Use to count a graph.
	$y = mx + b$	Use this form to find slope of a given line.

To write the equation of a line:

$$y - y_1 = m(x - x_1)$$

Horizontal line:	$y = b$
Vertical line:	$x = a$
Parallel lines:	Same slope
Perpendicular lines:	Slopes are opposite reciprocals.

Mathematical Models:

Mathematical models can be used to give a mathematical description of a real-world situation, and these models are used to help predict what will happen in real-world situations. Often these models are graphs or equations.

Steps used with mathematical models are:

1. Define a real-world problem.
2. Collect data.
3. Plot this collected data.
4. Construct a model that best represents the data.
5. Use the model to predict a real-world outcome.

If the predictions turn out to be incorrect, the model must be changed or discarded. Many models are continuously being revised. For example, a mathematical model that gives an accurate prediction of length of life is changing frequently as medical treatments and medicines improve life expectancy.

Linear functions can sometimes be used as mathematical models. We try to find a function that represents, with the greatest accuracy, data from experimentation and observation, reasoning, and common sense. When we plot data, we see what is called a **scatterplot.** Then we try to find the equation of a line that best fits the data.

Linear Regression

> **Linear Regression:**
> **a process that finds the equation of a line of *best fit* from given data. The linear regression line is a unique line that best describes the behavior of data.**

Calculators are used to find a linear regression for a given set of data. See Chapter 6, Example 2 for an example of finding a linear regression.

Section 1.3 Exercises

Find the slope and the *y*-intercept of the given equations:

1. $y = \dfrac{2}{5}x - 5$

2. $f(x) = -x + 4$

3. $y = \dfrac{3}{4}$

4. $x = -\dfrac{2}{3}$

5. $f(x) = 7 - \dfrac{1}{2}x$

6. $y = 4 - \dfrac{2}{9}x$

7. $2x + 3y = 12$

8. $3x - 2y = 18$

9. $y = 3$

10. $x = 8$

11. $4x + 5y = 12$

12. $3x - 5y + 10 = 0$

Graph the given line using the slope and intercept method and the given equation:

13. $y = \dfrac{1}{4}x - 1$

14. $y = \dfrac{2}{3}x + 1$

15. $f(x) = 4x - 1$

16. $f(x) = -3x + 5$

17. $2x - 4y = 8$

18. $3x + 2y = -3$

19. $x + 3y = 15$

20. $4y - 6x = -4$

Write the equation of a line in slope-intercept form using the given.

21. $m = 4$, *y*-intercept (0, 3)

22. $m = -\dfrac{2}{3}$, *y*-intercept (0, 2)

23. $m = -3$, *y*-intercept (0, 4)

24. $m = \dfrac{2}{9}$, *y*-intercept (0, 5)

25. $m = -3.5$, *y*-intercept $(0, -2)$

26. $m = \dfrac{2}{5}$, contains $(3, -2)$

27. $m = -\dfrac{2}{3}$, contains (4, 3)

28. $m = 2$, contains $(1, -3)$

29. $m = -3$, contains $(-2, 3)$

30. $m = -\dfrac{3}{4}$, contains $(-1, -2)$

31. contains $(-1, 3)$ and $(2, 5)$

32. contains $(2, 0)$ and $(5, 7)$

33. contains $(6, 1)$ and $(-1, 4)$

34. Contains $(-2, 2)$ and $(-1, 3)$

35. Contains $(0, 5)$ and $(2, 3)$

36. Contains $(-3, 0)$ and $(0, 1)$

Write equations of the horizontal and vertical lines that pass through the given point.

37. $(0, -2)$ 38. $\left(-\dfrac{4}{5}, 1\right)$

39. $(1, 2)$ 40. $(0, 0)$

Are the pairs of lines parallel, perpendicular or neither?

41. $y = \dfrac{2}{3}x - 5$ 42. $y = \dfrac{3}{4}x - 5$

$\quad\quad y = -\dfrac{2}{3}x + 5$ $y = 7 + .75x$

43. $y = -\dfrac{1}{4}x$ 44. $2x - 4y = -2$

$\quad\quad y = -4x + 2$ $2x + 4y = 3$

45. $y = 4x - 6$ 46. $y = 4 - x$

$\quad\quad 4y = 8 - x$ $y = x + 6$

Write two equations in slope-intercept form for a line passing through the given point. One line is parallel to the given line, and the other is perpendicular to the given line.

47. $(-1, 4)$ $f(x) = 2x + 5$

48. $(3, 5)$ $y = \dfrac{2}{3}x + 2$

49. $(-3, -1)$ $2x + y = 6$

50. $(4, 2)$ $y = 2.4(x - 2) + 1$

51. $(3, -2)$ $x = -1$

52. $(3, -2)$ $y = -1$

True or false?

53. The lines $x = -2$ and $y = 4$ are perpendicular.

54. The lines $y = 3x + 4$ and $y = -3x + 5$ are parallel.

55. The lines $x = -1$ and $x = 1$ are perpendicular.

56. The lines $y = 2x + 4$ and $y = 2x - 4$ are perpendicular.

Section 1.4 Additional Functions

Increasing, Decreasing and Constant Functions

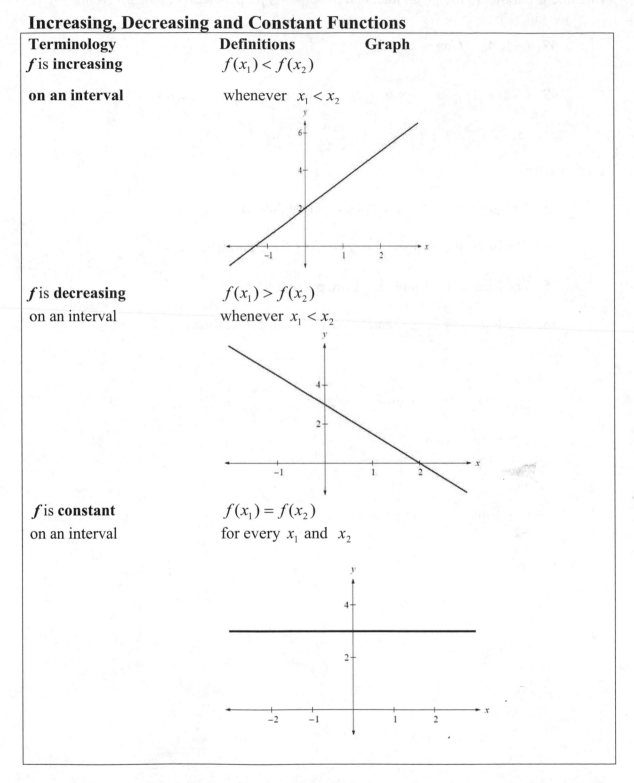

Terminology	Definitions	Graph
f is **increasing** on an interval	$f(x_1) < f(x_2)$ whenever $x_1 < x_2$	
f is **decreasing** on an interval	$f(x_1) > f(x_2)$ whenever $x_1 < x_2$	
f is **constant** on an interval	$f(x_1) = f(x_2)$ for every x_1 and x_2	

An example of an increasing function is any line with a positive slope and an example of a decreasing function is any line with a negative slope. An example of a constant function is $f(x) = c$ which is a horizontal line and has a slope of zero.

44

Example 1: Determine the intervals on which the function in the given figure is

     a. increasing   b. decreasing   c. constant

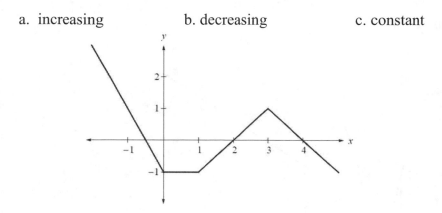

Solution:

   Slope cannot be both positive and negative at a point at the same time, so a function cannot be both increasing and decreasing at any one point. Thus we must use open intervals that do not contain the point where functions turn to express increasing and decreasing functions. The x-values are **always** used to define our intervals. We will look for intervals where the y-values are changing.

     a. For x-values (domain values) from $x = 1$ to $x = 3$, the y-values (range values) are increasing. The function is increasing on the interval (1, 3).

     b. For x-values from -2 to 0, y-values are decreasing; y-values also decrease for x-values from 3 to 5. The function is decreasing on the intervals $(-2, 0)$ and (3, 5).

     c. For x-values from 0 to 1 the value of y is constant. The function is constant on the interval (0, 1).

Curves:

Curves do not have slopes, but you will learn later that the slope of a line tangent to the graph of a curve, at a point, is used to determine if a function is increasing, decreasing, or constant at the point.

If the slope is found to be positive at a point, the function is increasing at that point; if the slope is found to be negative, the function is decreasing at that point.

Relative Maximum and Minimum Values.

Look at the graph below.

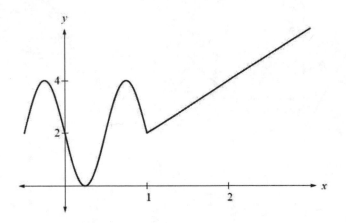

The graph has "highs" and "lows" at different *x*-values.

The values of the given function at $f(-0.25)$ and $f(0.75)$ are called **relative maxima (the plural of maximum is maxima).**

The value of the function at the point $f(0.25)$ is called a **relative minima (the plural of minimum is minima).**

Relative Maxima and Minima

Given a function *f(x)* and some *c*-value in the domain of *f*.

Then:
    f(c) is a relative maximum value if there exists an open interval I containing c
        such that $f(c) \geq f(x)$, for every *x* in I; and

    f(c) is a relative minimum if there exists an open interval I containing c
        such that $f(c) \leq f(x)$, for every *x* in I.

An easy way to think of relative maxima and minima is:
    If *f(c)* is the highest point in some open interval, there is a relative maximum at *c*.
    If *f(c)* is the lowest point in some open interval, there is a relative minimum at *c*.

In order to find relative maxima and minima in an algebra course a graphing calculator can be used. See Chapter 6, Example 3 for such a problem.

More Models of Functions:

Example 2: Two buses leave the same location at the same time. One travels East at a speed of 55 mph and the other travels North at a speed of 60 mph. Express the distance between the two buses as a function of time.

Solution: The easiest way to look at this problem is to draw a picture of the buses after a certain time like 2 hours.

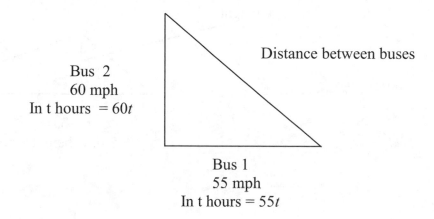

Bus 2
60 mph
In t hours $= 60t$

Distance between buses

Bus 1
55 mph
In t hours $= 55t$

We can find the distance that each bus travels by multiplying the mph of each by the number of hours each travels.

Bus 1 would travel a distance of 55 mph times 2 hours which is 110 miles.

Bus 2 would travel a distance of 60 mph times 2 hours which is 120 miles.

If we draw a diagram of the buses, the figure is a right triangle, so the Pythagorean Theorem will give the distance between them. From this theorem we know that the square of the hypotenuse equals the sum of the squares of the two legs: $a^2 + b^2 = c^2$.

We will define the distance of Bus 1 as $55t$ where t is any amount of time and the distance of Bus 2 will be $60t$.

The function can be represented as:

$$[d(t)]^2 = (55t)^2 + (60t)^2$$

$$d(t) = \sqrt{3025t^2 + 3600t^2} \quad = \quad \sqrt{6625t^2} \ = \ 81.39t$$

Since distance is never a negative number, we only use the positive root.

Example 3: A family has a small triangular plot of ground to use for a garden. The base of the triangle to be used must be 3 times as long as the height of the triangle.

Define the area of the garden plot as a function of the height.

Solution: First draw a picture of the garden plot.

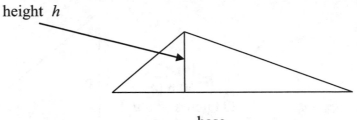

height h

base
3 time height $= 3h$

Remember that the area of a triangle is found by: Area $= \dfrac{1}{2}$ base times height.

The area function becomes:

$$A(h) = \frac{1}{2}(3h)(h)$$

$$= \frac{3}{2}h^2 \ .$$

Section 1.4 Exercises:

Determine the intervals on which the function is increasing, decreasing and constant. Estimate any relative maxima or minima of the function.

1. $f(x) = x^2$ 2 $f(x) = x^2 + 2$

3. $f(x) = x^2 - 3$ 4. $f(x) = 4x$

5. $f(x) = 3$ 6. $f(x) = |x|$

7. $f(x) = 2x + 1$ 8. $f(x) = -2x + 1$

9. $f(x) = |x| + 2$ 10. $f(x) = -|x|$

11. The Smiths have 100 feet of fencing with which to enclose a rectangular flower bed. If the bed is x feet long, express the bed's area as a function of the length.

12. A soccer team is designing a triangular flag for their games. The length of the base is 5 inches more that the height, h. Express the area of the flag as a function of the height.

13. An airplane is preparing to land at the local airport. The airplane's altitude is 5000ft. The slant distance from the plane to the airport is d feet. Express the horizontal distance h as a function of d.

14. A pool company is designing a rectangular pool. If the perimeter of the pool is 160 feet, and the length of the pool is x feet long, express the area of the pool as a function of the length.

15. A farmer has 400 yards of fencing to enclose a rectangular plot. If the width of the plot is w, express the area of the plot as a function of w.

Section 1.5 Function Algebra

In this section we will add, subtract, multiply and divide functions and obtain new functions.

Sums, Differences, Products and Quotients:

If $f(x) = x + 3$ and $g(x) = x^2$ then

$\quad f(2) = 2 + 3 = 5$ and $g(2) = 4$

$\quad f(2) + g(2) = 5 + 4 = 9$

$\quad f(2) - g(2) = 5 - 4 = 1$

$\quad f(2) * g(2) = 5 * 4 = 20$

$\quad$ and

$$\frac{f(2)}{g(2)} = \frac{5}{4}$$

Any sum, difference, product and quotient of $f(x)$ and $g(x)$ may be calculated as long as x is in the domain of **both** f and g and $g(x) \neq 0$ in the quotient $\dfrac{f(x)}{g(x)}$.

Sums, Differences, Products and Quotients of Functions

If f and g are functions and x is in the domain of both functions, then

$\quad (f + g)(x) = f(x) + g(x)$

$\quad (f - g)(x) = f(x) - g(x)$

$\quad (fg)(x) = f(x) * g(x)$

$\quad \dfrac{f}{g}(x) = \dfrac{f(x)}{g(x)}, \; g(x) \neq 0.$

Example 1: Given that $f(x) = x+2$ and $g(x) = \sqrt{x+1}$.

Find   a. $(f+g)(x)$

       b. $(f+g)(4)$

       c. $(f+g)(-3)$

Solution:

    a. $(f+g)(x) = f(x) + g(x)$

$$= x+2+\sqrt{x+1}$$

    b. $f(4) = 4+2 = 6$ and $g(4) = \sqrt{4+1} = \sqrt{5}$

$(f+g)(4) = f(4) + g(4)$

$$= 6 + \sqrt{5}$$

    c. $f(-3) = -3 + 2 = -1$ and $g(-3) = \sqrt{-3+1} = \sqrt{-2}$ and is not a real number.

From our examination of $g(x)$ we realize that -3 is not in the domain of $g(x)$.
Thus, $(f+g)(-3)$ does not exist.

Domain of sum, difference, product:

The domain of $(f+g)(x)$, $(f-g)(x)$ and $(fg)(x)$ is the intersection of the domains of the functions f and g.

The intersection of two domains is the set of numbers that is in both domains.

Example 2: Given that $f(x) = x^2 - 9$ and $g(x) = x+3$, find:

    a. the domain of $(f+g)(x)$, $(f-g)(x)$, $(fg)(x)$ and $\dfrac{f}{g}(x)$

    b. $(f+g)(x)$ c. $(f-g)(x)$

    d. $(fg)(x)$ e. $\dfrac{f}{g}(x)$ f. $(gg)(x)$

Solution:

a. The domain of f is the set of all real numbers $(-\infty, \infty)$.

The domain of g is also the set of all real numbers $(-\infty, \infty)$.

The domain of $f+g$, $f-g$ and fg is the intersection of the domains of f and g. It is the set of numbers that are in **both** domains and for this example is the set of all real numbers.

The domain of $\frac{f}{g}$ is also the intersection but it also must not include any numbers that would make the function g equal zero.

If $g(x) = x+3$, then $g(-3)$ would result in a denominator of zero.

Thus the domain must exclude -3 and is written in interval form as $(-\infty,-3)\cup(-3,\infty)$.

   b. $(f+g)(x) = f(x)+g(x) = (x^2-9)+(x+3) = x^2+x-6$

   c. $(f-g)(x) = f(x)-g(x) = (x^2-9)-(x+3) = x^2-x-12$

   d. $(f*g)(x) = f(x)*g(x) = (x^2-9)(x+3) = x^3+3x^2-9x-27$

   e. $(f/g)(x) = \dfrac{f(x)}{g(x)} = \dfrac{x^2-9}{x+3} = \dfrac{(x+3)(x-3)}{x+3} = x-3, x \neq -3$

   f. $(gg)(x) = g(x)*g(x) = (x+3)^2 = x^2+6x+9$

Difference Quotient:

The Difference Quotient (or the average rate of change) is used often in the study of calculus, and it is important to be able to find and simplify this quotient.

The Difference Quotient is defined as:
$\dfrac{f(x+h)-f(x)}{h}$ or $\dfrac{f(a+h)-f(a)}{h}$

Example 3: For the function $f(x) = x^2-2x-8$, find the difference quotient $\dfrac{f(x+h)-f(x)}{h}$.

Solution:
First we will find $f(x+h)$. We will replace x with $x+h$ in the given function.

$$\begin{aligned} f(x+h) &= (x+h)^2 - 2(x+h) - 8 \\ &= (x^2+2xh+h^2) - 2x - 2h - 8 \\ &= x^2+2xh+h^2 - 2x - 2h - 8 \end{aligned}$$

Now we will evaluate the Difference Quotient:

$$\frac{f(x+h)-f(x)}{h} =$$

$$= \frac{(x^2+2xh+h^2-2x-2h-8)-(x^2-2x-8)}{h}$$

$$= \frac{2xh-2h+h^2}{h} \quad \textit{combine like terms}$$

$$= \frac{h(2x-2+h)}{h} \quad \textit{factor}$$

$$= 2x-2+h \quad \textit{reduce}$$

Composite Functions:

The **Composite Function** $f \circ g(x)$ of two functions f and g is defined by

$$f \circ g(x) = f(g(x)).$$

The domain of $f \circ g$ is the set of all x in the domain of g such that $g(x)$ is in the domain of f.

Example 4: Given $f(x)=3x-4$ and $g(x)=x^2-2x+6$. Find the following.

    a. $(f \circ g)(x)$ b. $(g \circ f)(x)$

    c. $(f \circ g)(5)$ d. $(g \circ f)(5)$

Solution:

    a. $(f \circ g)(x) = f(g(x))$ We will substitute $g(x)$ for x in $f(x)$.

$$= 3(x^2-2x+6)-4$$

$$= 3x^2-6x+18-4$$

$$= 3x^2-6x+14$$

b. $(g \circ f)(x) = g(f(x))$ we will substitute $f(x)$ for x in $g(x)$

$$= (3x-4)^2 - 2(3x-4) + 6$$

$$= 9x^2 - 24x + 16 - 6x + 8 + 6$$

$$= 9x^2 - 30x + 30$$

c. $(f \circ g)(5) = f(g(5)) = f(5^2 - 2*5 + 6)$

$$= f(21) = 3(21) - 4 = -4 + 63$$
$$= 59$$

d. $(g \circ f)(5) =$
$$g(f(5)) = g(3*5 - 4)$$

$$= g(11) = 11^2 - 2*11 + 6$$

$$= 105$$

A graphing calculator can be used to check both c and d. See Chapter 6, Example 4.

Note:

$$\underline{f(g(x)) \neq g(f(x))}$$

except in special cases when the two functions are inverses of one another.

Example 5: If $f(x) = 2x - 4$ and $g(x) = \sqrt{x}$, find the following.

a. $(f \circ g)(x)$ b. $(g \circ f)(x)$

c. find the domain of $f \circ g$ and $g \circ f$

Solution:

a. $(f \circ g)(x) = f(g(x)) = 2\sqrt{x} - 4$

b. $(g \circ f)(x) = g(f(x)) = \sqrt{2x - 4}$

c. We can see that the domain of f is $(-\infty, \infty)$ and the domain of g is $[0, \infty)$. To find the domain of $f \circ g$, look first at the domain of g which is $x \geq 0$. The output from these numbers will be within the domain of f. Since f can input any real number, then any output that comes from g will be okay. Thus all of the domain of g can be input. Thus, the domain of $f \circ g$ is $[0, \infty)$.

To find the domain of $(g \circ f)(x)$, first look at the domain of f which is all real numbers. The outputs from f with all real numbers as inputs will also be all real numbers. These outputs of f will be the inputs for g but these cannot be negative. We will need:

$$2x - 4 \geq 0 \quad \text{or} \quad x \geq 2.$$

The domain of $(g \circ f)(x)$ is $[2, \infty)$.

Example 6: Given $f(x) = \dfrac{1}{x+2}$ and $g(x) = \dfrac{4}{x}$, find the following.

    a. $(f \circ g)(x)$ b. $(g \circ f)(x)$

    c. find the domain of $f \circ g$ and $g \circ f$

Solution:

a. $(f \circ g)(x) = f(g(x)) = \dfrac{1}{\dfrac{4}{x} + 2} = \dfrac{1}{\dfrac{4 + 2x}{x}} = \dfrac{x}{4 + 2x} = \dfrac{x}{2(2 + x)}$

b. $(g \circ f)(x) = g(f(x)) = \dfrac{4}{\dfrac{1}{x + 2}} = 4(x + 2)$

c. The domain of f is $x \neq -2$ and the domain of g is $x \neq 0$. When we look for the domain of $f \circ g$, we see that zero is not in the domain of g, so 0 is not in the domain of $f \circ g$.

The domain of f cannot contain -2, so the output of g must not be -2. Set $g = -2$ and solve.

$$\frac{4}{x} = -2$$

$$-2x = 4 \qquad \text{or} \qquad x = -2$$

From this calculation, we know that in the domain of f $x \neq -2$, and we also know that in the domain of g $x \neq 0$.
The domain of $f \circ g$ would thus be:

$$(-\infty, -2) \cup (-2, 0) \cup (0, \infty).$$

To find the domain of $g \circ f$, we know from the domain of f that $x \neq -2$.

Thus -2 is not in the domain of $g \circ f$

Since the domain of g is $x \neq 0$ then,

$$f(x) = 1/x + 2 \text{ cannot equal zero because the numerator is 1.}$$

Thus there is no restriction. The domain of $g \circ f$ is $(-\infty, -2) \cup (-2, \infty)$.

Decomposing a Function

When we decompose a function our goal is to try to express the given function as a composition of two functions.

Example 7: If $f(x) = \sqrt{3x - 5}$, find $g(x)$ and $h(x)$ such that

$$f(x) = (g \circ h)(x)$$

Solution: The best way to approach decomposing a function is to carefully examine the given function and try to find a way to represent it as two functions.

If we examine the given function for this example, we see that $(3x - 5)$ could be one function and then we could take the square root of that function.

We can let $g(x) = \sqrt{x}$ and $h(x) = 3x - 5$.

Next, we must check to see if our two functions satisfy the required composition.

Our problem stated that our composition should be

$$f(x) = (g \circ h)(x)$$

$$= g(h(x)) = g(3x-5) = \sqrt{3x-5}$$

which is our original function given in the problem.

Example 8: If $f(x) = (x-4)^7$, find $g(x)$ and $h(x)$ such that

$$f(x) = (g \circ h)(x)$$

Solution: To approach decomposing this function, carefully examine the given function and try to find a way to represent it as two functions.

When we examine f, we see that $f(x)$ raises $(x-4)$ to the 7th power.

Two functions that can be used for the composition are

$$g(x) = x^7 \quad \text{and} \quad h(x) = (x-4).$$

Next, we must check to see if our two functions satisfy the required composition.

Our problem stated that our composition should be

$$f(x) = (g \circ h)(x)$$

$$= g(h(x)) = g(x-4) = (x-4)^7$$

which is our original function given in the problem.

Section 1.5 Exercises

Given: $f(x) = 2x^2$ and $g(x) = 4x + 3$, find the following:

1. $(f + g)(4)$

2. $(f - g)(0)$

3. $(fg)((-\frac{1}{2})$

4. $(fg)(\frac{1}{2})$

5. $(\frac{f}{g})(\sqrt{2})$

6. $(\frac{g}{f})(0)$

7. $(g + g)(2)$

8. $(g - f)(-2)$

9. $(\frac{f}{g})(-2)$

10. $(f + g)(-\frac{1}{4})$

For each pair of functions below find:

$$(f + g)(x),\ (f - g)(x),\ (fg)(x),\ (ff)(x),\ \frac{f}{g}(x),\ (gg)(x)\ \text{and}\ \frac{g}{f}(x)?$$

11. $f(x) = 3x - 2$ $\quad g(x) = 4 - 2x$

12. $f(x) = 2x - 3$ $\quad g(x) = x^2 + 3$

13. $f(x) = \sqrt{x + 1}$ $\quad g(x) = x - 2$

14. $f(x) = \sqrt{x}$ $\quad g(x) = x^2$

15. $f(x) = |x|$ $\quad g(x) = x - 2$

16. $f(x) = \dfrac{2}{x - 1}$ $\quad g(x) = \dfrac{1}{2 - x}$

For each given function f, find and simplify the difference quotient:

$$\frac{f(x + h) - f(x)}{h}.$$

17. $f(x) = 2x^2 - 1$

18. $f(x) = 4 - 2x$

19. $f(x) = 3x^2 + 4x - 5$

20. $f(x) = 2x^3 - 4x^2$

Given that $f(x) = 4x - 1$ and $g(x) = x^2 - x - 6$, find the following.

21. $(f \circ g)(-2)$ 22. $(g \circ f)(-1)$

23. $(f \circ g)(0)$ 24. $(f \circ f)(2)$

Find $(f \circ g)$, $(g \circ f)$ and the domain of each of the following.

25. Given $f(x) = x + 4$ and $g(x) = x - 2$.

26. Given $f(x) = \dfrac{1}{x}$ and $g(x) = x$.

Find $f(x)$ and $g(x)$ if $h(x) = (f \circ g)(x)$.

27. $h(x) = (7 - x)^3$ 28. $h(x) = \dfrac{1}{(x-3)^6}$

29. $h(x) = (\sqrt{x} - 4)^2$ 30. $h(x) = \sqrt[4]{(x-2)^3}$

Section 1.6 Transformations

Symmetry: A graph is symmetric if there is an axis or a point that can be drawn so that the graph will mirror itself across this axis or point.

If the coordinate plane is folded along the y-axis, and if the graph that lies on the left half of the plane coincides with the graph on the right, then the graph is **symmetric with respect to the y-axis.**

A graph is **symmetric with respect to the y-axis** provided that the point $(-x, y)$ is on the graph whenever the point (x, y) is on the graph.

Points that have the same y-value and opposite x-values are **reflections of each other across the y-axis.**

The two points $(4, 1)$ and $(-4, 1)$ are reflections across the y-axis.

A graph is **symmetric with respect to the x-axis** provided that the point $(x, -y)$ is on the graph whenever the point (x, y) is on the graph.

When the graph is folded along the x-axis, points above and below the x-axis coincide. The two points $(3, 6)$ and $(3, -6)$ are reflections across the x-axis.

A graph **is symmetric with respect to the origin** provided that the point $(-x, -y)$ is on the graph whenever the point (x, y) is on the graph.

Rather than folding the graph along either axis, we can see reflection across the origin by rotating the graph 180° and the result will coincide with the original figure.

Given the point $(5, -2)$, its reflection across the origin would be the point $(-5, 2)$.

Example 1. Test to see if $x^2 + y^2 = 9$ is symmetric with respect to the x-axis, the y-axis and/or the origin.

Solution:

    1. Test for symmetry with respect to the x-axis: replace y with $-y$

$$x^2 + y^2 = 9 \qquad \text{given equation}$$
$$x^2 + (-y)^2 = 9 \qquad \text{substitute and simplify}$$
$$x^2 + y^2 = 9$$

        The resulting equation is the same as the original so the graph is symmetric with respect to the x-axis.

    2. Test for symmetry with respect to the y-axis: replace x with $-x$

$$x^2 + y^2 = 9 \qquad \text{given equation}$$
$$(-x)^2 + y^2 = 9 \qquad \text{substitute and simplify}$$
$$x^2 + y^2 = 9$$

        The resulting equation is the same as the original so the graph is symmetric with respect to the y-axis.

    3. Test for symmetry with respect to the origin: replace x with $-x$ and y with $-y$

$$x^2 + y^2 = 9 \qquad \text{given equation}$$
$$(-x)^2 + (-y)^2 = 9 \qquad \text{substitute and simplify}$$
$$x^2 + y^2 = 9$$

        The resulting equation is the same as the original so the graph is symmetric to the origin.

This problem can be solved using a graphing calculator. To see this problem, see Chapter 6, Example 5.

Example 2

Test to see if $y = x^2 + 4$ is symmetric with respect to the x-axis, the y-axis and/or the origin.

Solution:

1. Test for symmetry with respect to the x-axis: replace y with $-y$.

   $y = x^2 + 4$ given equation

   $(-y) = x^2 + 4$ substitute and simplify

   $-y = x^2 + 4$

   The resulting equation is not the same as the original equation. Thus the graph is not symmetric with respect to the x-axis.

2. Test for symmetry with respect to the y-axis: replace x with $-x$.

   $y = x^2 + 4$ given equation

   $y = (-x)^2 + 4$ substitute and simplify

   $y = x^2 + 4$

   The resulting equation is the same as the original equation so the graph is symmetric with respect to the y-axis

3. Test for symmetry with respect to the origin: replace x with $-x$ and y with $-y$.

   $y = x^2 + 4$ given equation

   $(-y) = (-x)^2 + 4$ substitute and simplify

   $-y = x^2 + 4$

   The resulting equation is not the same as the original equation. Thus the graph is not symmetric with respect to the origin.

This example can be solved using a graphing calculator. See Chapter 6, Example 6.

Even and Odd Functions:

Even and Odd Functions:

   <u>**An even function**</u> **is a function that is symmetric with respect to the y-axis.**

   or $f(x) = f(-x)$ **for every x in the domain of f.**

   <u>**An odd function**</u> **is a function that is symmetric with respect to the origin.**

   or $f(-x) = -f(x)$ **for every x in the domain of f.**

   A function cannot be both even and odd except for the function $f(x)=0$.

How to test for an even/odd function:

Given a function $f(x)$
1. Find $f(-x)$ by replacing x with $-x$ in the given function. Simplify.
   If $f(x) = f(-x)$, then the given function is even.

2. Find $-f(x)$ by multiplying the given function by -1. Simplify.
   If $f(-x) = -f(x)$, then the given function is odd.

Example 3: Are the given functions even, odd or neither?

   a. $f(x) = 2x^5 - x^3 + 4x$ b. $f(x) = 4x^4 + x^2$

Solution:

   a. $f(x) = 2x^5 - x^3 + 4x$

   1. $f(-x) = 2(-x)^5 - (-x)^3 + 4(-x)$
       $f(-x) = -2x^5 + x^3 - 4x$

   We see that $f(x) \neq f(-x)$ and the function is not even

   2. $-f(x) = -(2x^5 - x^3 + 4x)$
       $-f(x) = -2x^5 + x^3 - 4x$

   We see that $f(-x) = -f(x)$ and the function is odd.

   b. $f(x) = 4x^4 + x^2$
         $f(-x) = 4(-x)^4 + (-x)^2$
         $f(-x) = 4x^4 + x^2$

   We see that $f(x) = f(-x)$,   and the function is even.

See Chapter 6, Example 7 for this example solved with a graphing calculator.

Transformations of Functions:

We need to be able to recognize certain graphs and the functions they represent. Several common functions are shown below.

Identity function: $f(x) = x$

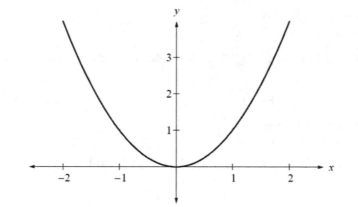

Square function: $f(x) = x^2$

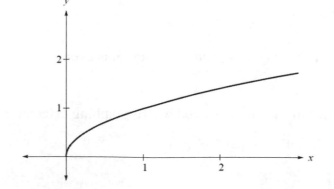

Square root function: $f(x) = \sqrt{x}$

Cubic function: $f(x) = x^3$

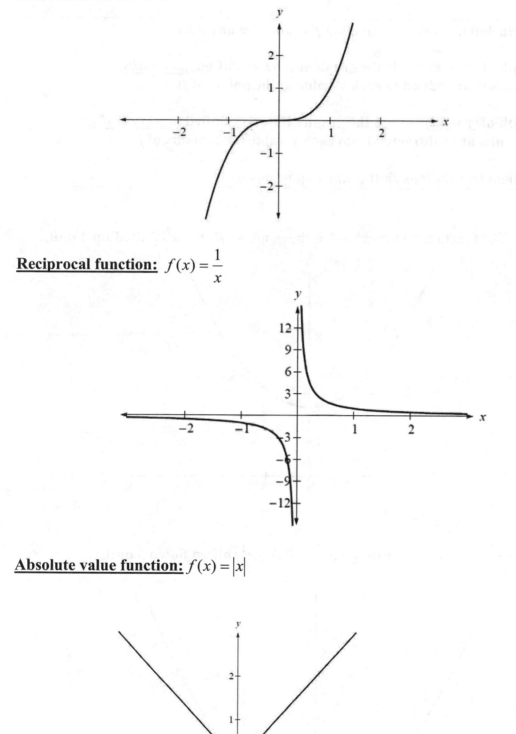

Reciprocal function: $f(x) = \dfrac{1}{x}$

Absolute value function: $f(x) = |x|$

Next we will learn how to shift these basic functions.

Vertical Translations:

Vertical Translation: For any function $f(x)$ and for any $c \neq 0$,

  Graph of $y = f(x) + c$ is the graph of $y = f(x)$ shifted _up c units_,
    c units are added to each y-value of the points of $f(x)$.

  Graph of $y = f(x) - c$ is the graph of $y = f(x)$ shifted _down c units_,
    c units are subtracted from each y-value of all points of $f(x)$.

  Vertical translations shift graphs up or down.

Example 4. The function $f(x) = x^2 + 4$ is the graph of $f(x) = x^2$ **shifted up 4 units.**

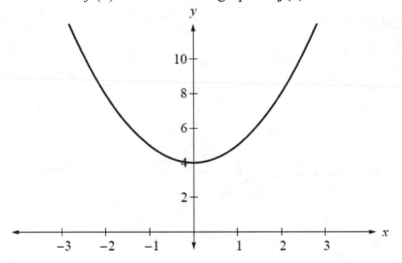

and the function $f(x) = x^2 - 3$ is the graph of $f(x) = x^2$ **shifted down 3 units**

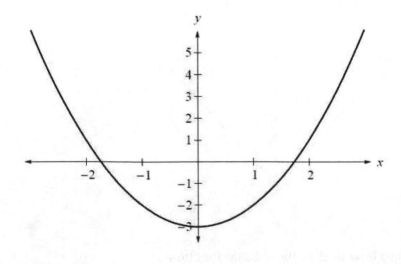

Horizontal Translations:

Horizontal Translation: For any function $f(x)$ and for any $c \neq 0$,

Graph of $y = f(x - c)$ is the graph of $y = f(x)$ shifted *right c units*, **c units are added to each x-value of the points of f(x).**

Graph of $y = f(x + c)$ is the graph of $y = f(x)$ shifted *left c units*. **c units are subtracted from each x-value of the points of f(x).**

Horizontal translations shift graphs left or right.

Example 5: The graph of $f(x - 2) = (x - 2)^2$ is the graph of $f(x) = x^2$ **shifted right 2 units,**

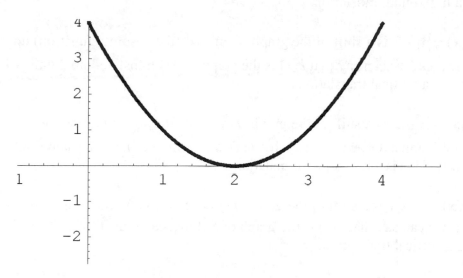

and the graph of $f(x + 3) = (x + 3)^2$ is the graph of $f(x) = x^2$ **shifted left 3 units**

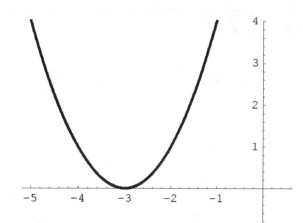

Example 6: For each of the given, describe how each graph can be obtained from one of the basic graphs shown earlier.

    a. $h(x) = x^2 - 4$ b. $h(x) = (x-3)^2$

    c $h(x) = |x| + 2$ d. $h(x) = |x-2|$

    e. $h(x) = x^3 + 1$ f. $h(x) = (x-3)^3$

Solution:

    a. $h(x) = x^2 - 4$ is a shift of the graph $f(x) = x^2$ (the square function) down 4 units. Or, we can say that $h(x)$ is the graph of $f(x)$ translated down 4 units. This is a vertical translation.

    b. $h(x) = (x-3)^2$ is a shift of the graph $f(x) = x^2$ (the square function) right 3 units. Or, we can say that $h(x)$ is the graph of $f(x)$ translated right 3 units. This is a horizontal translation.

    c. $h(x) = |x| + 2$ is a shift of the graph $f(x) = |x|$ (the absolute function) up 2 units. Or, we can say that $h(x)$ is the graph of $f(x)$ translated up 2 units. This is a vertical translation.

    d. $h(x) = |x-2|$ is a shift of the graph $f(x) = |x|$ (the absolute function) right 2 units. Or, we can say that $h(x)$ is the graph of $f(x)$ translated right 2 units. This is a horizontal translation.

    e. $h(x) = x^3 + 1$ is a shift of the graph $f(x) = x^3$ (the cube function) up 1 unit. Or, we can say that $h(x)$ is the graph of $f(x)$ translated up 1 unit. This is a vertical translation.

    f. $h(x) = (x-3)^3$ is a shift of the graph $f(x) = x^3$ (the cube function) right 3 units. Or, we can say that $h(x)$ is the graph of $f(x)$ translated right 3 units. This is a horizontal translation.

This example can be solved using the graphing calculator to get a view of the graph and its translation. See Chapter 6, Example 8.

Reflections

Graphs can be reflected across the x-axis and the y-axis. When a graph is reflected, it is shifted across an axis, line or point. The new graph is called a reflection.

To reflect $f(x)$ across the x-axis,
   graph $-f(x)$.
To reflect $f(x)$ across the y-axis,
   graph $f(-x)$.
If a point (x, y) is on the graph of $f(x)$,
   then $(x, -y)$ is on the graph $y = -f(x)$,
   and $(-x, y)$ is on the graph $y = f(-x)$.

If $f(x) = x^2$ the graph is

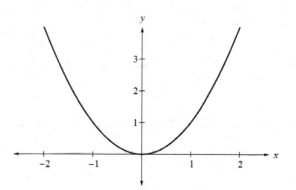

then $g(x) = -f(x)$ reflects across the x-axis.

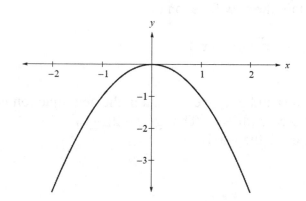

69

If $f(x) = x^3$, the graph is

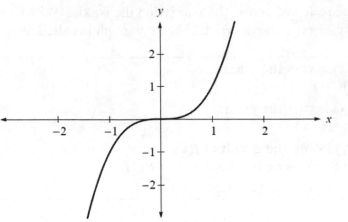

then $g(x) = f(-x)$ reflects across the y-axis.

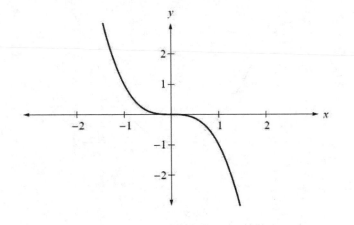

Example 7: If a function $f(x)$ is defined as $f(x) = 2x^3 - 3x$, describe what translations and/or were used to obtain the new function g:

$$g(x) = 2(-x)^3 - 3(-x)$$

Solution:

      If we compare $f(x)$ and $g(x)$, we see that in the new function $g(x)$ the variable x has been replaced with $-x$. Thus $g(x) = 2(-x)^3 - 3(-x)$ is a reflection of the function f across the y-axis.

Vertical Stretching and Shrinking

To obtain the graph $y = cf(x)$ for some real number c, we <u>multiply the y-coordinates</u> of the points on the graph of $y = f(x)$ by c.

For example if $y = 3f(x)$, we would multiply each y-coordinate by 3; If $y = \dfrac{1}{3}f(x)$, we multiply each y-coordinate by $\frac{1}{3}$.

This process is referred to as **vertically stretching** the graph of f if $\mid c \mid$ is > 1, or **vertically shrinking** the graph when $0 < \mid c \mid < 1$.

Given the function $y = f(x)$.

$y = cf(x)$ if $\mid c \mid > 1$ then the graph of f is <u>**vertically stretched**</u> by a factor of c

if $0 < \mid c \mid < 1$ then the graph of f is <u>**vertically shrunk**</u> by a factor of c.

Horizontal Stretching and Shrinking

To obtain the graph $y = f(cx)$ for some real number c, we <u>divide the x-coordinates</u> of the points on the graph of $y = f(x)$ by c.

This process is referred to as **horizontally shrinking** the graph of f for $\mid c \mid > 1$, or **horizontally stretching** the graph when $0 < \mid c \mid < 1$.

Given the function
$y = f(x)$

$y = f(cx)$ if $\mid c \mid > 1$
then the graph of f is <u>**horizontally shrunk**</u> by a factor of $\dfrac{1}{c}$

if $0 < \mid c \mid < 1$
then the graph of f is <u>**horizontally stretched**</u> by a factor of $\dfrac{1}{c}$.

Example 8:

Given $y = f(x)$ for some function f. Describe what changes occur to the graph of f with each of the following:

a. $g(x) = 3f(x)$ b. $g(x) = \frac{1}{3}f(x)$ c. $g(x) = f(4x)$

d. $g(x) = f(\frac{1}{8}x)$ e. $g(x) = -f(x)$ f. $g(x) = f(-x)$

Solution:

a. $g(x) = 3f(x)$: this graph is of the form $cf(x)$, and we know that this is a vertical change. Since $|3| > 1$, we know this is a stretch. Thus, $g(x)$ is a vertical stretching of the graph of f by a factor of 3.

b. $g(x) = \frac{1}{3}f(x)$: this graph is of the form $cf(x)$, and we know that this is a vertical change. Since $0 < |\frac{1}{3}| < 1$, we know this is a shrinking. Thus, $g(x)$ is a vertical shrinking of the graph of f by a factor of $\frac{1}{3}$.

c. $g(x) = f(4x)$: this graph is of the form $f(cx)$, and we know this is a horizontal change. Since $|4| > 1$, we know this is a horizontal shrink. Thus, $g(x)$ is a horizontal shrinking of the graph of f by a factor of $\frac{1}{4}$.

d. $g(x) = f(\frac{1}{8}x)$: this graph is of the form $f(cx)$, and we know this is a horizontal change. Since $|\frac{1}{8}| < 1$, we know this is a horizontal stretching. Thus, $g(x)$ is a horizontal stretching of the graph of f by a factor of 8.

e. $g(x) = -f(x)$: this is a reflection and $g(x)$ is a reflection across the x-axis

f. $g(x) = f(-x)$: this is a reflection and $g(x)$ is a reflection across the y-axis. The table below is a table describing transformations and their results.

TRANSFORMATIONS of $y = f(x)$:

Vertical Translation: $y = f(x)$ + or $-c$

$y = f(x) + c$ is the graph of f **shifted up c units.**
$y = f(x) - c$ is the graph of f **shifted down c units.**

Horizontal Translation: $y = f(x$ + or $-c)$

$y = f(x + c)$ is the graph of f shifted **left c units.**
$y = f(x - c)$ is the graph of f shifted **right c units.**

Vertical Stretching or Shrinking : $y = cf(x)$

For $|c| > 1$ a **vertical stretch.**
$0 < |c| < 1$ **a vertical shrink.**

Horizontal Stretching or Shrinking; $y = f(cx)$

For $|c| > 1$ **a horizontal shrink.**
$0 < |c| < 1$ **a horizontal stretch.**

Reflections:
$y = -f(x)$ is a reflection of f **across the x-axis.**
$y = f(-x)$ is a reflection of f **across the y-axis.**

Exercises 1.6

Draw the graph of a function that is

1. symmetric with respect to the x-axis
2. symmetric with respect to the y-axis
3. symmetric with respect to the origin

Determine whether the given equations are symmetric with respect to the x-axis, the y-axis, the origin, or none.

4. $y = |x| + 3$ 5. $y = |x|$

6. $y = |x + 2|$ 7. $4y = 2x + 6$

8. $2x + 3 = 2y$ 9. $3y = x^2 - 4$

10. $x^2 + 1 = 4y$ 11. $y = 4$

12. $y = \dfrac{2}{x}$ 13. $y = -2x^3$

Find the point that is symmetric to the given point with respect to the x-axis, the y-axis, the origin.

14. $(-4, 3)$ 15. $(\frac{1}{2}, 0)$

16. $(-2, -3)$ 17. $(2, \frac{1}{3})$

18. $(0, -2)$ 19. $(5, -4)$

Determine algebraically whether the function is even, odd, or neither.

20. $f(x) = 4x^3$ 21. $f(x) = 4x^3 + 3$

22. $f(x) = x^5$ 23. $f(x) = x^6$

24. $f(x) = \sqrt[3]{x}$ 25. $f(x) = \dfrac{1}{x}$

26. $f(x) = \dfrac{1}{2x^2}$ 27. $f(x) = \sqrt{x + 2}$

For each of the given functions, describe how each graph can be obtained from the graph of $f(x) = x^2$.

28. $f(x) = x^2 + 2$ 29. $f(x) = -x^2$

30. $f(x) = x^2 - 3$ 31. $f(x) = (x + 2)^2$

32. $f(x) = (x - 4)^2$ 33. $f(x) = 3x^2$

34. $f(x) = -(x + 3)^2$ 35. $f(x) = (x - 4)^2 - 3$

Chapter 1 Summary

Functions

Each member of the domain corresponds to **exactly** one member of the range.

Domain: input values
Range: output values
Test for function: Vertical Line Test

Slopes/Lines

Slope:

$$m = \frac{y_2 - y_1}{x_2 - x_1}$$

Slope-Intercept Equation:

$$y = mx + b$$

Point-Slope Equation:

$$y - y_1 = m(x - x_1)$$

Horizontal Line: $y = b$

Vertical Line: $x = a$

Parallel Lines: $m_1 = m_2$. if $b_1 \neq b_2$

Perpendicular Lines:

$$m_1\, m_2 = -1 \qquad \text{or}$$

vertical and horizontal lines

Algebra for Functions

Sum: $(f + g)(x) = f(x) + g(x)$

Difference: $(f - g)(x) = f(x) - g(x)$

Product: $(fg)(x) = f(x) * g(x)$

Quotient: $(\frac{f}{g})(x) = \frac{f(x)}{g(x)}, \;\; and\; g(x) \neq 0$

Composition: $(f \circ g)(x) = f(g(x))$
$(g \circ f)(x) = g(f(x))$

Symmetry Tests

x-axis: replace y with $-y$, get equivalent equation

y-axis: replace x with $-x$, get equivalent equation

origin: replace x with $-x$ and replace y with $-y$
and get an equivalent equation

Transformations

Vertical Translation:	$y = f(x) \pm c$
Horizontal Translation:	$y = g(x \pm c)$
Reflection across x-axis	$y = -f(x)$
Reflection across y-axis	$y = f(-x)$
Horizontal Stretching/Shrinking	$y = f(cx)$
Vertical Stretching/Shrinking	$y = cf(x)$

Chapter 1 Review:

In problems 1 and 2 is the given relation a function? Find the domain and range.
1. {(2, 3), (4, 5), (6, 5), (2, 7)
2. {(2, 4), (2, 5), (2, 6), (2, 7)}

For problems 3 – 5 is the given graph a function?
3.

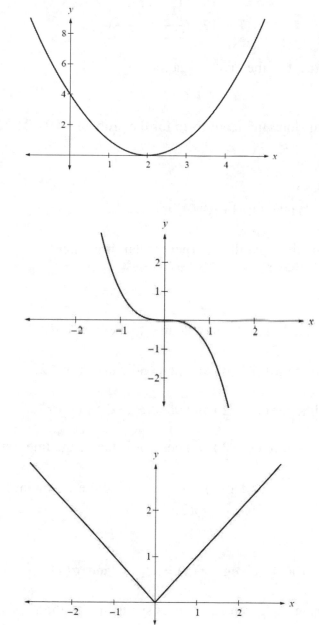

4.

5.

Find the domain of the following functions.

6. $f(x) = 5x - 3x^2$

7. $f(x) = \dfrac{2}{x}$

8. $f(x) = \dfrac{2}{x^2 - x - 6}$

9. $|x - 4|$

Given the function $f(x) = x^2 - 2x + 1$, find the following.

10. $f(2)$

11. $f(-2)$

12. $f(y + 2)$

13. $f(0)$

Find the slope of the line containing the given points.

14. $(2, -3), (4, -1)$

15. $(1, 3), (7, 3)$

16. $(2, 5), (2, 4)$

17. $\left(\dfrac{1}{3}, \dfrac{2}{3}\right), \left(-\dfrac{1}{8}, \dfrac{5}{8}\right)$

18. Find the slope and y-intercept of the given equation.
$$-3x - 2y = 9$$

Write the equation of a line in slope-intercept form for the problems 19 - 21.

19. $m = -4$, y-intercept $(0, 3)$

20. $m = -\dfrac{1}{3}$, y-intercept $(0, 4)$

21. contains the points $(2, -3)$ and $(-1, -1)$

For problems 22 and 23 are the lines parallel, perpendicular or neither?

22. $2x - 3y = 9$

23. $y - 2x = 4$
$\quad 4x = 6y + 12$

$\qquad y = 2x + 6$

24. Find the equation of the line thru $(1, 0)$ and parallel to the line $y - 2x = 4$.

25. Find the equation of the line thru $(2, -4)$ and perpendicular to $y - 2x = 4$.

26. Find the equation of the line thru $(1, -2)$ and parallel to the line $y = 7$.

27. Find the equation of the line thru $(1, -2)$ and perpendicular to the line $y = 7$.

For problems 28 - 30 $f(x) = \sqrt{x + 2}$ and $g(x) = x^2 - 2$. Find the following:

28. $(f + g)(2)$

29. $(f - g)(2)$

30. $(ff)(1)$

31. Find $(f \circ g)(x)$ and $(g \circ f)(x)$ given $f(x) = x^2 + x$ and $g(x) = x - 3$

Determine algebraically whether the given equation is symmetric to the x-axis, the y-axis and the origin.

32. $x^2 + 2y^2 = 1$

33. $x^2 + y^2 = 9$

34. $x + 2y = 3$

35. $y = x^2$

36. $y = -x^3$

37. $y = x^4$

38. $y = |x| + 2$

39. $y = |x + 2|$

Write an equation for a function that has a graph that is:

40. shaped as $y = x^2$ but shifted 4 units down and 3 units left

41. shaped as $y = |x|$ stretched horizontally by a factor of 3 and shifted up 2 units.

CHAPTER 2

Equations, Inequalities and Functions

2.1 Linear Equations and Functions

2.2 Complex Numbers

2.3 Quadratic Equations and Functions

2.4 Graphs of Quadratic Functions

2.5 Rational, Radical, Absolute Value Equations

2.6 Linear Inequalities

Section 2.1: Linear Equations and Functions

Equation

Equation: A statement in which two expressions are set equal.

To **solve an equation** means to find all values so that when substituted into the equation in place of the variable make the equation a true statement. A number that is a solution to an equation is said to **satisfy the equation**. All solutions of an equation make up the **solution set of the equation**.

Linear Equation

A linear equation in one variable is an equation that can be written in the form:

$$ax + b = 0$$

where a and b are real numbers with $a \neq 0$.

We can use the Addition Property of Equality and/or the Subtraction Property of Equality to solve equations.

Addition Property of Equality

Addition Property of Equality:

Adding the same number to both sides of an equation does not change the solution to the equation:

If $a = b$,   then $a + c = b + c$.

Subtraction Property of Equality

Subtraction Property of Equality:

Subtracting the same number from both sides of an equation does not change the solution to the equation:

If $a = b$,   then $a - c = b - c$.

Example 1: Solve the equation: $x - 3 = 5$.

Solution: Given:
$$x - 3 = 5$$
$$x - 3 + 3 = 5 + 3 \qquad \text{Addition Property of Equality}$$
$$x = 8 \qquad \text{Combine like terms.}$$

Check:
$$x - 3 = 5$$
$$8 - 3 = 5$$
$$5 = 5 \qquad \textbf{True statement}$$

We will also use the Multiplication Property of Equality, the Division Property of Equality, and the Distributive Property to solve equations.

Multiplication Property of Equality:
Multiplying both sides of an equation by the same nonzero number does not change the solution to the equation:

If $\quad a = b \quad$ and $\quad c \neq 0 \quad$ then $\quad ac = bc$.

Distributive Property:
For any real numbers m, n, and p,
$$m(n + p) = mn + mp \quad \text{and} \quad m(n - p) = mn - np$$

Division Property of Equality:
Dividing both sides of an equation by the same nonzero number does not change the solution to the equation:

If $\quad a = b \quad$ and $\boldsymbol{c \neq 0}$ $\qquad$ then $\qquad \dfrac{a}{c} = \dfrac{b}{c}$.

Reminder:
$$\frac{ac + bc}{c} = \frac{(a + b)c}{c} = a + b.$$

Example 2: Solve the equation $4x - 3 = 2$.

Solution: Given
$$4x - 3 = 2$$
$$4x - 3 + 3 = 2 + 3 \qquad \text{Addition Property}$$
$$4x = 5 \qquad \text{Combine like terms.}$$
$$\frac{4}{4}x = \frac{5}{4} \qquad \text{Division Property}$$

$$x = \frac{5}{4}$$

Check:

$$4x - 3 = 2$$

$$4\left(\frac{5}{4}\right) - 3 = 2$$

$$5 - 3 = 2$$

$$2 = 2 \qquad \textbf{True statement}$$

We can solve Example 1 as well as Example 2 using a graphing calculator. See Chapter 6, Example 9.

Example 3.   Solve $2(4 - 2x) = 5 - 3(x + 1)$.

Solution: Given : $2(4 - 2x) = 5 - 3(x + 1)$

$$
\begin{array}{ll}
8 - 4x = 5 - 3x - 3 & \text{Distributive Property} \\
8 - 4x = 2 - 3x & \text{Combine like terms.} \\
8 - 4x + 4x = 2 - 3x + 4x & \text{Addition Property} \\
8 = 2 + x & \text{Combine like terms.} \\
8 - 2 = 2 - 2 + x & \text{Addition Property} \\
6 = x &
\end{array}
$$

Check:

$$2(4 - 2x) = 5 - 3(x + 1)$$
$$8 - 4x = 5 - 3x - 3$$
$$8 - 4 * 6 = 5 - 3 * 6 - 3$$
$$8 - 24 = 5 - 18 - 3$$
$$-16 = -16 \qquad \textbf{True statement}$$

A graphing calculator can be used to solve Example 3. See Chapter 6, Example 10.

Zeros of Linear Functions

An input of c to a function f is called a <u>zero of the function</u> if the output for the function is zero when the input is c. That is, c is a zero of function f if $f(c) = 0$.

Zeros

Real zeros of a function are the input values to the function that will make $f(x) = 0$.

These values are also the x-value of the x-intercepts of the graph.

A <u>linear function</u> is given by $f(x) = ax + b$ where a and b are constants ($a \neq 0$).

If we look at the linear function $f(x) = 2x + 4$, we see that $f(-2) = 2(-2) + 4 = 0$. Thus we know that -2 is a zero of the given function.

A linear function has at most one zero.

If we graph the function $f(x) = 2x + 4$,

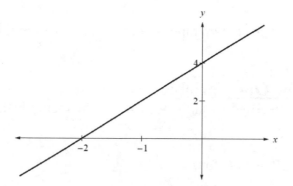

we can see that the zero which is -2 is the x-coordinate of the point where the graph intersects the x-axis.

The x-intercept of the graph is the point $(-2, 0)$.

If we are given a linear function $f(x) = ax + b$ ($a \neq 0$), we set the function equal to zero and find the solution to this equation which will give us the zero of the function.

The zero of the function $f(x) = ax + b$ ($a \neq 0$) is the solution to the equation $ax + b = 0$.

Example 4. Find the zero of the function $f(x) = 6x - 3$.

Solution: To find the zeros of a function we must find the value of x such that $f(x) = 0$.

We find this x-value by setting $f(x)$ equal to zero and solving for x.

$$6x - 3 = 0 \qquad \text{Set the function} = 0.$$

$$6x = 3 \qquad \text{Add 3 to both sides.}$$

$$x = \frac{3}{6} = \frac{1}{2} \qquad \text{Divide both sides by 6.}$$

Check:
$$f(x) = 6x - 3$$

$$f\left(\frac{1}{2}\right) = 6\left(\frac{1}{2}\right) - 3 = 0$$

$x = \dfrac{1}{2}$ is the **zero of the linear function** since $f\left(\dfrac{1}{2}\right) = 0$.

See Chapter 6, Example 11 for the graphic solution to the given problem in Example 4.

Solving Formulas for One Variable

To solve formulas for a specified variable, we can use the methods that we use to solve linear equations.

Example 5: Solve $A = P + Prt$ for r.

Solution:

　　　　To solve for r we will isolate r.

$A = P + Prt$	Given
$A - P = P + Prt - P$	Subtract P from both sides.
$A - P = Prt$	Combine like terms.
$\dfrac{A - P}{Pt} = r$	Divide both sides by Pt.

Example 6:   Solve $M = 4t + 2p$ for p.

Solution:　　To solve for p we will isolate p.

$M = 4t + 2p$	Given
$M - 4t = 4t + 2p - 4t$	Subtract $4t$ from both sides.
$M - 4t = 2p$	Combine like terms.
$\dfrac{M - 4t}{2} = p$	Divide both sides by 2.

We can also reduce the answer we just found by splitting the answer into two fractions and reducing each fraction.

$$\frac{M}{2} - \frac{4t}{2} = \frac{M}{2} - 2t = p$$

The two solutions: $\dfrac{M - 4t}{2}$ *and* $\dfrac{M}{2} - 2t$ *are equivalent*.

(*) Steps to Solve Equations:

1. Eliminate parentheses using distribution.

2. Collect like terms on each side of the equation.

3. Use Add/Subtract to isolate the variable

4. Use multiply/divide to make coefficient of $x = +1$ (FOR Fractions-mult by reciprocol!!)

Watch Signs

Example 7:   Solve $T = 6pr + rd$ for r.

Solution:

To solve for r we will isolate r:

$$T = 6pr + rd$$

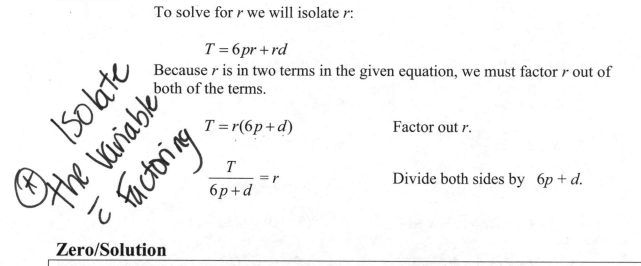

Because r is in two terms in the given equation, we must factor r out of both of the terms.

$$T = r(6p + d)$$ Factor out r.

$$\frac{T}{6p + d} = r$$ Divide both sides by $6p + d$.

Zero/Solution

Zero of a Function and **Solution of an Equation**
To find the zero of $f(x)$, set $f(x) = 0$ and solve.
The solution of the equation is the zero of the function.
The zero of $f(x)$ is the x-value of the x-intercept of the graph of $f(x)$.

Section 2.1 Exercises.

Solve the equations in problems 1 – 14.

1. $3x + 3 = 24$

2. $2t - 4 = 9$

3. $2x - 7 = 0$

4. $5p = 0$

5. $4 - p = 6$

6. $5 - 3x = 11$

7. $x + 2 = 2x - 5$

8. $2 + p = 2p + 1$

9. $5x + 4 = 3x + 10$

10. $4m - 3 = m + 6$

11. $5x + 4 - 2x = 2x - x + 14$

12. $8(5x + 3) = 6(2x - 5)$

13. $3(2t - 2) + 6 = 4(t - 2)$

14. $4(2x + 3) = 6(2x - 1)$

Find the zero of each linear function in problems 15 – 20.

15. $f(x) = x + 3$

16. $f(x) = 4x + 8$

17. $f(x) = 5 - x$

18. $f(x) = 3x + 12$

19. $f(x) = 7 - 3x$

20. $f(x) = 6 - x$

In problems 21 – 32 solve for the given variable.

21. $A = \frac{1}{2}bh$ for h

22. $A = \frac{1}{2}bh$ for b

23. $y = mx + b$ for b

24. $y = mx + b$ for m

25. $P = 2L + 2W$ for L

26. $P = 2L + 2W$ for W

27. $T = pcd + de$ for d

28. $T = pcd + de$ for e

29. $2x + 3y = 6$ for x

30. $2x + 3y = 6$ for y

31. $m = n + nde$ for n

32. $t = v - wv$ for v

Section 2.2 Complex Numbers

Some functions have zeros that are not real numbers; $f(x) = \sqrt{-1}$ is one example.
To solve the equation $x^2 + 1 = 0$, we see that $x^2 = -1$ or $x = \pm\sqrt{-1}$. But $\sqrt{-1}$ has no meaning since there is no real number that when multiplied by itself will result in -1.

There is an extension of the number system, called **complex numbers**, in which $x^2 = -1$ does have two solutions.

Complex Numbers

Complex numbers are formed by adding the imaginary unit i to the real number system.

Definition of i:

$i = \sqrt{-1}$ and $i^2 = -1$

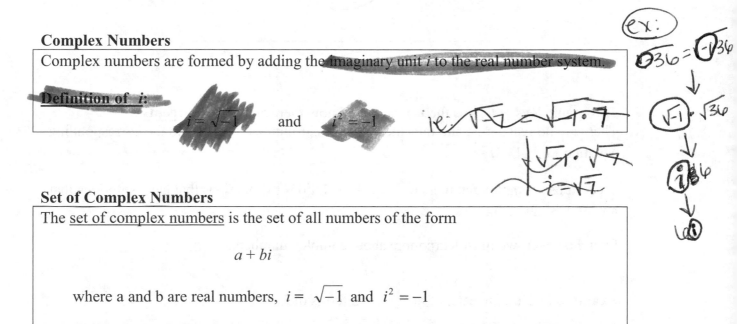

Set of Complex Numbers

The set of complex numbers is the set of all numbers of the form

$$a + bi$$

where a and b are real numbers, $i = \sqrt{-1}$ and $i^2 = -1$

Imaginary Numbers

Imaginary Numbers:

In the **complex number $a + bi$,**

a is called the real part of the number and

b is called the imaginary part if $b \neq 0$.

The **number bi is called an imaginary number**.

Ex. $(3+4i) + (-2+6i)$
$= 3+4i+2+6i$
$3-2+4i+6i$
$1+10i$

Look at the graph of the function $f(x) = x^2 + 1$ shown below.

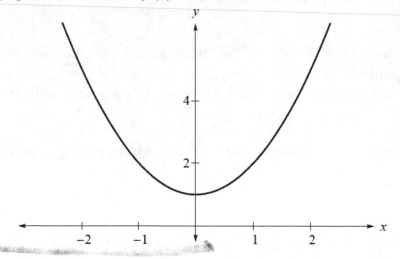

This graph <u>does not cross</u> the x-axis so we know there are <u>**no x-intercepts**</u>.
There are no real zeros, and thus there are no real-number solutions to the corresponding
equation $x^2 + 1 = 0$.

We will use complex numbers to write the solutions to equations that have solutions that
are <u>not real numbers</u>.

First, however, we must learn more about complex numbers.

Example 1: Rewrite each of the given in terms of i

    a. $\sqrt{-6}$ b. $\sqrt{-25}$ c. $-\sqrt{-10}$

    d. $-\sqrt{-49}$ e. $\sqrt{-32}$

Solution:

    a. $\sqrt{-6} = \sqrt{-1*6} = \sqrt{-1} * \sqrt{6} = i\sqrt{6}$ or $\sqrt{6}\,i$

    b. $\sqrt{-25} = \sqrt{-1*25} = \sqrt{-1} * \sqrt{25} = 5i$

    c. $-\sqrt{-10} = -\sqrt{-1*10} = -\sqrt{-1} * \sqrt{10} = -i\sqrt{10}$ or $-\sqrt{10}\,i$
    d. $-\sqrt{-49} = -\sqrt{-1*49} = -\sqrt{-1} * \sqrt{49} = -i*7 = -7i$

    e. $\sqrt{-32} = \sqrt{-1*32} = \sqrt{-1}*\sqrt{32} = i\sqrt{16*2} = i*4\sqrt{2} = 4i\sqrt{2}$ or $4\sqrt{2}\,i$

Addition and Subtraction of Complex Numbers

Complex numbers follow the commutative, associative, and distributive rules. We can add and subtract complex numbers just as we do binomials. We collect the real parts together and the imaginary parts together in the same way that we collect like terms in binomials.

Addition: $(a+bi)+(c+di) = a+bi+c+di = (a+c)+(b+d)i$

Subtraction: $(a+bi)-(c+di) = a+bi-c-di = (a-c)+(b-d)i$

Example 2. Add, subtract and simplify when possible.

     a. $(7+4i)+(9+5i)$ b. $(6+3i)-(8-6i)$

Solution:

     a. $(7+4i)+(9+5i) = 7+4i+9+5i = 7+9+4i+5i = 16+9i$

     b. $(6+3i)-(8-6i) = 6+3i-8+6i = 6-8+3i+6i = -2+9i$

The preceding problem can be solved using a graphing calculator. See Chapter 6, Example 12.

Multiplication of Complex Numbers

When multiplying imaginary numbers, we must convert them into their imaginary form using i before multiplying. Remember that the definition of i tells us that $i = \sqrt{-1}$.

We must also remember that $i^2 = -1$.

$$\sqrt{-3} * \sqrt{-5} = \sqrt{-1*3} * \sqrt{-1*5}$$
$$= \sqrt{-1} * \sqrt{3} * \sqrt{-1}\sqrt{5}$$
$$= i\sqrt{3} * i\sqrt{5} = i^2\sqrt{15} = -1\sqrt{15} = -\sqrt{15}$$

Note: $\sqrt{-3} * \sqrt{-5} = \sqrt{-3*-5} = \sqrt{15}$ is **INCORRECT**. <u>Always factor out $\sqrt{-1}$ before multiplying.</u>

Multiplication of Imaginary Numbers

Multiplication:

Two imaginary numbers: $(bi)(di) = bdi^2 = bd(-1) = -bd$

Two complex numbers: $(a+bi)(c+di) = ac + adi + bci + bdi^2$
$$= ac + i(ad + bc) + bd(-1)$$
$$= (ac - bd) + (ad + bc)i$$

Example 3. Multiply and simplify each of the following.

     a. $\sqrt{-9} * \sqrt{-100}$ b. $\sqrt{-49} * \sqrt{-1}$

Solution:

     a. $\sqrt{-9} * \sqrt{-100} = \sqrt{-1} * \sqrt{9} * \sqrt{-1} * \sqrt{100}$
$$= i * 3 * i * 10$$
$$= i^2 * 30$$
$$= -1 * 30$$
$$= -30$$

     b. $\sqrt{-49} * \sqrt{-1} = \sqrt{-1} * \sqrt{49} * \sqrt{-1} * \sqrt{1}$
$$= i * 7 * i * 1$$
$$= i^2 * 7$$
$$= (-1) * 7$$
$$= -7$$

Example 4. Multiply and simplify each of the following.

     a. $(1-3i)(1+2i)$ b. $(4-2i)^2$

Solution:

     a. $(1-3i)(1+2i) = 1 + 2i - 3i - 6i^2$ Use foil
$$= 1 - i - 6(-1) \qquad i^2 = -1$$
$$= 1 - i + 6 = 7 - i$$

     b. $(4-2i)^2 = (4-2i)(4-2i)$ Use foil
$$= 16 - 8i - 8i + 4i^2$$
$$= 16 - 16i + 4(-1) \qquad i^2 = -1$$
$$= 16 - 16i - 4$$
$$= 12 - 16i$$

We can use a graphing calculator to multiply complex numbers. See Chapter 6, Example 13.

Simplification of Powers of *i*

Reminder:

$$i = \sqrt{-1} \qquad\qquad i^5 = i(i^4) = i(1) = i$$
$$i^2 = -1 \qquad\qquad i^6 = i(i^5) = i(i) = i^2 = -1$$
$$i^3 = i^2 * i = (-1)i = -i \qquad\qquad i^7 = i(i^6) = i(-1) = -i$$
$$i^4 = (i^2)^2 = (-1)^2 = 1 \qquad\qquad i^8 = (i^4)^2 = (1)^2 = 1$$

Note the pattern in the values of *i* in the table above.

The values of the powers of *i* rotate through the values $\sqrt{-1}, -1, -i,$ and 1 and then the values are repeated.

Values of *i* Raised to Any Power

To find the values of *i* raised to any power:
1. Divide the exponent of *i* by 4.
2. Set the original value equal to *i* raised to the power of <u>the remainder</u>.
3. The original value is equal to the value of this new power of *i*.

Example 5: Simplify each of the following.

    a. i^{25} b. i^{38} c. i^{51} d. i^{60}

Solution:

    a. Simplify i^{25}:   25 divided by 4 = 6 with remainder of 1

$$i^{25} = i^1 = i$$

    b. Simplify i^{38} 38 divided by 4 = 9 with remainder of 2

$$i^{38} = i^2 = -1$$

    c. Simplify i^{51} 51 divided by 4 = 12 with remainder of 3

$$i^{51} = i^3 = -i$$

d. Simplify i^{60} 60 divided by 4 = 15 with remainder of zero

$$i^{60} = i^0 = 1$$

Conjugate of a Complex Number

Definition of the Conjugate of a Complex Number:

If $a+bi$ is a complex number, then its conjugate is $a-bi$.

Examples:

Complex Number	Conjugate
$4+3i$	$4-3i$
$6-2i$	$6+2i$
$5i$	$-5i$
4	4

Properties of Conjugates of Complex Numbers:

Addition: $(a+bi)+(a-bi) = 2a$

Multiplication:
$$(a+bi)(a-bi) = a^2 - abi + abi - b^2i^2$$
$$= a^2 - b^2(-1)$$
$$= \boldsymbol{a^2 + b^2}$$

The product of a complex number and its conjugate is a real number.

Example 6: Multiply the following.

a. $(4+2i)(4-2i)$ b. $(3i)(-3i)$

Solution:

a. $(4 + 2i)(4 - 2i) = 16 - 8i + 8i - 4i^2$
$$= 16 - 4(-1)$$
$$= 16 + 4 = 20$$

b. $(3i)(-3i) = -9i^2 = -9(-1) = 9$

Division of Complex Numbers

Think of division as simplifying the quotient of two complex numbers. We can look at this type of simplification as **rationalizing the denominator,** since we are multiplying both the numerator and denominator of the given quotient by the conjugate of the denominator. See Example 7 below.

Example 7. Express in the form $a+bi$, where a and b are real numbers

a. $\dfrac{1}{4+3i}$

b. $2 - i$ divided by $3 - 4i$

Solution:

a. $\dfrac{1}{4+3i} = \dfrac{1}{4+3i} * \dfrac{4-3i}{4-3i} = \dfrac{4-3i}{16+9} = \dfrac{4}{25} - \dfrac{3}{25}i$

b. First we write the problem in fraction form and multiply by 1, using the complex conjugate of the denominator to form a fraction of 1.
The conjugate of the denominator is $3 + 4i$.

We will use: $\dfrac{3+4i}{3+4i} = 1$

$$\dfrac{2-i}{3-4i} = \dfrac{2-i}{3-4i} * \dfrac{3+4i}{3+4i} = \dfrac{6+8i-3i-4i^2}{9+16} = \dfrac{10}{25} + \dfrac{5}{25}i = \dfrac{2}{5} + \dfrac{1}{5}i$$

Reminder: To divide complex numbers, we write the operation of division as a complex quotient (fraction). We need to change this fraction so that there are no imaginary numbers in the denominator. We can accomplish this by multiplying the complex quotient by a fraction which contains the conjugate of the quotient's denominator as both a numerator and denominator. This fraction is equal to 1 since it has the same numerator and denominator.

To divide complex numbers using a graphing calculator, see Chapter 6, Example 14.

Section 2.2 Exercises

Simplify and write each answer in $a+bi$ form where a and b are real numbers.

1. $(4+3i)+(6+2i)$

2. $(-2+4i)+(5+3i)$

3. $(-3-2i)+(4+4i)$

4. $(-8+i)+(2i-1)$

5. $(-4-i)+(-2-i)$

6. $(4+\sqrt{-4})+(5-\sqrt{-9})$

7. $(3-\sqrt{-16})+(2+\sqrt{-4})$

8. $(4-3i)-(2+2i)$

9. $(12+7i)-(6-i)$

10. $(3-2i)-(5-4i)$

11. $(-4-2i)-(-3-i)$

12. $(-4-3i)-(-3-4i)$

13. $2i(3-4i)$

14. $2i(6i-4)$

15. $-4i(-6+2i)$

16. $-5i(-2-3i)$

17. $(2+3i)(1+4i)$

18. $(3i+1)(2i+5)$

19. $(3-4i)(2-6i)$

20. $(4-3i)(2-5i)$

21. $(-2-3i)(-5-i)$

22. $(-3-2i)(-4+2i)$

23. $(4-\sqrt{-9})(5+\sqrt{-36})$

24. $(3-\sqrt{-25})(2-\sqrt{-16})$

25. $(3+2i)^2$

26. $(2-4i)^2$

27. $\dfrac{5-2i}{2+3i}$

28. $\dfrac{4-i}{2-i}$

29. $\dfrac{1+i}{1-i}$

30. $\dfrac{4-2i}{5+i}$

Simplify each of the following:

31. i^{31}

32. i^{18}

33. i^{68}

34. i^{101}

Section 2.3 Quadratic Equations and Functions

Quadratic Equation

An equation that can be written in the form
$$ax^2 + bx + c = 0$$
where a, b, and c are real numbers with a $\neq 0$ is a **quadratic equation**.

An equation with an x^2 term as its highest term (2nd degree) is called a quadratic equation.

Standard Form:

A quadratic equation written in the form $ax^2 + bx + c = 0$ is in standard form.

Quadratic Function

A function that can be written in the form
$$f(x) = ax^2 + bx + c$$
where a, b, and c are real numbers with a $\neq 0$ is a **quadratic function**.

Roots/Zeros

The **zeros** of a quadratic function $f(x) = ax^2 + bx + c$ are the solutions of the associated quadratic equation $ax^2 + bx + c = 0$. These solutions can also be called **roots** of the equation.

Quadratic functions can have real number or imaginary number zeros and quadratic equations can have real number or imaginary number solutions.

If the zeros of a quadratic function are real numbers, they are also the first coordinate of the x-intercepts of the graph of the quadratic function.

The two principals below are helpful in solving quadratic equations.

Principal of Zero Products:
If $ab = 0$, then either $a = 0$ or $b = 0$.
If either $a = 0$ or $b = 0$, then $ab = 0$.

Principal of Square Roots:
If $x^2 = k$ then $x = \sqrt{k}$ or $x = -\sqrt{k}$.

To Solve Quadratic Equations:

Methods for solving quadratic equations

1. **Factor method.** The equation is rewritten in standard form and then is factored. Using the Principle of Zero Products, the factors are set equal to zero and solved. The results are the solutions to the quadratic equation.
   See Factor Notes found in the Algebra Review located at the front of this book.

2. **Square root method.** This method is used when the first degree term equals zero. The x^2 term is isolated, and then the square root is taken of both sides of the equation using the Principle of Square Roots.

3. **Complete the Square Method.** Explained in example 3.

4. **Quadratic Formula.** Explained in example 6.

Example 1. Solve $x^2 - 3x + 2 = 0$.

Solution. Given $\quad x^2 - 3x + 2 = 0$

We will factor the equation. (Remember we want to find two numbers whose product is positive 2 and whose sum is equal to negative 3.)

$$(x-2)(x-1) = 0 \qquad \text{Factor.}$$
$$x - 2 = 0 \quad \text{or} \quad x - 1 = 0 \qquad \text{Set each factor} = \text{zero.}$$
$$x = 2 \qquad \text{or} \quad x = 1 \qquad \text{Solve.}$$

Check: $x = 2$: $(2)^2 - 3(2) + 2 = 0$

$$4 - 6 + 2 = 0$$
$$0 = 0 \qquad \text{True statement}$$

$x = 1$: $(1)^2 - 3(1) + 2 = 0$

$$1 - 3 + 2 = 0$$
$$0 = 0 \qquad \text{True statement}$$

This equation can also be solved with a graphing calculator. See Chapter 6, Example 15.

Example 2. Solve $3x^2 - 15 = 0$.

Solution: Given

$$3x^2 - 15 = 0 \qquad \text{Use Square Root method since there is not a first degree term.}$$
$$3x^2 = 15 \qquad \text{Isolate } x^2.$$
$$x^2 = 5 \qquad \text{Divide both sides by 3.}$$
$$x = \sqrt{5} \qquad \text{or} \qquad x = -\sqrt{5} \qquad \text{Take square root of both sides.}$$

Check: $x = \sqrt{5}$ $3(\sqrt{5})^2 - 15 = 0$

$\qquad\qquad\qquad\quad 3 * 5 - 15 = 0$

$\qquad\qquad\qquad\qquad 0 = 0$ $\qquad\qquad$ True

$\qquad\quad x = -\sqrt{5}$ $3(-\sqrt{5})^2 - 15 = 0$

$\qquad\qquad\qquad\quad 3 * 5 - 15 = 0$

$\qquad\qquad\qquad\qquad 0 = 0$ $\qquad\qquad$ True

Number of Solutions of a Quadratic Equation

A quadratic equation can have **two real number solutions, one real number solution or two complex number solutions (no real solutions).**

Example 3.   Solve $x^2 + 6 = 0$.

Solution: We will solve this equation using the square root method since the equation does not contain a first degree term.

$\qquad\qquad x^2 + 6 = 0$

$\qquad\qquad x^2 = -6$ $\qquad\qquad\qquad$ Isolate the x^2 term.

$\qquad\qquad x = \pm\sqrt{-6}$ $\qquad\qquad$ Take the square root of both sides.

$\qquad\qquad x = \pm i\sqrt{6}$ $\qquad\qquad\;$ Write the solutions as a complex. number.

Because the solutions are imaginary numbers instead of real numbers, the graph has no x-intercepts.

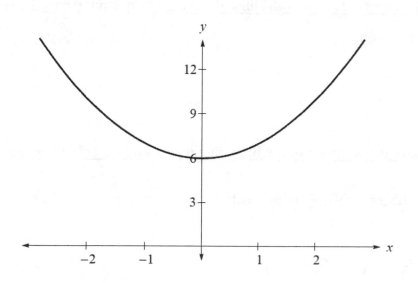

Note: the graph **does not** cross the x-axis and shows **no real solutions.**

99

Complete the Square Method

> Any quadratic equation can be solved using the square root property if it is first written in the form: $(x+n)^2 = k$ for suitable numbers n and k.
>
> Complete the square to get a quadratic equation into this form.

It is easier to understand the complete the square method by working an example. The steps used in the complete the square method are shown in Example 4 below.

Example 4: Solve $9x^2 - 12x - 1 = 0$.

Solution: We need to find constants n and k so that the given equation can be written in the form $(x+n)^2 = k$. If we expand $(x+n)^2$ we find $x^2 + 2xn + n^2$, and the coefficient of x^2 is 1.

Step1: **Get a leading coefficient of 1** in the given equation.

 We will multiply both sides of the given equation by 1/9.

$$x^2 - \frac{4}{3}x - \frac{1}{9} = 0$$

Step 2: **Add the constant $\frac{1}{9}$ to both sides of the equation** leaving only 2 terms on the left side of the equation.

$$x^2 - \frac{4}{3}x = \frac{1}{9}$$

Step 3. **Calculate the number that will make the left side a perfect square**.

 To find that number we take $\frac{1}{2}$ of the coefficient of the x-term.

$$\frac{1}{2} * (-\frac{4}{3}) \quad = \quad -\frac{2}{3}$$

Step 4: **Square the new number and add to both sides** of the equation.

$$\left(-\frac{2}{3}\right)^2 = \frac{4}{9}$$ Square this new number.

$$x^2 - \frac{4}{3}x + \frac{4}{9} = \frac{1}{9} + \frac{4}{9}$$ Add the squared number to both sides.

Step 5: **Factor the left side into a binomial (two terms) square**.

$$\left(x - \frac{2}{3}\right)^2 = \frac{5}{9}$$ Factor.

Step 6: **Use the square root property and rationalize the denominator**.

$$x - \frac{2}{3} = \pm\sqrt{\frac{5}{9}}$$

$$x - \frac{2}{3} = \pm\frac{\sqrt{5}}{3}$$ then $$x = \frac{2}{3} \pm \frac{\sqrt{5}}{3}$$

Complete the Square Method to solve $ax^2 + bx + c = 0$, $a \neq 0$.
1. Transform the equation into standard form and then put it into descending exponent order.
2. If $a \neq 1$, divide each term by a, then rewrite the equation so that the constant is alone on one side of the equal sign.
3. Complete the square by taking one-half of the coefficient of x, squaring that number, and adding this squared number to both sides of the equation.
4. Write one side of the equation as the square of a binomial.
5. Use the square root property.
6. Solve for the variable.

Example 5.   Solve $2x^2 - 3x - 1 = 0$ by completing the square.

Solution: Given:
$$2x^2 - 3x - 1 = 0$$

$$x^2 - \frac{3}{2}x - \frac{1}{2} = 0$$ Multiply all terms by $\frac{1}{2}$ so the coefficient of

x is 1.

$$x^2 - \frac{3}{2}x = \frac{1}{2} \qquad \text{Add } \frac{1}{2} \text{ to both sides.}$$

Complete the square $\dfrac{1}{2}\left(-\dfrac{3}{2}\right) = -\dfrac{3}{4}$ and $\left(-\dfrac{3}{4}\right)^2 = \dfrac{9}{16}$

Add this number to both sides.

$$x^2 - \frac{3}{2}x + \frac{9}{16} = \frac{1}{2} + \frac{9}{16}$$

$$\left(x - \frac{3}{4}\right)^2 = \frac{17}{16} \qquad \text{Factor and simplify.}$$

$$x - \frac{3}{4} = \pm\frac{\sqrt{17}}{4} \qquad \text{Take the square root of both sides.}$$

$$x = \frac{3}{4} \pm \frac{\sqrt{17}}{4} \qquad \text{or} \qquad x = \frac{3 \pm \sqrt{17}}{4}$$

Quadratic Formula:

The quadratic formula can be used to find the solutions on <u>any quadratic equation</u> if the equation is transformed into standard form: $ax^2 + bx + c = 0$.

The solutions of the quadratic equation $ax^2 + bx + c = 0$, where $a \neq 0$, are

$$x = \frac{-b \pm \sqrt{b^2 - 4ac}}{2a}$$

Example 6. Solve $x^2 - 4x + 1 = 0$ using the quadratic formula.

Solution: The coefficients of the given equation give us: $a = 1$, $b = -4$, and $c = 1$. Substitute these values into the quadratic formula.

$$x = \frac{-b \pm \sqrt{b^2 - 4ac}}{2a} \qquad \text{Quadratic formula}$$

$$x = \frac{-(-4) \pm \sqrt{(-4)^2 - 4(1)(1)}}{2(1)}$$

$$x = \frac{4 \pm \sqrt{16-4}}{2} = \frac{4 \pm \sqrt{12}}{2} = \frac{4 \pm 2\sqrt{3}}{2} = \frac{2(2 \pm \sqrt{3})}{2}$$

$$x = 2 \pm \sqrt{3}$$

The solutions are: $2+\sqrt{3}$ and $2-\sqrt{3}$.

This problem can be solved using a graphing calculator. See Chapter 6, Example 16.

Example 7. Solve $3x^2 - x + 2 = 0$ using the quadratic formula.

Solution: From the given coefficients, we see that $a = 3$, $b = -1$, and $c = 2$. Use the quadratic formula and substitute these values into the formula.

$$x = \frac{-(-1) \pm \sqrt{(-1)^2 - 4(3)(2)}}{2(3)}$$

$$x = \frac{1 \pm \sqrt{1-24}}{6}$$

$$x = \frac{1 \pm \sqrt{-23}}{6}$$

Notice that $\sqrt{-23}$ is not a real number and we will use i to write the answers as complex numbers.

$$x = \frac{1 \pm i\sqrt{23}}{6}$$

The two solutions are both complex numbers.

The Discriminant

The quantity under the radical in the quadratic formula, $b^2 - 4ac$, is called the **discriminant.**

The value of the discriminant can be used to determine whether the solutions will be rational, irrational, or complex numbers as well as how many solutions there are.

Solutions

Discriminant	Number of solutions	Type
Positive, perfect square	two	rational
Positive, not perfect square	two	irrational
Zero	one	rational
Negative	two	complex

In this case the two solutions are complex conjugates.

In Example 6, the equation is $x^2 - 4x + 1 = 0$ and the discriminant is equal to 12 indicating there are two irrational solutions.

In Example 7, the equation is: $3x^2 - x + 2 = 0$ and the discriminant is equal to -23 indicating there are two complex solutions.

Quadratic Type Equations

Some equations that are not quadratic can be solved in the same manner as a quadratic equation by using substitution to change the original equation into a quadratic equation.

An equation is called a **quadratic type** if it can be rewritten in the form:

$$au^2 + bu + c = 0 \qquad \text{where } a \neq 0 \text{ and } u \text{ is an appropriate substitute value.}$$

In this type of equation we first find a quadratic in terms of **u** by finding an appropriate value for **u** such that the substitution converts the given equation into a quadratic. Lastly after finding values for u, we solve for the solutions in term of the original variable.

Example 8. Solve $x^6 + 7x^3 = 8$.

Because the given equation is not a quadratic equation we must look for a way to solve it. We want to see if we can rewrite the equation as a quadratic in terms of u.
Look at the two exponents in the equation, and we see that $(x^3)^2 = x^6$. If this relationship of the middle term variable being the square root of the first term variable, we can solve the equation.

Solution:

$$x^6 + 7x^3 - 8 = 0 \qquad \text{Rewrite in standard form.}$$
$$\text{Let } u = x^3 \text{ and then } u^2 = x^6, \text{ and the equation becomes:}$$

$$u^2 + 7u - 8 = 0$$

$$(u + 8)(u - 1) = 0 \qquad \text{Factor.}$$

$$u = -8, u = 1 \qquad \text{Solve each factor for } u.$$

Since we originally let $u = x^3$, we now replace u with x^3 and solve for x.

$$x^3 = -8 \text{ and } x^3 = 1 \qquad \text{Take the cube root.}$$

$$x = -2, \text{ and } x = 1$$

Check: $(1)^6 + 7(1)^3 - 8 = 1 + 7 - 8 = 0 \qquad \text{true}$
$(-2)^6 + 7(-2)^3 - 8 = 64 - 56 - 8 = 0 \qquad \text{true}$

Both $x = -2$, and $x = 1$ are solutions.

Example 9.   Solve $x^4 - 5x^2 + 4 = 0$.

Solution: This is not a quadratic equation, but we can see that $(x^2)^2 = x^4$.
This equation can be written as a quadratic equation using u.

Let $u = x^2$ and then $u^2 = x^4$.

The original equation becomes:

$$u^2 - 5u + 4 = 0$$

$$(u-1)(u-4) = 0 \qquad\qquad \text{Factor.}$$

$$u = 1, u = 4 \qquad\qquad \text{Solve each factor for } u.$$

Replace u with x^2 and solve for x.

$$x^2 = 1 \text{ and } x^2 = 4 \qquad \text{Take the square root of both sides.}$$

$$x = \pm 1, \text{ and } x = \pm 2$$

Check:

$$(1)^4 - 5(1)^2 + 4 = 1 - 5 + 4 = 0 \qquad \text{True}$$
$$(-1)^4 - 5(-1)^2 + 4 = 1 - 5 + 4 = 0 \qquad \text{True}$$
$$(2)^4 - 5(2)^2 + 4 = 16 - 20 + 4 = 0 \qquad \text{True}$$
$$(-2)^4 - 5(-2)^2 + 4 = 16 - 20 + 4 = 0 \qquad \text{True}$$

All four values $x = \pm 1$, and $x = \pm 2$ are solutions.

Note: When you have equations with exponents of degree other than 2, it is helpful with solving these equations to try to convert the equations to quadratics by using the "u substitution".

Section 2.3 Exercises

Solve:

1. $x^2 - x - 20 = 0$

2. $x^2 - 6x + 8 = 0$

3. $2x^2 + x - 1 = 0$

4. $3x^2 - x - 2 = 0$

5. $3x^2 - 12x = 0$

6. $5x^2 - 10x = 0$

7. $5x^2 - 20 = 0$

8. $5x^2 = 25$

9. $4x^2 = 26$

10. $2x^2 - 12 = 0$

11. $7x^2 + 14 = 0$

12. $4x^2 + 12 = 0$

13. $5x^2 - 55 = 0$

14. $5x^2 + 55 = 0$

15. $3x^2 - 6 = 0$

16. $3x^2 = 6x$

17. $3x^3 + 5x^2 - 2x = 0$

18. $4x^3 + x^2 - 4x - 1 = 0$

Solve by completing the square.

19. $x^2 + 4x = 5$

20. $x^2 = 7x - 6$

21. $x^2 + 6x + 8 = 0$

22. $x^2 + 7x + 12 = 0$

Solve using the quadratic formula.

23. $x^2 - 7x = 18$

24. $x^2 + x + 3 = 0$

25. $x^2 + 3x - 1 = 0$

26. $8x^2 + 6 = 2x$

Find the discriminant and then determine what type of solutions exist.

27. $3x^2 = 6x + 7$

28. $5x^2 - 10x + 8 = 0$

29. $x^2 - 25 = 0$

Solve for x.

30. $x^4 - 4x^2 + 3 = 0$

31. $x - 3\sqrt{x} - 4 = 0$

Section 2.4 Graphs of Quadratic Functions

Graph of a Quadratic Function

The graph of a quadratic function is called a **parabola.** All functions of the form
$$y = ax^2 + bx + c$$
where a, b, and c are real numbers with a $\neq$ 0, have parabolas as their graphs.

The graph of $y = x^2$:

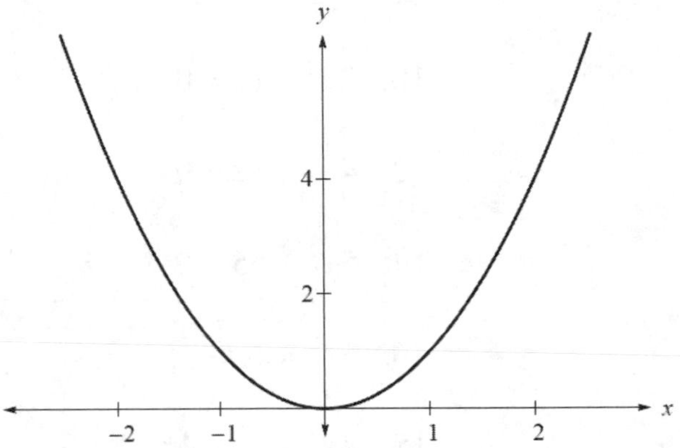

Parabolas are examples of graphs that are symmetric with respect to a line (the y-axis in the graph above).

This line of symmetry is called the **axis** of the parabola.

The point where the axis intersects the parabola is the **vertex** of the parabola.

The vertex is the point where the graph changes direction and might be the highest point, the maximum point, of the graph or it can be the lowest point, the minimum point.

Graphs of Parabolas:

$$y = a(x - h)^2 + k, \quad a \neq 0,$$

1. is a parabola with a vertex (h, k), and the vertical line $x = h$ is the axis of symmetry;

2. opens upward if $a > 0$ and the vertex is a minimum point
   and opens downward if $a < 0$ and the vertex is a maximum point;

3. is broader than $y = x^2$ if $0 < |a| < 1$ and narrower than $y = x^2$ if $|a| > 1$;

4. maximum/minimum value $= k$.

Example 1: Find the vertex, the axis of symmetry and the maximum or minimum value: $y = 5(x-3)^2 - 2$.

Solution: The function is in the form $y = a(x-h)^2 + k$ and we see that
$$a = 5, h = 3, and\ k = -2.$$

Vertex $= (h,\ k)$ $(3, -2)$
Axis of symmetry $x = h$ $x = 3$
Maximum value: None   because $a > 0$ so graph opens upward
Minimum value (k value of vertex): -2

Example 2: Find the vertex, the axis of symmetry and the maximum or minimum value: $f(x) = -3(x+4)^2 + 6$

Solution: This function is in the form $y = a(x-h)^2 + k$ and we see that
$$a = -3, h = -4, and\ k = 6$$

Vertex: $(h,\ k)$ $(-4, 6)$
Axis of symmetry: $x = h$ $x = -4$
Maximum (k value of vertex) $a < 0$, graph has a maximum: max is 6

Graphing Quadratic Functions of the type: $f(x) = ax^2 + bx + c, \quad a \neq 0$

We will transform the function from the given form into the form $a(x-h)^2 + k$ so that we can find the vertex, the axis of symmetry and the maximum/minimum value. Knowing these values, sketching the graph becomes much easier.

The process of completing the square can be used to change $ax^2 + bx + c$ to the form $a(x-h)^2 + k$. See Example 3 below.

Example 3: Find the vertex, the axis of symmetry, and the maximum or minimum value, and sketch the graph of $f(x) = x^2 - 6x + 7$.

Solution: To express $f(x) = x^2 - 6x + 7$ in the form $a(x-h)^2 + k$, complete the square on the terms involving x. Take half of the coefficient of x and square this value:

$$\left(\frac{-6}{2}\right)^2 = (-3)^2 = 9$$

Add and subtract the new number to the expression:
$$f(x) = x^2 - 6x + 9 - 9 + 7$$
$$= (x^2 - 6x + 9) - 9 + 7$$

$$f(x) = (x-3)^2 - 2$$ 　　　　This is now in the form $a(x-h)^2 + k$.

Vertex: $(3, -2)$

Axis of symmetry: $x = 3$

$a > 0$, parabola opens up and has a minimum point.

Minimum value of function: -2

The graph is:

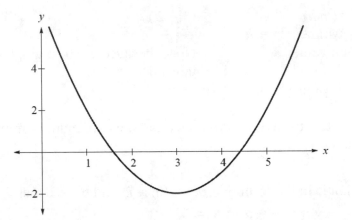

Note that this graph is a shift of the graph of $y = x^2$ right 3 units and down 2 units. The axis of symmetry does not show up as part of the graph but is instead a characteristic of the graph. The axis is an imaginary line that could be used to fold the graph in half such that the two halves of the graph would coincide.

This problem can be solved by graphing the given curve using a graphing calculator and then using the CALC function to solve for maximum or minimum.

Example 4: Find the vertex, the axis of symmetry, and the maximum or minimum value

of 　　$f(x) = \dfrac{x^2}{2} - 2x + 5$　 and sketch the graph of the function.

Solution: Complete the square to transform the function into $a(x-h)^2 + k$ form.

Begin by factoring $\dfrac{1}{2}$ out of the **first two terms**:

$$f(x) = \frac{1}{2}(x^2 - 4x) + 5$$

Next complete the square inside the parentheses. Half of -4 is -2 and $(-2)^2 = 4$. Add and subtract 4 inside the parentheses:

$$f(x) = \frac{1}{2}(x^2 - 4x + 4 - 4) + 5$$

Next use the distributive law to remove -4 from within the parentheses.

$$= \frac{1}{2}(x^2 - 4x + 4) - \frac{1}{2} * 4 + 5$$

$$f(x) = \frac{1}{2}(x-2)^2 + 3$$

Vertex: (2, 3)
Axis of Symmetry: $x = 2$
Minimum: 3

Graph:

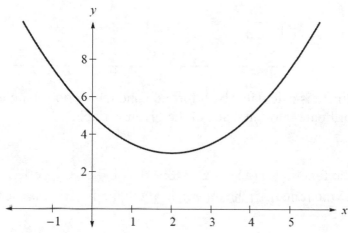

Example 5: Find the vertex, the axis of symmetry and the maximum or minimum value:
$f(x) = -2x^2 + 8x + 3$.

Solution: $f(x) = -2x^2 + 8x + 3$

$= -2(x^2 - 4x) + 3$	Factor -2 out of 1st two terms.
$= -2(x^2 - 4x + 4 - 4) + 3$	Complete the square.
$= -2(x^2 - 4x + 4) - 2*(-4) + 3$	Distribute.
$= -2(x-2)^2 + 11$	

Vertex: (2, 11)

Axis of Symmetry: $x = 2$

Maximum value $= 11$

Formula for Finding the Vertex of a Parabola

An alternative way to find the vertex is to use the formula shown below.

Formula for the Vertex of a Parabola:

The vertex of the graph of $f(x) = ax^2 + bx + c$ is given by:

$$\left(-\frac{b}{2a}, f\left(-\frac{b}{2a} \right) \right)$$

Note that the x-coordinate is calculated by a formula and the y-coordinate is found by substituting the x-coordinate into f in place of the given variable.

Example 6: Given the function $f(x) = -x^2 + 8x - 6$. Find a) the vertex, b) maximum or minimum value, c) the range, d) the intervals where the function is increasing and decreasing.

Solution:
a) Vertex: The coefficients of the terms tell us that $a = -1, b = 8, and\ c = -6$, use the above formula to find the x-coordinate of the vertex.

$$-\frac{b}{2a} = -\frac{8}{2(-1)} = 4$$

Substitute this x-value into f for x to obtain the y-coordinate of the vertex.
$$f(4) = -(4)^2 + 8(4) - 6 = 10$$

The vertex is (4, 10).

b) Maximum or Minimum value: Since a is negative, the graph opens down and the y-coefficient of the vertex which is 10 is the maximum value of the function.

c) Range: We can determine the range by thinking about what the graph would be and interpreting the graph. Because a is negative, we know the graph opens down, the vertex is a maximum, and the y-coefficient of the vertex gives us the largest value of the range. The range is $(-\infty, 10]$.

d) Since the graph opens down, the function values increase as we approach the vertex from the left and decrease as we move to the right from the vertex.

Increasing: $(-\infty, 4)$.
Decreasing: $(4, \infty)$.

The graph of our function $f(x) = -x^2 + 8x - 6$ is shown below:

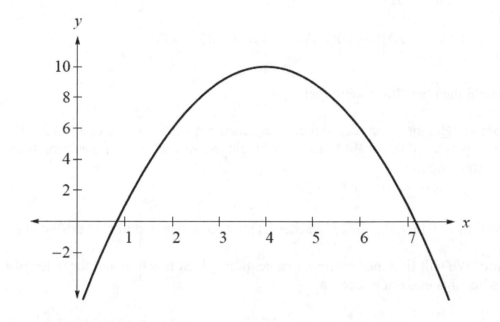

Applications

Many real-world problems involve finding the maximum or minimum value of a quadratic function.

Example 7: <u>Maximizing Area</u>. A gardener has 80 feet of fence to enclose a rectangular garden. What is the maximum area that the gardener can enclose? What will the dimensions of the garden be?

Solution: First make a drawing of the rectangular garden. Let w represent the width in feet. Then $\frac{1}{2}(80 - 2w)$ or $(40 - w)$ft. represents the length.

The Area of a rectangle is given by length times width.

$$A(w) = (40 - w)w$$

$$A(w) = -w^2 + 40w.$$

We have written a quadratic function, and we know that its graph is a parabola.

Since w^2 has a negative coefficient, the function opens down and has a **maximum value** at the vertex.

Find the vertex, which will be $(w, A(w))$.

113

$$w = -\frac{b}{2a} = -\frac{40}{2(-1)} = 20 \text{ ft.}$$

and $\quad A(20) = -(20)^2 + 40(20) = -400 + 800 = 400$

Area would then be: 400 square feet.

Example 8: <u>Height</u>. A model rocket is launched with an initial velocity of 50 ft/sec from the top of a hill that is 30 ft high. Its height in t seconds after it has been launched is given by the function:

$$s(t) = -16t^2 + 50t + 30$$

Find the time at which the rocket reaches its maximum height and find this height.

Solution: We will find the maximum value of the given function and the value of t (time) when this maximum occurs.

The function is a quadratic function and the coefficient of t^2 is negative. We know that the graph is a parabola, opens downward, and has a maximum value at the vertex.

Use the formla to find the vertex of the parabola. The first coordinate of the vertex is the time t when the rocket reaches its maximum height.

$$t = -\frac{b}{2a} = -\frac{50}{2(-16)} = 1.562$$

The second coordinate of the vertex is the maximum height of the rocket.

$$s(1.562) = -16(1.562)^2 + 50(1.562) + 30 = 69.062$$

The time that the maximum height is reached is: 1.562 seconds, and the maximum height is: 69.062 feet.

Now let's graph this function.

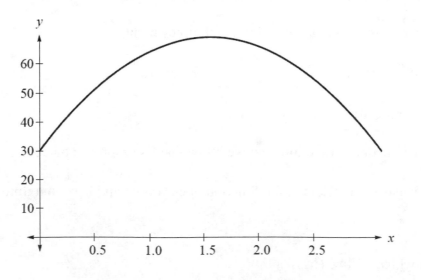

114

Section 2.4 Exercises

For the problems 1 − 11 find: a) the vertex; b) the axis of symmetry; c) determine if there is a maximum or minimum value and find that value.

1. $f(x) = x^2 - 4x - 12$

2. $g(x) = x^2 + 6x - 7$

3. $f(x) = x^2 - 8x + 12$

4. $f(x) = x^2 - 4x + 3$

5. $g(x) = 3x^2 + 9x + 12$

6. $f(x) = -x^2 - 6x + 2$

7. $f(x) = -x^2 - 4x$

8. $g(x) = -x^2 + 4$

9. $f(x) = -3x^2 - 2x + 1$

10. $f(x) = -x^2 - 4x + 2$

11. $f(x) = 2x^2 - 4x + 5$

12. $g(x) = -x^2 + 6x - 6$

For problems 13 – 16, find: a) the vertex; b) determine if there is a maximum or minimum value and find that value; c) the range; d) intervals where the function is increasing and decreasing.

13. $f(x) = x^2 - 7x + 6$

14. $g(x) = x^2 - 4x - 5$

15. $g(x) = -2x^2 + 6x - 5$

16. $f(x) = -2x^2 - 4x + 16$

17. A ball is thrown directly upward from a height of 4 ft with an initial velocity of 30 ft/sec. The function $s(t) = -16t^2 + 30t + 4$ gives the height of the ball t seconds after it has been thrown. Determine the time at which the ball reaches its maximum height and find the maximum height.

18. A farmer wants to enclose a rectangular area, using the side of his barn as one side of the rectangle. What is the maximum area that he can enclose with 66 ft of fence? What should the dimensions be in order to give this area?

Section 2.5   Rational, Radical and Absolute Value Equations

Rational Equation

Rational Equation: an equation that contains a rational expression.

The first step in solving a rational equation is to eliminate fractions:
  multiply by the Common Denominator (called LCD) in order to
  make all of the denominators equal to one.

Example 1. Solve $\dfrac{1}{2} - \dfrac{x-2}{3} = \dfrac{1}{6}$

Solution: We see that the equation contains fractions, and we realize that the equation is easier to solve if we can eliminate these fractions. To do this we will find the LCD of the three fractions in the problem by looking at the denominators (2, 3, and 6). To find the LCD we must find a number that has all three denominators as factors. The LCD is 6. When we multiply each side of the equation by 6 and simplify, the fractions are gone.

$$\frac{1}{2} - \frac{x-2}{3} = \frac{1}{6} \qquad\qquad \text{Given}$$

$$6*\left(\frac{1}{2} - \frac{x-2}{3}\right) = 6*\left(\frac{1}{6}\right) \qquad\qquad \text{Multiply by LCD of 6.}$$

$$6*\left(\frac{1}{2}\right) - 6*\left(\frac{x-2}{3}\right) = 6*\left(\frac{1}{6}\right) \qquad\qquad \text{Distribute.}$$

$$3 - 2(x-2) = 1 \qquad\qquad \text{Simplify.}$$

$$3 - 2x + 4 = 1 \qquad\qquad \text{Distribute.}$$

$$7 - 2x = 1 \qquad\qquad \text{Combine like terms.}$$

$$-2x = -6 \qquad\qquad \text{Subtract 7 from each side.}$$

$$x = 3 \qquad\qquad \text{Divide both sides by } -2.$$

Check: Substitute 3 into the original equation for x and see if equation is true.

$$\frac{1}{2} - \frac{3-2}{3} \quad = \quad \frac{1}{2} - \frac{1}{3} \quad = \quad \frac{3}{6} - \frac{2}{6} = \frac{1}{6}$$

The solution to the equation is 3.   This problem can be solved using a graphing calculator. See Chapter 6, Example 17.

Example 2: Solve: $\dfrac{1}{x}+\dfrac{1}{6}=\dfrac{1}{4}$

Solution: Because the equation contains fractions, our first step will be to eliminate these. To do this we must find the Lowest Common Denominator of the three denominators. The LCD for x, 6, and 4 must be a term that has factors of all three of the denominators, and we see that it is $12x$. Multiply each side of the equation by $12x$.

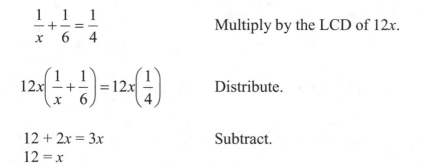

$$\frac{1}{x}+\frac{1}{6}=\frac{1}{4}$$ Multiply by the LCD of $12x$.

$$12x\left(\frac{1}{x}+\frac{1}{6}\right)=12x\left(\frac{1}{4}\right)$$ Distribute.

$$12+2x=3x$$ Subtract.
$$12=x$$

Check:

$$\frac{1}{12}+\frac{1}{6} \quad = \quad \frac{1}{12}+\frac{2}{12} \quad = \quad \frac{3}{12} \quad = \quad \frac{1}{4}$$

The solution to the equation is 12.

Remember:

1. Use the LCD to remove the fractions in a rational <u>EQUATION</u>. This is not appropriate if we have an expression rather than an equation.

2. Always check rational equations because not all possible solutions found by multiplying by the LCD are valid solutions.

Extraneous Solution:

<u>Extraneous Solution</u>:
    A number that appears to be a solution to an equation but results in a zero in the denominator of the equation or results in a false or undefined solution is called an <u>extraneous solution</u>.

Example 3. Solve the equation: $\dfrac{1}{x} + \dfrac{1}{x-3} = \dfrac{x-2}{x-3}$.

Solution: The LCD for x and $x-3$ is $x(x-3)$

Notice that $x = 3$ is NOT a possible solution of the equation because this value would make a denominator have a value of zero which is undefined.

$$\dfrac{1}{x} + \dfrac{1}{x-3} = \dfrac{x-2}{x-3} \qquad\qquad \text{Given}$$

$$x(x-3)*\dfrac{1}{x} + x(x-3)*\dfrac{1}{x-3} = x(x-3)*\dfrac{x-2}{x-3} \qquad \text{Multiply by LCD.}$$

$$x-3+x = x(x-2) \qquad\qquad \text{Simplify.}$$

$$2x-3 = x^2 - 2x$$

$$0 = x^2 - 4x + 3 \qquad\qquad \text{Quadratic}$$

$$0 = (x-3)(x-1)$$

$$x-3 = 0 \qquad \text{or} \qquad x-1 = 0$$

$$x = 3 \qquad\quad \text{or} \qquad x = 1$$

If $x = 3$, the denominator of $x-3$ has a value of 0. This is not valid.

If $x = 1$, the original equation is satisfied.
The only solution to the equation is 1.

We can use a graphing calculator to check the possible solutions. See Chapter 6, Example 18.

Radical Equations

Radical Equation:
    any equation that includes a variable under a radical sign.

Principal of Powers: If $a = b$, then $a^n = b^n$.
We will use this principal to help us solve radical equations.

The Squaring Property is Used to Solve Radical Equations

Squaring Property of Equality:

Both sides of an equation may be squared, but all solutions must be verified so that any extraneous solutions are eliminated.

If an equation involves radicals, we often raise both sides to a positive power. The solutions of the new equation always contain the solutions of the given equation. In some cases however, the new equation has solutions that are **not solutions** to the original equation. These are called extraneous solutions. **As a result, check all solutions in the given radical equation.**

To solve Radical Equations:
1. **Isolate the radical first;**
2. **Raise both sides to a power that will remove the radical sign;**
3. **Solve for the variable;**
4. **Check.**

Example 4: Solve $\sqrt{x^2 - 16} = 3$

Solution: <u>Always isolate the radical first.</u>

$$\sqrt{x^2 - 16} = 3 \qquad\qquad \text{Given}$$

$$\left(\sqrt{x^2 - 16}\right)^2 = 3^2 \qquad\qquad \text{Principal of Powers}$$

$$x^2 - 16 = 9$$

$$x^2 = 25 \qquad\qquad \text{Solve.}$$

$$x = \pm 5$$

Check each solution:
$$\sqrt{5^2 - 16} = \sqrt{25 - 16} = \sqrt{9} = 3$$

$$\sqrt{(-5)^2 - 16} = \sqrt{25 - 16} = 3$$

Both 5 and -5 are solutions.

Example 5: Solve $x = \sqrt{2x+3}$

Solution:

$x = \sqrt{2x+3}$ Given

$x^2 = \left(\sqrt{2x+3}\right)^2$ Principal of Powers

$x^2 = 2x+3$

$x^2 - 2x - 3 = 0$ Factor to solve.

$(x-3)(x+1) = 0$

$x - 3 = 0$ or $x + 1 = 0$

$x = 3$ or $x = -1$

Check: $x = 3$ or $x = -1$

$3 = \sqrt{2*3+3}$ $-1 = \sqrt{2(-1)+3}$

$3 = \sqrt{9}$ or $-1 = \sqrt{1}$

Correct   Incorrect

Because -1 does not satisfy the original equation, it is an extraneous solution.
The only solution is 3.

Example 6: Solve: $x + 2 = \sqrt{-2-3x}$

Solution:

$x + 2 = \sqrt{-2-3x}$ Given

$(x+2)^2 = \left(\sqrt{-2-3x}\right)^2$ Principal of Powers

$x^2 + 4x + 4 = -2 - 3x$

$x^2 + 7x + 6 = 0$

$(x+6)(x+1) = 0$

$x + 6 = 0$ or $x + 1 = 0$

$x = -6$ or $x = -1$

Check: $\qquad\qquad x = -6 \qquad\qquad\qquad\qquad x = -1$

$$-6+2 = \sqrt{-2-3(-6)} \qquad -1+2 = \sqrt{-2-3(-1)}$$

$$-4 = \sqrt{16} \qquad\qquad\qquad 1 = \sqrt{1}$$

$$\text{Incorrect} \qquad\qquad\qquad\qquad \text{Correct}$$

The solution -6 does not check. **The only solution to the original equation is** -1.

If an equation has two radicals, rewrite the equation so that the radicals are on opposite sides of the equal sign. It is often necessary to raise both sides to a power more than once.

Example 7: Solve $\sqrt{x-3} = 5 - \sqrt{x+2}$.

Solution: $\qquad\qquad \sqrt{x-3} = 5 - \sqrt{x+2} \qquad\qquad$ Given

$$(\sqrt{x-3})^2 = \left(5 - \sqrt{x+2}\right)^2 \qquad \text{Square both sides.}$$

$$x - 3 = \left(5 - \sqrt{x+2}\right)\left(5 - \sqrt{x+2}\right) \qquad \text{Use foil.}$$

$$x - 3 = 25 - 5\sqrt{x+2} - 5\sqrt{x+2} + (x+2)$$

$$x - 3 = 25 - 10\sqrt{x+2} + x + 2$$

$$-30 = -10\sqrt{x+2} \qquad\qquad \text{Combine like terms.}$$

$$3 = \sqrt{x+2} \qquad\qquad\qquad \text{Isolate the radical.}$$

$$3^2 = (\sqrt{x+2})^2 \qquad\qquad \text{Square both sides again.}$$

$$9 = \overset{.}{x} + 2$$

$$x = 7$$

Check: $\qquad\qquad \sqrt{x-3} = 5 - \sqrt{x+2} \qquad\qquad$ Given

$$\sqrt{7-3} = 5 - \sqrt{7+2} \qquad\qquad \text{Substitute 7 for } x.$$

$$\sqrt{4} = 5 - \sqrt{9}$$

$$2 = 5 - 3$$

$$2 = 2$$

The solution is 7.

Absolute Value Equations

For $a > 0$ and some algebraic expression X: $|X| = a$ means:

$$X = a \quad \text{or} \quad X = -a.$$

Solving Absolute Value Equations

To Solve Equations with Absolute Value Terms :

1. Isolate the absolute value term so that $\left|\text{expression}\right| = a$.

2. For $a > 0$, and
$$\left|\text{expression}\right| = a \quad \text{the absolute value symbols are}$$
$$\text{removed by:}$$

$$\text{expression} = a \qquad \text{or} \qquad \text{expression} = -a$$

Example 8:   Solve: $|x| = 8$.

Solution: Given $|x| = 8$

$$x = 8 \quad \text{or} \quad x = -8$$

Check: $|x| = 8$ $|x| = 8$

$|8| = 8$ $|-8| = 8$ Both answers are correct.

Example 9:   Solve $|x + 1| + 4 = 7$

Solution: $|x + 1| + 4 = 7$ Isolate the absolute symbol.

$$|x + 1| = 3$$

$$x + 1 = 3 \qquad \text{or} \qquad x + 1 = -3$$

$$x = 2 \qquad \text{or} \qquad x = -4$$

Check: For $x = 2$

$$|x + 1| + 4 = 7 \qquad\qquad \text{Given}$$

$$|2 + 1| + 4 = 7 \qquad\qquad \text{Substitute 2 for } x.$$

$$3 + 4 = 7$$

$$7 = 7$$

Correct

For $x = -4$

$$|x + 1| + 4 = 7 \qquad\qquad \text{Given}$$

$$|-4 + 1| + 4 = 7 \qquad\qquad \text{Substitute } -4 \text{ for } x.$$

$$|-3| + 4 = 7$$

$$3 + 4 = 7$$

$$7 = 7$$

Correct

The solutions are 2 and -4 since both of these solutions check.

Absolute value equations can be solved using a graphing calculator. See Chapter 6, Example 19.

Note: For rational, radical, and absolute value equations ALWAYS check your results. Extraneous results often appear in these three types of equations, and the extraneous results must be removed from the solution set.

Section 2.5 Exercises

Solve the given equations.

1. $\dfrac{1}{4} + \dfrac{1}{6} = \dfrac{1}{y}$

2. $\dfrac{3}{x} + \dfrac{1}{2} = \dfrac{3}{4}$

3. $\dfrac{1}{x} + \dfrac{1}{2} = \dfrac{3}{4}$

4. $\dfrac{4}{y} - \dfrac{1}{2} = 3$

5. $\dfrac{1}{t} + \dfrac{1}{5} = \dfrac{t-1}{5t} + \dfrac{3}{10}$

6. $\dfrac{2}{x} + \dfrac{1}{4x} = \dfrac{5}{8}$

7. $\dfrac{x}{2} = \dfrac{5}{x+3}$

8. $\dfrac{x}{3} = \dfrac{6}{x+7}$

9. $\dfrac{x-1}{x^2-4} + \dfrac{1}{x-2} = \dfrac{x+4}{x+2}$

10. $\dfrac{17+y}{y^2-1} - \dfrac{y-2}{y-1} = \dfrac{1}{y+1}$

11. $\dfrac{1}{x-1} + \dfrac{2}{x} = \dfrac{x}{x-1}$

12. $\dfrac{4}{m} + \dfrac{3}{m-3} = \dfrac{m}{m-3} - \dfrac{1}{3}$

13. $\dfrac{5}{x+2} - \dfrac{x-1}{x-3} = -\dfrac{2}{x-3}$

14. $\dfrac{5}{x-3} - 1 = \dfrac{x+7}{2x-6}$

15. $\dfrac{1}{x} = \dfrac{1}{x^3}$

16. $\dfrac{2}{x} = \dfrac{2}{x^2}$

17. $\sqrt{3x-1} = -5$

18. $\sqrt{3x-4} = -9$

19. $\sqrt{x} = x$

20. $\sqrt{x-2} = x$

21. $y+1 = \sqrt{2y+10}$

22. $\sqrt{2y+18} = y-3$

23. $|x| = 4$

24. $|x| = -4$

25. $|x+3| = 6$

26. $|x+4| = 8$

27. $|x-3| = 7$

28. $|x| = 0$

29. $|x+2| + 4 = 6$

30. $|2x+6| = 4$

Section 2.6: Linear Inequalities

Inequality

Inequality:

An inequality says that one expression is <u>greater than</u>, <u>greater than or equal to</u>, <u>less than</u>, or <u>less than or equal to</u> another.

An inequality uses the following symbols: $<$, $>$, $\leq$, $\geq$

A value of the variable for which the inequality is true is a <u>solution</u> of the inequality.

The <u>solution set</u> of an inequality is the set of all solutions to the inequality.

<u>Equivalent inequalities</u> are inequalities that have the same solution set.

The techniques used to solve inequalities are very similar to those used to solve equations.

Properties of Inequalities:

If P, Q, and R are algebraic expressions, then:

$P < Q$ and $P + R < Q + R$ are equivalent.
$P > Q$ and $P + R > Q + R$ are equivalent.
(The same expression may be added to both sides of an inequality.)

If $R > 0$, then $P < Q$ and $PR < QR$ are equivalent.
If $R > 0$, then $P > Q$ and $PR > QR$ are equivalent.
(The same <u>positive</u> expression may be multiplied to both sides of an inequality.)

If $R < 0$, then $P < Q$ and $PR > QR$ are equivalent.
If $R < 0$, then $P > Q$ and $PR < QR$ are equivalent.
(The same <u>negative</u> expression may be multiplied to both sides of an inequality, as long as the direction of the inequality is changed.)

Remember: If both sides of an inequality are multiplied by a negative number, then the <u>direction of the inequality is reversed.</u>

Linear Inequality

Examples 1 and 2 below are examples of a linear inequality.

Solutions to inequalities are written in interval form.

Example 1: Solve: $2x - 4 < 6 - 3x$ and graph the solution. Give answer in interval form.

Solution:

$2x - 4 < 6 - 3x$	Given
$5x - 4 < 6$	Add $3x$ to both sides.
$5x < 10$	Add 4 to both sides.
$x < 2$	Divide both sides by 5.

The solution in interval form is: $(-\infty, 2)$.

Graph:

This problem can be solved using a Graphing Calculator. See Chapter 6, Example 20.

Example 2: Solve $-26 - 14x > 20x + 8$ and graph. Give answer in interval form.

Solution:

$-26 - 14x > 20x + 8$	Given
$-26 - 34x > 8$	Subtract $20x$ from both sides.
$-34x > 34$	Add 26 to both sides.
$x < -1$	Divide both sides by -34. Change direction of inequality.

The solution in interval form is: $(-\infty, -1)$.

Graph:

Compound Inequality:

A Compound Inequality is formed when two inequalities are joined using the word "and" or "or".

Example: $-5 < 2x + 3$ and $2x + 3 \leq 7$

These can be combined into one compound inequality:

$-5 < 2x + 3 \leq 7$

Example 3: Solve $-5 < 2x + 3 \leq 7$. Sketch the graph and give the solution in interval form.

Solution: Solve this inequality by isolating the variable in the middle term.

$$-5 < 2x + 3 \leq 7 \qquad \text{Given}$$

$$-8 < 2x \leq 4 \qquad \text{Subtract 3 from each part.}$$

$$-4 < x \leq 2 \qquad \text{Divide by 2.}$$

The solution in interval form is: $(-4, 2]$.

Graph:

Example 4: Solve $2x - 5 \leq -3$ or $2x - 5 > 3$ and sketch graph.

Solution: Solve this type of inequality by solving each part separately.

$$2x - 5 \leq -3 \quad \text{or} \quad 2x - 5 > 3 \qquad \text{Given}$$

$$2x \leq 2 \quad \text{or} \quad 2x > 8 \qquad \text{Add 5 to both sides in each.}$$

$$x \leq 1 \quad \text{or} \quad x > 4 \qquad \text{Divide both sides by 2.}$$

The solution in interval form is: $(-\infty, 1] \cup (4, \infty)$.

Graph:

Inequalities Containing Absolute Values

Properties of Absolute Value Inequalities:

1. $|a| < b$ can be written as $-b < a < b$

2. $|a| > b$ can be written as $a < -b$ **or** $a > b$

3. $|a| \leq b$ can be written as $-b \leq a \leq b$

4. $|a| \geq b$ can be written as $a \leq -b$ **or** $a \geq b$

Solutions to inequalities containing absolute value symbols are written in interval form.

Example 5: Romove the absolute value symbols.

$|x| < 5$ can be written as $-5 < x < 5$

$|x| \geq 3$ can be written as $x \leq -3$ or $x \geq 3$

$|3x + 2| < 6$ can be written as $-6 < 3x + 2 < 6$

Example 6: Solve $|3x + 2| < 6$

Solution: $|3x + 2| < 6$ Given

$-6 < 3x + 2 < 6$ Rewrite without absolute symbols.

$-8 < 3x < 4$ Subtract 2 from all parts.

$-\dfrac{8}{3} < x < \dfrac{4}{3}$ Divide by 3.

The solution in interval form is: $\left(-\dfrac{8}{3}, \dfrac{4}{3}\right)$.

Example 7: Solve the equation: $|4x + 4| \geq 8$ and graph the solution set. Give the solution in interval form.

Solution:

$$|4x + 4| \geq 8 \qquad \text{Given}$$

$$4x + 4 \geq 8 \quad \text{or} \quad 4x + 4 \leq -8 \qquad \text{Remove absolute symbols.}$$

$$4x \geq 4 \quad \text{or} \quad 4x \leq -12 \qquad \text{Subtract 4.}$$

$$x \geq 1 \quad \text{or} \quad x \leq -3 \qquad \text{Divide by 4.}$$

The solution in interval form is: $(-\infty, -3] \cup [1, \infty)$.

The graph is:

Section 2.6 Exercises

Solve and graph the following.

1. $x + 5 < 4x - 10$

2. $2x - 6 \leq 3x + 4$

3. $4x - 4 - 2x \geq 2 - 4x + 10$

4. $10 - 4y \leq 3y - 4$

5. $-\frac{1}{3}x \leq \frac{5}{4} + \frac{5}{6}x$

6. $2x(x - 4) < 2(x^2 - 4)$

Solve the following, and write the solution in interval form.

7. $-4 \leq x + 1 < 5$

8. $3 \leq x - 4 \leq 5$

9. $-2 \leq x - 3 < 4$

10. $-2 < x + 2 < 4$

11. $-4 \leq -2x < 8$

12. $-3 < \frac{1}{2}(3x - 6)$

13. $2x < 10$ or $x + 4 > 16$

14. $2x + 2 < 6$ or $2x + 2 \geq 16$

15. $x + 10 \leq 1/3$ or $x - 20 \geq \frac{1}{2}$

16. $|x| < 4$

17. $|x| < 6$

18. $|x| > 9$

19. $|x + 3| < 6$

20. $|x + 4| < 7$

21. $|x + 7| \geq 9$

22. $|x + 2| > 6$

23. $|x - 1/4| < 6$

24. $|3x| > 6$

25. $|2x + 4| \leq 10$

26. $|4 - 3x| > 8$

27. $|x + 4/3| \leq 8/3$

28. $\left|\frac{2x + 1}{5}\right| > 10$

29. $\left|\frac{2x - 2}{3}\right| > 8$

30. $|2x + 3| < 5$

Chapter 2 Summary

Tools for Solving Equations:

      Addition Property of Equality
          If $a = b$, then $a + c = b + c$

      Subtraction Property of Equality
          If $a = b$, then $a - c = b - c$

      Multiplication Property of Equality

          If $a = b$, then $ac = bc \ (c \neq 0)$

      Division Property of Equality

          If $a = b$, then $a/c = b/c \ (c \neq 0)$

      Square Root Property of Equality
          If $a = b$, then $\sqrt{a} = \sqrt{b}$

      Power Property of Equality
          If $a = b$, then $a^n = b^n$

Zero of a Function:

      Given function, f. If a is input into the function as the variable and
      the result is $f(a) = 0$, then a is a zero of the function.

Complex Number: $a + bi$, a and b real, $i = \sqrt{-1}$, $i^2 = -1$

Imaginary Number: $a + bi$, $b \neq 0$

Complex Conjugates: $a + bi$ and $a - bi$

Quadratic Equations: $ax^2 + bx + c = 0, a \neq 0, a, b, c \ real$

Quadratic Function: $f(x) = ax^2 + bx + c, a \neq 0, a, b, c \ real$

Quadratic Formula: for $ax^2 + bx + c = 0, a \neq 0$

$$x = \frac{-b \pm \sqrt{b^2 - 4ac}}{2a}$$

Tools for Solving Inequalities:

Addition Property of Inequalities
If $P < Q$, then $P + R < Q + R$
If $P \leq Q$, then $P + R \leq Q + R$
If $P > Q$, then $P + R > Q + R$
If $P \geq Q$, then $P + R \geq Q + R$

Multiplication Property of Inequalities
For $R > 0$ (R is positive):
If $P < Q$, then $PR < QR$
If $P \leq Q$, then $PR \leq QR$
If $P > Q$, then $PR > QR$
If $P \geq Q$, then $PR \geq QR$

For $R < 0$ (R is negative):
If $P < Q$, then $PR > QR$
If $P \leq Q$, then $PR \geq QR$
If $P > Q$, then $PR < QR$
If $P \geq Q$, then $PR \leq QR$

Absolute Value Equations and Inequalities
For $b > 0$

$|a| = b$ can be written as $a = b$ or $a = -b$

$|a| < b$ can be written as $-b < a < b$

$|a| > b$ can be written as $a < -b$ or $a > b$

Chapter 2 Review

Solve the equations.

1. $5x - 4 = 1$

2. $2x - 5 = 5x + 7$

3. $4(x - 2) = 2(x + 3)$

4. $(2x - 1)(3x + 2) = 0$

5. $x^2 + x - 6 = 0$

6. $3x^2 = 8 - 2x$

7. $4x^2 = 20$

8. $x^2 - 6 = 0$

Find the zeros of the each function.

9. $f(x) = 6x - 24$

10. $f(x) = x - 5$

11. $f(x) = 3 - 9x$

12. $f(x) = x^2 + 2x + 1$

13. $f(x) = x^2 - 2x - 24$

14. $f(x) = 2x^2 + 5x - 3$

Solve.

15. $\dfrac{4}{x + 2} + \dfrac{2}{x - 1} = 0$

16. $\dfrac{3}{x} + \dfrac{2}{x + 1} = 0$

17. $\sqrt{3x + 2} = \sqrt{5x + 1}$

18. $-1 = \sqrt{x - 4} - \sqrt{x - 1}$

19. $|x - 3| = 4$

20. $|2x + 3| = 15$

Solve, graph and write solution in interval form.

21. $-4 \le 2x + 1 \le 5$

22. $-1 < 2x - 3 \le 7$

23. $3x < -6$ or $x + 2 > 5$

24. $4x + 2 \le 6$ or $2x \ge 10$

25. $|4x - 1| < 3$

26. $|x + 5| \ge 3$

27. Solve $V = lwh$ for h

28. Solve $v = \sqrt{3gp}$ for g

Express in terms of i.

29. $-\sqrt{-20}$

30. $\sqrt{-6} * \sqrt{-12}$

133

31. $\dfrac{\sqrt{-36}}{-\sqrt{-64}}$

32. $\sqrt{-48} * \sqrt{-12}$

For problems 33 – 36 perform the indicated operation, simplify, and write in $a + bi$ form.

33. $(4 + 2i)(5 + i)$

34. $(4 - 2i) - 2(-3i)$

35. $\dfrac{2 - 3i}{1 - 2i}$

36. $\dfrac{3 - i}{3 + i}$

Solve using the quadratic formula.

37. $3x^2 - 10x - 8 = 0$

38. $y^2 - 4y + 10 = 0$

39. $x^2 - 3x = 18$

40. $x^4 - 3x^2 + 2 = 0$

CHAPTER 3

POLYNOMIAL AND RATIONAL FUNCTIONS

Section 3.1 Polynomial Functions

Polynomial Function

Polynomial Function:

A polynomial function of degree n is a function of the form:

$$f(x) = a_n x^n + a_{n-1} x^{n-1} + \ldots\ldots + a_1 x + a_0$$

for real numbers $a_n, a_{n-1}, \ldots\ldots, a_1$ and a_0; with $a_n \neq 0$

and exponents that are whole numbers.

Leading Coefficient : the first nonzero coefficient, a_n

Leading Term : the term $a_n x^n$

Degree : is the exponent of the leading term which is n

The coefficients of a polynomial function are real numbers and the exponents are whole numbers.

Examples of Polynomial Functions:

Function	Degree	Leading term	Leading Coefficient	Example
Constant	0	4.3	4.3	$f(x) = 4.3$
Linear	1	$2x$	2	$f(x) = 2x - 3$
Quadratic	2	$3x^2$	3	$f(x) = 3x^2 + x - 4$
Cubic	3	x^3	1	$f(x) = x^3 + 2x^2 - 3x + 5$
Quartic	4	$4x^4$	4	$f(x) = 4x^4 + x^2 - x + 2$

The constant function $f(x) = 0$ has <u>no degree</u> since $f(x) = 0 = 0x = 0x^2 = 0x^7 = 0x^{49}$.

Examples of NON-POLYNOMIAL Functions:

$$f(x) = \frac{2}{x} + 10\,; \qquad f(x) = x^{\frac{1}{3}} + 4\,; \qquad f(x) = \sqrt{x}$$

QUADRATIC FUNCTION

We will look at an example of a quadratic function to see some of the characteristics of quadratic functions.

Function: $f(x) = x^2 - 2x - 8$
$$= (x-4)(x+2)$$

Graph:

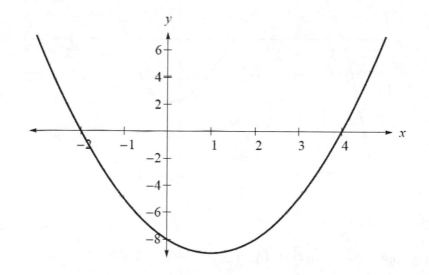

Zeros: $4,\ -2$

x-intercepts: $(4, 0), (-2, 0)$

y-intercept: $(0, -8)$

Minimum: -9 at $x = 1$

Maximum: none

Domain: $(-\infty,\ +\infty)$ All real numbers

Range: $[-9, \infty)$

CUBIC FUNCTION:

We will next look at the characteristics of a cubic function.

Function: $f(x) = x^3 + 3x^2 - x - 3$

$= (x+3)(x+1)(x-1)$

Graph:

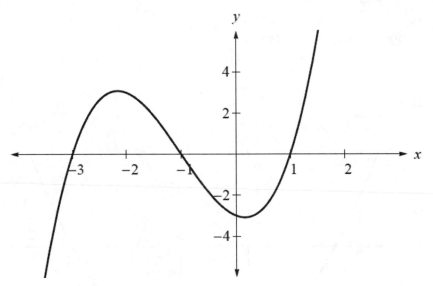

Zeros: $-3, -1, 1$

x-intercepts: $(-3, 0), (-1, 0), (1, 0)$

y-intercept: $(0, -3)$

Relative Minimum: -3.08 at $x = 0.155$

Relative Maximum: 3.08 at $x = -2.15$

Domain: $(-\infty, +\infty)$ All real numbers

Range: $(-\infty, +\infty)$ All real numbers

Notes on the Graph of a Polynomial:

1. The graph is <u>continuous</u> with no breaks, jumps, or holes.

2. The graph is <u>smooth</u> with no sharp corners.

3. The domain is all real numbers $(-\infty, \infty)$.

Leading Term & End Behavior:

As the variable x becomes very large and approaches infinity or becomes very small and approaches minus infinity, the behavior of the graph of a polynomial function is called the **end behavior** of the graph.

<u>The **leading term** and the **degree** of a polynomial function **determines its end behavior**.</u>

Notice: The polynomial function must be rewritten with the **degree of the exponents in descending order** in order to determine the degree of a function. The largest exponent is in the leading term and is the degree of the function.

<u>EVEN DEGREE</u>:
Look at the graphs below.
Notice that the first 3 graphs are graphs of functions of <u>even degree</u> with <u>positive leading coefficients</u>. We see that the y-values of points get very large as x gets very small and also the y-values get very large as x gets very large.

$f(x) = 3x^2$

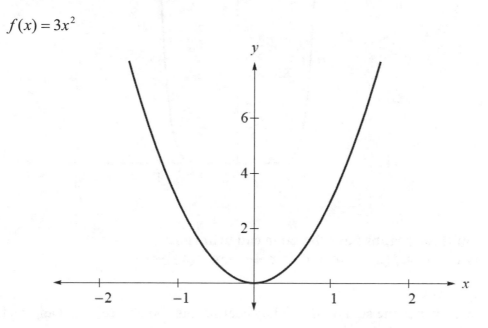

$f(x) = 2x^6$

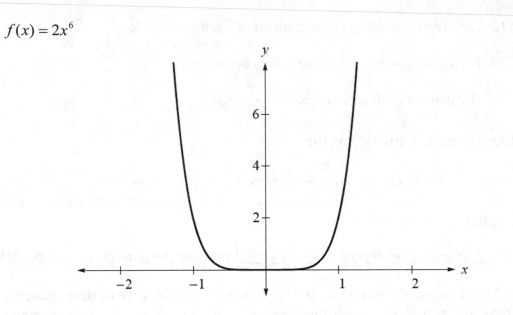

$f(x) = 5x^{10}$

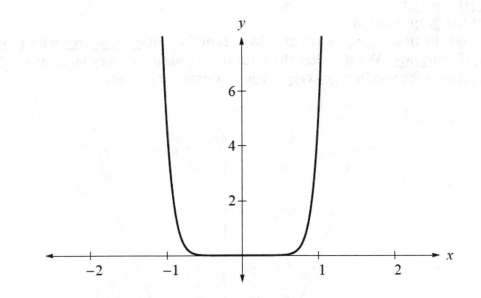

All three of these graphs have the same end behavior.
That is as $x \longrightarrow \infty, f(x) \rightarrow \infty$ and as $x \longrightarrow -\infty, f(x) \rightarrow \infty$.

Now we will change the sign of the leading coefficients and obsere what happens to the graphs.

The next 3 graphs are graphs of functions of <u>even degree</u> with <u>negative leading coefficients</u>. The y-values of points get very small as x gets very small and also get very small as x gets very large.

$f(x) = -3x^2$

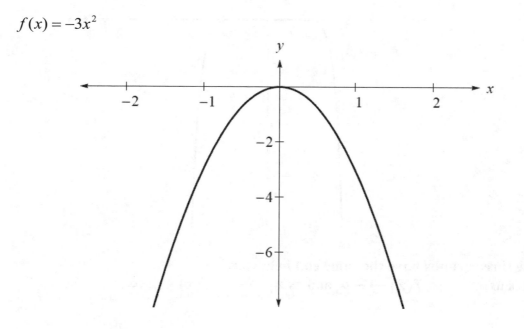

$f(x) = -2x^6$

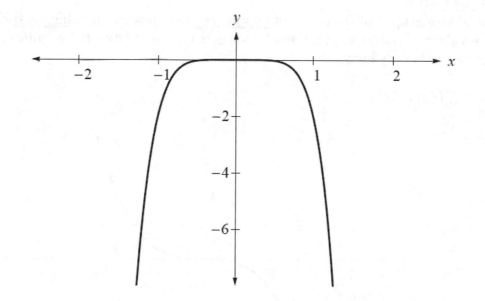

141

$f(x) = -5x^{10}$

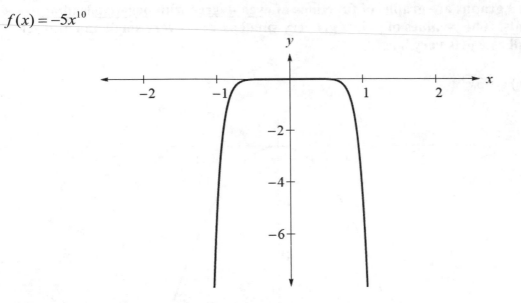

These three graphs have the same end behavior.
That is as $x \longrightarrow \infty, f(x) \rightarrow -\infty$ and as $x \longrightarrow -\infty, f(x) \rightarrow -\infty$.

Let's see what the end behavior of functions of odd degree.

ODD DEGREE:
Look at two graphs of functions of <u>odd degree</u> with <u>positive leading coefficients</u>.
The y-values of points get very small as x gets very small and the y-values get very large as x gets very large.

$f(x) = 3x^3$

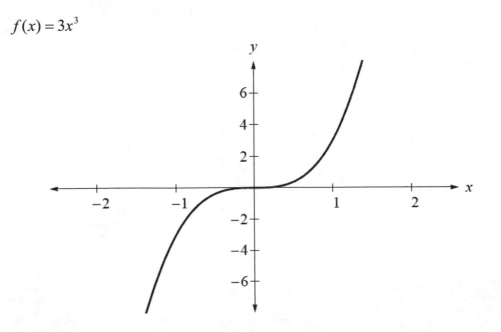

142

$$f(x) = 2x^7$$

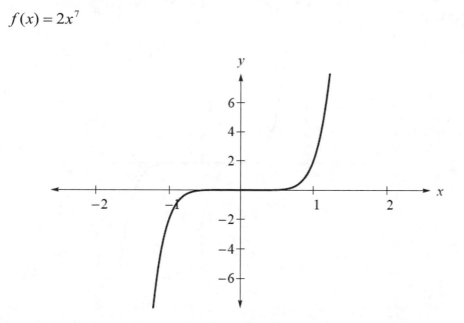

Both of these graphs have the same end behavior.
That is as $x \longrightarrow \infty, f(x) \to \infty$ and as $x \longrightarrow -\infty, f(x) \to -\infty$.

Next, we will **change the sign of the leading coefficients** of these odd degree graphs:

Look at two graphs of functions of <u>odd degree</u> with <u>negative leading coefficients</u>.
The y-values of the points get very large as x gets very small and the y-values get
very small as x gets very large.

$$f(x) = -3x^3$$

$$f(x) = -2x^7$$

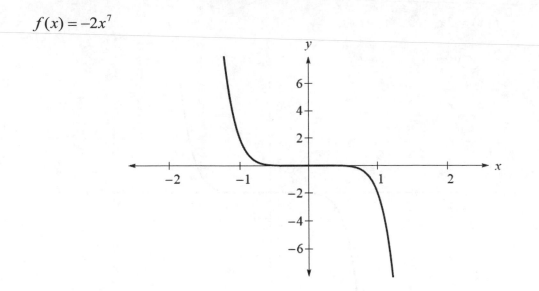

These last two graphs have the same end behavior. As x gets very large, y gets very small; and as x gets very small, y-values get very large.

That is as $x \longrightarrow \infty, f(x) \rightarrow -\infty$ and as $x \longrightarrow -\infty, f(x) \rightarrow \infty.$

Summary of the End Behavior of Polynomial Functions

Leading-Term Information about the Graphs

If $a_n x^n$ is the term of a polynomial function with $a_n \neq 0$ and **n** is the highest degree in the function then:

Degree Even:
Leading Coefficient Positive: the end behavior approaches $+ \infty$

Leading Coefficient Negative: the end behavior approaches $-\infty$

Degree Odd:
Leading Coefficient Positive:
as x approaches $-\infty$, the end behavior approaches $-\infty$
as x approaches $+\infty$, the end behavior approaches $+\infty$

Leading Coefficient Negative:
as x approaches $-\infty$, the end behavior approaches $+\infty$
as x approaches $+\infty$, the end behavior approaches $-\infty$

Example 1: Using the leading-term information, match each of the following functions with one of the graphs below:

a. $f(x) = 2x^4 - x^3 + 1$

b. $f(x) = -2x^3 - x^2 + 2x + 1$

c. $f(x) = 3x^5 + x + 2$

d. $f(x) = -4x^6 + x^5 - 2x^3$

1.

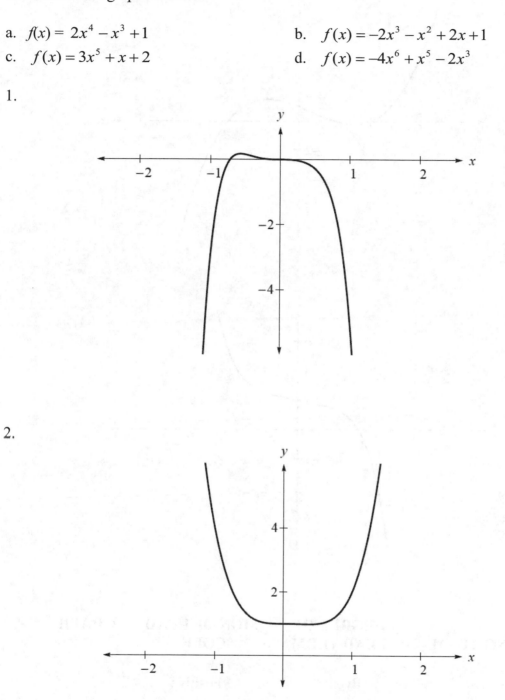

2.

3.

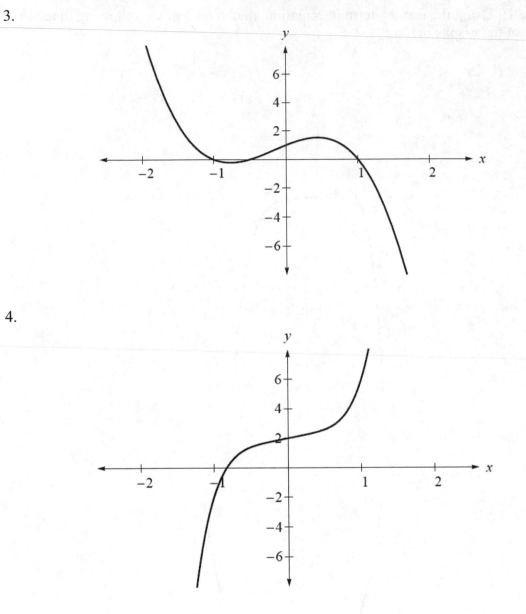

4.

Solution:

	LEADING TERM	DEGREE OF LEAD TERM	SIGN OF LEAD COEF	GRAPH
a)	$2x^4$	Even	Positive	2
b)	$-2x^3$	Odd	Negative	3
c)	$3x^5$	Odd	Positive	4
d)	$-4x^6$	Even	Negative	1

Zeros of a Polynomial Function

Zeros of a Polynomial Function

Given: $f(x) = x^2 - 2x - 3$

To find the zeros, set $f(x) = 0$ and solve.

$$x^2 - 2x - 3 = 0$$
$$(x - 3)(x + 1) = 0$$
$$x - 3 = 0 \qquad x + 1 = 0$$
$$x = 3, \ -1$$

Solutions of $f(x) = 0$ are zeros of the given function.

Zeros: $3, \ -1$

The zeros are the x-coordinates of the x-intercepts in the graph of the function.

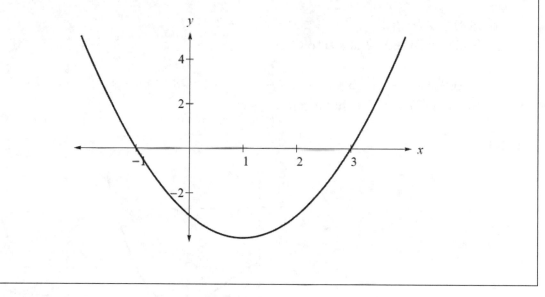

<u>Factor Theorem</u>: For polynomial $f(x)$, if $f(a) = 0$, then $(x - a)$ is a factor of $f(x)$. We will use the Factor Thereom on the next few examples.

Example 2: Find the zeros of $f(x) = (x + 3)(x + 2)(x - 1)$.

Solution: $\qquad f(x) = (x + 3)(x + 2)(x - 1) \qquad\qquad$ Given

$\qquad\qquad\quad (x + 3)(x + 2)(x - 1) = 0 \qquad\qquad$ Set $f(x) = 0$ and solve

$\qquad\qquad\quad x + 3 = 0 \qquad x + 2 = 0 \qquad x - 1 = 0$

$\qquad\qquad\quad x = -3, \ -2, 1$

147

The zeros of $f(x)$ are $-3, -2, 1$ and

$$f(-3) = 0; \quad f(-2) = 0; \quad f(1) = 0$$

> If a is a real zero of a function then $f(a) = 0$,
> $(a, 0)$ is an x-intercept of the graph of the function.

Example 3: If $g(x) = x^3 - 2x^2 - x + 2$, are 2 and 3 zeros of $g(x)$?

Solution: $g(x) = x^3 - 2x^2 - x + 2$ Given

To decide if each number, c, is a zero, we will find the values of $g(c)$.

$g(2) = 2^3 - 2(2)^2 - 2 + 2 = 8 - 8 - 2 + 2 = 0$
Since $g(2) = 0$, 2 is a zero of $g(x)$.

$g(3) = 3^3 - 2(3)^2 - 3 + 2 = 27 - 18 - 3 + 2 = 8$
Since $g(3) \neq 0$, 3 is not a zero of $g(x)$.

Graph :

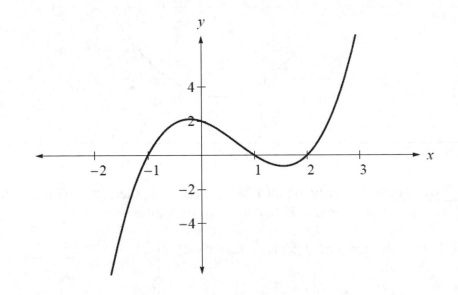

Example 4: Find the zeros of

$$f(x) = 3(x+2)(x-2)(x-2)(x-2)$$
$$= 3(x+2)(x-2)^3$$

Solution: To find the zeros, we set $f(x) = 0$, then set the factors $= 0$, and we can solve for the zeros.

$$x+2 = 0 \qquad x-2 = 0$$
$$x = -2, 2$$

The zeros of $f(x)$ are -2 and 2.

Example 5: Find the zeros of

$$g(x) = -(x-3)(x-3)(x+4)(x+4)$$

$$= -(x-3)^2(x+4)^2$$

Solution: To find the zeros, we set $f(x) = 0$, then set the factors $= 0$, and we can solve for the zeros.

$$x+4 = 0 \qquad x-3 = 0$$

$$x = -4, 3$$

The zeros of $f(x)$ are -4 and 3.

Multiplicity: **The multiplicity of an item is the number of times that item appears in an event.**

Looking back at Example 4 and Example 5, we see that several factors occur more than once.

In Example 4 the factor $(x-2)$ occurs three times. The zero found from this factor, 2, has a **multiplicity of 3**. The factor $(x+2)$ occurs once. The zero found from this factor, -2, has a **multiplicity of 1**.

In Example 5 the factor $(x-3)$ occurs twice. The zero found from this factor, 3, has a **multiplicity of 2**. The factor $(x+4)$ occurs twice. The zero found from this factor, -4, has a **multiplicity of 2**.

Multiplicity Relationship to the *x*-intercepts of Graphs

<u>Multiplicity Relationship to Graphs</u>:

Multiplicity of a zero is either odd or or it is even.

If $(x-a)^k$ where $k \geq 1$, is a factor of a polynomial function and $(x-a)^{k+1}$ is not a factor and:

if k is <u>odd</u>, then the graph crosses the axis at $(a, 0)$;

if k is <u>even</u>, then the graph is tangent to the axis at $(a, 0)$.

If a graph is **tangent to an axis,** it touches the axis but does not cross it.

Example 6: Find the zeros of $f(x) = x^3 - 2x^2 - 4x + 8$ and describe the graph at these zeros.

Solution:

$f(x) = x^3 - 2x^2 - 4x + 8$ Given

$f(x) = x^2(x-2) - 4(x-2)$ Factor by grouping

$= (x-2)(x^2-4)$

$= (x-2)(x-2)(x+2)$

$= (x-2)^2(x+2)$

The zeros are:

2 with a multiplicity of 2, and -2 of a multiplicity of 1.

At the *x*-intercept $(2, 0)$ the graph is tangent to the axis because the multiplicity is an even number.

At the *x*-intercept $(-2, 0)$ the graph crosses the axis because the multiplicity is an odd number.

Next we wil graph the function $f(x) = x^3 - 2x^2 - 4x + 8$.

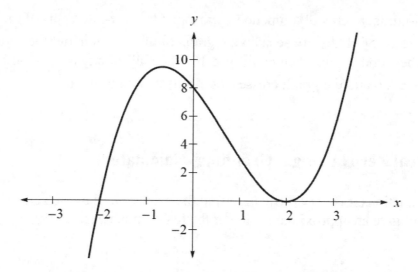

This problem can be solved using a graphing calculator. See Chapter 6, Example 21.

Example 7:   Find the zeros of $f(x) = x^4 + 3x^2 - 54$ and describe the graph at
these zeros

Solution: $f(x) = x^4 + 3x^2 - 54$ Given

$f(x) = (x^2 + 9)(x^2 - 6)$ Factor

$x^2 + 9 = 0$ and $x^2 - 6 = 0$ Solve each factor

$x^2 = -9$ $x^2 = 6$

$x = \pm\sqrt{-9} = \pm 3i$ $x = \pm\sqrt{6}$

The zeros are $\pm 3i$ and $\pm\sqrt{6}$ all with multiplicity of 1.
Look at the graph of the function from Example 7:

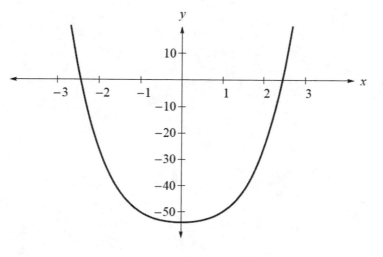

Only the real-number zeros of a function correspond to the x-intercepts of the graph. The real-number zeros of $\pm\sqrt{6}$ are seen on the graph of the function, but the zeros $\pm 3i$ are not real-numbers and are not seen on the graph. The multiplicity is 1, an odd number, for the two zeros $\pm\sqrt{6}$ and the graph crosses the x-axis at both of them.

Finding Real Zeros Using a Graphing Calculator:

With many functions it is very difficult to find the exact values of the zeros. A graphing calculator will give an approximate value of the real-number zeros.

See Chapter 6, Example 22 for an example of such a function.

Section 3.1 Exercises

Tell whether the given polynomial is constant, linear, quadratic, cubic, or quartic and find the leading term, the leading coefficient, and the degree of the polynomial.

1. $f(x) = 3x^4 - 7x + 5$

2. $g(x) = 12x^3 - 4$

3. $f(x) = 0.3x - 2.3$

4. $h(x) = -3$

5. $g(x) = 134x^2 + x - 2$

6. $f(x) = -6x^2 - 2x$

7. $h(x) = -3x^3 - x^2 + 5x$

8. $f(x) = 4 - x$

9. $f(x) = -5$

10. $f(x) = 17x - x^2$

Describe the end behavior of the graph of each function.

11. $f(x) = -5x^3 - 2x + 4$

12. $g(x) = 0.5x^4 + 0.3x^3 - .0.7x$

13. $h(x) = -2x^6 + 8x^4$

14. $f(x) = 2x^5 - 3x^6$

15. $g(x) = 10 + 2x^5 + x$

16. $h(x) = 2x - 3x^4 + 2x^5$

Find the zeros of the polynomial function and state the multiplicity of each function.

17. $f(x) = (x-3)^2(x-4)$

18. $g(x) = (x^2 - 4)^3$

19. $h(x) = -3(x-2)(x-2)(x-2)(x+2)$

20. $f(x) = x^3(x-5)^2(x+1)$

21. $f(x) = -2(x-1)^2(x+5)^3 x^4$

22. $g(x) = x^4 - 17x^2 + 16$

3.2   Graphs of Polynomial Functions

Graphs

If a polynomial function $f(x)$ of degree n is graphed, the graph will have:

at most n real x-intercepts and thus no more than $\underline{n \ \text{real zeros}}$;

at most $n-1$ turning points called relative maxima and minima.

Maxima/minima occur when the graph of the function changes from decreasing to increasing or from increasing to decreasing.

Example 1:   Graph the polynomial function $f(x) = -3x^4 + 6x^3$

Solution:

Step 1: Use the leading term to find the end behavior of the graph:

The leading term is $-3x^4$.

The degree, 4, is even, and the coefficient, -3, is negative.

These two facts tell us that the end behavior is:
As $x \to \infty$, the graph $\to -\infty$

As $x \to -\infty$, the graph $\to -\infty$.

The graph will look **somewhat like**:

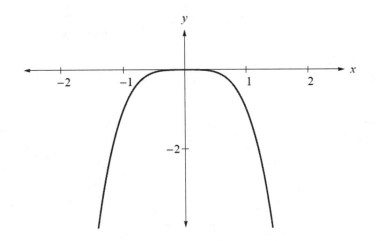

Step 2: Find the zeros by setting $f(x) = 0$. Remember that the zeros of a function are the first coordinate of the x-intercept.

$$-3x^4 + 6x^3 = 0$$

$$-3x^3(x-2) = 0 \qquad\qquad\qquad \text{Factor to solve}$$

$$-3x^3 = 0 \qquad\qquad x - 2 = 0 \qquad \text{Principal of zero products}$$

$$x = 0 \quad \text{or} \quad x = 2$$

The zeros are: 0 with multiplicity of 3, and 2 with multiplicity 1.

Step 3: Find the intercepts.

The zeros are the x-coordinates of the x-intercepts, and the y-coordinates at the x-intercepts are zero.

x-intercepts are: (0, 0) and (2, 0).

To find the y-intercept, find $f(0)$ to know the y-coordinate.
The x-coordinates at the y-intercepts are zero.

$$f(x) = -3x^4 + 6x^3$$
$$f(0) = -3(0)^4 + 6(0)^3 = 0$$

The y-intercept is: (0, 0).

Step 4: Use the zeros to divide the x-axis into intervals and find whether the graph is above or below the x-axis in each interval.

The zeros are 0 and 2, so the intervals will be

$$(-\infty, 0) \qquad (0, 2) \qquad (2, \infty)$$

Choose a test value in each interval and find the value of the function within each interval at the chosen test point.

Interval	Test value	Function value	Sign	Location
$(-\infty, 0)$	-2	-96	$-$	Below x-axis
$(0, 2)$	1	3	$+$	Above x-axis
$(2, \infty)$	3	-81	$-$	Below x-axis

These test points also give points on the graph:

$$(-2, -96); \quad (1, 3); \quad (3, -81)$$

Step 5: Find a few more points on the graph. Choose values of x and solve for $f(x)$ to get points.

x	$f(x)$	point
-1	-9	$(-1, -9)$
1	3	$(1, 3)$
1.5	5.06	$(1.5, 5.06)$

Step 6: Check the multiplicity of the zeros:

0: multiplicity is 3 (odd), so the graph crosses the axis at this zero;

2: multiplicity is 1 (odd), so the graph crosses the axis at this zero.

Step 7: Using the information found in Steps 1 thru 6, draw the graph.

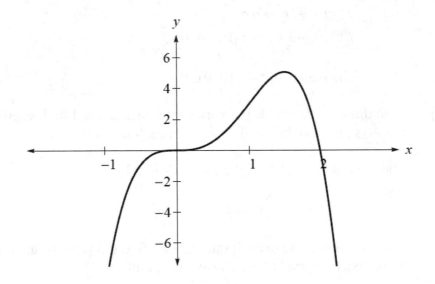

156

Guide for Graphing a Polynomial Function

Guide for Graphing a Polynomial Function:

1. Determine the end behavior of the graph using the leading term.

2. Find the zeros of the function by solving $f(x) = 0$.
   Find the x-intercepts using the zeros as the first coordinate.

3. Find the y-intercept by finding $f(0)$.

4. Divide the x-axis into intervals using the zeros and then use a test
   point to find the sign of the function value in each repective interval.

5. Find additional points if needed to determine the general shape of the graph.

6. Use the multiplicity of each zero to see if the graph crosses the x-axis or
   is tangent to it at the zero.

7. Draw the graph.

Example 2. Graph the polynomial function $f(x) = x^3 + x^2 - 4x - 4$.

Solution:

1. The leading term is x^3. The degree is 3, which is odd, and the coefficient is
   positive. The end behavior is:
   $$\text{as } x \to -\infty, f(x) \to -\infty \qquad \text{and} \quad \text{as } x \to \infty, f(x) \to \infty$$
   The graph will look **somewhat like**:

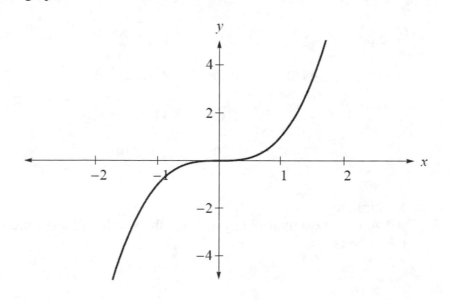

2. Find the zeros by solving $f(x) = 0$.

$$x^3 + x^2 - 4x - 4 = 0$$
$$x^2(x+1) - 4(x+1) = 0 \qquad\qquad \text{Factor.}$$

$$(x^2 - 4)(x+1) = 0 \qquad\qquad \text{Factor.}$$

$$(x-2)(x+2)(x+1) = 0$$

The zeros are -2, -1, and 2, and each has multiplicity of 1.

The x-intercepts: (using the zeros) are $(-2, 0)$, $(-1, 0)$, and $(2, 0)$.

3. The y-intercept:
   To find the y-intercept, solve $f(0)$.
   $$f(0) = 0^3 + 0^2 - 4(0) \quad = \quad -4$$

   y-intercept: $(0, -4)$

4. Divide the x-axis into intervals:

Interval	Test value	Function value	Sign	Location
$(-\infty, -2)$	-3	-10	$-$	below axis
$(-2, -1)$	$-3/2$	0.88	$+$	above axis
$(-1, 2)$	1	-6	$-$	below axis
$(2, \infty)$	3	20	$+$	above axis

5. Add points:

x	$f(x)$	point
$-1/2$	-0.88	$(-1/2, -0.88)$
$1/2$	-5.63	$(1/2, -5.63)$
3	20	$(3, 20)$

6: Multiplicity:
   All zeros have a multiplicity of 1 and the graph will cross the x-axis at the three zeros.

7. Draw the graph:

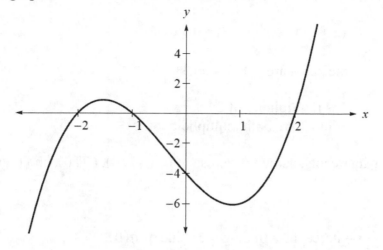

Example 3:   Graph the polynomial function $g(x) = (x+1)(x-1)^2(x-3)$.

Solution: Expand the function (multiply factors): $g(x) = x^4 - 4x^3 + 2x^2 + 4x - 3$

1. The leading term is x^4, and the degree is 4 which is even, and the coefficient is positive. The end behavior is:

    as $x \to -\infty, g(x) \to \infty$ and   as $x \to \infty, g(x) \to \infty$

    The graph will look **somewhat like**:

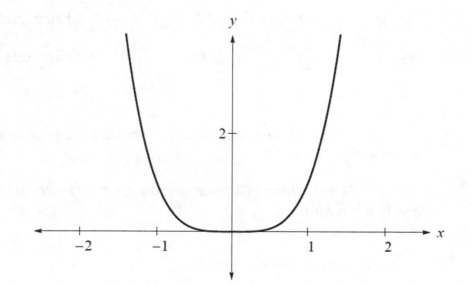

2. Find the zeros by solving $g(x) = 0$.

$$(x+1)(x-1)^2(x-3) = 0$$

the zeros are -1, 1, and 3

1 is multiplicity of 2;
-1 and 3 are both multiplicity of 1

x-intercepts, using the zeros, are $(-1, 0)$, $(1, 0)$, and $(3, 0)$.

3. Find the y-intercept by finding the value of $g(0)$.
$$g(0) = (0 + 1)(0 - 1)^2(0 - 3)$$
$$= (1)(1)(-3) = -3$$

y-intercept is $(0, -3)$.

4. Divide the x-axis into intervals using the zeros.

Interval	Test value	Function value	Sign	Location
$(-\infty, -1)$	-2	45	$+$	above axis
$(-1, 1)$	0	-3	$-$	below axis
$(1, 3)$	2	-3	$-$	below axis
$(3, \infty)$	4	45	$+$	above axis

5. Multiplicity:
zeros of -1 and 3 have multiplicity of 1 (odd) and the graph crosses x-axis at these zeros.

zero of 1 is multiplicity of 2 (even) and the graph is tangent to the x-axis at this zero.

If necessary, find extra points to graph.

6. Draw the graph.

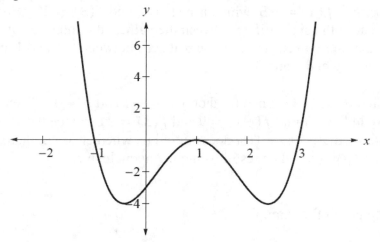

The Intermediate Value Theorem

The graphs of polynomial functions are unbroken curves; there are no gaps. In most cases the domain of a polynomial function is $(-\infty, \infty)$. Now consider a polynomial function $F(x)$. If you determine that $F(a) > 0$ and $F(b) < 0$, what would the graph of $F(x)$ look like in the interval $[a, b]$. There **must** be a point between **a and b** (we will call that value **c**) where $F(c) = 0$.

The Intermediate Value Theorem:

If $P(x)$ is a polynomial function with only real coefficients, and if for real numbers a and b where $a \neq b$, and if $P(a)$ and $P(b)$ are of opposite sign: then there exists at least one real zero between **a** and **b**.

Example 4: Use the intermediate value theorem to determine whether the given function has a real zero between the given numbers:

$$f(x) = x^3 + 2x^2 - 8x \qquad \text{between } -1 \text{ and } 1, \text{ and between } 1 \text{ and } 3$$

Solution: Find $f(-1)$, $f(1)$, and $f(3)$.

$$f(-1) = (-1)^3 + 2(-1)^2 - 8(-1) = 9$$

$$f(1) = (1)^3 + 2(1)^2 - 8(1) = -5$$

$$f(3) = (3)^3 + 2(3)^2 - 8(3) = 21$$

161

Now check for differences in signs between the points: $f(-1) = 9$ which is positive, $f(1) = -5$ which is negative, and $f(3) = 21$ which is positive. Because the signs differ between the values, the Intermediate Value Theorem tells us that there exists at least one real zero between -1 and 1 and at least one real zero between 1 and 3.

What if instead we had used only $a = -1$ and $b = 3$? Then we would have found $f(-1) = 9$ and $f(3) = 21$. Since these are the same sign, the Intermediate Value Test does not tell us whether or not there are zeros between the two points. The result would be inconclusive.

Look at the graph for example 4 :

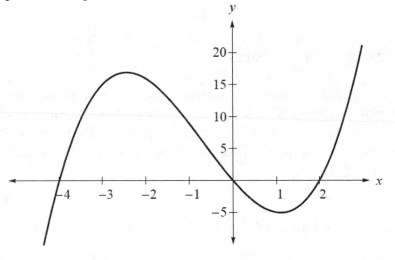

Example 5: . Use the Intermediate Value Theorem to determine whether the given function has a real zero between the given numbers:

$$f(x) = x^4 - 5x^3 \qquad\qquad \text{between 2 and 3}$$

Solution: Find $f(2)$ and $f(3)$ and see if they have different signs

$$f(2) = (2)^4 - 5(2)^3 = -24 \qquad\qquad f(3) = (3)^4 - 5(3)^3 = -54$$

Both are negative, but this does not necessarily mean that there is no zero between them. It is impossible to determine if the given function has a real zero between the two numbers.

Section 3.2 Exercises

For each function in problems $1-6$ find:
    a. the maximum number of real zeros that the function can have;
    b. the maximum number of x-intercepts that the graph can have;
    c. the maximum number of turning points that the graph can have.

1. $f(x) = x^6 - 2x^2 + 8$ 2. $f(x) = -x^4 + x^2 - x^6 + 5$

3. $f(x) = 1/2x^3 + 4x^2$ 4. $f(x) = x^8 - 2x^6 + 4x - 8$

5. $f(x) = -2x - x^5$ 6. $f(x) = -5x^4 + 4x^3 - 2x - 6$

For each function in problems $7-12$ find:
    a. the end behavior of the graph;
    b. the y-intercept.

7. $f(x) = 3/4x^2 - 6$ 8. $f(x) = -2x^4 - 3x^3 - 6x^2 - 2$

9. $f(x) = x^3 - 3x^2 + x - 2$ 10. $f(x) = -2x^5 - x^4 + x^2 + 3$

11. $f(x) = x^9 - x^8 + x + 4$ 12. $f(x) = 5$

Graph each of the polynomial functions using the Guide for graphing polynomials.

13. $f(x) = -2x^3 - 4x^2$ 14. $f(x) = x^5 - 6x^3$

15. $f(x) = -x(x-2)^2(x+1)(x+2)$ 16. $f(x) = x(x-1)(x+1)(x+2)$

Using the Intermediate Value Theorem, determine, if possible, if there is a real zero between the two given numbers.

17. $f(x) = x^3 + 5x^2 - 6x - 11$;   for -2, and 1

18. $f(x) = x^3 + 6x^2 - 8x - 10$;   for 1, and 2

19. $f(x) = 3x^2 - x - 7$;   for -3, and 0

20. $f(x) = -2x^2 - 4x + 6$;   for -4, and -2

Section 3.3   Division of Polynomials

To determine if some number k is a factor of a larger number P, we divide P by k. If the result has no remainder (remainder is zero), then we know that the number k is indeed a factor of P. We use a similar method to find the factors of a polynomial, and then we can find the zeros of that polynomial.

Dividing Polynomials:

We will begin our study of division by using long division with polynomials.

Remainder Theorem

Remainder Theorem:
   For any polynomial $P(x)$ and any number k, there exists a unique
   polynomial $Q(x)$ and number R, the remainder, such that:
$$P(x) \ = \ (x-k) \ * \ Q(x) \ + \ R \qquad \text{and} \qquad P(k) = R$$
The second statement: $P(k) = R$ will be used often.

Example 1.   Use long division to determine if $(x + 2)$ and $(x - 2)$ are factors of:
$$P(x) = x^3 - 3x + 2$$

Solution: Notice that there is no 2nd degree term in the given polynomial. Before dividing, we will add a term of $0x^2$ to the polynomial: $P(x) = \ x^3 + 0x^2 - 3x + 2$

In our example $(x + 2)$ is the **divisor** and $x^3 + 0x^2 - 3x + 2$ is the **dividend**.

Divide by the factor $(x + 2)$:

$$
\begin{array}{r}
x^2 - 2x + 1 \\
x+2 \overline{\smash{\big)}\, x^3 + 0x^2 - 3x + 2} \\
\underline{x^3 + 2x^2} \\
-2x^2 - 3x \\
\underline{-2x^2 - 4x} \\
x + 2 \\
\underline{x + 2} \\
0
\end{array}
$$

Quotient is $x^2 - 2x + 1$

Remainder is 0

Because the remainder is zero, we know that $(x + 2)$ is a factor.

Next we will divide by the other factor $(x-2)$.

$$
\begin{array}{r}
x^2+2x+1 \\
x-2\overline{)x^3+0x^2-3x+2} \\
\underline{x^3-2x^2} \\
2x^2-3x \\
\underline{2x^2-4x} \\
x+2 \\
\underline{x-2} \\
4
\end{array}
$$

Quotient is x^2+2x+1

Remainder is 4

We find a remainder of 4 rather than zero, so $(x-2)$ is not a factor.

Use the Remainder Theorem with the polynomial function given in Example 1:

$$P(k)=x^3-3x+2$$

$$P(-2)=(-2)^3-3(-2)+2=-8+6+2=0$$

$$P(2)=(2)^3-3(2)+2\ =\ 8-6=4$$

These values are the same as the remainders we found in Example 1. Rather than having to use long division, we can **use the Remainder Theorem to test for zeros**.

Synthetic Division:

We will often use the Remainder Theorem to find factors of a polynomial. We will also use an abbreviated long division technique to divide polynomials called **synthetic division**.

Example 2: Look at the two examples below. We will divide using long division and then we will use an abbreviated version with only the number coefficients

$$(5x^3 - 6x^2 - 28x - 2) \div (x + 2)$$

$$
\begin{array}{r}
5x^2 - 16x + 4 \\
x + 2 \overline{)\,5x^3 - 6x^2 - 28x - 2} \\
\underline{5x^3 + 10x^2} \\
-16x^2 - 28x \\
\underline{-16x^2 - 32x} \\
4x - 2 \\
\underline{4x + 8} \\
-10
\end{array}
\qquad
\begin{array}{r}
5 - 16 + 4 \\
1 + 2 \overline{)\,5 - 6 - 28 - 2} \\
\underline{5 + 10} \\
-16 - 28 \\
\underline{-16 - 32} \\
4 \quad -2 \\
\underline{4 \; + \; 8} \\
-10
\end{array}
$$

Notice that the numbers in these two examples are quite similar.

We will abbreviate the second division even further as an example of **synthetic division**.

Synthetic Division: An easy way to undertand synthetic division is to see the technique used in a problem.

Lets look at the solution for Example 2 above using synthetic division.

Since the divisor is $x + 2$, we set the divisor equal to zero and solve and get -2 which we will use as our abbreviated divisor

Begin by writing the division using only the coefficients:

$$-2\rfloor \; 5 \; -6 \; -28 \; -2$$

Next, bring down the 5

$$
\begin{array}{r}
-2\rfloor \; 5 \; -6 \; -28 \; -2 \\
\hline
5
\end{array}
$$

Now, multiply 5 by -2, get -10 which we put in row 2 under -6 and add to the first row.

$$
\begin{array}{r}
-2\rfloor \; 5 \; -6 \; -28 \; -2 \\
\quad\; -10 \\
\hline
5 \; -16
\end{array}
\qquad \text{add}
$$

166

Next multiply -16 by -2 and get 32 which we place in row 2 below -28 and add the two rows.

$$
\begin{array}{r|rrrr}
-2 & 5 & -6 & -28 & -2 \\
   &   & -10 & 32 & \\
\hline
   & 5 & -16 & 4 &
\end{array}
$$

Finally we multiply 4 by -2 and we get -8. Add this to -2, and get

$$
\begin{array}{r|rrrr}
-2 & 5 & -6 & -28 & -2 \\
   &   & -10 & 32 & -8 \\
\hline
   & 5 & -16 & 4 & -10
\end{array}
$$

The coefficients of the quotient polynomial and the remainder are read directly from the bottom row. The quotient is $5x^2 - 16x + 4$, and the remainder is -10. Notice that the degree of the quotient is one less than the original polynomial.

The result of the division in the example of synthetic division is written in factored form as:

$$
\begin{aligned}
5x^3 - 6x^2 - 28x - 2 &= (x+2)(5x^2 - 16x + 4) + (-10) \\
P(x) \qquad\qquad &= \ (x - k) \ * \ Q(x) \qquad + \quad R
\end{aligned}
$$

Example 3   Given that $f(x) = 3x^4 - 5x^3 - 2x^2 + x - 4$, find $f(6)$.

Solution: From the Remainder Theorem, $f(6)$ is equal to the remainder when $f(x)$ is divided by $x - 6$. We can use synthetic division to find the remainder.

$$
\begin{array}{r|rrrrr}
6 & 3 & -5 & -2 & 1 & -4 \\
  &   & 18 & 78 & 456 & 2742 \\
\hline
  & 3 & 13 & 76 & 457 & 2738
\end{array}
$$

From the bottom row we see that the quotient is $3x^3 + 13x^2 + 76x + 457$ with a remainder of 2738.
From the remainder theorem $f(6) = 2738$

Check: To check we will see if $f(6)$ does equal the remainder we found above.
$$
f(x) = 3x^4 - 5x^3 - 2x^2 + x - 4
$$
$$
f(6) = \ 3(6)^4 - 5(6)^3 - 2(6)^2 + (6) - 4 = 2738
$$

In Example 3 with $f(x) = 3x^4 - 5x^3 - 2x^2 + x - 4$, $f(6)$ can also be found using a graphing calculator. See Chapter 6, Example 23.

Example 4: If $f(x) = x^3 + 4x^2 - 9x - 36$, is 3 a zero of $f(x)$?

Solution: We will see if $(x - 3)$ is a factor of $f(x)$ and thus 3 is a zero of the function. We can use synthetic division with the Remainder Theorem to find $f(3)$.

$$
\begin{array}{r|rrrr}
3 & 1 & 4 & -9 & -36 \\
 & & 3 & 21 & 36 \\
\hline
 & 1 & 7 & 12 & 0
\end{array}
$$

The remainder is 0. The Remainder Theorem tells us that $f(3) = 0$. Since the remainder is zero, the number 3 is a zero of the function.

The Factor Theorem

The Factor Theorem:

The polynomial $(x - k)$ is a factor of the polynomial $P(x)$
if and only if $P(k) = 0$.

Example 5: Given $f(x) = 6x^3 + 19x^2 + 2x - 3$. Find the factors of $f(x)$ and then solve the equation $f(x) = 0$.

Solution: Since we do not know a method for factoring this function, use the Remainder Theorem to look for factors. Try $(x - 1)$. Use synthetic division to test if $f(1) = 0$

$$
\begin{array}{r|rrrr}
1 & 6 & 19 & 2 & -3 \\
 & & 6 & 25 & 27 \\
\hline
 & 6 & 25 & 27 & 24
\end{array}
$$ remainder is 24

Synthetic division gives us a remainder 24, and from the Remainder Theorem we know that $f(1) = 24$. Since $f(1) \neq 0$, $x - 1$ <u>is not a factor</u>.

We will look at the possible factor $(x + 3)$:

$$
\begin{array}{r|rrrr}
-3 & 6 & 19 & 2 & -3 \\
 & & -18 & -3 & 3 \\
\hline
 & 6 & 1 & -1 & 0
\end{array}
$$

We see that the remainder is 0.

Since $f(-3) = 0$, we know that $(x+3)$ <u>is a factor</u>.

$$f(x) = 6x^3 + 19x^2 + 2x - 3 \qquad \text{Given}$$

$$f(x) = (x+3)(6x^2 + x - 1)$$ Use the last line from synthetic division.

$$f(x) = (x+3)(3x-1)(2x+1)$$ Now factor the degree 2 factor.

Next, we set the factors of $f(x) = 0$ and then we can set each factor equal to zero.

$$(x+3)(3x-1)(2x+1) = 0$$

$$x + 3 = 0 \qquad 3x - 1 = 0 \qquad 2x + 1 = 0$$

We solve each of these equations to find the solutions.

$$x = -3, \ \frac{1}{3}, \ -\frac{1}{2}$$

The solutions to the equation $6x^3 + 19x^2 + 2x - 3 = 0$ are: $-3, \ \dfrac{1}{3}, \ -\dfrac{1}{2}.$

Example 5 can be solved using a graphing calculator. See Chapter 6, Example 24.

Look at the graph below of the function: $\quad f(x) = x^3 - 7x - 6$.

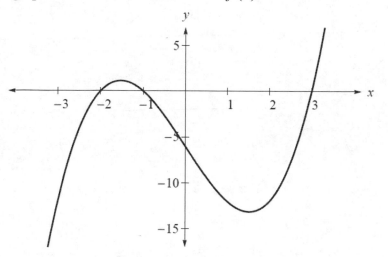

From the graph we can see that the zeros are $-2, -1,$ and 3.

The graph shows the zeros and we can deduce much from this information. We now know:

-2 is a solution of $f(x) = 0$

-2 is a zero of $f(x)$

$f(-2) = 0$

$(-2, 0)$ is an x-intercept of the graph

0 is the remainder when $f(x)$ is divided by $x + 2$

$(x + 2)$ is a factor of f

The numbers -1 and 3 could also be used in place of -2 in the statements above.

Using this knowledge we can write $f(x)$ as a product of linear factors:

$$f(x) = (x + 2)(x + 1)(x - 3).$$

Section 3.3 Exercises

Use long division to decide whether the second polynomial is a factor of the first.

1. $4x^2 + 2x + 42$, $x - 3$

2. $-3x^2 - 4x + 2$, $x + 2$

3. $x^3 + 2x^2 - 3$, $x - 1$

4. $2x^3 + x + 2$, $x + 2$

5. $4x^3 + 6x^2 - 5x - 2$, $x + 2$

6. $2x^4 + 5x^3 - 2x^2 + 5x + 3$, $x + 3$

In the following, a polynomial $P(x)$ and a divisor $d(x)$ are given. Use long division to find the quotient $Q(x)$ and the remainder $R(x)$ when $P(x)$ is divided by $d(x)$.

7. $P(x) = x^3 - 27$, $d(x) = x + 2$

8. $P(x) = x^3 + x^2 + x - 8$, $d(x) = x - 1$

9. $P(x) = 2x^3 - 3x^2 - 5x + 4$, $d(x) = x - 2$

10. $P(x) = 3x^2 + 8x + 5$, $d(x) = x + 3$

Use synthetic division to decide whether or not the given number is a zero of the given polynomial.

11. 12, $P(x) = x^2 + 2x - 120$

12. 2, $P(x) = x^3 - 3x^2 + 4x - 4$

13. 4, $P(x) = 2x^3 - 6x^2 - 9x + 4$

14. -3, $P(x) = x^3 + 2x^2 - x + 6$

Use synthetic division to find the quotient and the remainder.

15. $(x^3 - 64) \div (x - 4)$

16. $(2x^4 + x^3 - 15x^2 + 3x) \div (x + 3)$

17. $(x^3 + 2x^2 + x - 5) \div (x - 2)$

18. $(x^3 + x^2 - x - 1) \div (x + 1)$

Use synthetic division to find the given function value.

19. $f(x) = 2x^4 + x^3 - 10x^2 - 2$, $f(-2)$

20. $f(x) = x^3 - 3x^2 + 4x + 2$, $f(4)$

Factor the polynomial and solve the equation $f(x) = 0$.

21. $f(x) = x^3 + x^2 - 4x - 4$

22. $f(x) = x^3 + 2x^2 - 9x - 18$

Section 3.4   Zeros of Polynomial Functions

In a polynomial function P and a value k, we know from the Remainder Theorem, that if $P(k) = 0$, then the remainder when $P(x)$ is divided by $(x - k)$ is equal to zero. This means that $(x - k)$ is a factor of $P(x)$. Conversely, if $(x - k)$ is a factor of $P(x)$, then $P(k)$ will equal 0.

Factor Theorem

Factor Theorem:

> The polynomial $(x - k)$ is a factor of the polynomial $P(x)$ if and only if $P(k) = 0$.

Example 1. Is $(x - 1)$ a factor of $f(x) = 2x^4 + 3x^2 - 5x + 6$?

Solution: By the Factor Theorem, $(x - 1)$ is a factor of $f(x)$ only if $f(1) = 0$.

Use synthetic division and the Remainder Theorem to determine the remainder R when $f(x)$ is divided by $(x - 1)$.

$$
\begin{array}{r|rrrrr}
1 & 2 & 0 & 3 & -5 & 6 \\
  &   & 2 & 2 & 5 & 0 \\
\hline
  & 2 & 2 & 5 & 0 & 6
\end{array}
\qquad \text{remainder is 6}
$$

Since the remainder is 6, $f(1) = 6$, and $(x - 1)$ is **not** a factor of $f(x)$.

Example 2. Is $(x - i)$ a factor of $f(x) = 3x^3 + (-4 - 3i)x^2 + (5 + 4i)x - 5i$?

Solution: The only way $(x - i)$ can be a factor of $f(x)$ is if $f(i) = 0$.

Use synthetic division and the Remainder Theorem to determine the remainder when $f(x)$ is divided by $(x - i)$.

$$
\begin{array}{r|rrrr}
i & 3 & -4 - 3i & 5 + 4i & -5i \\
  &   & 3i   & -4i   & 5i \\
\hline
  & 3 & -4   & 5   & 0
\end{array}
\qquad \text{remainder is 0}
$$

Since the remainder is 0, we know that $f(i) = 0$, and $(x - i)$ is a factor of $f(x)$.

We can write:

$$f(x) = (x - i)(3x^2 - 4x + 5)$$

Notice that $3x^2 - 4x = 5$ is the quotient from the synthetic division above.

Fundamental Theorem of Algebra

Fundamental Theorem of Algebra:

Every polynomial of degree n with $n \geq 1$ has at least one zero in the set of complex numbers.

$$P(x) = (x - k) * Q(x)$$

Remember that any real number can be written as a complex number with an imaginary part.

$$4 = 4 + 0i$$

The Fundamental Theorem and the Factor Theorem can be used to factor $Q(x)$ in the same way. If $P(x)$ has degree n and repeating the process n times gives:

$$P(x) = a_n(x - k_1)(x - k_2)\ldots(x - k_n)$$

where a_n is the leading coefficient of $P(x)$. Each of these factors leads to a zero of $P(x)$, so $P(x)$ has n zeros $k_1, k_2, k_3, \ldots, k_n$.

A polynomial of <u>degree n</u> has <u>at most n distinct zeros</u>.

Finding Polynomials when Given Zeros

If we are given several numbers, we can find a polynomial function with those numbers as zeros. Example 3 demonstrates how to find a polynomial function when the zeros are known.

Example 3: Find a polynomial function of degree 3 with real coefficients, having the zeros of 1, $2i$, and $-2i$.

Solution: The given zeros show that the polynomial function has factors of
$(x - 1)$, $(x - 2i)$, and $(x + 2i)$.

Write a function using these factors.

$$f(x) = a_n(x-1)(x-2i)(x+2i)$$ let $a_n = 1$ for the simplest function

$$= (x-1)(x^2+4)$$ Multiply $(x-2i)(x+2i)$

$$= x^3 - x^2 + 4x - 4$$ Multiply

Notice that the coefficients of $f(x)$ are real numbers even though there were two zeros that were purely imaginary.

Example 4: Find a polynomial of degree 4 with -1 as a zero of multiplicity 3, and 0 as a zero of multiplicity 1.

Solution: Again we will let $a_n = 1$ in order to get the simplest possible function.

$$f(x) = (x+1)^3(x-0) = (x+1)^3 x$$
$$= x^4 + 3x^3 + 3x^2 + x$$

Conjugate Zeros Theorem

<u>Conjugate Zeros Theorem</u>

If $P(x)$ is a polynomial having <u>only real coefficients</u> and if
$\qquad a + bi$ is a zero of $P(x)$,
then the complex conjugate
$\qquad a - bi$ is also a zero of $P(x)$.
This is not true if the coefficients are not real.

If $P(x)$ is a polynomial having <u>only rational coefficients</u> and if
$\qquad a + b\sqrt{c}$ is a zero of $P(x)$ and irrational,
then the conjugate
$\qquad a - b\sqrt{c}$ is also a zero of $P(x)$.
Where a, b and c are rational numbers, but $\sqrt{c}$ is an irrational number.

Example 5: If a polynomial function of degree 6 with rational coefficients has
$-2+4i$, $-3i$, and $1-\sqrt{2}$ as three of its zeros. Find the other zeros.

Solution: Since the coefficients are rational (and thus real as well), the function must also have zeros that are conjugates of the given zeros:
$$-2-4i, \quad 3i, \quad \text{and } 1+\sqrt{2}$$

These are the only zeros of the polynomial since the degree is given as six.

Example 6:   Find a polynomial function of lowest possible degree having real coefficients and zeros of 2 and $2 - i$.

Solution: Because one of the given zeros is a complex number, then its conjugate $2 + i$ also must be a zero, so the polynomial has at least 3 zeros, 2, $2 - i$, and $2 + i$. Since we want the lowest degree, these will be the only zeros, and the degree of the polynomial function will be 3.

The three factors must be:

$$(x-2)(x-(2-i))(x-(2+i)) \quad \text{or} \quad (x-2)(x-2+i)(x-2-i)$$

and

$$f(x) = (x-2)(x-(2-i))(x-(2+i))$$

$$f(x) = (x-2)(x-2+i)(x-2-i) = (x-2)(x^2 - 4x + 5)$$

$$f(x) = x^3 - 6x^2 + 13x - 10$$

Rational Zeros of Polynomial Functions

Often it is difficult to find the zeros of a polynomial function. The following theorem gives a useful method for finding a set of possible zeros of a polynomial with integer coefficients.

Rational Zeros Theorem

<u>Rational Zeros Theorem</u>

Let $P(x) = a_n x^n + a_{n-1} x^{n-1} + \ldots + a_1 x + a_0$, $a_n \neq 0$ be a polynomial with integer coefficients.

If p/q is a *zero of* $P(x)$ and p/q is in lowest terms:

then p is a factor of the constant term a_0

and q is a factor of the leading coefficient a_n

Example 7: Given $f(x) = 2x^4 - 11x^3 + 14x^2 - 11x + 12$. Find all rational zeros.

Solution: If p/q is a rational zero of the function, by the Rational Zeros theorem p must be a factor of $a_0 = 12$ and q must be a factor of $a_4 = 2$.

The possible values of p are: $\pm 1, \pm 2, \pm 3, \pm 4, \pm 6$ or ± 12

The possible values of q are: ± 1 or ± 2.

The possible rational zeros are found by forming all possible quotients of the form p/q:

$$\pm 1, \ \pm 1/2, \ \pm 2, \ \pm 3, \ \pm 3/2, \ \pm 4, \ \pm 6, \ \text{or} \ \pm 12$$

We do not know if any of these numbers are zeros, but if $f(x)$ does have any rational zeros, they will be in this list.

The proposed zeros can be tested using synthetic division. From this testing, we find that 4 is a zero:

$$
\begin{array}{r|rrrrr}
4 & 2 & -11 & 14 & -11 & 12 \\
  &   & 8 & -12 & 8 & -12 \\
\hline
  & 2 & -3 & 2 & -3 & 0
\end{array}
$$
remainder is 0.

We can now look for zeros of the simpler polynomial we find with synthetic division because $f(x) = (x - 4)(2x^3 - 3x^2 + 2x - 3)$.

$$Q(x) = 2x^3 - 3x^2 + 2x - 3$$

Any rational zero of $Q(x)$ will have a numerator of $\pm 3, \pm 1$ and a denominator of $\pm 2, \pm 1$

Thus, any rational zeros of $Q(x)$ will be in this list:

$$\pm 3, \ \pm \frac{3}{2}, \ \pm 1, \ \pm \frac{1}{2}$$

Again using synthetic division and trial and error we find that $\dfrac{3}{2}$ is a zero

$$(3/2) \; \bigg| \quad 2 \quad -3 \quad \quad 2 \quad -3$$
$$\underline{\quad\quad\quad\quad\quad 3 \quad\quad 0 \quad\quad 3 \quad}$$
$$\quad\quad\quad 2 \quad\quad 0 \quad\quad 2 \quad\quad 0 \quad\quad\quad\quad\quad\quad \text{remainder is } 0$$

Now we have $f(x) = (x-4)(2x-3)(2x^2+2)$.

The quotient is $2x^2 + 2$, which, by the quadratic formula, has i and $-i$ as zeros. These are imaginary zeros. The real zeros of the function are:

$$4 \text{ and } \frac{3}{2}$$

So, $f(x) = (x-4)(2x-3)(x-i)(x+i)$.

Test these zeros first using synthetic division.

In a problem like Example 7, you can use a graphing calculator to graph the function and see if any of the zeros of the graph are close to the possible zeros.

Chapter 6, Example 25 is an example of the use of a graphing calculator to find real zeros. The above problem can be solved in the same manner.

Descartes' Rule of Signs, stated below, gives a useful test for finding the number of positive or negative real zeros of a given polynomial.

The function to be tested must be written in **descending or ascending order** with no zero terms added.

Descartes' Rule of Signs

Descartes' Rule of Signs:

If *f(x)* is a polynomial function with real coefficients:

a. The number of positive real zeros of *f(x)* is either equal to the number of variations that occur in the signs of the coefficients of *f(x)*, or is less than the number of variations by a positive even integer.

b. The number of negative real zeros of *f(x)* is either equal to the number of variations in the signs of the coefficients of *f(−x)*, or is less than the number of variations by a positive even integer.

Example 8:
What does Descartes' Rule of Signs tell about the zeros of:
$$P(x) = x^5 - 3x^2 + x - 4?$$

Solution:

The number of positive sign variances in $P(x)$ is 3.

This tells us that the number of positive real zeros is either 3 or less than 3 by a factor of 2, (i.e. $3 - 2, 3 - 4, 3 - 6 \ldots$). So there are either 3 or 1 positive real zeros.

$P(-x) = -x^5 - 3x^2 - x - 4$.
The number of sign variations in $P(-x)$ is zero.
There are **no** negative real zeros.

Because the degree of $P(x)$ is 5, there are 5 total zeros:

Total zeros: 5

Positive zeros	3	or	1
Negative zeros	0	or	0
Imaginary zeros	2	or	4

Section 3.4 Exercises

Find a polynomial function of degree 3 with the given numbers as zeros.

1. $-1, 3, 5$

2. $-3, 4i, -4i$

3. $4, i, -i$

4. $\sqrt{3}, -\sqrt{3}, 3$

5. $1+\sqrt{2}, 1-\sqrt{2}, -4$

6. $2+5i, 2-5i, -3$

7. $-2, 0, 3$

8. $-1/2, 0, 3/2$

9. Find a polynomial function of degree 5 with -2 as a zero of multiplicity 3, 0 as a zero of multiplicity 1, and 2 as a zero of multiplicity 1.

10. Find a polynomial of degree 4 with -1 as a zero of multiplicity 1, 4 as a zero of multiplicity 2, and -2 as a zero of multiplicity 1.

Suppose that a polynomial function of degree 4 with rational coefficients has the given numbers as zeros. Find the other zeros.

11. $-2, \sqrt{3}, 4$

12. $-2i+3, -\sqrt{5}$

13. $2i, 0, -4$

14. $-2-i, 2-\sqrt{5}$

Suppose that a polynomial function of degree 5 with rational coefficients has the given numbers as zeros. Find the other zeros.

15. $-\frac{1}{2}, \sqrt{3}, -2i$

16. $-3, 0, 3, -2i$

Find a polynomial function, of lowest degree, with rational coefficients and $a_n = 1$ that has the given numbers as its zeros.

17. $2+i, 3$

18. $-3i, 2$

19. $\sqrt{2}, -3i$

20. $\sqrt{3}, -i$

List all possible rational zeros of each function:

21. $f(x) = 4x^5 - x^3 + 2$

22. $f(x) = 4x^3 - 3x^2 + 4x - 8$

Find all zeros of each given function:

23. $f(x) = x^3 - 8x^2 + 17x - 4$

24. $f(x) = 12x^3 + 20x^2 - x - 6$

25. $f(x) = x^4 + 2x^3 - 13x^2 - 38x - 24$

Section 3.5   Rational Functions

Rational Function

Rational Function:

A rational function is a function of the form $\qquad f(x) = \dfrac{p(x)}{q(x)}$

where $p(x)$ and $q(x)$ are polynomials and $q(x) \neq 0$
The domain of a rational function is the set of all x-values for which $q(x) \neq 0$.

Since any values of x such that $q(x) = 0$ cannot be part of the domain of the function, a rational function has one or more discontinuities (breaks) in its graph.

Examples of rational functions:

1   $f(x) = \dfrac{1}{x}$ where x $\neq$ 0.

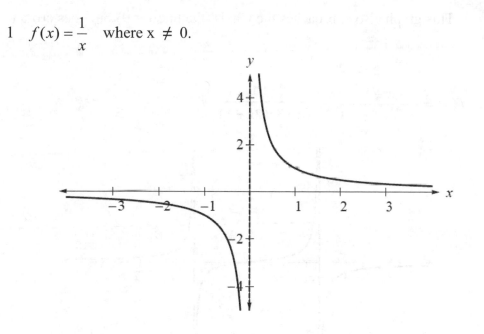

The graph **approaches** the y-axis as the values of x get near to zero.
The graph gets very close to the y-axis but does not cross it. Remember
That the y-axis is the line $x = 0$.
The domain of this function is the set of all real numbers except 0. Notice
that f is an odd function, and thus the graph is symmetric with respect to
the origin.

181

2. $f(x) = \dfrac{1}{x^2}$ where x ≠ 0

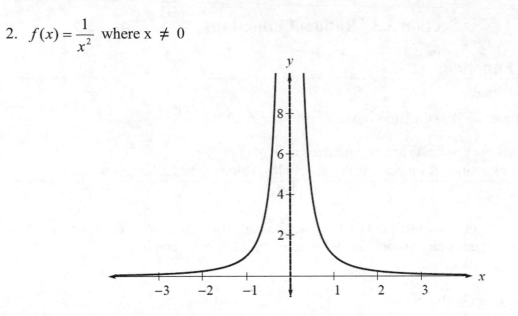

This graph also approaches the y-axis (the line x = 0) but does cross it.

3. $f(x) = \dfrac{x+1}{2x^2 + 5x - 3} = \dfrac{x+1}{(x+3)(2x-1)}$

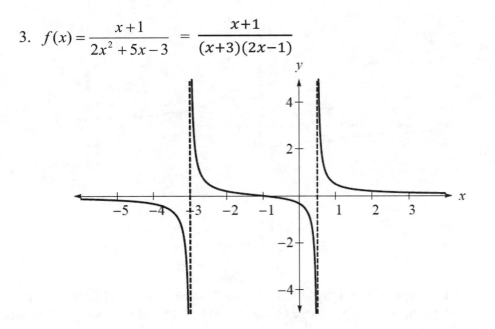

The graph of this function does not cross the lines $x = -3$ and $x = \dfrac{1}{2}$.

4. $f(x) = \dfrac{x+3}{x-2}$

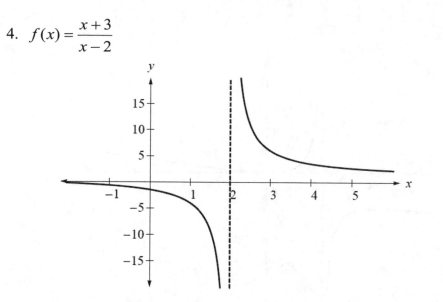

The graph of this function does not cross the line $x = 2$.

5, $f(x) = \dfrac{3x^2 - 3x - 6}{x^2 + 8x + 16}$

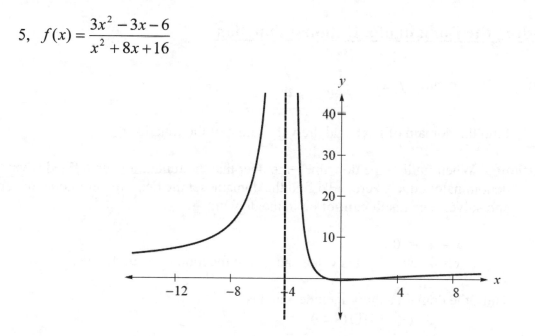

The graph does not cross the line $x = -4$.

6. $f(x) = \dfrac{x^2}{x+2}$

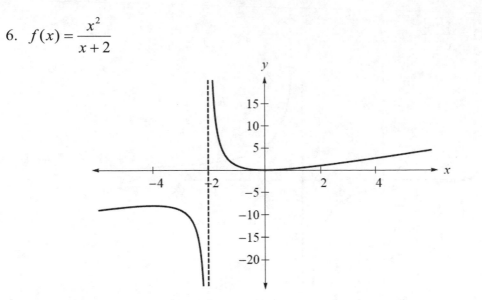

The graph of this function does not cross the line $x = -2$.

Finding the Domain of a Rational Function

Example 1: Given: $f(x) = \dfrac{1}{x-4}$

Find the domain of $f(x)$ and draw the graph of the function.

Solution: When finding the domain, remember that the function is undefined when the denominator equals zero. To find the domain, set the denominator equal to zero and solve. The result **cannot** be in the domain.

$$x - 4 = 0$$
$$x = 4 \qquad \text{this value causes the function to be undefined}$$

Thus, the domain cannot include 4 and is:
$$(-\infty, 4) \cup (4, \infty)$$

To graph the function, notice that the function is the graph of

$$f(x) = \dfrac{1}{x} \qquad \text{shifted to the right 4 units.}$$

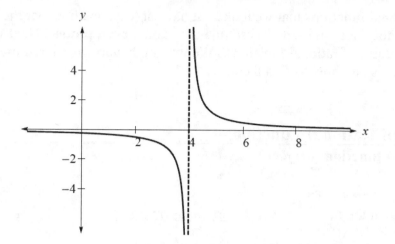

See Chapter 6, Example 26 for this problem solved with a graphing calculator.

Example 2: Using the previous graphs 1 thru 6 shown at the start of this section, find the domain of each of these functions.

Solution:

$$f(x) = \frac{1}{x}$$ Domain: $(-\infty, 0) \cup (0, \infty)$

$$f(x) = \frac{1}{x^2}$$ Domain: $(-\infty, 0) \cup (0, \infty)$

$$f(x) = \frac{x+1}{2x^2 + 5x - 3}$$ Domain: $(-\infty, -3) \cup (-3, 1/2) \cup (1/2, \infty)$

$$f(x) = \frac{x+3}{x-2}$$ Domain: $(-\infty, 2) \cup (2, \infty)$

$$f(x) = \frac{3x^2 - 3x - 6}{x^2 + 8x + 16}$$ Domain: $(-\infty, -4) \cup (-4, \infty)$

$$f(x) = \frac{x^2}{x+2}$$ Domain: $(-\infty, -2) \cup (-2, \infty)$

185

Each of the rational functions that we looked at have at least one line that the graph approaches but does not intersect. These lines are called **asymptotes**. Next we will learn about the asymptotes of rational functions. We will study vertical, horizontal, and oblique asymptotes and how to find them.

Asymptotes of Rational Functions

For the rational function $y = f(x)$

If $|f(x)| \rightarrow \infty$ as $x \rightarrow a$
then the line $x = a$ is a <u>vertical asymptote.</u>

If $f(x) \rightarrow a$ as $|x| \rightarrow \infty$
then the line $y = a$ is a <u>horizontal asymptote.</u>

To Find Vertical Asymptotes

<u>To Find Vertical Asymptotes</u>:

set the denominator of the function equal to 0 and solve for x.

If a is a zero of the denominator and not a zero of the numerator, then the line $x = a$ is a vertical asymptote.

As stated, we find vertical asymptotes using the denominator of a rational function.

Example 3: Find the vertical asymptotes for the graph of each of the following functions:

a. $f(x) = \dfrac{4x}{x^2 + 2x - 15}$　　　　b. $f(x) = \dfrac{x+3}{x^3 - 2x}$

Solution:

a. $f(x) = \dfrac{4x}{x^2 + 2x - 15}$

Set the denominator equal to zero and solve for x to find the zeros of the denominator.

$$x^2 + 2x - 15 = 0$$
$$(x+5)(x-3) = 0$$
$$x + 5 = 0 \qquad x - 3 = 0$$
$$x = -5 \qquad x = 3$$

The zeros of the denominator are: -5, 3.
The only zero of the numerator is $x = 0$ and is not a zero of the denominator.

The vertical asymptotes are $x = -5$ and $x = 3$.

b. $f(x) = \dfrac{x + 3}{x^3 - 2x}$

We see that -3 is the only zero of the numerator.
We must set the denominator equal to 0 to find the zeros of the denominator.

$$x^3 - 2x = 0$$
$$x(x^2 - 2) = 0 \qquad\qquad \text{Factor and solve the factors}$$
$$x = 0 \quad x^2 - 2 = 0$$
$$x = 0 \quad x = \pm\sqrt{2}$$

The zeros of the denominator are: 0, $\sqrt{2}$, $-\sqrt{2}$ and these are not zeros of the numerator.
The vertical asymptotes are: $x = 0$; $x = \sqrt{2}$; $x = -\sqrt{2}$

To Find Horizontal Asymptotes

To Find Horizontal Asymptotes**:**
     a. If the **numerator has a lower degree than the denominator**, there is
         a horizontal asymptote at:
$$y = 0$$
     b. If the **numerator and the denominator have the same degree,** use the

         coefficients of each to form a fraction: $\dfrac{a_n}{b_n}$ where a_n is the

         numerator leading coefficient, and b_n is the denominator leading
         coefficient.

         There is a horizontal asymptote at:

$$y = \frac{a_n}{b_n}$$

If the **degree of the numerator is greater than the degree of the denominator,**
     there is no horizontal asymptote.

Example 4: Find the horizontal asymptotes for the graph of each of the following:

a. $f(x) = \dfrac{2x-6}{x^3-1}$

b. $f(x) = \dfrac{2x^2+1}{3x^2-1}$

Solution:

a. $f(x) = \dfrac{2x-6}{x^3-1}$

The degree of the numerator is 1 and is lower than the degree of the denominator which is 3. Therefore there is a horizontal asymptote at $y = 0$.

b. $f(x) = \dfrac{2x^2+1}{3x^2-1}$

Since the numerator and denominator both have a degree of 2, form a fraction using the coefficients of the term of the highest degree in each: $\dfrac{2}{3}$.

Therefore there is a horizontal asymptote at $y = \dfrac{2}{3}$.

Facts about Asymptotes

Facts about Asymptotes:

Vertical asymptotes occur at the x-values of the zeros of the denominator that are not a zero of the numerator.

The graph never crosses a vertical asymptote.

The line $y = 0$ (the x-axis) is a horizontal asymptote when the degree of the numerator is less than the degree of the denominator.

When the degree of the numerator and denominator are the same, the line :

$$y = \frac{\text{leading coefficient of numerator}}{\text{leading coefficient of denominator}} \quad \text{is a } \textbf{horizontal} \text{ asymptote.}$$

A graph may cross a horizontal asymptote but does not always.

An **oblique** asymptote occurs when the degree of the numerator is 1 greater than the degree of the denominator. Use synthetic divison to find an oblique asymptote.

A graph **never** has both an oblique asymptote and a horizontal asymptote.

188

Example 5. Find all asymptotes of: $\dfrac{2x-6}{x^3-1}$.

Solution: From the denominator we see that 3 is a zero of the denominator but not a zero of the numerator, and :

$x = 3$ is a vertical asymptote.

The degree of the numerator is 1 more than the degree of the denominator. We will look for an oblique asymptote:

Using synthetic division:

$$f(x) = \frac{x^2+1}{x-3} = x+3+\frac{10}{x-3}$$

As x gets very large, the remainder fraction is very small, and the graph will approach the line (this line is the quotient in the divison):
$y = x+3$ is an oblique asymptote.

The graph of Example 5 is:

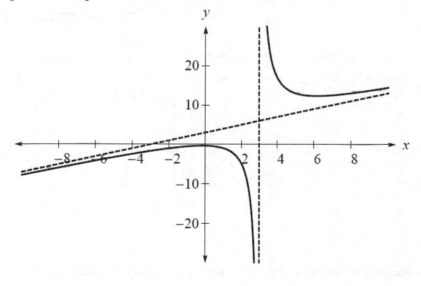

Example 6: Given: $f(x) = \dfrac{3x^2-2x-1}{x-3}$ Find all asymptotes.

Use any zero of the demoninator to find a vertical asymptote: set x equal to that value. We must also find the zeros of the numerator to insure that numerator and denominator do not have a common zero.

Solution: We factor the numerator into $(3x+1)(x-1)$. These are not factors of the denominator.

From the denominator, the line $x = 3$ is a vertical asymptote.

Use the degrees of the numerator and denominator to find other asymptotes. The degree of the numerator is 1 greater than the degree of the denominator, and so we will look for an oblique asymptote.

Check for oblique asymptote using division, and we find that:

$$\frac{3x^2 - 2x - 1}{x - 3} = 3x + 7 + \frac{20}{x - 3}$$

From the above quotient, we find that $y = 3x + 7$ is an oblique asymptote.

The graph of the given function is:

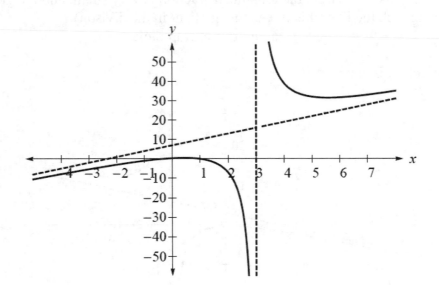

Notice that the two asymptotes that we found previously are seen in this graph.

Our findings: Vertical Asymptote: $x = 3$, and Oblique Asymptote: $y = 3x + 7$

Steps for Graphing Rational Functions

Steps for Graphing Rational Functions:

1. Find any vertical asymptotes using the zeros of the denominator that are are not zeros of the numerator.

   Sketch any asymptotes found.

2. Determine any other asymptotes: either horizontal or oblique.
   Sketch any asymptotes found.

3. Find any intercepts.
   for the x-intercepts, let $y = 0$
   and
   for the y-intercept, let $x = 0$.

4. Plot a few selected points ….. at least one in each region of the domain determined by any vertical asymptotes.

5. Draw the graph.

Section 3.5 Exercises

Find any vertical, horizontal, or oblique asymptotes for the following functions:

1. $f(x) = \dfrac{2}{x-4}$

2. $f(x) = \dfrac{-3}{x+1}$

3. $f(x) = \dfrac{x+3}{x-2}$

4. $f(x) = \dfrac{x-5}{2-x}$

5. $f(x) = \dfrac{4x+5}{5x-3}$

6. $f(x) = \dfrac{5x}{x-2}$

7. $f(x) = \dfrac{3}{x^2-4}$

8. $f(x) = \dfrac{-2}{x^2-x-6}$

9. $f(x) = \dfrac{x^2-3}{x+1}$

10. $f(x) = \dfrac{x^2+9}{x-1}$

11. $f(x) = \dfrac{(x-1)(x+3)}{(x-2)(3x-1)}$

12. $f(x) = \dfrac{2(x+1)(x-4)}{(4x-2)(x+2)}$

13. $f(x) = \dfrac{2x^2-4}{x^2+1}$

14. $f(x) = \dfrac{-4x^2+12}{x^2+4}$

Sketch the graph of the following functions:

15. $f(x) = \dfrac{3}{4+x}$

16. $f(x) = -\dfrac{6}{x^2}$

17. $f(x) = \dfrac{1}{x^2+2}$

18. $f(x) = \dfrac{x+1}{x-2}$

19. $f(x) = \dfrac{2x}{x^2+3x+2}$

20. $f(x) = \dfrac{x-2}{x^2-4x+3}$

Find a rational function that satisfies the given conditions. Answers many vary.

21. Vertical asymptotes $x = -3$, $x = 2$.

22. Vertical asymptotes $x = -2$, $x = 3$; horizontal asymptote: $y = 4/3$; x-intercept $(1, 0)$.

Section 3.6   Polynomial and Rational Inequalities

Quadratic Inequality

Quadratic Inequality:

A quadratic inequality is an inequality that can be written in the form

$$ax^2 + bx + c < 0$$

for real numbers $a \neq 0$, b, and c.

The symbol $<$ can be replaced with $>$, $\leq$, or $\geq$.

Examples of quadratic inequalities:

$$3x^2 - 2x + 4 > 0 \qquad\qquad -x^2 + 4x \leq 7 \qquad\qquad -4x^2 > 12$$

A quadratic inequality is one type of polynomial inequality. Other examples of polynomial inequalities are:

$$3x > 2 \qquad\qquad 2x^4 + 2x^2 - x \leq 9 \qquad\qquad x^3 + 2x^2 > x - 3$$

If the inequality sign is replaced with an equal sign, the inequality becomes an equation. When this equation is solved, the results help in finding the solutions to the inequality.

Example 1:   Solve: $x^3 - 4x > 0$.

Solution:

In this problem we are looking for all values of x which make the given polynomial greater than zero. This means that we are looking for intervals where the graph of the function $f(x) = x^3 - 4x$ has POSITIVE values.

We begin by finding the zeros of the function.

$$x^3 - 4x = 0 \qquad\qquad \text{Set the inequality} = 0.$$

$$x(x^2 - 4) = 0 \qquad\qquad \text{Factor.}$$

$$x(x - 2)(x + 2) = 0$$

These three factors give us the zeros which are − 2, 0, and 2.

Use the zeros to divide the x-axis into 4 intervals:

$$(-\infty,-2), \quad (-2,0), \quad (0,2), \quad \text{and} \quad (2,\infty).$$

These intervals formed on the x-axis by the zeros are used to solve the problem. We will choose a test value within each interval and determine the sign of the function for each test value. This will tell us the value of the function over each interval.

INTERVAL	TEST VALUE	SIGN OF $f(x)$
$(-\infty,-2)$	$f(-4)=-48$	negative
$(-2,0)$	$f(-1)=3$	**positive**
$(0,2)$	$f(1)=-3$	negative
$(2,\infty)$	$f(4)=48$	**positive**

The original problem was to solve: $x^3-4x>0$.

Since the inequality sign says "polynomial" $>$ 0, the problem asks for those intervals where the polynomial is **positive**. From our chart, we find two intervals where the values are positive. The solution is the union of these two intervals:

$$(-2,0) \cup (2,\infty)$$

Look at the graph of $f(x)=x^3-4x$.

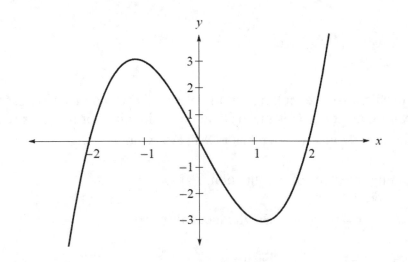

We see that the function values are positive when the graph is above the x-axis: between x values of -2 and 0 and also from values of x greater than 2. Thus the graph verifies our solution of $(-2,0) \cup (2,\infty)$.

The problem in Example 1 can be solved using a graphing calculator. See Chapter 6, Example 27.

Steps Used To Solve a Polynomial Inequality

To solve a polynomial inequality:

1. Use addition/subtraction so that one side of the inequality is zero.

2. Replace the inequality symbol with an equal sign and solve $P(x) = 0$.

3. Use the solutions to divide the x-axis into intervals.

4. Choose a test value in each interval and determine the sign of the polynomial.

5. Select the intervals that make the inequality a true statement.

6. Include the endpoints of the intervals in the solution if the inequality symbol is $\geq$ or $\leq$.

Example 2: Solve $2x^4 - 3x^3 - 5x^2 \leq -x - 1$

Solution:

In order to solve the inequality, we need to have zero on the right side of the inequality. We will add $x + 1$ to both sides:

$$2x^4 - 3x^3 - 5x^2 + x + 1 \leq 0$$

We begin by finding the zeros of $f(x) = 2x^4 - 3x^3 - 5x^2 + x + 1$

$$2x^4 - 3x^3 - 5x^2 + x + 1 = 0$$

Using previously discussed techniques and synthetic division, we find that the zeros to be:

$$-1, \quad 1 - \sqrt{2}, \quad 1/2, \quad 1 + \sqrt{2}$$

195

Now we can form intervals on the x-axis and pick test points in each interval:

$$(-\infty, -1) \quad (-1, 1 - \sqrt{2}), \quad (1 - \sqrt{2}, 1/2) \quad (1/2, 1 + \sqrt{2}), \quad (1 + \sqrt{2}, \infty)$$

INTERVAL	TEST VALUE	SIGN OF $f(x)$
$(-\infty, -1)$	$f(-3) = 196$	positive
$(-1, 1 - \sqrt{2})$	$f(-1/2) = -1/4$	**negative**
$(1 - \sqrt{2}, 1/2)$	$f(0) = 1$	positive
$(1/2, 1 + \sqrt{2})$	$f(1) = -4$	**negative**
$(1 + \sqrt{2}, \infty)$	$f(5) = 756$	positive

The function is negative over two of our intervals, and our solution is the union of these.

$$[-1, 1 - \sqrt{2}] \cup \left[\frac{1}{2}, 1 + \sqrt{2} \right]$$

To solve Example 2 using a graphing calculator, see Chapter 6, Example 28.

Rational Inequalities

Rational Inequalities:

    Inequalities that contain rational expressions are called rational inequalities.

Example 3: Solve the rational inequality $\dfrac{x-2}{x+2} \geq \dfrac{x+3}{x-1}$.

Solution: The method above will work, but we need a few more steps to solve rational inequalities. Notice that if $x = -2$ or $x = 1$, the result would be a denominator equal to zero.

Begin by subtracting $\dfrac{x+3}{x-1}$ from both sides so that the right side is zero.

$$\frac{x-2}{x+2} - \frac{x+3}{x-1} \geq 0 \qquad \text{Multiply both sides by LCD } (x+2)(x-1).$$

$$(x+2)(x-1)\left(\frac{x-2}{x+2}\right) - (x+2)(x-1)\left(\frac{x+3}{x-1}\right) \geq (x+2)(x-1)(0)$$

Now we have an equivalent function:

$$f(x) = (x-1)(x-2) - (x+2)(x+3)$$

Find the zeros of $f(x)$:

$$(x-1)(x-2) - (x+2)(x+3) = 0 \qquad \text{Simplify.}$$

$$x^2 - 3x + 2 - (x^2 + 5x + 6) = 0$$

$$x^2 - 3x + 2 - x^2 - 5x - 6 = 0$$

$$-8x - 4 = 0$$

$$-8x = 4$$

$$x = -\frac{1}{2}$$

<u>Critical values</u> are: (1) x-values where our function $f(x)$ is zero; or (2) values not in the domain of our original inequality.

Values not in the domain of this example are: -2 and 1, and the function zero is $-\frac{1}{2}$.

The critical values are: -2, $-\frac{1}{2}$, and 1 and we use these to wrote our intervals.

The intervals of the x-axis would be:

$$(-\infty, -2) \qquad (-2, -1/2) \qquad (-1/2, 1) \qquad and \qquad (1, \infty)$$

INTERVAL	TEST VALUE	SIGN OF $f(x)$
$(-\infty, -2)$	$f(-4) = 2.8$	**positive**
$(-2, -1/2)$	$f(-1) = -2$	negative
$(-1/2, 1)$	$f(0) = 2$	**positive**
$(1, \infty)$	$f(3) = -2.8$	negative

197

Remember that we are solving:

$$\frac{x-2}{x+2} - \frac{x+3}{x-1} \geq 0$$

Our chart shows us that 2 of the intervals contain positive values for our $f(x)$.

The solution to the inequality is the union of the two positive valued intervals:
$$(-\infty, -2) \cup [-1/2, 1).$$

We must use a bracket for the zero of $-\frac{1}{2}$ to show that this value is included in the solution interval since the symbol $\geq$ is used .

To solve Example 3 using a graphing calculator, see Chapter 6, Example 29.

To Solve a Rational Inequality

To solve a rational inequality:

1. Use addition/subtraction to get zero on one side of the equation.

2. Replace the inequality symbol with an equal sign to find the zeros of the equivalent function found in Step 1.

3. Find the undefined values for the variable (zeros of the denominators).

4. The critical values are the zeros of the inequality and the undefined values.

5. Use the critical values to divide the x-axis into intervals.

6. Choose a test value in each interval and determine the sign.

7. Pick the intervals that make the given inequality a true statement.

8. If the inequality symbol is $\leq$ or $\geq$ the zeros should be included in the interval.

Section 3.6 Exercises

Given: $f(x) = x^2 + 3x - 18$ Solve each:

1. $f(x) = 0$

2. $f(x) > 0$

3. $f(x) \geq 0$

4. $f(x) \leq 0$

5. $f(x) < 0$

6. $f(x) \neq 0$

Solve the given inequalities.

7. $(x+1)(x-2) > 0$

8. $(x-5)(x-3) \leq 0$

9. $x^2 - x - 12 > 0$

10. $x^2 - x - 12 \leq 0$

11. $x^2 > 36$

12. $x^2 < 4$

13. $x^2 + 6x + 16 < 8$

14. $2x^2 - 9x > -4$

15. $x^3 - 5x \leq 0$

16. $x^3 - 16x \geq 0$

17. $\dfrac{x-3}{x+6} \leq 0$

18. $\dfrac{x+1}{x-3} > 0$

19. $\dfrac{4}{x+1} < \dfrac{2}{x+3}$

20. $\dfrac{x+3}{x-5} \leq 1$

Chapter 3 Summary

Polynomial Function:

$$f(x) = a_n x^n + a_{n-1} x^{n-1} + \ldots\ldots + a_1 x + a_0$$

End Behavior:

The leading term of the polynomial functions demonstrates its end behavior.

<u>Degree Even:</u>

Leading Coefficient Positive: the end behavior approaches $+\infty$

Leading Coefficient Negative: end behavior approaches $-\infty$

<u>Degree Odd:</u>

Leading Coefficient Positive:

as x approaches $-\infty$, the end behavior approaches $-\infty$

as x approaches $+\infty$, the end behavior approaches $+\infty$

Leading Coefficient Negative:

as x approaches $-\infty$, the end behavior approaches $+\infty$

as x approaches $+\infty$, the end behavior approaches $-\infty$

The Intermediate Value Theorem:

If $P(x)$ is a polynomial function with only real coefficients, and if for real numbers a and b, $P(a)$ and $P(b)$ are opposite in sign, then there exists at least one real zero between a and b.

Division of Polynomials:

For any polynomial $P(x)$ and any number k, there exists a unique polynomial $Q(x)$ and number R such that:

$$P(x) = (x-k) * Q(x) + R$$

The Remainder Theorem:

If $P(x)$ is divided by $(x-k)$, then the remainder is $P(k)$.

The Factor Theorem:

The polynomial $(x-k)$ is a factor of the polynomial $P(x)$ if $P(k) = 0$.

Fundamental Theorem of Algebra:
> Every polynomial of degree n, $n \geq 1$, has at least one complex zero.
> $$P(x) = (x - k) * Q(x)$$

Conjugate Zeros Theorem
> If $P(x)$ is a polynomial having <u>only real coefficients</u> and if
>> $a + bi$ is a zero of $P(x)$,
>
> then the conjugate
>> $a - bi$ is also a zero of $P(x)$.
>
> If $P(x)$ is a polynomial having <u>only rational coefficients</u> and if
>> $a + b\sqrt{c}$ is a zero of $P(x)$,
>
> then the conjugate
>> $a - b\sqrt{c}$ is also a zero of $P(x)$.

Rational Zeros Theorem
> Let $P(x) = a_n x^n + a_{n-1} x^{n-1} + \ldots + a_1 x + a_0$, $a_n \neq 0$ be a
> polynomial with integer coefficients.
> If p/q is a zero of $P(x)$ and p/q is in lowest terms:
>> then p is a factor of the constant term a_0
>> and q is a factor of the leading coefficient a_n

Decartes' Rule of Signs:
> If $f(x)$ is a polynomial function with real coefficients:
> a. The number of positive real zeros of $f(x)$ is either equal to the number of sign variations that occur in the coefficients of $f(x)$, or is less than the number of variations by a positive even integer.
> b. The number of negative real zeros of $f(x)$ is either equal to the number of sign variations of $f(-x)$, or is less than the number of variations by a positive even integer.

<u>Rational Function:</u>
A function of the form
> $$f(x) = \frac{p(x)}{q(x)}$$ where $p(x)$ and $q(x)$ are polynomials and $q(x) \neq 0$

Asymptotes:
> For the rational function $y = f(x)$
> If $\left| f(x) \right| \to \infty$ as $x \to a$

then the line $x = a$ is a <u>vertical asymptote.</u>
If $f(x) \to a$ as $\left| x \right| \to \infty$
then the line $y = a$ is a <u>horizontal asymptote.</u>

Graphing Rational Functions:
1. Find any vertical asymptotes using the zeros of the denominator, and determine that they are not also zeros of the numerator. Sketch any asymptotes found.
2. Determine any other asymptotes: either horizontal or oblique. Sketch any asymptotes found.
3. Find any intercepts.
    For x-intercepts, let $y = 0$ and
    for y-intercept, let $x = 0$.
4. Plot a few selected points ….. at least one in each region of the domain determined by any vertical asymptotes.
5. Draw the graph.

To solve a polynomial inequality:
1. Use addition/subtraction to get zero on one side of the inequality.
2. Replace the inequality symbol with an an equal sign and solve.
3. Use the solutions to divide the x-axis into intervals.
4. Choose a test value in each interval and determine the sign of the equation over that interval.
5. Pick the intervals that make the given inequality a true statement.
6. Include the endpoints of the intervals in the solution if the inequality symbol is $\geq$ or $\leq$.

To solve a rational inequality:
1. Use addition/subtraction to get 0 on one side.
2. Replace the inequality symbol with an $=$ and find the zeros.
3. Find the undefined values for the variable (found as the zeros of the denominators).
4. The critical values are the zeros and the undefined values.
5. Use the critical values to divide the x-axis into intervals.
6. Choose a test value in each interval and determine the sign.
7. Pick the intervals that make the inequality symbol a true statement.
8. If the inequality symbol is $\leq$ or $\geq$ the zeros should be included in the interval.

Chapter 3 Review

Sketch the graph and find the zeros, relative maxima, relative minima, the domain and range.

1. $f(x) = x^2 - 4$

2. $f(x) = x^3$

3. $f(x) = (x-1)^2$

Classify the function as constant, linear, quadratic, cubic, or quartic. Find the leading term, the leading coefficient, and the degree.

4. $f(x) = 2 + 5x - 7x^3$ 5. $f(x) = 3x - 37x^4$

6. $f(x) = 17x - 2$ 7. $f(x) = 4$

8. $f(x) = 2x - 12 + 3x^2$

Describe the end behavior of the graph of the given function.

9. $f(x) = 7x^5 - 12x$ 10. $f(x) = -6x^8 + 1$

Find the zeros and the multiplicity of each function.

11. $f(x) = (x-2)^3 (x)(x+2)^2$

12. $f(x) = x^4 - 10x^2 + 9$

13. $f(x) = x^3 + 3x^2 - 25x - 75$

Use the intermediate value theorem to decide if possible whether the function has a zero between the two given values.

14. $f(x) = 4x^2 - 8x - 3$; -2 and 0 15. $f(x) = 2x^3 - 6$; 2 and 3

Use synthetic division to find the quotient and the remainder.

16. $(x^3 + 3x^2 - 12x + 4) \div (x - 3)$ 17. $(x^4 - 16) \div (x - 2)$

Use synthetic division to determine if the given numbers are zeros of the function.

18. 1, −2; $f(x) = x^3 - 3x^2 - 6x + 8$ 19. $-\sqrt{2}, 3$; $f(x) = 4x^2 - 8$

Factor the polynomial and then solve the equation $f(x) = 0$.

20. $f(x) = x^4 + 5x^2 - 36$

21. $f(x) = x^3 + x + 3x^2 + 3$

Find a polynomial of lowest degree with rational coefficients with the given numbers as some of the zeros.

22. $\sqrt{5}$ 23. $i, -2$

Solve each of the following inequalities.

24. $x^2 - 25 < 0$

25. $x^2 > 6x - 9$

26. $\dfrac{x-3}{x+1} < 0$

CHAPTER 4

EXPONENTIAL AND LOGARITHMIC FUNCTIONS

Section 4.1 Inverses of Functions

Certain arithmetic operations are inverse operations. If we start with a number x, add 4 to our number, and then subtract 4, the result is our original number x. The operations of addition and subtraction are inverse operations. Some functions also have inverse functions. Next we will see how to find the inverse function of a given function.

In this section we will start with a given function and obtain the inverse of the function if that inverse exists. If we go from the output of a function back to its input, we have an inverse relation. If this relation is a function, then we have an inverse function.

Let's look at a simple relation g that consists of three ordered pairs:

Given: $g = \{(-3, 3), (-2, 5), (0, 9)\}$

If we switch the values of the x and y coordinates, the relation that results is called the **inverse** of the relation g:

Inverse of $g = \{(3, -3), (5, -2), (9, 0)\}$

Inverse Relation of Ordered Pairs

Inverse Relation of Ordered Pairs:

To find the inverse of a relation of ordered pair, interchange the first and second coordinates of each ordered pair in the relation.

Example 1. Given the relation $h = \{(4, 7), (1, 6), (0, 3)\}$. Find the inverse relation.

Solution: We find the inverse relation by interchanging the coordinates of the ordered pairs.

Inverse of $h = \{(7, 4), (6, 1), (3, 0)\}$.

If we were to plot the three original points, and then plot the three inverse points, we would see that the pairs in the inverse are reflections of the original points across the line $y = x$.

Inverse Relation of an Equation

Inverse Relation of an Equation:

The inverse relation of an equation is found by interchanging the variables in the original equation.

Example 2. Find an inverse equation for the given equation: $y = x^2 - 3x$.

Solution: We find the inverse relation by interchanging the variables x and y:

$$x = y^2 - 3y$$

Look at the graphs of the two equations in Example 2:

Given equation:

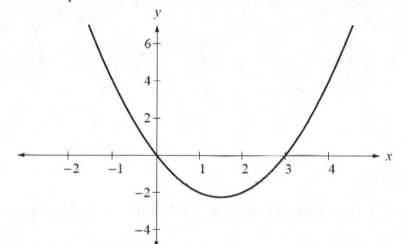

Inverse equation:

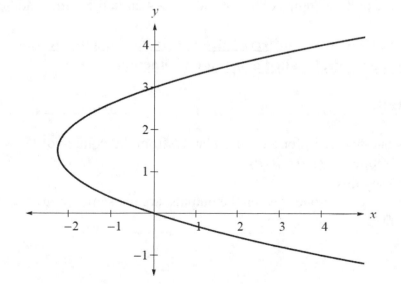

207

Graphing these two graphs on one axis we see that the graph of the given equation and its inverse are reflections across the line $y = x$.

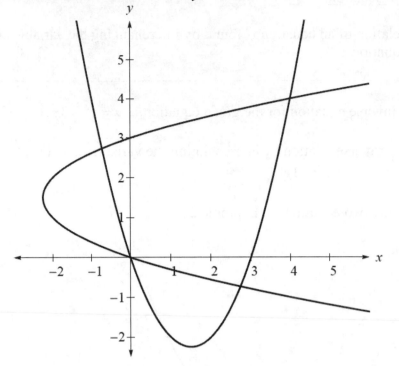

One-to-One Functions

For the function $y = 3x - 4$, two different input values of x result in two different output values for y.

In contrast, for the function $y = x^2$, two different input values of x can result in the same output value for y. For example, inputs of $x = 4$ and $x = -4$ give the same result of 16.

A function such as $y = 3x - 4$, where __different elements from the domain lead to different elements in the range, is called a one-to-one function.__

One-to-one Function

One-to-one **Function**:
> A function f is one-to-one if, for elements a and b from the domain of f,
> $$a \neq b \quad \text{implies} \quad f(a) \neq f(b).$$
> Another way to say this:
> > a function is one-to-one if when the outputs are the same, so are the inputs:
> > $$f(a) = f(b) \quad \text{implies} \quad a = b.$$

To Prove that a function is one-to-one:
show that if $f(a) = f(b)$, then $a = b$.

Inverse of a function

Inverse of a function:

If the inverse of a function is ALSO a function, it is called "f inverse" and symbolically is written as:
$$f^{-1}$$
Note: this is **not** an exponent.

Example 3. Determine if the following function is one-to-one:

$$f(x) = 2x - 4$$

Solution: We need to show that $f(a) = f(b)$ implies $a = b$.

So, for some a and b in the domain of f, we assume $f(a) = f(b)$.

$2a - 4 = 2b - 4$	Set $f(a) = f(b)$.
$2a = 2b$	Add 4 to both sides.
$a = b$	Divide both sides by 2.

Because we set $f(a) = f(b)$ and proved $a = b$, our function is one-to-one.

One-to-one Functions and Their Inverses

One-to-one Functions and Their Inverses:

If a function is one-to-one, then its inverse, f^{-1}, is also a function.

The <u>domain</u> of a one-to-one function f is the <u>range</u> of its inverse f^{-1}.

The <u>range</u> of a one-to-one function f is the <u>domain</u> of its inverse f^{-1}.

Functions which are **strictly increasing** or **strictly decreasing** over their domains are one-to-one functions.

Example 4. Given the function $f(x) = -2x + 6$. Prove that f is one-to-one.

Solution: We must give a formal proof since the problem said "prove". We will assume that $f(a) = f(b)$ and then show that $a = b$.

$$f(a) = -2a + 6 \qquad \text{and} \qquad f(b) = -2b + 6$$

$$-2a + 6 = -2b + 6 \qquad\qquad \text{Set } f(a) = f(b)$$

$$-2a = -2b \qquad\qquad\qquad \text{Subtract 6 from both sides}$$

$$a = b \qquad\qquad\qquad\qquad \text{Divide by negative 2}$$

Since the assumption $f(a) = f(b)$ results in $a = b$, we proved that the given function f is one-to-one.

One way to show that a function is **not** one-to-one, is to find a pair of unequal input values that result in the same function output value.

Example 5. Given $f(x) = \sqrt{25 - x^2}$, show that this function is not one-to-one.

Solution: We will look for a two different input values for x that result in the same function output value.

$$f(4) = \sqrt{25 - 4^2} = \sqrt{25 - 16} = \sqrt{9} = 3$$
$$f(-4) = \sqrt{25 - (-4)^2} = \sqrt{25 - 16} = \sqrt{9} = 3$$
Since x-values of $4 \neq -4$, but $f(4) = f(-4)$,
we know that $f(x)$ is not one-to-one.

Horizontal Line Test

Horizontal Line Test:

If any horizontal line intersects the graph of a function at more than one point, then the function is not one-to-one.

Use the horizontal line test to determine if a function is one-to-one.

A graphing calculator can be used to determine whether a function is one-to-one. See Chapter 6, Example 30.

How to Find the Inverse of a Function

How to Find the Inverse of a Function:

If a function f is one-to-one, the inverse can be found by these steps:

1. Replace $f(x)$ with y.

2. Interchange x and y.

3. Solve for y.

4. Replace y with $f^{-1}(x)$.

Example 6: Given the one-to-one function $f(x) = 2x - 6$. Find its inverse.

Solution: Given $f(x) = 2x - 6$

$$y = 2x - 6 \qquad \text{Replace } f(x) \text{ with } y.$$

$$x = 2y - 6 \qquad \text{Interchange } x \text{ and } y.$$

$$x + 6 = 2y \qquad \text{Solve for } y.$$

$$\frac{x+6}{2} = y$$

$$f^{-1}(x) = \frac{x+6}{2}$$

Example 7. Given $f(x) = x^3$.

a. Determine whether f is one-to-one.

b. If f is one-to-one, find the inverse of f.

Solution:

a. We know that the graph of $f(x) = x^3$ is:

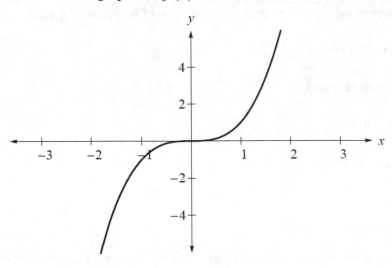

The function is one-to-one because it passes the horizontal line test, and it is also increasing over its domain.

b. $f(x) = x^3$

$y = x^3$ Replace $f(x)$ with y.

$x = y^3$ Interchange x and y.

$y = \sqrt[3]{x}$ Solve for y.

$f^{-1}(x) = \sqrt[3]{x}$

Composition of a Function and its Inverse

Composition of a Function and its Inverse:

If a function f is one-to-one, then f^{-1} is its inverse and:

$(f^{-1} \circ f)(x) = f^{-1}(f(x)) = x$ for any x in the domain of f

and

$(f \circ f^{-1})(x) = f(f^{-1}(x)) = x$ for any x in the domain of f^{-1}

f^{-1} is the unique function for the properties to hold.

Example 8.   Given $f(x) = 3x + 7$ and $f^{-1}(x) = \dfrac{x-7}{3}$, use composition of functions to show that f^{-1} is the inverse of f.

Solution: Find $(f^{-1} \circ f)(x)$ and $(f \circ f^{-1})(x)$.

$$(f^{-1} \circ f)(x) = f^{-1}(f(x))$$
$$= f^{-1}(3x + 7) = \frac{(3x+7)-7}{3} = \frac{3x}{3} = x$$

$$(f \circ f^{-1})(x) = f(f^{-1}(x))$$
$$= f\left(\frac{x-7}{3}\right) = 3\left(\frac{x-7}{3}\right) + 7 = x - 7 + 7 = x$$

Since $(f^{-1} \circ f)(x) = x = (f \circ f^{-1})(x)$, we see that f^{-1} is the inverse of f.

Limiting the Domain
If the inverse of a function is not a function, we can in certain cases, limit the domain of the given function to allow the inverse to be a function.

Look at the function $y = x^2$: We know that this is the equation of a parabola and we will graph the equation.

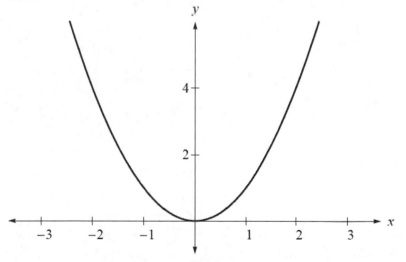

Using the graph of a parabola with the horizontal line test, we find that the given function is not one-to-one and has no inverse.

However, **the domain** in $f(x) = x^2$ **can be limited** so that $f^{-1}(x)$ is a function. We will limit the domain to be $[0, \infty)$.

Look at the graphs of $f(x) = x^2, x \geq 0, and \ f^{-1} = \sqrt{x}$

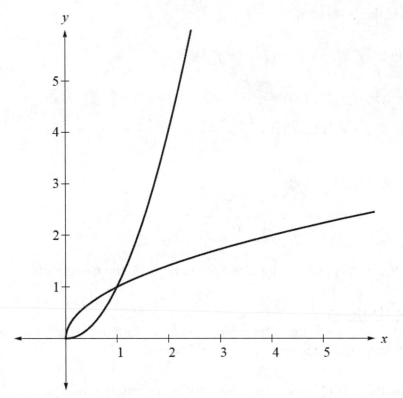

Note the reflection across the line $y = x$.

Exercises 4.1

Find the inverse relation for the following:

1. $\{(5,4),(-2,3),(4,7)\}$ 2. $\{(0,-2),(-3,-3),(-1,5)\}$

3. $y = 3x + 2$ 4. $2x^2 + 3y^2 = 6$

5. $y = 2x^2 - 1x$ 6. $x^4 y = 8$

7. $x = y^2 + 7y$ 8. $x = 4y + 9$

Sketch the graph of the given equation, and then reflect the graph across the line $y = x$ to see the graph of the inverse.

9. $y = 2x - 1$ 10. $y = x^2 + 3$

11. $x = -2y - 3$ 12. $x = y^2$

Prove that the following functions are one-to-one.

13. $f(x) = 4x - 3$ 14. $f(x) = x^3 + 2$

Show that the following functions are not one to one by giving an example of two input values for x which give the same output value.

15. $f(x) = x^2 + 2$ 16. $f(x) = x^4$

Use the horizontal line test to see which of the following are graphs of one-to-one functions:

17. $f(x) = 3 - x^2$

18. $f(x) = \dfrac{1}{x}$

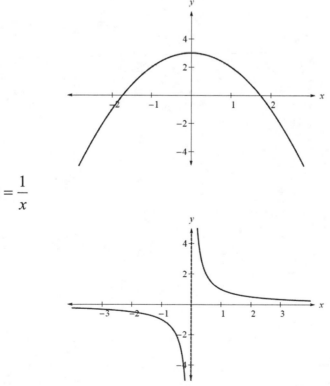

215

19. $f(x) = \dfrac{1}{x^2}$

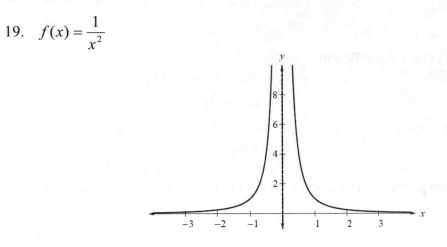

Graph the following using a table of values, and determine if the given function is a one-to-one function.

20. $f(x) = 4x + 1$ 　　　　　　　　21. $f(x) = x^2 + 1$

Determine if the given function is one-to-one. If it is, find its inverse.

22. $f(x) = x^3 + 2$ 　　　　　　　　23. $f(x) = \dfrac{1}{x}$

24. $f(x) = x^2 - 3$ 　　　　　　　　25. $f(x) = 4x - 2$

26. $f(x) = 2 - x^2$, domain is $[0, \infty)$

Section 4.2   Exponential Functions

Properties of Exponents

Properties of Exponents:

For $a > 0$ where a is a real number and $a \neq 1$, and any real number x:

1. a^x is a unique real number;

2. $a^b = a^c$ if and only if $b = c$;

3. if $a > 1$ and $m < n$ then $a^m < a^n$;

4. if $0 < a < 1$ and $m < n$ then $a^m > a^n$.

We will now define an exponential function: $f(x) = a^x$ where x is a real number and the base, a, is not 1 but is positive.

The domain of this function is the set of all real numbers

Exponential Function

The function:
$$f(x) = a^x, \quad a > 0 \quad \text{and} \quad a \neq 1,$$

is the **exponential function** with base a.

Notice: if $a = 1$, the function is the constant function $f(x) = 1$.

From the properties above we see that an exponential function always has a positive base.

Graphs of Exponential Functions:

Look at the following two graphs showing exponential functions:

I. $f(x) = 2^x$

The base of the exponential function $f(x) = 2^x$ is 2. This graph can be sketched by finding ordered pairs that satisfy the given function. Let $x = -2, -1, 0, 1, 2, 3$; and find $f(x)$ values for each and sketch the graph.

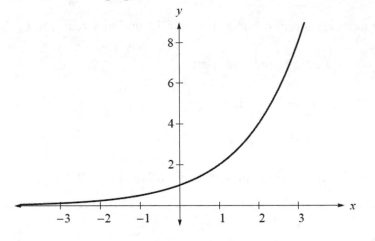

We can see from the above graph that the function $f(x) = 2^x$ has a domain of all real numbers and a range of all positive numbers. The x-axis is a horizontal asymptote.

The graph of $f(x) = 2^x$ is **typical** of graphs of $f(x) = a^x$ where $a > 1$. For larger values of a, the graphs rise more steeply, but the general shape is similar to the above graph.

Now look at a second exponential function:

II. $f(x) = \left(\dfrac{1}{2}\right)^x$ This graph can be sketched by using ordered pairs.

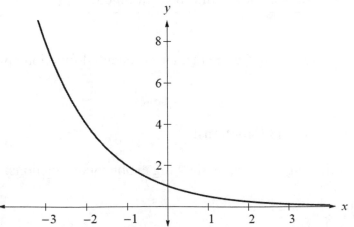

The base of the exponential function $f(x) = \left(\dfrac{1}{2}\right)^x$ is $\dfrac{1}{2}$. Looking at the graph, we can see that the domain is all real numbers, and the range is all positive numbers. The x-axis is a horizontal asymptote.

The graph of $f(x) = \left(\dfrac{1}{2}\right)^x$ is **typical** of graphs of $f(x) = a^x$ where $0 < a < 1$.

The graphs of $f(x) = 2^x$ and $f(x) = \left(\dfrac{1}{2}\right)^x$ are **mirror images** of each other with respect to the y-axis.

Using the horizontal line test on these graphs, we can see that __exponential functions are one-to-one__.

To graph other exponential functions, we can use translations and reflections of the above two graphs.

Example 1. Sketch the graph of the function $f(x) = 2^{x-4}$.

Solution: From our study of translations, we know that the graph of this function is the graph of the function $f(x) = 2^x$ shifted **right 4 units.**

Let $x = -2, -1, 0, 1, 2, 3$; and find $f(x)$ values for each

The graph would be:

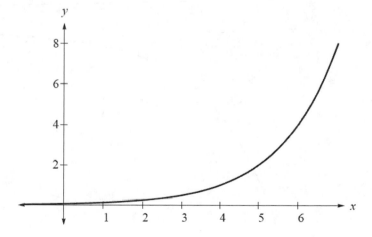

A graphing calculator can be used to verify your results.

Example 2. Sketch the graph of the function $f(x) = 2^x - 2$.

Solution: From our study of translations we know that the graph of this function is the graph of the function $f(x) = 2^x$ shifted **down 2 units.**

The graph would be:

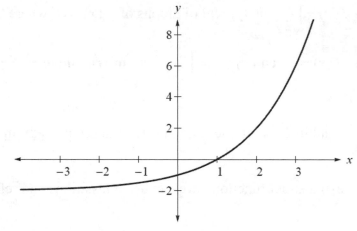

Notice that in the translation, $y = -2$ is a horizontal asymptote.
A graphing calculator can be used to verify your results.

Example 3. Sketch the graph of the function $f(x) = 4 - 2^{-x}$.

Solution: The graph of this function is the graph of the function $f(x) = 2^x$ **reflected across the y-axis, and then reflected across the x-axis and then shifted up 4 units.**

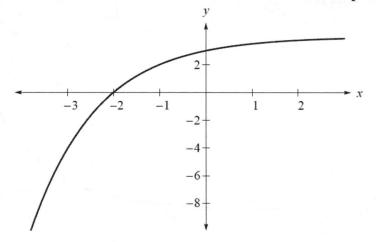

A graphing calculator can be used to verify the results.

One of the most useful exponential functions is the compound interest function.

Compound Interest

If P dollars is deposited into an account paying a rate of interest r compounded n times per year, then after t years the account will contain the amount A given by the equation:

$$A = P\left(1 + \frac{r}{n}\right)^{nt}$$

Example 4. If $10,000 is deposited at 10% interest compounded quarterly, define a function of time with the given money, compounding time, and interest. Then find the amount of money in the account at the end of 10 years.

Solution: Interest compounded quarterly is compounded every quarter year, or 4 times per year.

$$P = 10,000, \quad r = 10\% = 0.10, \quad n = 4$$

$$A(t) = 10,000\left(1 + \frac{0.10}{4}\right)^{4t}$$

Now, for 10 years, let $t = 10$ in the defined function:

$$A(10) = 10,000\left(1 + \frac{0.10}{4}\right)^{4*10} = 10,000(1.025)^{40}$$

Using a calculator we find:

$$A(10) = \$26,850.64$$

If the problem above in the last example had not given us the number of years and instead had given us the amount of money we hoped to earn and then asked how many years it would take for the deposit to reach this amount, we would solve for t.

A graphing calculator can be used to solve this type of problem.
See Chapter 6, Example 31.

Euler's Number

Let's look again at our compound interest formula:

$$A = P\left(1 + \frac{r}{n}\right)^{nt}$$

Suppose we can find an investment that will pay 100% interest, so that $r = 1$.

However, with such a great rate, we are only able to invest $1.00. P would also = 1

Also we can only invest for 1 year so t would = 1.

Our compound interest formula would be:

$$A = \left(1 + \frac{1}{n}\right)^n$$

Use this formula and let the compound number n increase to a large number and see what happens.

See the chart shown.

n	$\left(1 + \dfrac{1}{n}\right)^n$
1	2
2	2.25
5	2.48832
10	2.59374
25	2.66584
50	2.69159
100	2.70481
500	2.71557
1,000	2.71692
10,000	2.71815
1,000,000	2.71828

Look at the table we calculated. The results imply that as n increases, the value of $(1 + \frac{1}{n})^n$ gets closer and closer to some number. The number each of our calculations is approaching is called **Euler's Number. We use the symbol e to represent this number**.

Euler's Number

Euler's Number: $e = 2.718281828\ldots$

The number **e is a non-repeating, non-terminating number**, which means that we say e is an <u>irrational number</u>.

Since **e** is a fixed number, we can raise it to the power of x.

The function $f(x) = e^x$ has the graph:

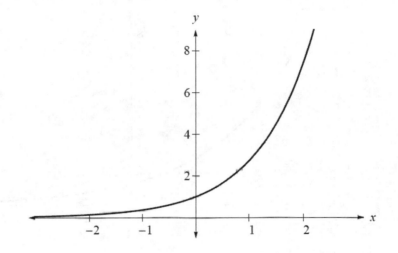

Remember that e is a number slightly larger than 2. Thus the graph looks very similar to the graph of $f(x) = 2^x$.

The function $f(x) = e^{-x}$ has the graph:

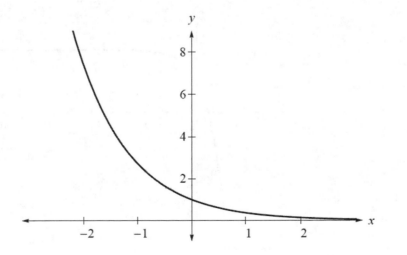

Example 5. Sketch the graph of the following functions. Describe how each graph can be obtained from the graph of $y = e^x$

    a. $f(x) = e^{-1/4x}$ b. $f(x) = 2 - e^{-3x}$ c. $f(x) = e^{x+1}$

Solution:

    a. The graph of $f(x) = e^{-1/4x}$ is a horizontal stretch of the graph of $f(x) = e^x$ and then reflected across the y-axis.

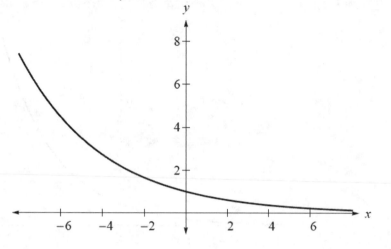

    b. The graph of $f(x) = 2 - e^{-3x}$ is a horizontal shrinking of the graph of $f(x) = e^x$, then reflected across the y-axis, and then across the x-axis and finally a translation up 2 units.

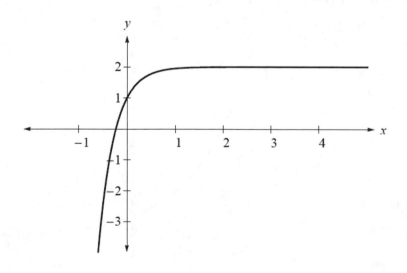

c. The graph of $f(x) = e^{x+1}$ is a translation of the graph of $f(x) = e^x$ shifted to the left 1 unit.

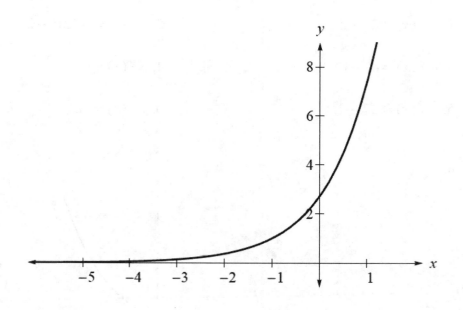

Section 4.2 Exercises

Use what you know about graphs of exponential functions to match the functions below with one of the graphs shown below.

1. $f(x) = 2^x - 2$

2. $f(x) = (1/2)^x + 2$

3. $f(x) = e^x + 1$

4. $f(x) = e^{x+2}$

5. $f(x) = 3^{-x} - 1$

6. $f(x) = -e^x$

a.

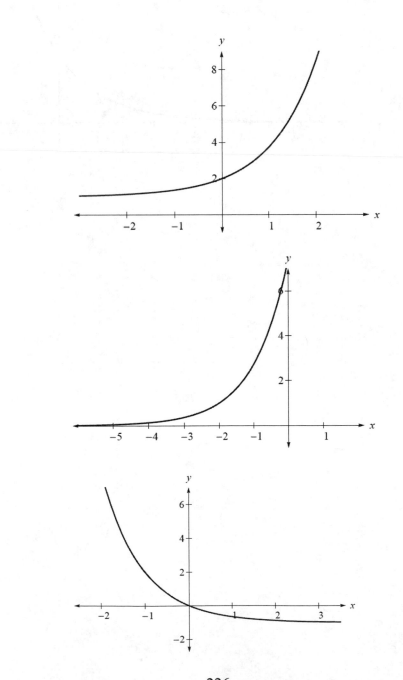

b.

c.

d.

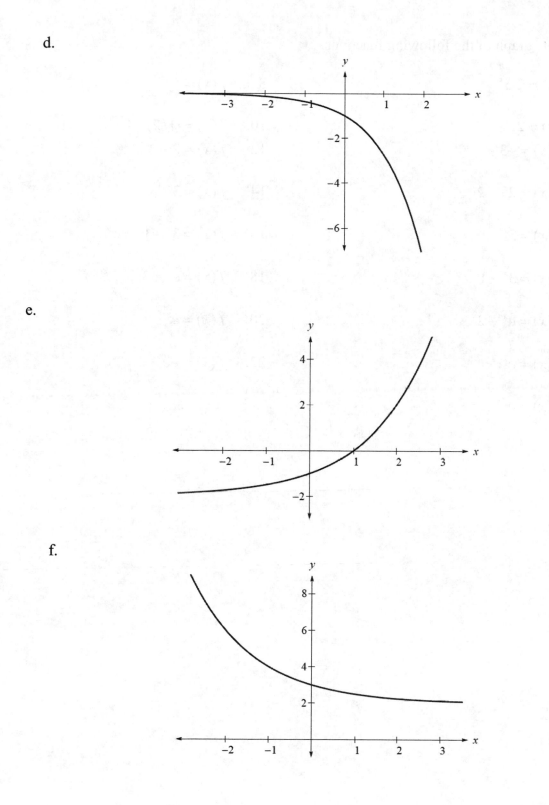

e.

f.

Sketch the graph of the following functions.

7. $f(x) = 2.5^x$

8. $f(x) = 5^x$

9. $f(x) = 2^{-x}$

10. $f(x) = (1/2)^x$

11. $f(x) = -3^x$

12. $f(x) = 2 - 2^x$

13. $f(x) = 2^x - 2$

14. $f(x) = 3^{x+1}$

15. $f(x) = 3^{x-1}$

16. $f(x) = 3^x + 1$

17. $f(x) = 3^x - 1$

18. $f(x) = e^x + 3$

19. $f(x) = e^x - 2$

20. $f(x) = e^{x+3}$

21. $f(x) = e^{x-2}$

22. $f(x) = -e^x$

23. $f(x) = e^{-x}$

Section 4.3   Logarithmic Functions

In Section 4.2 we learned that the exponential function $f(x) = a^x$, when $0 < a < 1$ or when $a > 1$, is a one-to-one function. Since the function is one-to-one, we realize that it will have an inverse function. Next we will look at the inverse functions of exponential functions.

The inverse of the exponential function with base a is called the **logarithmic function with base a** and we symbolize this function as **$\log_a$**.

These value is written $\log_a(x)$ or $\log_a x$ and is read "the logarithm of x with base a".

Definition of $\log_a$

Definition of $\log_a$

Let a be a positive real number, and $a \neq 1$. The logarithm of x with base a is defined by:

$$y = \log_a x \qquad \text{if and only if} \qquad x = a^y$$

for every $x > 0$ and every real number y.

The two equations in the definition, $y = \log_a x$ and $x = a^y$, are equivalent. The bases are the same in both equations.

The first form is called the **logarithmic form:** $\qquad \log_a x = y$

The second form is called the **exponential form:** $\qquad a^y = x$

Think of $\log_a x$ as: "the power to which we raise a to get x".

Example 1. Find the value of $y = \log_2(8)$.

Solution:

If we change from the logarithmic form to the exponential form, we get $2^y = 8$. We can easily solve this form of the equation for y since $2^3 = 8$.

From our original equation, $y = \log_2(8)$, and the fact that we found y equivalent to 3, our equation in logarithmic form is:

$$\log_2(8) = 3.$$

Graphs of logarithm functions:

From Section 4.2, we saw that the graph of $y = a^x$ where $a > 1$ is:

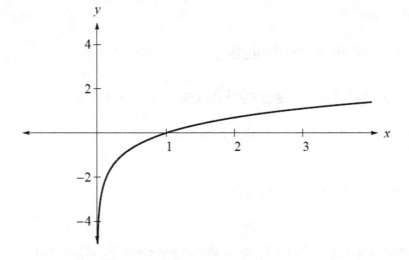

The domain of this function is all real numbers, and the range is all positive real numbers. The graph is increasing and has a horizontal asymptote of the x-axis. The y-intercept is $(0,1)$ and there is no x-intercept.

Now let's examine the graph of $y = \log_a x$ where $a > 1$:

The domain of y is all positive numbers, and the range is all real numbers. The graph is increasing and has a vertical asymptote of the y-axis. The x-intercept is $(1, 0)$ and there is no y-intercept. Remember that the domain of a function is the range of its inverse, and the range of the function is the same as the domain of its inverse.

Since the exponential function and the logarithm function are inverses of each other, we can put the two graphs on the same set of axes:

230

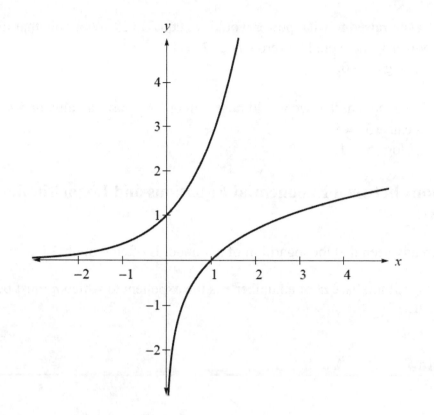

Recall that graphs of inverse functions are reflections across the line $y = x$.

Example 2: Find the value of each of the following:

    a. $\log_{10}(1000)$ b. $\log_2 16$ c. $\log_{16} 4$

    d. $\log_7 1$ e. $\log_5 5$

Solution:

    a. The exponent to which we raise 10 to obtain 1,000 is 3, ($10^3 = 1000$).

             $\log_{10}(1000) = 3.$

    b. The problem asks to what power we would raise the number 2 so that we get
        value of 16. We know that $2^4 = 16$

             $\log_2 16 = 4.$

    c. We know that $4 = \sqrt{16} = 16^{1/2}$. The exponent to which we would raise 16
        so that we get 4 is $\dfrac{1}{2}$. Remember that fractional exponents represent roots.

             $\log_{16} 4 = \dfrac{1}{2}$

231

d. Seven raised to what power would we equal to 1? We know that the only
    power value would be zero since $7^0 = 1$.

$$\log_7 1 = 0.$$

e. The exponent that we would raise 5 in order to have a value of 5 is 1
    because $5^1 = 5$.

$$\log_5 5 = 1.$$

Conversions between Exponential Equations and Logarithmic Equations:

We have already seen that the logarithm of a number is often thought of as an exponent.
Thus:

the logarithm, base a, of a number x is the exponent to which a must be raised to
obtain x.

Conversion

Conversion:

$$\log_a x = y \qquad \text{is the same as} \qquad x = a^y$$

1. The bases are the same in both forms.

2. The y in the log form becomes the exponent in the exponential form.

Example 3. Convert the following exponential equations to equivalent logarithmic
equations.

a. $27 = 3^x$ 　　　　　　b. $10^{-2} = 0.01$ 　　　　　　c. $e^m = 17$

Solution:

a. $27 = 3^x \qquad \rightarrow \qquad \log_3 27 = x$

b. $10^{-2} = 0.01 \qquad \rightarrow \qquad \log_{10}(0.01) = -2$

c. $e^m = 17 \qquad \rightarrow \qquad \log_e 17 = m$

Example 4. Convert the following logarithmic equations to exponential equations.

        a. $\log_2 16 = 4$ b. $\log_a R = 6$ c. $x = \log_n P$

Solution:

        a. $\log_2 16 = 4$ $\rightarrow$ $2^4 = 16$

        b. $\log_a R = 6$ $\rightarrow$ $a^6 = R$

        c. $x = \log_n P$ $\rightarrow$ $n^x = P$

Common Logarithm

<u>Common Logarithm</u>

     Common logarithms are logarithms with a base of 10.

     The symbol log without a written base implies the common logarithm and the base is understood to be 10.

     $\log x \;\; = \;\; \log_{10} x.$

Chapter 6, Example 32 shows an example of a problem using a calculator to evaluate a common logarithm.

Natural Logarithms

<u>Natural Logarithm</u>**:**

     A logarithm with a base of e is a natural logarithm.

     The abbreviation " ln " is used to represent a natural logarithm.

     $\log e^x = \ln x$

See Chapter 6, Example 33 for finding natural logarithms using a graphing calculator.

Sometimes it is necessary to change the base of a logarithm. The following formula allows us to do so.

Change of Base Theorem

> **Change of Base Theorem:**
>
> If x is any positive number and if a and b are positive numbers, $a \neq 1$, $b \neq 1$, then
>
> $$\log_a x = \frac{\log_b x}{\log_b a}$$

Example 5. Find $\log_3 7$ using common logarithms and a calculator.

Solution:

$$\log_3 7 = \frac{\log_{10} 7}{\log_{10} 3} \qquad \text{Use change of base formula.}$$

$$= 1.771243749$$

Example 6. Find $\log_3 7$ using natural logarithms and a calculator.

Solution:

$$\log_3 7 = \frac{\log_e 7}{\log_e 3} = \frac{\ln 7}{\ln 3}$$

$$= 1.771243749$$

Graphs of Logarithmic Functions

Example 7.   Graph $y = f(x) = \log_6 x$.

Solution: Remember that the equation $y = \log_6 x$ is equivalent to the exponential form of this equation: $x = 6^y$.

We will make a table by choosing values for y and calculating the x-values.

$x = 6^y$	y	
1	0	$x = 6^y , = 6^0 = 1$
6	1	$x = 6^y , = 6^1 = 6$
36	2	$x = 6^y , = 6^2 = 36$
216	3	$x = 6^y , = 6^3 = 216$
1/6	-1	$x = 6^y , = 6^{-1} = \dfrac{1}{6}$
1/36	-2	$x = 6^y , = 6^{-2} = \dfrac{1}{36}$

Plotting the points we found above, the graph is:

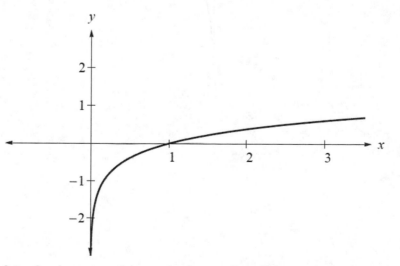

The graph can also be found using a graphing calculator. See Chapter 6, Example 33.

235

Example 8.   Make a table, and sketch the graph of $y = f(x) = \ln x$.

Solution:

x	$y = \ln x$
0.5	-0.69314
1	0.0
2	0.69314
3	1.09861
4	1.38629
5	1.60944

The graph found using the points from the table is: $f(x) = \ln x$

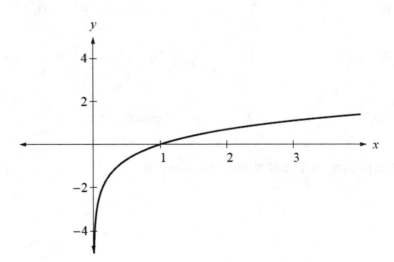

Example 9. Using your knowledge of translations, sketch the graph of $f(x) = \ln(x+3)$.

Solution: We will sketch the graph of $f(x) = \ln x$ shifted left 3 units.

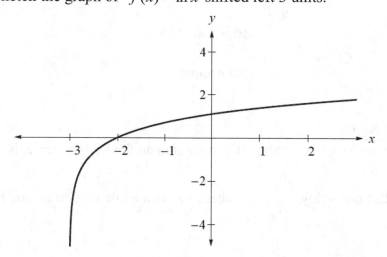

Applications

Decibel Rating
The loudness of sounds is measured in units called **decibels**. To measure with this unit, an intensity of I_0 is assigned to a very faint sound, called the **threshold sound**. If a certain sound has intensity I, then the decibel rating of this louder sound is:

$$\text{Decibels} = 10 * \log_{10} \frac{I}{I_0}$$

Example 10. Find the decibel rating of a sound having an intensity of $100\ I_0$

Solution: Use the formula above to find the decibel rating.

$$\textbf{Decibels} = 10 * \log_{10} \frac{I}{I_0}$$

$$= 10 * \log_{10} \frac{100 I_0}{I_0} \qquad \text{Substitute } 100\ I_0 \text{ for } I.$$

$$= 10 * \log_{10} 100 \qquad \text{Reduce.}$$

$$\text{let } \log_{10} 100 = x$$

237

$$\text{then} \quad 10^x = 100 \qquad \text{Use exponential form.}$$

$$\text{and} \quad x = 2$$

$$= \quad 10 * x = \quad 10 * 2$$

$$= \quad 20 \text{ decibels}$$

Richter Scale

The intensity, I, of an earthquake, measured on the Richter scale, is

$$\textbf{Richter} = \log_{10} \frac{I}{I_0} \qquad \text{where} \quad I_0 \text{ is the intensity of an small size earthquake.}$$

Example 11. Find the Richter scale rating of an earthquake having an intensity of $1,000,000 \, I_0$.

Solution: $\quad \text{Richter} = \log_{10} \frac{I}{I_0}$

$$= \log_{10} \frac{1,000,000 I_0}{I_0} \qquad \text{Substitute } 1,000,000 \, I_0 \text{ for } I.$$

$$= \log_{10} 1,000,000 \qquad \text{Reduce.}$$

$$\text{let} \quad \log_{10} 1,000,000 = x$$

$$\text{then} \quad 10^x = 1,000,000 \qquad \text{Change to exponential form.}$$

$$\text{and} \quad x = 6$$

$$\text{Richter} = \quad 6$$

The magnitude of the earthquake was 6 on the Richter Scale.

Section 4.3 Exercises

Sketch the graph of each of the following:

1. $x = 3^y$

2. $x = 5^y$

3. $x = (1/4)^y$

4. $x = (3/4)^y$

5. $y = \log_2 x$

6. $y = \log_5 x$

7. $f(x) = \log x$

8. $f(x) = \log_e x$

Find the value of each of the following without the use of a calculator.

9. $\log_2 32$

10. $\log_3 81$

11. $\log_6 36$

12. $\log_7 49$

13. $\log 1$

14. $\log 1000$

15. $\log 0.01$

16. $\log_2 (1/8)$

17. $\ln 0$

18. $\ln 1$

19. $\ln e$

20. $\log 0$

21. $\log 100$

22. $\log 10$

23. $\log_4 4^3$

24. $\log \sqrt{100}$

25. $\log_4 \sqrt[3]{4}$

26. $\log_{25} 5$

27. $\ln e^{1/2}$

28. $\ln \sqrt{e}$

Convert each of the following equations to a logarithmic equation.

29. $10^4 = 10,000$

30. $e^4 = z$

31. $m^t = 4$

Convert the following equations to an exponential equation.

32. $\log_4 4 = 1$

33. $\log 8 = 0.9031$

34. $\ln 15 = 2.7081$

35. $\log_a R = p$

36. $\log_b R^4 = q$

Find the logarithm value using common logarithms with the change-of-base formula.

37. $\log_3 24$

38. $\log_7 24$

39. Find the decibel ratings of the following sounds, having intensities as given.

a. whisper, $115\,I_0$

b. truck, $1{,}200{,}000{,}000\,I_0$

c. rock music, $895{,}000{,}000{,}000\,I_0$

d. jet takeoff, $109{,}000{,}000{,}000{,}000\,I_0$

40. Find the Richter Scale ratings of earthquakes having the following intensities.

a. $1000\,I_0$

b. $1{,}000{,}000\,I_0$

4.4 Logarithmic Function Properties

Properties of Logarithms

<u>Properties of Logarithms</u>

If y and z are any positive real numbers, r is any real number, a is any positive real number, and $a \neq 1$, then:

(1) $\log_a yz = \log_a y + \log_a z$ Product Rule

(2) $\log_a \dfrac{y}{z} = \log_a y - \log_a z$ Quotient Rule

(3) $\log_a y^r = r * \log_a y$ Power Rule

(4) $\log_a a = 1$

(5) $\log_a 1 = 0$

(6) $\log_a a^y = y$

(7) $a^{\log_a y} = y$

The properties of logarithms for the special cases of base ten (the common logarithm) and base equal to e (natural logarithm) are written as shown below:

Common logarithms	Natural logarithms
(1) $\log(yz) = \log y + \log z$	(1) $\ln(yz) = \ln y + \ln z$
(2) $\log \dfrac{y}{z} = \log y - \log z$	(2) $\ln \dfrac{y}{z} = \ln y - \ln z$
(3) $\log u^c = c \log u$	(3) $\ln u^c = c \ln u$

Example 1. Express each product as a sum of logarithms.

  a. $\log_5(7*3)$ b. $\log_3(5*2)$ c. $\log_9(6*4)$

Solution:

  a. $\log_5(7*3) = \log_5 7 + \log_5 3$

  b. $\log_3(5*2) = \log_3 5 + \log_3 2$

  c. $\log_9(6*4) = \log_9 6 + \log_9 4$

Example 2. Express each quotient as the difference of logarithms.

  a. $\log_5 \dfrac{2}{3}$ b. $\log_6 \dfrac{4}{3}$ c. $\log_9 \dfrac{8}{5}$

Solution:

  a. $\log_5 \dfrac{2}{3} = \log_5 2 - \log_5 3$

  b. $\log_6 \dfrac{4}{3} = \log_6 4 - \log_6 3$

  c. $\log_9 \dfrac{8}{5} = \log_9 8 - \log_9 5$

Example 3. Use the Power Rule to express each of the following as a product.

  a. $\log_a 7^{-4}$ b. $\log_a \sqrt[3]{5}$ c. $\ln x^5$

Solution:

  a. $\log_a 7^{-4} = -4\log_a 7$

  b. $\log_a \sqrt[3]{5} = \log_a 5^{\frac{1}{3}} = \dfrac{1}{3}\log_a 5$

  c. $\ln x^5 = 5\ln x$

Using the Properties of Logarithms

Example 4. Use the properties of logarithms to rewrite each of the following:

a. $\log_a \dfrac{pq}{r^3}$ b. $\log_a \sqrt[4]{n^3}$ c. $\log_b \sqrt{\dfrac{x^3 y^6}{z^4}}$

Solution:

a. $\log_a \dfrac{pq}{r^3} = \log_a p + \log_a q - \log_a r^3 = \log_a p + \log_a q - 3\log_a r$

b. $\log_a \sqrt[4]{n^3} = \log_a n^{3/4} = \dfrac{3}{4}\log_a n$

c. $\log_b \sqrt{\dfrac{x^3 y^6}{z^4}} = \dfrac{1}{2}\log_b \dfrac{x^3 y^6}{z^4}$

$\qquad\qquad = \dfrac{1}{2}\left(\log_b x^3 + \log_b y^6 - \log_b z^4\right)$

$\qquad\qquad = \dfrac{1}{2}\left(3\log_b x + 6\log_b y - 4\log_b z\right)$

$\qquad\qquad = \dfrac{3}{2}\log_b x + \dfrac{6}{2}\log_b y - \dfrac{4}{2}\log_b z$

$\qquad\qquad = \dfrac{3}{2}\log_b x + 3\log_b y - 2\log_b z$

Example 5. Use the properties of logarithms to rewrite as a single logarithm:

a. $\log_4 (x+3) + \log_4 x - \log_4 3$

b. $4\log_a n - 2\log_a p$

c. $\dfrac{1}{2}\log_7 m + \dfrac{5}{2}\log_7 2n - \log_7 m^2 n$

Solution:

a. $\log_4 (x+3) + \log_4 x - \log_4 3 = \log_4 \dfrac{(x+3)x}{3}$

b. $4\log_a n - 2\log_a p \;=\; \log_a n^4 - \log_a p^2 \;=\; \log_a \dfrac{n^4}{p^2}$

c. $\dfrac{1}{2}\log_7 m + \dfrac{5}{2}\log_7 2n - \log_7 m^2 n$

$$=\; \log_7 m^{1/2} + \log_7 (2n)^{5/2} - \log_7 m^2 n$$

$$=\; \log_7 \dfrac{m^{1/2}(2n)^{5/2}}{m^2 n}$$

$$=\; \log_7 \dfrac{2^{5/2} n^{3/2}}{m^{3/2}} \qquad =\; \log_7 \sqrt{\dfrac{32n^3}{m^3}}$$

Example 6. Assume that $\log_{10} 2 = 0.3010$ *and* $\log_{10} 3 = 0.4771$, and find the following.

a. $\log_{10} 6$ b. $\log_{10} 4$ c. $\log_{10} 9$

d. $\log_{10} \dfrac{1}{2}$ e. $\log_{10} 5$ f. $\log_{10} \dfrac{3}{2}$

Solution: Since we only have values for the logarithm of 2 and 3, we must convert each argument into new arguments that are factors of the numbers 2 and/or 3.

a. $\log_{10} 6 \;=\; \log(3*2) = \log 3 + \log 2 = 0.3010 + 0.4771 = 0.7781$

b. $\log_{10} 4 \;=\; \log 2^2 = 2\log 2 = 2(0.3010) = 0.6020$

c. $\log_{10} 9 \;=\; \log 3^2 = 2\log 3 = 2(0.4771) = 0.9542$

d. $\log_{10} \dfrac{1}{2} \;=\; \log 1 - \log 2 = 0 - 0.3010 = -0.3010$

e. $\log_{10} 5 \;=\; \log \dfrac{10}{2} = \log 10 - \log 2 = 1 - 0.3010 = 0.699$

f. $\log_{10} \dfrac{3}{2} \;=\; \log 3 - \log 2 = 0.4771 - 0.3010 = 0.1761$

Example 7. Simplify each of the following.

     a. $\log_a a^5$ b. $\ln e^t$ c. $\log 10^p$

     d. $10^{\log 4r}$ e. $e^{\ln 6}$

Solution:

     a. $\log_a a^5 = 5\log_a a = 5$

     b. $\ln e^t = t\ln e = t$

     c. $\log 10^p = p\log 10 = p$

     d. $10^{\log 4r} = 4r$

     e. $e^{\ln 6} = 6$

Section 4.4 Exercises

Express each product as a sum of logarithms.

1. $\log_4(17*12)$ 2. $\log_a(4*19)$

3. $\log_m 12T$ 4. $\log_r yz$

5. $\ln 3x$ 6. $\ln st$

Express each quotient as a difference of logarithms.

7. $\log_a \dfrac{m}{n}$ 8. $\ln \dfrac{a}{x}$

Express each as a product.

9. $\log_9 x^4$ 10. $\log_a y^7$

11. $\log_n T^{-4}$ 12. $\ln \sqrt{7}$

Express each as a sum and/or difference of logarithms.

13. $\log_7 5rs^3t^6$ 14. $\log_a \dfrac{r^3 t^9}{c^2 d^8}$

15. $\log_b \sqrt{\dfrac{x^8}{y^5 z^3}}$ 16. $\ln \sqrt[3]{\dfrac{p^6 q^9}{a^4 c^7}}$

Express each as one logarithm and simplify.

17. $\log_b 30 + \log_b 4$ 18. $\log 10 + \log 100$

19. $\dfrac{1}{2}\log_b x + 3\log_b w - 5\log_b q$ 20. $\ln x^5 - 3\ln \sqrt[3]{x}$

If $\log_b 2 = 0.3010$, $\log_b 5 = 0.6990$ and $\log_b 7 = 0.8451$, find each of the following.

21. $\log_b 14$ 22. $\log_b 49$

23. $\log_b \dfrac{2}{7}$ 24. $\log_b 70$

4.5 Logarithmic and Exponential Equations

Solving Logarithmic Equations

We will look at two types of equations containing logarithmic expressions.

Type 1: This type of logarithmic equation contains **only** logarithmic expressions. To solve this type of equation, we use the fact that a logarithmic function is one-to-one. The result of this is the following:

> If $x > 0$, $y > 0$, $a > 0$ and $a \neq 1$, then
>
> $$\text{if } \log_a x = \log_a y \quad \text{then} \quad x = y$$

We will use the following techniques to solve this type of logarithmic equation:

To Solve Type 1 Logarithmic Equations

To solve type 1 logarithmic equations:

1. Use the properties of logarithms to combine all logs on the left of the equal sign into 1 log expression.

2. Use the properties of logarithms to combine all logs on the right of the equal sign into 1 log expression.

   The result will be in this form: $\log_a \{\text{expression 1}\} = \log_a \{\text{expression 2}\}$.

3. from the statement above, we can then set

   expression 1 = expression 2

4. Solve the resulting equation.

Example 1:   Solve: $\log_4 (2x - 3) = \log_4 12 - \log_4 3$.

Solution: This is a **type 1** logarithmic equation. We will use the steps above.

$$\log_4 (2x - 3) = \log_4 12 - \log_4 3$$

$$\log_4(2x-3) = \log_4 \frac{12}{3} \qquad \text{Change difference of the logs into a quotient.}$$

$$\log_4(2x-3) = \log_4 4 \qquad \text{Simplify.}$$

$$2x-3 = 4 \qquad \text{Set log arguments equal.}$$

$$2x = 7 \qquad \text{Solve equation.}$$

$$x = 7/2$$

Example 2. Solve: $4\log_2 x = 3\log_2 2$.

Solution:
$$4\log_2 x = 3\log_2 2$$

$$\log_2 x^4 = \log_2 2^3 \qquad \text{Use exponent log properties.}$$

$$x^4 = 2^3 \qquad \text{Set log arguments equal.}$$

$$x = \sqrt[4]{8}$$

Example 3. Solve: $\ln x - \ln(x+1) = 3\ln 4$.

Solution:
$$\ln x - \ln(x+1) = 3\ln 4$$

$$\ln \frac{x}{x+1} = \ln 4^3 \qquad \text{Use properties of logs.}$$

$$\frac{x}{x+1} = 64 \qquad \text{Set log arguments equal.}$$

$$x = 64(x+1) \qquad \text{Solve the equation.}$$

$$x = 64x + 64$$

$$-63x = 64$$

$$x = -\frac{64}{63} \quad \text{or} \quad \text{No Solution}$$

The answer of $-\dfrac{64}{63}$ that we found is not a solution because when the answer is substituted into the given equation, we would be trying to take the logarithm of a negative number. **The log of a negative value is not defined**.

Example 3 can be solved using a graphing calculator. See Chapter 6, Example 35.

Now, we will look at a second type of logarithmic equation.

Type 2: This type of logarithmic equation contains logarithmic expressions but it also contains terms that are not logarithmic expressions.

To Solve Type 2 Logarithmic Equations

To solve type 2 logarithmic equations:

1. Use algebra to arrange all of the logarithmic expressions on one side of the equal sign.

2. Use the properties of logs to combine all of the logarithmic expressions into one logarithm.

3. Use algebra to place all of the non-logarithmic expressions on the other side of the equal sign

   The result of these steps will be: $\log_a \{\text{expression}\} = \text{number}$

4. Transform this result from the logarithmic form to the exponential form.

5. Solve.

Example 4.   Solve: $\log_2 (x + 7) + \log_2 x = 3$.

Solution: This is a **type 2** logarithmic equation because the term on the right side of the equal sign does not include a logarithm. We will use the steps above.

$\log_2 (x + 7) + \log_2 x = 3$

$\log_2 [x(x + 7)] = 3$ Use properties to combine logs.

$x(x + 7) = 2^3$ Transform to exponential form.

$$x^2 + 7x = 8$$ Distribute.

$$x^2 + 7x - 8 = 0$$ Solve the equation.

$$(x + 8)(x - 1) = 0$$ Factor.

$$x = -8, 1$$

Now check both of these solutions.
We cannot take the logarithm of a negative number, and substitution of $x = -8$ would result in such. The only solution to Example 4 is $x = 1$.

Example 4 can be solved using a graphing calculator. See Chapter 6, Example 36.

Example 5. Solve: $\log_4 x = -1$.

Solution: The equation is a **type 2** logarithmic equation. Use that method for solving.

$$\log_4 x = -1$$

$$4^{-1} = x$$ Transform to exponential form.

$$x = \frac{1}{4}$$ Remove negative exponent.

Check: $\log_4 x = -1$

$$\log_4 \frac{1}{4} = -1$$

$$\log_4 4^{-1} = -1$$

$$-1 = -1$$

This problem can be solved using a graphing calculator. See Chapter 6, Example 37.

Example 6. Solve: $\log_3(x + 3) + \log_3(x + 5) = 1$.

Solution:

$$\log_3(x + 3) + \log_3(x + 5) = 1$$ Type 2

$$\log_3[(x+3)(x+5)] = 1 \qquad\qquad \text{Use properties.}$$

$$(x+3)(x+5) = 3^1 \qquad\qquad \text{Transform.}$$

$$x^2 + 8x + 15 = 3 \qquad\qquad \text{Use F O I L.}$$

$$x^2 + 8x + 12 = 0 \qquad\qquad \text{Solve.}$$

$$(x+6)(x+2) = 0$$

$$x = -6, -2$$

Check: $\log_3(x+3) + \log_3(x+5) = 1$

   For $x = -6$

$\log_3(-6+3) + \log_3(-6+5)$.

   This value results in taking the log of a negative number which is undefined.

For $x = -2$

$\log_3(-2+3) + \log_3(-2+5)$

$\log_3 1 + \log_3 3$

$0 + 1 = 1$

The only solution is $x = -2$.

Example 6 can be solved using a graphing calculator. See Chapter 6, Example 38

Solving Exponential Equations

Equations are called <u>exponential equations</u> when variables occur in the exponents.

Some equations, such as $3^{2x} = 81$, can be written so that each side has the same base raised to an exponent:

$$3^{2x} = 81$$

$$3^{2x} = 3^4$$

Equations with Exponentials of the Same Base

> Equations with Exponentials of the Same Base:
>
> if $a > 0$ and $\neq 1$, then
>
> if $a^r = a^s$ then $r = s$

The last rule states that when bases are the same, then the exponents are equal. We will try to reduce the bases to the same value. Then we can set the exponents equal to each other and solve the resulting equation.

if $\qquad 3^{2x} = 3^4$

then $\qquad\qquad 2x = 4 \qquad$ and $\qquad x = 2$

We were able to solve this problem because we were given both sides of the equation with the same base.

Example 7. Solve: $2^{4x-11} = 32$.

Solution:

$2^{4x-11} = 32$

$2^{4x-11} = 2^5$ $\qquad\qquad\qquad$ Convert both sides to the same base.

$4x - 11 = 5$ $\qquad\qquad\qquad$ Set exponents equal.

$4x = 16$ $\qquad\qquad\qquad$ Solve.

$x = 4$

Check:

$2^{4x-11} = 32$
$2^{4(4)-11}$
$2^{16-11} \quad = \quad 2^5 \quad = \quad 32$

Example 7 can be solved using a graphing calculator. See Chapter 6, Example 39.

When an exponential equation problem is such that we are **unable** to convert both sides to the same base, we must use a different method to solve the problem.

To Solve Exponential Equations with Different Bases

To Solve Exponential Equations with Different Bases:

1. Isolate the exponential term.

2. Take the natural or common logarithm of both sides.

3. Use exponent operations for logarithms to solve for the variable.

Example 8. Solve: $3^x = 22$.

Solution:

$3^x = 22$

We cannot reduce both sides to the same base, so we will take the logarithm of both sides.

$\log 3^x = \log 22$ Take the common log of both sides.

$x \log 3 = \log 22$ Use exponent property.

$x = \dfrac{\log 22}{\log 3}$ This is the exact value of x.

Use a calculator to approximate the answer.

$x = 2.8136$.

Example 8 can be solved using a graphing calculator. See Chapter 6, Example 40.

Example 9. Solve: $2 = e^{0.4t}$.

Solution:

$2 = e^{0.4t}$

$\ln 2 = \ln e^{0.4t}$ Take the natural log of both sides.

$\ln 2 = 0.4t \ln e$ Use exponent property.

$\ln 2 = 0.4t$ $\ln e = 1$.

$t = \dfrac{\ln 2}{0.4}$ This is the exact value of t.

Use a calculator to approximate the solution.

$x = 1.7329$.

Example 9 can be solved using a graphing calculator. See Chapter 6, Example 41.

Example 10. Solve $e^x + e^{-x} - 8 = 0$.

Solution:

$$e^x + e^{-x} - 8 = 0$$

In this problem there is more than one term with a variable in the exponent. To begin with we will solve this problem for e^x.

$e^x + \dfrac{1}{e^x} - 8 = 0$ Change from negative exponent to positive.

$e^{2x} + 1 - 8e^x = 0$ Multiply both sides by e^x to remove fraction.

To simplify our equation, let $u = e^x$ and then $u^2 = e^{2x}$.

$u^2 - 8u + 1 = 0$ Solve for u.

$u = \dfrac{-(-8) \pm \sqrt{(-8)^2 - 4(1)(1)}}{2(1)}$ Use quadratic formula.

$u = \dfrac{8 \pm \sqrt{60}}{2} = \dfrac{8 \pm 2\sqrt{15}}{2}$

$u = 4 \pm \sqrt{15}$

$e^x = 4 \pm \sqrt{15}$ Replace u with e^x.

We have an exponential equation and will solve for x by taking the natural log of both sides.

$\ln e^x = \ln(4 \pm \sqrt{15})$

$x = \ln(4 \pm \sqrt{15})$ Recall that $\ln e^x = x$.

Using a calculator to approximate the solutions, we find:

$$x = 2.0634 \text{ and } -2.0634.$$

Example 10 can be solved using a graphing calculator. See Chapter 6, Example 42.

Section 4.5 Exercises

Solve the following exponential equations.

1. $4^x = 64$

2. $2^{5x} = 16$

3. $3^x = 28$

4. $4^{4x-8} = 128$

5. $81 = 3^{4x} * 9^{2x}$

6. $37^x = 74$

7. $2^{3x-1} = 1/2$

8. $e^r = 10,000$

9. $e^{-0.4t} = 0.06$

10. $3^{2x} = 4^{x-1}$

11. $(5.3)^x = 52$

12. $e^x + e^{-x} = 4$

Solve the given logarithmic equations.

13. $\log_4 x = 9$

14. $\log x = -6$

15. $\ln x = 2$

16. $\log_2(8 + 4x) = 6$

17. $\log x + \log(x - 3) = 1$

18. $\log_2(x + 5) - \log_2(x + 1) = \log_2 x$

19. $2\ln(x + 3) - \ln(x + 1) = 3\ln 2$

20. $\log_3(3x) = \log_3 x + \log_3(4 - x)$

21. $\ln(x + 2) = \ln e^{\ln 2} - \ln x$

22. $\log_4(x + 1) = 2 + \log_4(3x - 2)$

23. $\log_8(x - 5) = 2/3$

24. $\log \sqrt{x} = \log(x - 6)$

Section 4.6   Applications

Law of Growth or Decay Formula

Law of Growth (or Decay) Formula:

Let q_0 be the value of a quantity q at the time $t = 0$ (q_0 is the initial value of q)

If q changes instantaneously at a rate proportional to its current value, then
$$q = q_0 e^{rt}$$

if $r > 0$, r is called **the rate of growth**, and if $r < 0$, r is called **the rate of decay** .

The next several examples show applications of exponential and logarithmic equations.

Example 1.   Population Growth:

Suppose the function

$$P(t) = 100,000 e^{.3t}$$

gives the population of a certain city at time t measured in years. In how many years will the population of the city double?

Since we see in the given function that the population of the city is 100,000 when $t = 0$, we want to find the value of t for which $P(t) = 200,000$.

Replace $P(t)$ with 200,000 in the original function and we then have:

$$200,000 = 100,000\, e^{.3t}$$

or

$$2 = e^{.3t}$$

We want to solve for t, but the variable is part of an exponent. We have an exponential equation, and to solve it we take the natural logarithms of both sides of the equation.

$$\ln 2 \;=\; \ln e^{.3t}$$

$$\ln 2 = 0.3t \ln e \qquad\qquad \text{Use properties.}$$

$$\ln 2 \;=\; 0.3t \qquad\qquad \text{Recall } \ln e = 1.$$

and $$t = \frac{\ln 2}{0.3}$$ This is the exact value answer.

Using a calculator, we calculate that $t = 2.3105$ years.

Example 2. Half-life of a Radioactive Substance:

Suppose the amount, $I(t)$, in grams of a certain radioactive substance at a time t is given by

$$I(t) = I_0 e^{-2t}$$

where I_0 is the amount of the substance initially (when $t = 0$) and t is measured in days.

We want to find the *half-life* of the substance, that is, the time it takes for half of a given amount of the substance to decay.

We need to find the time t that must elapse for $I(t)$ to be reduced to a value equal to $\frac{I_0}{2}$.

We must write the given function using $\frac{I_0}{2}$ for $I(t),$ and then solve for t.

$$\left(\frac{1}{2}\right) I_0 = I_0 e^{-2t}$$

Divide both sides by I_0 :
$$\frac{1}{2} = e^{-2t}$$

Take the natural logarithm of both sides.

$$\ln \frac{1}{2} = \ln e^{-2t}$$

Use the properties of logarithms.

$$\ln \frac{1}{2} = -0.2t \ln e$$

Remember that $\ln e = 1$.
$$\ln \frac{1}{2} = -0.2t$$

$$t = \frac{-\ln\frac{1}{2}}{0.2}$$ Answer is the exact value.

Using a calculator, we find that

$$t = 3.4657 \quad \text{or} \quad \text{approximately } 3.466 \text{ days.}$$

Example 3.   Carbon 14 Dating:

Carbon 14 is a radioactive isotope of carbon which has a half-life of about 5600 years. The earth's atmosphere contains much carbon, mostly in the form of carbon dioxide, with small traces of carbon 14. Most of this atmospheric carbon is in the form of the non-radioactive isotope carbon 12. The ratio of carbon 14 to carbon 12 is virtually constant in the atmosphere.

However, as a plant absorbs carbon dioxide from the air in the process of photosynthesis, the carbon 12 stays in the plant while the carbon 14 decays by conversion to nitrogen. Thus, the ratio of carbon 14 to carbon 12 is smaller in the plant than it is in the atmosphere. Even when the plant is eaten by an animal, this ratio will continue to decrease. Based on these facts, a method of dating objects called *carbon 14 dating* has been developed.

Let R be the (nearly constant) ratio of carbon 14 to carbon 12 found in the atmosphere. Let r be the ratio found in a fossil.

It can be shown that the relationship between R and r is given by

$$\frac{R}{r} = e^{\frac{t\ln 2}{5600}}$$

where t is the age of the fossil in years.

If we verify the formula for $t = 0$, we get:

$$\frac{R}{r} = e^0 = 1$$

Since the ratio equals 1, it follows that $R = r$, so that the ratio in the fossil is the same as the ratio in the atmosphere. This is true only when $t = 0$.

Let's verify the formula for $t = 5600$.

$$\frac{R}{r} = e^{\frac{t \ln 2}{5600}}$$

$$\frac{R}{r} = e^{\ln 2} = 2 \qquad \text{and} \qquad r = \frac{1}{2} R$$

From this last result, we see that the ratio in the fossil is half the ratio in the atmosphere. Since the half-life of carbon 14 is 5600 years, we expect only half of it to remain at the end of that time. Thus, the formula gives the correct result for $t = 5600$.

Example 4.   Continuously Compounded Interest:

The formula for calculating continuously compounded interest is given by:

$$A = Pe^{rt}$$

where P is the principal, r is the annual interest rate expressed as a decimal, t is the number of years of investment, and A is the amount after t years.

Suppose \$30,000 is deposited in a money market account that pays interest at the rate of 5% per year compounded continuously. Find the balance in the account after 6 years. We use the formula above with the values given in the example.

$$A = Pe^{rt}$$

$$P = 30{,}000 \qquad r = 0.05 \qquad t = 6$$

Substitute in values.

$$A = 30{,}000\, e^{0.05(6)} \; = \; 30{,}000\, e^{0.3} \qquad \text{This is the exact value.}$$

Using a calculator, we can find the approximate value for A.

$$A = \$40{,}495.76$$

Example 5. Suppose $10,000 is invested at an interest rate of r, compounded continuously, and grows to an amount of $14,190.68 in 5 years.

Find the interest rate at which the original $10,000 was invested.

Solution: Given: $P = 10,000$ $A = 14190.68$ $t = 5$

$$A = Pe^{rt}$$

$$14,190.68 = 10,000\,e^{5r}$$

$$\frac{14190.68}{10,000} = e^{5r}$$

$$1.419068 = e^{5r}$$

$$\ln 1.419068 = \ln e^{5r}$$

$$\ln 1.419068 = 5r$$

$$r = \frac{\ln 1.419068}{5} \qquad\qquad \text{This is the exact value.}$$

Use a calculator to approximate the value of r.

$$r = 0.07000 = 7\%$$

The last example can be solved using a graphing calculator. See Chapter 6 , Example 43.

Section 4.6 Exercises

1. The 1980 population of the United States was approximately 231 million, and the population has been growing continuously at a rate of about 1.03% per year. Predict the population in the year 2025 if the growth trend continues.

2. The 1985 population estimate for India was 766 million, and the population has been growing continuously at a rate of about 1.8% per year. Assuming that this rapid growth rate continues, estimate the population of India in the year 2025.

3. In fishery science, the collection of fish that results from one annual reproduction is called a cohort. It is usually assumed that the number of fish $N(t)$ still alive after t years is given by an exponential function. For one type of fish, $N(t) = N_0 e^{-0.15t}$, where N_0 is the initial size of the cohort. If the cohort for a specific year is 25 million, how many of that cohort will be alive after 10 years?

4. The amount of a radioactive substance present at time t measured in seconds is $A(t) = 4000e^{-.5t}$. Find the half-life of the substance. Half-life is the amount of time it takes for one-half of the substance to decay.

5. Find the half-life of a radioactive specimen if the amount y in grams present at time t in days is $y = 2000e^{-.5t}$

6. The number of rabbits in a colony is describe by $y = y_0 e^{.5t}$ where t represents time in months and y_0 is the rabbit population when $t = 0$. If $y_0 = 200$, find the rabbit population at time $t = 5$.

7. Refer to problem 6 above. How long will it take for the number of rabbits to quadruple?

8. Suppose an Egyptian mummy is discovered in which the ratio of carbon 14 to carbon 12 is about one-fourth the ratio found in the atmosphere. About how long ago did the Egyptian die? Refer to Example 3 in this section.

9. If the ratio of carbon 14 to carbon 12 in an object is 1/5 the atmospheric ratio, how old is the object? Refer to Example 3 in this section.

10. Using the formula given in Example 3, if an object is found that contains 20% of the normal amount of carbon 14, how old is the object?

11. Use the formula given in Example 3 to solve the formula for t.

12. If $20,000 is deposited into an account that is compounded continuously at an interest rate of 5%, what amount of money will be in the account after 10 years?

13. If $40,000 is invested in an account that pays interest compounded continuously at 4% interest, how long will it take to double the initial investment?

14. Using the formula for compounded continuously interest: $A = Pe^{rt}$, solve for r.

15. Using the formula for compounded continuously interest: $A = Pe^{rt}$, solve for t.

Chapter 4 Summary

To find Inverse Relations:
1. **Given Ordered Pairs: interchange coordinates**
2. **Given Equation: interchange the variables**
3. **Given Graph: Reflect across the line $y = x$**

One-to-One Functions:
To "**Prove**": If $f(a) = f(b)$, then show $a = b$
To "**Show**": Horizontal Line test

Inverse of a Function:
1. **Replace $f(x)$ with y**
2. **Interchange x and y**
3. **Solve for y**
4. **Replace y with f^{-1}**

Composition of a Function and its Inverse:
$(f^{-1} \circ f)(x) = f^{-1}(f(x)) = x$ for any x in the domain of f
$(f \circ f^{-1})(x) = f(f^{-1}(x)) = x$ for any x in the domain of f^{-1}

Exponential function:
$$f(x) = a^x, \quad a > 0 \quad \text{and} \quad a \neq 1, \text{ and real number } x.$$

Interest: Compound: $A = P\left(1 + \dfrac{r}{n}\right)^{nt}$

Compound Continuously: $A = Pe^{rt}$

Euler's number e: = 2.718281828

Logarithm/Exponential Form: $y = \log_a x$ **if and only if**
$x = a^y$

Change of Base Theorem: $\log_a x = \dfrac{\log_b x}{\log_b a}$

Properties of Logarithms

(1) $\log_a yz = \log_a y + \log_a z$

(2) $\log_a \dfrac{y}{z} = \log_a y - \log_a z$

(3) $\log_a y^r = r * \log_a y$

(4) $\log_a a = 1$

(5) $\log_a 1 = 0$

(6) $\log_a a^y = y$

(7) $a^{\log_a y} = y$

To solve logarithmic equations:

   When: $\log_a$ {expression 1} = $\log_a$ {expression 2},

      set expression 1 = expression 2.

   When: $\log_a$ {expression } = number,

      transform the result from the logarithmic form to the
      exponential form.

To solve exponential equations:

   1. When: $a^r = a^s$, then $r = s$
   2. Isolate the exponential term and
         take the natural or common logarithm of both sides.

Chapter 4 Review

Find the inverses of the given relations.

1. $\{(1, -2), (4, 1), (7, 4), (10, 7)\}$

Find an equation of the inverse relation for each.

2. $y = -3x + 4$ 3. $y = 2x^2 + 3x + 1$

Which of the following functions is one-to-one?

4. $f(x) = 4x - 2$ 5. $f(x) = 4x^2 - 2x$

6. $f(x) = 4x^3 - 2$

Find the inverse of the following functions.

7. $f(x) = 4 - 3x$ 8. $f(x) = \sqrt[3]{x - 2}$

9. $f(x) = e^x$ 10. $f(x) = \log x$

Match the equations listed with one of the graphs below:

11. $f(x) = \log_2 x$ 12. $f(x) = \log_3(x + 2)$

13. $f(x) = (2/3)^x$ 14. $f(x) = 4^x + 2$ 15. $f(x) = e^x - 3$

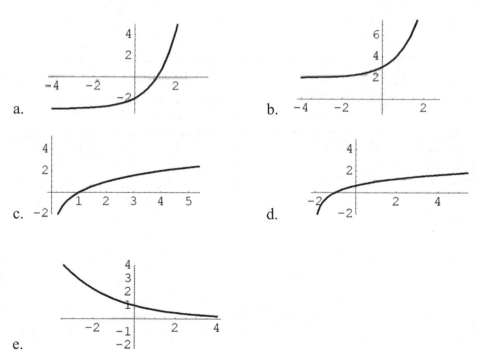

a.   b.

c.   d.

e.

Find the value of each of the following without using a calculator.

16. $\log_8 64$ 17. $\log 1{,}000$

18. $\ln e^2$ 19. $\log 10^3$

Convert each equation to an exponential equation.

20. $\log_3 x = 2$ 21. $\log_b M = N$

Convert each equation to a logarithmic equation.

22. $5^{-2} = 1/25$ 23. $e^x = 40$

Use the change of base formula to find the logarithm value.

24. $\log_4 10$

Express in terms of sums and differences of logarithms.

25. $\log \dfrac{x^2 y^4}{z^5}$

Solve each equation.

26. $\log_3 x = 4$ 27. $4^{x-1} = 8^x$

28. $\log_x 32 = 5$ 29. $\log_2 x + \log_2 (x-6) = 4$

30. $\log x^2 - \log x = 0$

CHAPTER 5

SYSTEMS OF EQUATIONS AND INEQUALITIES

Section 5.1 Linear Systems of Equations with Two Variables

System of Equations

System of Equations:

      Any set of 2 or more equations is a **system of equations**.

      The solution set of a system is the set of solutions that satisfy all of the equations;
           that is it is the intersection of the solution sets of the individual equations.

      An example of a system of equations is:
$$2x + y = 8$$
$$x - y = 1$$

Linear Equations

Linear Equations are first degree equations; that is, there are no variables raised to an exponent higher than one.

Remember that the solution set of a linear equation in two variables is an infinite set of ordered pairs which are the points on the graph of the equation; these points form a straight line. The solution set of a system is the points that are common to all of the equations in the system. Another way to think of the solution set of a system is to view it as the intersection of the graphs of the two equations. There are three possibilities for the solution set of a system of two linear equations with two variables: **one point**, **no points**, or **infinite points**.

A. <u>One Point</u>:
$$2x - y = 4$$
$$x + y = 5$$

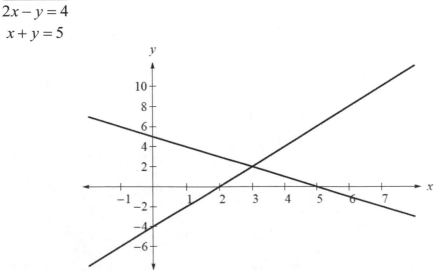

The solution to the system is the intersection of the two lines.
From the graph we can see that the solution to the given system is the point (3, 2).

B. <u>No Points:</u>

$$3x + 2y = -4$$
$$3x + 2y = 3$$

If we put each of these into slope-intercept form we can readily see the slope of each line and the y-intercept. We will solve each equation for y.

$$3x + 2y = -4 \qquad\qquad\qquad 3x + 2y = 3$$
$$2y = -3x - 4 \qquad\qquad\qquad 2y = -3x + 3$$
$$y = -\frac{3}{2}x - 2 \qquad\qquad\qquad y = -\frac{3}{2}x + \frac{3}{2}$$
$$m = -\frac{3}{2}, \ y\text{-intercept} = -2 \qquad\qquad m = -\frac{3}{2}, \ y\text{-intercept} = \frac{3}{2}$$

Since the slopes are the same, we know that the lines are parallel. We can easily graph them using the slope and the y-intercepts.

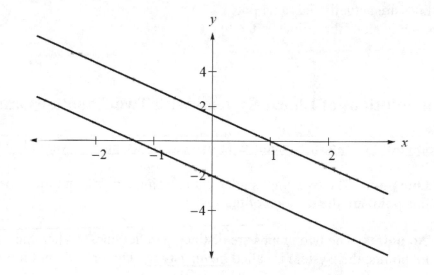

Since these two lines are parallel and do not intersect, we know that there is no solution for this system.

C. Infinite Points:

$$x + y = 5$$
$$2y = -2x + 10$$

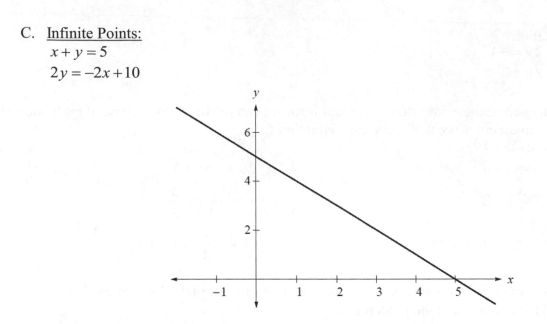

These two lines are actually the same line.
The solution set is all of the points on the line.

Graphs of Solutions of Linear Systems with Two Equations and Two Variables

Graphs of Solutions of Linear Systems with two equations and two variables:

1. **One point**: The two graphs intersect in a single point, and the coordinates of this point are the solution of the system.

2. **No points:** The two graphs are distinct, parallel lines. When the solution is no points, the system is called **inconsistent.** The lines do not intersect and have no common points. There is no solution.

3. **Infinite points:** The graphs are the same line. In this situation, the equations are **dependent**. There are infinite solutions to this system which are the points of the line.

Solving a System of Linear Equations with Two Variables

Methods used to solve a system of linear equations with two variables:

1. Graph both equations and find the point of intersection.

2. Use the Substitution Method.

3. Use the Addition Method

Graphing Method:

1. Graph each line.
2. Find the point of intersection which is the solution to the system.

When we graph a system of equations, we can usually see the approximate solution of a linear system.
It is difficult to determine the exact values of the solution of the system by looking at the graph unless a graphing calculator is used.

Substitution Method:

1. Solve one of the equations for one of the variables.
2. Substitute this solution into the other equation which will result in an equation in only one variable.
3. Find the solution to the new equation found in step 2.
4. Substitute the solution found in step 3 back into one of the original equations to find the value of the other variable.
5. Check the solution in both of the given equations.

Example 1. Use the substitution method to solve the given system.

$$x + y = 2 \qquad (1)$$
$$x + 3y = -2 \qquad (2)$$

Solution:

Solve equation (1) for x.

$$x = 2 - y$$

Substitute this solution into equation in place (2) of x.

$$(2 - y) + 3y = -2$$

$$2 - y + 3y = -2 \qquad \qquad \text{Remove parentheses.}$$

$$2 + 2y = -2 \qquad \qquad \text{Collect like terms.}$$

$$2y = -4 \qquad \qquad \text{Subtract 2 from both sides.}$$

$$y = -2 \qquad \qquad \text{Divide.}$$

Substitute -2 back into the first equation for y and solve for x.
$$x - 2 = 2 \qquad \text{or} \quad x = 4$$
The solution to the given system is the point of intersection $(4, -2)$.

Check: Given $x + y = 2$ (1)

                 $x + 3y = -2$ (2)

     (1) $4 + (-2) =$ Substitute solution values into equation 1.

              $2 = 2$ True

     (2) $4 + 3(-2) =$ Substitute solution values into equation 2.

              $4 - 6 = -2$

              $2 = 2$ True

The solution is correct because both equations are true statements using the solution as variable values.

Addition (sometimes called "Elimination") Method:

1. Multiply the two equations by suitable numbers, so that when the equations are added, one of the variables is eliminated.
2. Add the two new equations so that the result is a new equation in only one variable.
3. Solve this single variable equation.
4. Substitute the solution back into one of the original equations to obtain the value of the second variable.
6. Check the solution in both of the given equations.

Example 2: Use the addition method to solve the given system.

$$3x + 4y = 5$$
$$2x + 3y = 4$$

Solution: If we multiply the first equation by -2 and the second equation by 3, the coefficients of x will be the same in both equations but with **opposite signs**. When we add the two equations, we eliminate x.

$$-6x - 8y = -10$$
$$6x + 9y = 12$$

Add the two new equations.

$$y = 2$$

Substitute this value into the first equation in place of y.

$$3x + 4(2) = 5$$

Solve for the other variable.
$$3x + 8 = 5$$
$$3x = -3$$
$$x = -1$$
The solution is $(-1,\ 2)$.

Check: Given $3x + 4y = 5$
   $2x + 3y = 4$

   Replace the variables with the solution values.

(1)	$3(-1) + 4(2) =$	$-3 + 8 =$	$5 = 5$	True
(2)	$2(-1) + 3(2) =$	$-2 + 6 =$	$4 = 4$	True

Example 2 can be solved using a graphing calculator as shown in Chapter 6, Example 44.

Example 3.   Solve the given system using the addition method.

$$-3x + 2y = 4$$
$$6x - 4y = 7$$

Solution: We will be able to eliminate the x variable when adding if we multiply the first equation by 2.

$$-6x + 4y = 8$$
$$6x - 4y = 7$$

Adding the two equations, we get

$$0 = 15$$

Both variables are eliminated and the result is the **false statement** $0 = 15$. Because this is a false statement, there is no solution to this system, and we know that the lines are parallel. This given system is inconsistent.

Example 4.   Solve the given system using the addition method.

$$4x - y = -2$$
$$-4x + y = 2$$

Solution: We do not need to multiply either equation because we can see that if we add The equations we will eliminate the x-variable .

Adding the two equations, we get:
$$0 = 0$$

Both variables were eliminated and the result is the **true statement:** $0 = 0$. The true statement tells us that there is a solution and is an infinite number of points. (The graph of the equations are the same line.) This given system is dependent.

Applications

Example 5. The owner of a golf shop ordered 10 putters and 12 drivers for $1150. In a second purchase he ordered 4 putters and 3 drivers for $325. Find the cost of each putter and of each driver.

Solution: Write a system of equations to solve this problem.

Let:
$$x = \text{the cost of a putter}$$

$$y = \text{the cost of a driver}$$

Use the data from the first purchase to write one equation.

$$10x + 12y = 1150$$

Use the data from the second purchase to write a second equation.

$$4x + 3y = 325$$

The two equations together form a system of equations which we will solve.

$$10x + 12y = 1150$$
$$4x + 3y = 325$$

Looking at the system we see that if we multiply the second equation by -4, we will eliminate the y variable when we add the two equations.

$$10x + 12y = 1150$$
$$-16x - 12y = -1300$$

Add the two equations.

$$-6x = -150$$

Solve this new equation by dividing both sides of the equation by -6.

$$x = 25$$

Substitute 25 for x into the first equation.

$$10(25) + 12y = 1150$$

Solve this latest equation to find the value of y.

$$250 + 12y = 1150$$

$$12y = 900 \qquad \text{then} \qquad y = 75$$

Thus, the cost of each putter is $25, and the cost of each driver is $75.

Example 6. John has $30,000 which he wishes to invest. With part of his money he buys shares in a mutual fund that pays interest of 9% per year. He invests the rest of his money in municipal bonds paying interest of 10% per year. After one year John earns interest of $2820. How much is invested at each rate?

Solution: Write a system of equations to solve this problem.

Let
$\quad x =$ the amount of money invested at 9%
$\quad y =$ the amount of money invested at 10%

Write the first equation about the total money invested.

$$x + y = 30000$$

The second equation will calculate the interest earned in 1 year.

$$0.09x + 0.10y = 2820$$

The system of equations is the two equations we wrote:
$$x + y = 30000$$
$$0.09x + 0.10y = 2820$$

Looking at our equations, we see that if we will multiply the first equation by -9 and the second equation by 100, we will eliminate one variable.

$$-9x - 9y = -270000$$

$$9x + 10y = 282000$$

Adding and eliminating x, we find the value of y.

$$y = 12000$$

Substituting this value for y into the first equation, we find x.

$$x + 12000 = 30000$$

$$x = 18000$$

John invested $18,000 at 9% and $12,000 at 10%.

Example 6 can be solved using a graphing calculator. See Chapter 6, Example 45.

Example 7. Six hundred tickets were sold for a school play. The price of an adult ticket was $3.00, and the price of a child's ticket was $1.00. If $1400 was collected in ticket sales, how many tickets of each kind were sold?

Solution: Write a system of equations to solve this problem.

Let

$x =$ the number of adult tickets sold
$y =$ the number of child tickets sold

Write the first equation about the total number of the tickets.

$$x + y = 600$$

Write the second equation about the money.

$$3.00x + 1.00y = 1400$$

Our two equations form a system of equations for the given problem.

$$x + y = 600$$
$$3x + 1y = 1400$$

To solve the system, use the addition method.

We can eliminate one variable by multiplying the first equation by -3.

$$-3x - 3y = -1800$$
$$3x + y = 1400$$

276

Add the equations, and eliminate x.

$$-2y = -400 \qquad \text{Solve for } y.$$
$$y = 200$$

Substitute this value of y into the first equation to find x.

$$x + 200 = 600$$

$$x = 400$$

The solution shows that 400 adult tickets and 200 child tickets were sold.

This example can be solved using a graphing calculator. See Chapter 6, Example 46.

Section 5.1 Exercises

Solve each system graphically.

1. $\begin{aligned} x+y&=3 \\ 2x+y&=5 \end{aligned}$
2. $\begin{aligned} x+y&=1 \\ 3x-y&=3 \end{aligned}$
3. $\begin{aligned} x+2y&=6 \\ 3x+y&=3 \end{aligned}$

4. $\begin{aligned} x-2y&=0 \\ 2x-3y&=2 \end{aligned}$
5. $\begin{aligned} x+y&=0 \\ 2x-2y&=-4 \end{aligned}$
6. $\begin{aligned} 2x-3y&=3 \\ 3x+y&=10 \end{aligned}$

Solve each system using the substitution method.

7. $\begin{aligned} x+y&=5 \\ 2x-y&=4 \end{aligned}$
8. $\begin{aligned} 2x-3y&=1 \\ 4x+y&=-5 \end{aligned}$
9. $\begin{aligned} y+2x&=6 \\ 4x-y&=6 \end{aligned}$

10. $\begin{aligned} 2x+4y&=6 \\ 3x-y&=2 \end{aligned}$
11. $\begin{aligned} 2x-4y&=-4 \\ 3x+2y&=10 \end{aligned}$
12. $\begin{aligned} 3x-3y&=3 \\ 4x+4y&=12 \end{aligned}$

Solve each system using the addition method.

13. $\begin{aligned} x+3y&=5 \\ x-3y&=-1 \end{aligned}$
14. $\begin{aligned} x+2y&=8 \\ x+2y&=4 \end{aligned}$
15. $\begin{aligned} 3x+4y&=6 \\ 4x-3y&=8 \end{aligned}$

16. $\begin{aligned} 2x+y&=7 \\ 3x-2y&=7 \end{aligned}$
17. $\begin{aligned} 2x-3y&=10 \\ -4x+6y&=15 \end{aligned}$
18. $\begin{aligned} 6x-4y&=14 \\ 4x+3y&=11 \end{aligned}$

19. $\begin{aligned} 0.5x-0.4y&=1 \\ 0.3x+0.2y&=0.6 \end{aligned}$

20. On July 4th Six Flags Amusement Park sold 35,000 tickets and collected $1,375,000 in ticket sales. If adult tickets sold that day for $50 and child tickets sold for $35, how many tickets of each kind were sold?

21. On October 12th Six Flags Amusement Park sold 15,000 tickets and collected $510,000 in ticket sales. If adult tickets sold that day for $40 and child tickets sold for $30, how many tickets of each kind were sold?

22. How much low-fat milk which is 3% butterfat should be mixed with milk that is 14% butterfat to get 25 gallons of low-fat milk that is 8.72% butterfat?

23. How much saline solution that is 20% saline must be added to a second solution which is 2% saline to produce twenty-five gallons of a mixture that is 5.6% saline?

24. If Abby has $20,000 to invest, she will split the total amount between two funds. One fund will pay 7% and the other pays 4%. How much will he invest in each to have a profit of $1250?

Section 5.2 Linear Systems with Three Variables

Ordered Triple

The solution of a linear equation of the form:

$$Ax + By + Cz = K \qquad \text{(an equation with three variables)}$$

is an **ordered triple** $(x,\ y,\ z)$.

An example of a triplet solution to an equation would be:

the triple $(1,\ 2,\ 4)$ is a solution of the equation $2x + 3y - z = 4$.

The solution set of such an equation is an infinite number of ordered triples.

Solving a System with Three Variables

To solve a system with three or more variables use the addition method repeatedly:

To Solve a System with Three Variables:
1. Eliminate the same variable from each of two pairs of equations.
2. Then using the resulting equations, eliminate another variable.
3. The result of step 2 will be an equation containing only one variable.
4. Solve this equation for the value of the variable.
5. Substitute this value into one of the resulting equations found in step 1.
6. Solve for the second variable.
7. Substitute both of the values of the variables back into one of the original equations to find the value of the third variable.
8. It is helpful to number the equations as you go.

Let's look at an example.

Example 1. Solve the given system:

$$
\begin{array}{lll}
2x + y - z = 2 & \text{equation} & (1) \\
x + 3y + 2z = 1 & \text{equation} & (2) \\
x + y + z = 2 & \text{equation} & (3)
\end{array}
$$

Solution:

We choose to eliminate x first from equations (1) and (2). Multiply both sides of equation (2) by -2.

Add equations (1) and (2).

$$2x + y - z = 2 \qquad\qquad \text{equation (1)}$$
$$-2x - 6y - 4x = -2 \qquad \text{equation (2) multiplied by } -2$$
$$\overline{\qquad\qquad\qquad}$$
$$-5y - 5z = 0 \qquad\qquad \text{Call this new equation (4).}$$

The variable x must be eliminated again from a different pair of equations. Let's use equations (2) and (3). Multiply both sides of equation (2) by -1 and add the result to equation (3).

$$-x - 3y - 2z = -1 \qquad \text{equation (2) multiplied by } -1$$
$$x + y + z = 2 \qquad\quad \text{equation (3)}$$
$$\overline{\qquad\qquad\qquad}$$
$$-2y - z = 1 \qquad\qquad \text{Call this new equation (5).}$$

Now solve the system formed by the two new equations (4) and (5). To eliminate z, multiply both sides of equation (4) by -1 and both sides of equation (5) by 5 and add these equations.

$$5y + 5z = 0 \qquad\qquad \text{equation (4) multiplied by } -1$$
$$-10y - 5z = 5 \qquad\quad \text{equation (5) multiplied by } 5$$
$$\overline{\qquad\qquad\qquad}$$
$$-5y = 5 \quad \text{or} \quad y = -1$$

Substitute -1 into equation (5) for y.

$$-2(-1) - z = 1$$

Solve for z: $\quad 2 - z = 1 \quad \rightarrow \quad -z = -1 \quad \rightarrow \quad z = 1$

To find x, substitute the values we found for the variables y and z into equation (3).

$$x + y + z = 2 \qquad\qquad \text{equation (3)}$$

$$x - 1 + 1 = 2 \qquad \text{or} \qquad x = 2$$

The ordered triple which is the solution of the given system is $(2, -1, 1)$.

Check:

Given $2x + y - z = 2$ equation (1)

           $x + 3y + 2z = 1$ equation (2)

           $x + y + z = 2$ equation (3)

Substitute the solution values into each equation and check for a true statement.

(1)	$2x + y - z =$	$2(2) + (-1) - (1) =$	$4 - 2 = 2$	True
(2)	$x + 3y + 2z =$	$(2) + 3(-1) + 2(1) =$	$2 - 3 + 2 = 1$	True
(3)	$x + y + z =$	$(2) + (-1) + (1) =$	$2 - 1 + 1 = 2$	True

Example 2.   Solve the given system:

$$x - y + z = 0 \qquad\qquad \text{equation (1)}$$
$$x - 2y + 3z = -5 \qquad\qquad \text{equation (2)}$$
$$2x + 3y - z = 11 \qquad\qquad \text{equation (3)}$$

Solution:

Let's choose to eliminate z first using (1) and (2). Multiply both sides of equation (1) by -3. Then add equations (1) and (2).

$$-3x + 3y - 3z = 0 \qquad\qquad \text{equation (1) multiplied by } -3.$$
$$\underline{x - 2y + 3z = -5} \qquad\qquad \text{equation (2)}$$

$$-2x + y = -5 \qquad\qquad \text{Call this equation (4).}$$

The variable z must be eliminated again from a different pair of equations. Let's use (2) and (3). Multiply both sides of equation (3) by 3 and add the result to equation (2).

$$6x + 9y - 3z = 33 \qquad\qquad \text{equation (3) multiplied by 3}$$
$$\underline{x - 2y + 3z = -5} \qquad\qquad \text{equation (2)}$$

$$7x + 7y = 28 \qquad\qquad \text{Divide the new equation by 7.}$$

$$x + y = 4 \qquad\qquad \text{Call this equation (5).}$$

Solve the system formed by the two new equations (4) and (5). To eliminate y, multiply both sides of equation (5) by -1 and add these equations.

$$-x - y = -4$$
equation (5) multiplied by -1

$$-2x + y = -5$$
equation (4)

$$-3x = -9 \qquad \text{or} \qquad x = 3$$

Substitute 3 into equation (5) for x.

$$3 + y = 4 \qquad \text{or} \qquad y = 1$$

Use equation (1) to find z by substituting the x and y values for the variables x and y.

$$x - y + z = 0 \qquad\qquad\qquad \text{equation (1)}$$

$$3 - 1 + z = 0 \qquad \text{or} \qquad z = -2$$

The ordered triple which is the solution of the given system is (3, 1, -2).

Applications:

We encounter systems of equations with three or more variables in many areas. In science and business/finance fields, systems of equations are often used to solve problems.

Example 3. An organic farm is going to plant three crops on ten acres of land. Potatoes, corn and beans will be planted. The area acreage needed for corn is twice as much as the acreage needed for potatoes, and the beans crop will use two acres less than the acreage needed for the potatoes. Find the acreage used for each crop.

Solution:

Let x represent the acres used for the corn crop.
Let y represent the acres used for the bean crop.
Let z represent the acres used for the potato crop.

Since the total acreage used is 10, we have one equation.

$$x + y + z = 10 \qquad\qquad \text{equation (1)}$$

Using the statement from the problem: acreage needed for corn is twice as much as for potatoes, we get a second equation.

$$x = 2z \qquad\qquad \text{or}$$

$$x - 2z = 0 \qquad\qquad \text{equation (2)}$$

Using the statement from the problem: bean crop will use two acres less than the potatoes, we get a third equation.

$$y = z - 2 \qquad \text{or}$$
$$y - z = -2 \qquad\qquad\qquad\qquad \text{equation (3)}$$

We now have a system of three equations:

$$
\begin{aligned}
x + y + z &= 10 \qquad\qquad \text{equation (1)}\\
x - 2z &= 0 \qquad\qquad \text{equation (2)}\\
y - z &= -2 \qquad\qquad \text{equation (3)}
\end{aligned}
$$

Use equations (1) and (2) to eliminate x. Multiply equation (2) by -1 and add to equation (1).

$$
\begin{aligned}
x + y + z &= 10 \qquad\qquad \text{equation (1)}\\
-x \quad\; + 2z &= 0 \qquad\qquad \text{equation (2) times } -1\\
\hline
y + 3z &= 10 \qquad\qquad \text{new equation (4)}
\end{aligned}
$$

Use (3) and (4) to eliminate z Multiply (3) by -1 and add.

$$
\begin{aligned}
-y + z &= 2 \qquad\qquad \text{equation (3) times } -1\\
y + 3z &= 10 \qquad\qquad \text{equation (4)}\\
\hline
4z &= 12 \qquad \text{or} \qquad z = 3
\end{aligned}
$$

Substitute the value for z into equation (3) to find y.

$$y - 3 = -2 \qquad \text{or} \qquad y = 1$$

Use equation (1) to find x by substituting the values for the variables y and z.

$$x + 1 + 3 = 10 \qquad \text{or} \qquad x = 6$$

The solution is: 6 acres for corn, 1 acre for beans, and 3 acres for potatoes.

Example 4. Bethy has $25,000 she wishes to invest. She invests part of her money into an account paying 3% interest, part into a second account paying 4% interest, and the rest into an account paying 5% interest. After 1 year the total interest from her three accounts is $1060. She invested $1,000 more into the account paying 4% than in the account paying 3%. Find the amount of money invested in each account.

Solution:

Let x represent the amount invested in the 3% account.
Let y represent the amount invested in the 4% account.
Let z represent the amount invested in the 5% account.

Since the total money invested is 25,000, we have the first equation.

$$x + y + z = 25000 \qquad \text{equation (1)}$$

Since the total interest received is 1060, we have a second equation.

$$0.03x + 0.04y + 0.05z = 1060$$
$$\text{or}$$
$$3x + 4y + 5z = 106000 \qquad \text{equation (2)}$$

From the fact: she invested $1,000 more into the account paying 4% than in the account paying 3%, we have a third equation.

$$x + 1000 = y$$
$$\text{or}$$
$$x - y = -1000$$

We can write this equation as
$$x - y + 0z = -1000 \qquad \text{equation (3)}$$

We now have a system of three equations to solve for the solution to our problem.

$$x + y + z = 25000 \qquad \text{equation (1)}$$
$$3x + 4y + 5z = 106000 \qquad \text{equation (2)}$$
$$x - y + 0z = -1000 \qquad \text{equation (3)}$$

Use equations (1) and (2) to eliminate z. Multiply equation (1) by -5 and add to equation (2).

$$-5x - 5y - 5z = -125000 \qquad \text{equation (1) times } -5$$
$$\underline{3x + 4y + 5z = 106000} \qquad \text{equation (2)}$$

$$-2x - y = -19000$$

284

or

$$2x + y = 19000 \qquad \text{new equation (4)}$$

Add equations (3) and (4) to eliminate y.

$$x - y = -1000 \qquad \text{equation (3)}$$
$$\underline{2x + y = 19000} \qquad \text{equation (4)}$$

$$3x = 18000 \qquad \text{or}$$

$$x = 6,000$$

Substitute the value of 6000 for x into equation (3).

$$6000 - y = -1000 \qquad \text{or}$$

$$y = 7,000$$

Substitute values for x and y into equation (1).

$$6000 + 7000 + z = 25000 \qquad \text{or}$$

$$z = 12,000$$

Bethy invested $6,000 at 3%; $7,000 at 4%; and $12,000 at 5%.

Section 5.2 Exercises

Solve each of the following systems of equations.

1. $x + 2y - 3z = 1$
    $2x - y - z = -3$
    $3x + 3y + 2z = 16$

2. $3x + 4y - z = 7$
    $-2x + 5y + 4z = 2$
    $4x - 7y - 4z = 4$

3. $3x + y - z = 2$
    $-2x - 2y + 3z = -11$
    $x + 3y - 2z = 11$

4. $x + 2y - 3z = 2$
    $2x + 4y = -8$
    $2x + 2z = 4$

5. $2x - y + 2z = 7$
    $x + 2y - z = -9$
    $3x - 4y + 2z = 8$

6. $x + 2y - 3z = -8$
    $3x - y - 2z = 4$
    $4x - 2y - 5z = 5$

7. $3x + 5y + 4z = 1$
    $x + 4y - z = 5$
    $2x - 3y + 4z = -2$

8. $2x + y + z = 1$
    $4x - 2y + 2z = -6$
    $-6x + 3y + 3z = -3$

9. $2x + 2y + 3z = 3$
    $x + 3y + z = 0$
    $4x + 6y - 4z = -5$

10. $2x + y - 3z = 5$
    $x - 2y + 4z = 15$
    $3x + 4y + 2z = -5$

11. $x + 2y + 3z = 5$
    $2x + z = 3$
    $3y - 2z = 11$

12. $x - 2y + 3z = 6$
    $3x - y + 2z = 2$
    $2x - 3y - z = 7$

13. $2x + 4y - z = 3$
    $3x - 5y = -19$
    $4y - 10z = 18$

14. $x + 2y - z = 8$
    $2x - 6y + 2z = -1$
    $3x + 8y + 5z = 1$

15. Clay had $50,000 he wished to invest. He invested part of his money in bonds paying 4% interest, part in stocks paying 5% interest, and the rest of the money in a hedge fund with interest of 7%. His interest after one year was $2220. If he invested twice as much in bonds as he did in stocks, how much was invested in each type of investment?

16. The choir recently gave a performance for the community. Adult tickets sold for $3, senior tickets for $2 and child tickets for $1. A total of 825 tickets were sold for $1525. If the total of the adult and senior tickets sold were 400 tickets, how many of each were sold?

Section 5.3   Systems of Inequalities

Many mathematical descriptions of real situations are best expressed as inequalities rather than equalities. Quite often a system of inequalities is needed. We will draw a graph to see the solution of an inequality in two variables.

Linear Inequality in Two Variables

Linear Inequality in Two Variables:

A linear inequality in 2 variables is an inequality of the form:

$$Ax + By \leq C$$

where A, B, and C are real numbers with A and B not both equal to zero.

The symbols of inequalities can be: $\leq$, $<$, $\geq$, and $>$.

One solution of an inequality in two variables is an ordered pair (x, y).

The solution set of an inequality is the set of all ordered pairs that make the inequality a true statement.

Solutions of inequalities are written using Interval Notation.

The graph of an inequality is an easy way to see the solution set.

Examples of inequalities in two variables are:

$$3x - 4y < 18$$

$$2x + 36 \leq 12$$

$$x + 7y > 15$$

$$\frac{1}{2}x - \frac{2}{3}y \geq 6$$

The graph of a linear inequality turns out to be made up of a half-plane with its boundary, the line of the inequality, perhaps included.

287

Steps Used to Graph an Inequality with Two Variables

Steps used to graphing an inequality with two variables:

1. First graph the line that would result if the inequality sign were changed to an = sign.

2. This line, called the **boundary line**, will divide the graph into 2 half-planes. One of these half-planes is the solution set of the inequality.

3. To determine which half-plane (the one above or below the line) is the solution, pick a test point and see if the test point satisfies the given inequality.

4. If the test point satisfies the given inequality, shade the half-plane that includes the test point.

5. If the test point does not satisfy the given inequality, shade the other side of the line.

6. Make the line a solid line if the inequality symbol is either $\geq$ or $\leq$.

7. Make the line a dotted line if the inequality symbol is either $>$ or $<$.

Example 1. Graph $y < x + 4$.

Solution: Follow the steps above. First graph the line $y = x + 4$. Make a table to help you graph the line. The line will be a dotted line because of the given inequality symbol.

Pick a test point. Let's use the point $(0, 0)$. Does it satisfy the inequality?
$$(0) < (0) + 4 \qquad \text{or} \qquad 0 < 4$$
Since the point **does** satisfy the given inequality, shade the side of the line that **contains** our point $(0, 0)$.

The shaded area is the solution set to the inequality.

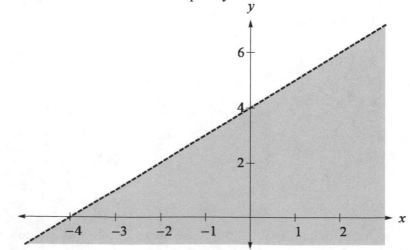

Example 2. Graph: $2x + y \leq 6$

Solution: First graph the line : $2x + y = 6$. Make a table to graph the line. The line will be solid since the $\leq$ symbol tells us to include the boundary line.

Pick a test point. Let's use the point (0, 0). Does it satisfy the inequality?

$$2(0) + (0) \leq 6 \quad \text{or} \quad 0 \leq 6$$

Since it does satisfy the given inequality, shade the side of the line that contains our point (0, 0).

The line is solid since the inequality symbol includes the equal sign.

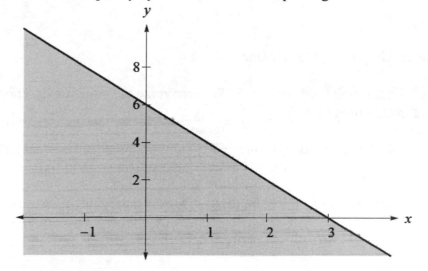

Example 2 can be solved using a graphing calculator. See Chapter 6, Example 47.

Example 3. Graph $x > 2$ on a plane.

Solution: First graph the line: $x = 2$. We recognize this to be a vertical line thru (2, 0).

The line should be dotted since the inequality does not contain the equal sign.

Pick a test point. Let's use the point (0, 0). Does it satisfy the inequality?

$$(0) > 2 \quad \text{or} \quad 0 > 2$$

Since it **does not** satisfy the given inequality, shade the side of the line that **does not** contain our point.

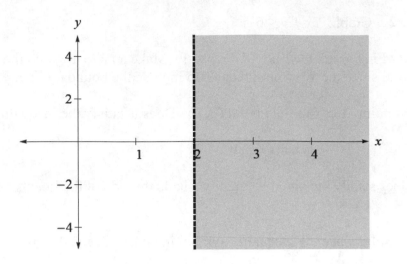

Example 4: Graph $y \leq 5$ on a plane.

Solution: First graph the line: $y = 5$. We recognize the equation as a horizontal line that goes through the point (0, 5).

The line should be solid since the inequality symbol contains the equal sign.

Pick a test point. Let's use the point (0, 0). Does it satisfy the inequality?

$$(0) \leq 5 \quad \text{or} \quad 0 \leq 5$$

Since the point (0, 0) **does** satisfy the given inequality, shade the side of the line that contains our point.

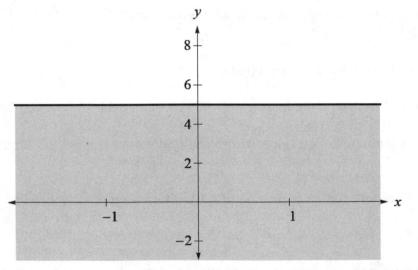

Systems of Linear Inequalities

The solution set of an inequality in two variables is usually a set whose graph is one or more regions of the coordinate plane. The solution set of a **system of inequalities**, such as

$$x + y < 4$$
$$3x - 2y \geq 6$$

is the intersection of the solution sets of each inequality. The solution of the given system is best visualized by its graph.

Graphing a System of Inequalities:

To graph the solution set of a system of inequalities, graph both inequalities on the same axes. Then shade the solution set for each inequality, and finally identify the solution of the system by shading heavily the region common to both solutions.

Example 5. Graph:
$$x + 2y \leq 6$$
$$x - y \geq 3$$

Solution: Graph the $x + 2y \leq 6$ by graphing $x + 2y = 6$ using a solid line. Use (0, 0) as the test point, find the half-plane that represents the solution, and shade that side.

Then graph $x - y \geq 3$ by graphing $x - y = 3$ using a solid line. Use (0, 0) as the test point; find the half-plane that represents the solution; and shade that side.

The solution set of the given system is the region of the plane that is shaded by **both** inequalities.

Note that the parts of the lines $x + 2y = 6$ and $x - y = 3$ that are included in the combined shaded areas are also within the solution set.

The easiest way to check your solution is to choose a test point within the intersection of the shaded areas to verify that this point will make both inequalities true statements.

Graph of

$$x + 2y \le 6$$
$$x - y \ge 3$$

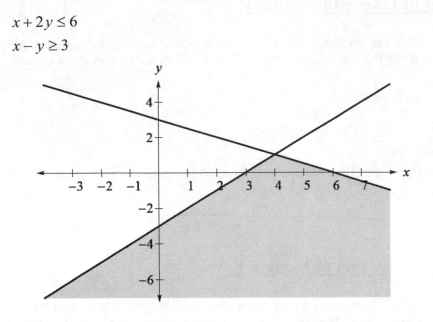

Check:
To check our graph we will select a test point in our shaded area. Let's use the point (4, 0).

Next check this point in both of the inequalities of the system.

$$x + 2y \le 6$$
$$x - y \ge 3$$

(1): $x + 2y \le 6$
    $(4) + 2(0) \le 6$
     $4 \le 6$ True

(2): $x - y \ge 3$
    $(4) - (0) \ge 3$
     $4 \ge 3$ True

Example 5 can be solved using a graphing calculator. See Chapter 6, Example 48.

Section 5.3 Exercises

Graph each given inequality.

1. $y > 3x$

2. $3y < x$

3. $y > x$

4. $y < x$

5. $x > -4$

6. $x < 5$

7. $y > 4$

8. $y < -3$

9. $2x - 3y \leq 6$

10. $3x + 2y \leq 12$

11. $x \leq -3$

12. $x \geq 5$

13. $y \leq -1$

14. $y \geq -2$

Graph each inequality in the system and then find the solution set.

15. $\begin{aligned} x + 2y > 2 \\ x - 2y < 4 \end{aligned}$

16. $\begin{aligned} 2x - y < 4 \\ x + 3y > -2 \end{aligned}$

17. $\begin{aligned} 3x - 4y \leq 3 \\ 2x + y \geq -2 \end{aligned}$

18. $\begin{aligned} x \leq 4 \\ y \geq 2 \end{aligned}$

Section 5.4   Solving Linear Systems Using Matrices

Suppose that you are the owner of a golf shop, and you receive the following shipments of golf balls from two golf ball makers: from Willis you receive 2 cases of white balls, 4 cases of yellow balls, and 8 cases of red balls; and from Boyd you receive 4 cases of white balls, 3 cases of yellow balls, and 11 cases of red balls.

We can rewrite the golf ball information in a chart so that it is easier to read.

<u>Golf Balls</u>

<u>Manufacturer</u>	white	yellow	red
Willis	2	4	8
Boyd	4	3	11

We can also remove identifying names and colors and reduce the chart to an array of numbers containing all of the golf ball shipment information. The following array contains all of our data:

$$\begin{bmatrix} 2 & 4 & 8 \\ 4 & 3 & 11 \end{bmatrix}$$

A rectangular array like this one is called a **matrix** (plural matrices). Notice the symbols we use to surround the array. These symbols signify a matrix.

Properties of a Matrix

<u>Properties of a Matrix</u>:

Each number in the matrix is called an **element** of the matrix.

The **rows** are the elements read horizontally, and the **columns** are the elements read vertical.

Matrices are classified by their **dimensions (often called order)**, that is, by the number of rows and columns that they contain. The above matrix has 2 rows and 3 columns and is called a "two by three" matrix and numerically is called a 2 x 3 matrix.

A matrix with p rows and q columns is said to be a "p by q" (p x q) matrix.

If the number of rows is equal to the number of columns, the matrix is a **square matrix.**

Matrices are useful in many areas of math, finance and science. When solving complicated systems of equations using matrices a computer can be helpful.

Element of a Matrix

An **element** of a matrix is one of the entries in the matrix. The address of an element is given by listing the row number and then the column number.

a_{ij} is the element of matrix A that occupies row i and column j.

Augmented Matrix

An **augmented matrix** is a combination of two matrices written as one. An example of an augmented matrix is show below:

$$\left[\begin{array}{cc|c} 1 & 2 & 3 \\ 4 & 5 & 6 \end{array}\right]$$

This augmented matrix is a combination of the two matrices:

$$\begin{bmatrix} 1 & 2 \\ 4 & 5 \end{bmatrix} \quad \text{and} \quad \begin{bmatrix} 3 \\ 6 \end{bmatrix}$$

Row Operations on Matrices

Row Operations on Matrices:

1. Any two rows can be interchanged.

2. All of the elements of a row can be multiplied by the same nonzero constant.

3. One row can be multiplied by a nonzero constant and then added to another row.

Solving Systems of Equations Using Matrices:

Gauss-Jordan Method of Solving Systems: this method is used to solve systems of equations.
Let's look at an example to understand how to use the Gauss-Jordan Method.
Example 1. Use the Gauss-Jordan method to solve the given linear system.

$$3x - y = 3$$
$$4x + 2y = 14$$

Solution:
The equations are in the needed form, $ax + by = c$, so we are ready to begin. We will use the given equations to write an augmented matrix.

$$\begin{bmatrix} 3 & -1 & | & 3 \\ 4 & 2 & | & 14 \end{bmatrix}$$

Use row operations to reduce the above matrix to one that looks like:

$$\begin{bmatrix} 1 & 0 & | & j \\ 0 & 1 & | & k \end{bmatrix}$$ **where j and k are real numbers.**

When we have this form for our matrix, we can translate the matrix from matrix form into two equations which will solve the given system. The two equations are:

$$x = j$$

$$y = k$$

These two equations then will tell us the values of the variables in the given system.

Begin with the augmented matrix from the given equations:

$$\begin{bmatrix} 3 & -1 & | & 3 \\ 4 & 2 & | & 14 \end{bmatrix}$$ Use row operations to **convert** it to $$\begin{bmatrix} 1 & 0 & | & j \\ 0 & 1 & | & k \end{bmatrix}.$$

It is easier to work on specific elements of the columns rather than rows to make this conversion. We can use any row operations to reduce the augmented matrix. Since the element in row 1, column 1 of the given matrix should be a one, multiply elements in row 1 by $\dfrac{1}{3}$. We now have the new matrix:

$$\begin{bmatrix} 1 & -\dfrac{1}{3} & | & 1 \\ 4 & 2 & | & 14 \end{bmatrix}$$

Compare our new matrix to the form we want, and we see that we need a zero for the element in row 2, column 1. To accomplish changing this element to zero, we will multiply row 1 by -4 and add the result to row 2. We then get a new matrix:

$$\begin{bmatrix} 1 & -\dfrac{1}{3} & | & 1 \\ 0 & \dfrac{10}{3} & | & 10 \end{bmatrix}$$

Looking at the new matrix we see that column 1 is in the form we want.

Next we will move to column 2 and work on the element in row 2, column 2. We want that element to be a one, so we will multiply elements in row 2 by $\frac{3}{10}$. Our new matrix is:

$$\begin{bmatrix} 1 & -\dfrac{1}{3} & \bigm| & 1 \\ 0 & 1 & \bigm| & 3 \end{bmatrix}$$

If we look again at the new matrix, we see that only one element needs changing. We want the element in row 1, column 2 to be a zero. We will multiply the elements in row 2 by 1/3 and add the result to row 1. We have a new matrix:

$$\begin{bmatrix} 1 & 0 & \bigm| & 2 \\ 0 & 1 & \bigm| & 3 \end{bmatrix}$$

Looking at the new matrix, we see that this matrix is now converted into the form we want. We will write our matrix in equation form, and the two equations give us the solution to the given system.

$$x = 2$$
$$y = 3$$

The only solution to the given system is the point (2, 3).

Check: Given $\begin{array}{l} 3x - y = 3 \\ 4x + 2y = 14 \end{array}$ We test our solution in each equation.

$$
\begin{array}{llll}
3x - y = & 3(2) - (3) = & 6 - 3 = 3 & \text{True} \\
4x + 2y = & 4(2) + 2(3) = & 8 + 6 = 14 & \text{True}
\end{array}
$$

Our solution is correct because it makes both equations true statements.

Notice: When we are converted our augmented equation into the desired form, we worked on columns. In each column we converted the element that we wanted to be a one first. After we had the one in the correct element, we used that element to convert the other elements in the column to zeros.

Example 2. Use the Gauss-Jordan method to solve the given system

$$x - y + 5z = -6$$
$$3x + 3y - z = 10$$
$$x + 3y + 2z = 5$$

Solution: We will begin by writing the augmented matrix from the given system.

$$\begin{bmatrix} 1 & -1 & 5 & | & -6 \\ 3 & 3 & -1 & | & 10 \\ 1 & 3 & 2 & | & 5 \end{bmatrix} \quad \text{We will } \textbf{convert it} \text{ to:} \quad \begin{bmatrix} 1 & 0 & 0 & | & j \\ 0 & 1 & 0 & | & k \\ 0 & 0 & 1 & | & m \end{bmatrix}.$$

Remember to work on columns. Start with column 1. There is already a one in row 1, column 1, so we will work to get a zero in row 2 of column 1. Multiply the elements of row 1 by -3 and add the result to row 2. Our new matrix is:

$$\begin{bmatrix} 1 & -1 & 5 & | & -6 \\ 0 & 6 & -16 & | & 28 \\ 1 & 3 & 2 & | & 5 \end{bmatrix}$$

Next, we see that we need a zero as the element in column 1, row 3. We must multiply the elements of row 1 by -1 and add the result to row 3. Our new matrix is:

$$\begin{bmatrix} 1 & -1 & 5 & | & -6 \\ 0 & 6 & -16 & | & 28 \\ 0 & 4 & -3 & | & 11 \end{bmatrix}$$

Column 1 is now in the correct form so we will move to column 2. We see that we need the element in column 2, row 2 to be a one. To get a one, we divide each element of row 2 by 6. Our new matrix is:

$$\begin{bmatrix} 1 & -1 & 5 & | & -6 \\ 0 & 1 & -\dfrac{8}{3} & | & \dfrac{14}{3} \\ 0 & 4 & -3 & | & 11 \end{bmatrix}$$

Look at the new matrix. We see that now, we need a zero as the element in row 1, column 2. Add row 2 to row 1 and place the result in row 1. The new matrix is:

$$\begin{bmatrix} 1 & 0 & \dfrac{7}{3} & | & -\dfrac{4}{3} \\ 0 & 1 & -\dfrac{8}{3} & | & \dfrac{14}{3} \\ 0 & 4 & -3 & | & 11 \end{bmatrix}$$

Look at the new matrix. Column 2 is not in the needed form yet.

298

We will use row operations to change the element in column 2, row 3 to a zero. Multiply the elements of row 2 by -4 and add the result to row 3. The new matrix is:

$$\left[\begin{array}{ccc|c} 1 & 0 & \dfrac{7}{3} & -\dfrac{4}{3} \\[2ex] 0 & 1 & -\dfrac{8}{3} & \dfrac{14}{3} \\[2ex] 0 & 0 & \dfrac{23}{3} & -\dfrac{23}{3} \end{array}\right]$$

Column 2 is now in the correct form, and we will move to column 3. We need the element in row 3, column 3 to be a one.

We will multiply the elements in row 3 by $\dfrac{3}{23}$. Our new matrix is:

$$\left[\begin{array}{ccc|c} 1 & 0 & \dfrac{7}{3} & -\dfrac{4}{3} \\[2ex] 0 & 1 & -\dfrac{8}{3} & \dfrac{14}{3} \\[2ex] 0 & 0 & 1 & -1 \end{array}\right]$$

Look at the new matrix. We next want the element in row 1, column 3 to be a zero.

Multiply the elements of row 3 by $-\dfrac{7}{3}$ and add the result to row 1. Our new matrix is:

$$\left[\begin{array}{ccc|c} 1 & 0 & 0 & 1 \\[2ex] 0 & 1 & -\dfrac{8}{3} & \dfrac{14}{3} \\[2ex] 0 & 0 & 1 & -1 \end{array}\right]$$

We must change the element in column 3, row 2 to a zero. Multiply the elements of row 3 by 8/3 and add the result to row 2. Our new matrix is:

$$\left[\begin{array}{ccc|c} 1 & 0 & 0 & 1 \\ 0 & 1 & 0 & 2 \\ 0 & 0 & 1 & -1 \end{array}\right]$$

Look at the new matrix . The matrix has been converted to the form we want, and we will use each row to write an equation.

The solution to the system is:
$$x = 1$$
$$y = 2$$
$$z = -1$$

The solution is the triplet $(1, \ 2, \ -1)$.

$$x - y + 5z = -6$$
Check: Given $\quad 3x + 3y - z = 10 \qquad$ Test each equation with the solution.
$$x + 3y + 2z = 5$$

$x - y + 5z =$ $\qquad$ $(1) - (2) + 5(-1) =$ $\qquad$ $1 - 2 - 5 = -6$

$3x + 3y - z =$ $\qquad$ $3(1) + 3(2) - (-1) =$ $\qquad$ $3 + 6 + 1 = 10$

$x + 3y + 2z =$ $\qquad$ $(1) + 3(2) + 2(-1) =$ $\qquad$ $1 + 6 - 2 = 5$

Example 3. Use the Gauss-Jordan method to solve the following system:

$$x + y = 2$$
$$3x + 3y = 7$$

Solution: Begin by writing the augmented matrix from the given system.

$$\begin{bmatrix} 1 & 1 & | & 2 \\ 3 & 3 & | & 7 \end{bmatrix}$$

Remember to work with columns. Begin with column 1. There is already a 1 in row 1, column 1, but a zero is needed in row 2 of column 1. Multiply each element of row 1 by -3 and add the result to row 2. Our new matrix is:

$$\begin{bmatrix} 1 & 1 & | & 2 \\ 0 & 0 & | & 1 \end{bmatrix}$$

Look at the new matrix. Column 1 is in the correct form, and we move to column 2. Our next step is to get a 1 in column 2, row 2. Because of the zeros, we are unable to do this step.

The equation corresponding to the second reduced row is:

$$0x \ + \ 0y \ = 1$$

and this equation has no solution. The solution to the system of equations is the empty set, and The system is inconsistent.

Row-Echelon Form of a Matrix:

A matrix is in row-echelon form if:

1. Unless the row has all 0's, the first nonzero element in the row is a 1.

2. For any 2 successive rows, the leading 1 in the upper row is to the left of the leading 1 in the lower row.

3. All of the rows that contain only zeros are at the bottom of the matrix.

Example 4. Which of the following matrices are in row-echelon form?

a. $\begin{bmatrix} 1 & -2 & 4 & | & 3 \\ 0 & 2 & 5 & | & 2 \\ 0 & 0 & 1 & | & 1 \end{bmatrix}$
b. $\begin{bmatrix} 1 & 0 & 0 & | & 2 \\ 0 & 0 & 1 & | & 3 \\ 0 & 0 & 0 & | & 0 \end{bmatrix}$
c. $\begin{bmatrix} 1 & 0 & | & 4 \\ 0 & 0 & | & 0 \end{bmatrix}$

d. $\begin{bmatrix} 1 & 0 & 2 & | & 3 \\ 0 & 1 & 1 & | & 2 \\ 0 & 1 & 0 & | & 1 \end{bmatrix}$
e. $\begin{bmatrix} 1 & 2 & 2 & | & 2 \\ 0 & 1 & 3 & | & 3 \\ 0 & 0 & 0 & | & 0 \end{bmatrix}$
f. $\begin{bmatrix} 1 & 0 & 3 & | & 2 \\ 0 & 1 & 2 & | & 3 \\ 0 & 0 & 1 & | & 5 \end{bmatrix}$

Solution: The matrices shown in b, c, e, and f are examples of row-echelon matrices because they follow the rules for such.

The matrix in example a is not in row-echelon form because the leading element in row 2 is not a one.

The matrix in example d is not in row-echelon form because the leading non-zero element in row 3 is not to the right of the leading non-zero element in row 2.

Requirements for Matrix Operations

Requirements for Matrix Operations:

Addition/ Subtraction of Two Matrices:
The two matrices must have an equal number of rows and an equal number of columns.

Multiplication of Two Matrices:
The number of columnss in the first matrix must be **exactly** equal to the number of rows in the second matrix. The result of the multiplication will be a matrix with the number of rows of the first matrix and the number of columns of the second matrix.

Section 5.4 Exercises

Write an augmented matrix for each of the following systems.

1. $2x - y = 4$
    $x + 3y = 4$

2. $x + 4y = 9$
    $3x - 2y = 8$

3. $x + 4y - 2z = 5$
    $x \qquad + 3z = 7$
    $2y + z = 4$

4. $3y - z = 5$
    $2x + 2y = 4$
    $x - 3y + 4z = 1$

Solve the systems of equations using the Gauss-Jordan method.

5. $2x + 3y = 7$
    $4x - 2y = 6$

6. $x + y = 4$
    $x - y = 0$

7. $3x + 4y = 4$
    $4x - 2y = -2$

8. $3x - 5y = 2$
    $x + 2y = 8$

9. $3x - 4y = 5$
    $x + 5y = 8$

10. $4x - y = 13$
    $3x + 3y = 6$

11. $3x + 2y - z = 4$
    $4x - y + 2z = 5$
    $2x - y - z = 0$

12. $2x + 3y + 2z = 1$
    $x - 5y + 3z = 7$
    $3x + y + 4z = 5$

13. $2x + 4y - 2z = 8$
    $3x + 2y + z = 0$
    $x + 3y - 3z = 8$

14. $3x + 4y - 2z = 6$
    $4x - 3y + z = 8$
    $x - y + 3z = 2$

15. $2x - y + 5z = 6$
    $x + 2y - 4z = 4$
    $3x - y + 2z = 5$

16. $3x + 3y + 4z = 12$
    $x - y + z = 1$
    $2x + 4y + 2z = 10$

17. $2x + y - z = 5$
    $x + 3y - z = 6$
    $3x - 2y - z = 2$

18. $2x + 3y - z = 5$
    $4x - y - 2z = 3$
    $6x - 3y - 7z = 7$

Section 5.5   Inverse Matrices

Multiplication of Matrices

Multiplication of Matrices:

If an m x n matrix A is multiplied by an n x p matrix B, the result in an m x p matrix C where each element c_{ij} in the product matrix C is:

$$c_{ij} = a_{i1}b_{1j} + a_{i2}b_{2j} + a_{i3}b_{3j} + \ldots + a_{in}b_{nj}$$

To accomplish the multiplication for each element, simultaneously move to the right along a row from matrix A and down a column of matrix B, multiplying each pair of elements and then adding the products of the pairs.

The number of columns of the first matrix must be the same as the number of rows in the second matrix. Hence, $AB \neq BA$, and in most cases, BA is not possible.

Example 1.   Find the product of the two given matrices:

$$A = \begin{bmatrix} 1 & 3 & -4 \\ 4 & 0 & -2 \end{bmatrix} \quad \text{and} \quad B = \begin{bmatrix} 5 & -4 & 2 & 0 \\ -1 & 6 & 3 & 1 \\ 7 & 0 & 5 & 8 \end{bmatrix}$$

Solution: Matrix A is a 2 x 3 matrix and B is a 3 x 4 matrix. The product $C = AB$ is a 2 x 4 matrix. Use the above rule for finding each element of the matrix C:

Row A	Column B	Element of C
R_1	C_1	$c_{11} = 1*5 + 3*(-1) + (-4)*7 = -26$
R_1	C_2	$c_{12} = 1*(-4) + 3*6 + (-4)*0 = 14$
R_1	C_3	$c_{13} = 1*2 + 3*3 + (-4)*5 = -9$
R_1	C_4	$c_{14} = 1*0 + 3*1 + (-4)*8 = -29$
R_2	C_1	$c_{21} = 4*5 + 0*(-1) + (-2)*7 = 6$
R_2	C_2	$c_{22} = 4*(-4) + 0*6 + (-2)*0 = -16$
R_2	C_3	$c_{23} = 4*2 + 0*3 + (-2)*5 = -2$
R_2	C_4	$c_{24} = 4*0 + 0*1 + (-2)*8 = -16$

We see that the multiplication:

$$AB = \begin{bmatrix} 1 & 3 & -4 \\ 4 & 0 & -2 \end{bmatrix} \begin{bmatrix} 5 & -4 & 2 & 0 \\ -1 & 6 & 3 & 1 \\ 7 & 0 & 5 & 8 \end{bmatrix} = \begin{bmatrix} -26 & 14 & -9 & -29 \\ 6 & -16 & -2 & -16 \end{bmatrix}.$$

Example 1 can be solved using a graphing calculator. See Chapter 6, Example 49.

Identity Property:

We know that the identity property of real numbers states that for any real number n,

$$(n)(1) = n \quad \text{and} \quad (1)(n) = n$$

The same idea is true for matrices.

If I is an identity matrix, then it follows that for any square matrix A plus the fact that A and I must be of the same order:

$$AI = A \quad \text{and} \quad IA = A$$

Identity Matrices

The symbol I_n is used to denote the square matrix of order n that has 1 in each position on the main diagonal and 0 everywhere else.

$$I_2 = \begin{bmatrix} 1 & 0 \\ 0 & 1 \end{bmatrix} \qquad I_3 = \begin{bmatrix} 1 & 0 & 0 \\ 0 & 1 & 0 \\ 0 & 0 & 1 \end{bmatrix}$$

From the identity rule for a matrix , we know that

$$AI_n = A = I_nA$$

Inverse of a Matrix

Inverse of a matrix:

If A is a square matrix of order n, that is, an $n \times n$ matrix, and if there exists a matrix B such that

$$AB = I_n = BA$$

then matrix B is the inverse of matrix A and is written as A^{-1}

Finding the Inverse of a Square Matrix

To find the inverse of a square matrix:

1. Make a matrix that is a combination of the given matrix followed by an identity matrix of the same order.

2. Use elementary row operations to change the new matrix so that the identity matrix portion appears as the first matrix of the combination.

3. The second section of the combined matrix is then the inverse.

Example 2. Find the inverse of the matrix A.

$$A = \begin{bmatrix} 2 & 4 \\ 1 & 5 \end{bmatrix}$$

Solution: We begin with step 1 above and combine matrix A with the I_2.

$$\left[\begin{array}{cc|cc} 2 & 4 & 1 & 0 \\ 1 & 5 & 0 & 1 \end{array} \right].$$

Next use row operations to convert the first two columns of the combined matrix into the identity matrix.

First switch rows 1 and 2 so that the element in row 1, column 1 will be a 1. We get the new matrix:

$$\left[\begin{array}{cc|cc} 1 & 5 & 0 & 1 \\ 2 & 4 & 1 & 0 \end{array} \right].$$

A zero is needed as the first element in row 2, column 1. Multiply each element of row 1 by -2 and add the result to the elements of row 2. The new matrix is:

$$\left[\begin{array}{cc|cc} 1 & 5 & 0 & 1 \\ 0 & -6 & 1 & -2 \end{array}\right].$$

Column 1 is in the correct form, and we move to column 2.
A one is needed as the element in row 2, column 2. We must divide each element of row 2 by -6. The new matrix is:

$$\left[\begin{array}{cc|cc} 1 & 5 & 0 & 1 \\ 0 & 1 & -\dfrac{1}{6} & \dfrac{1}{3} \end{array}\right].$$

A zero is needed as the element in row 1, column 2. Multiply each element of row 2 by -5 and add the result to row 1. The new matrix is:

$$\left[\begin{array}{cc|cc} 1 & 0 & \dfrac{5}{6} & -\dfrac{2}{3} \\ 0 & 1 & -\dfrac{1}{6} & \dfrac{1}{3} \end{array}\right].$$

The first portion of this matrix is now the identity matrix as stated in step 2 above. The second portion of the matrix is the inverse of the original matrix.

$$A^{-1} = \left[\begin{array}{cc} \dfrac{5}{6} & -\dfrac{2}{3} \\ -\dfrac{1}{6} & \dfrac{1}{3} \end{array}\right]$$

Example 2 can be solved using a graphing calculator. See Chapter 6, Example 50.

Example 3. Find A^{-1} if $A = \begin{bmatrix} 1 & 0 & 1 \\ 2 & -2 & -1 \\ 3 & 0 & 0 \end{bmatrix}$

Solution: Write the combination matrix:

$$\left[\begin{array}{ccc|ccc} 1 & 0 & 1 & 1 & 0 & 0 \\ 2 & -2 & -1 & 0 & 1 & 0 \\ 3 & 0 & 0 & 0 & 0 & 1 \end{array}\right]$$

We must convert the combined matrix to the form where the identity matrix is on the left and then we can find the inverse. We will begin with column 1. Since there is already a 1 as the element in row 1, column 1, move to row 2, column 1. This element should be zero. To convert this element to a zero, multiply the elements in row 1 by -2 and add the result to the elements of row 2. The new matrix is:

$$\left[\begin{array}{ccc|ccc} 1 & 0 & 1 & 1 & 0 & 0 \\ 0 & -2 & -3 & -2 & 1 & 0 \\ 3 & 0 & 0 & 0 & 0 & 1 \end{array}\right]$$

Look at the new matrix. The element in row 3, column 1 should be a zero. Multiply the elements in row 1 by -3 and add the result to the elements of row 3. The new matrix is:

$$\left[\begin{array}{ccc|ccc} 1 & 0 & 1 & 1 & 0 & 0 \\ 0 & -2 & -3 & -2 & 1 & 0 \\ 0 & 0 & -3 & -3 & 0 & 1 \end{array}\right]$$

We see that column 1 is in the identity form, and we move to column 2. To get a one as the element in row 2, column 2, multiply the elements in row 2 by $-\dfrac{1}{2}$. The new matrix is:

$$\left[\begin{array}{ccc|ccc} 1 & 0 & 1 & 1 & 0 & 0 \\ 0 & 1 & \dfrac{3}{2} & 1 & -\dfrac{1}{2} & 0 \\ 0 & 0 & -3 & -3 & 0 & 1 \end{array}\right]$$

Column 2 is as we want it, so we move to column 3. To get the element in row 3, column 3 as a one, divide the elements in row 3 by $-\dfrac{1}{3}$. The new matrix is:

$$\left[\begin{array}{ccc|ccc} 1 & 0 & 1 & 1 & 0 & 0 \\ 0 & 1 & \dfrac{3}{2} & 1 & -\dfrac{1}{2} & 0 \\ 0 & 0 & 1 & 1 & 0 & -\dfrac{1}{3} \end{array}\right]$$

Look at the new matrix. We need a zero in row 1, column 3. Multiply each element in row 3 by -1 and add the result to the elements in the first row. The new matrix is:

$$\left[\begin{array}{ccc|ccc} 1 & 0 & 0 & 0 & 0 & \dfrac{1}{3} \\ 0 & 1 & \dfrac{3}{2} & 1 & -\dfrac{1}{2} & 0 \\ 0 & 0 & 1 & 1 & 0 & -\dfrac{1}{3} \end{array}\right]$$

We see that a zero is needed as the element of row 2, column 3. Multiply each element in row 3 by $-\dfrac{3}{2}$ and add the result to row 2. The new matrix is:

$$\left[\begin{array}{ccc|ccc} 1 & 0 & 0 & 0 & 0 & \dfrac{1}{3} \\ 0 & 1 & 0 & -\dfrac{1}{2} & -\dfrac{1}{2} & \dfrac{1}{2} \\ 0 & 0 & 1 & 1 & 0 & -\dfrac{1}{3} \end{array}\right]$$

Look at our new matrix. The identity matrix elements are now in place on the left side of the matrix, and the inverse is seen on the right of the matrix. We can write the inverse matrix as:

$$A^{-1} = \left[\begin{array}{ccc} 0 & 0 & \dfrac{1}{3} \\ -\dfrac{1}{2} & -\dfrac{1}{2} & \dfrac{1}{2} \\ 1 & 0 & -\dfrac{1}{3} \end{array}\right].$$

Example 3 may be solved using a graphing calculator. See Chapter 6, Example 51.

Not all matrices have inverses. When attempting to find the identity matrix on the left side of an augmented matrix and a row of only zeros occurs, then an inverse matrix does not exist.

Using Matrix Inverses to Solve a System of Equations

The Inverse Method:

We can use the inverse of a matrix to help us solve systems of equations.

If we are given a system of two linear equations with two variables:

$$a_{11}x + a_{12}y = r_1$$
$$a_{21}x + a_{22}y = r_2$$

we can express this system in terms of the following matrices:

$$\begin{bmatrix} a_{11}x + a_{12}y \\ a_{21}x + a_{22}y \end{bmatrix} = \begin{bmatrix} r_1 \\ r_2 \end{bmatrix}.$$

Let $A = \begin{bmatrix} a_{11} & a_{12} \\ a_{21} & a_{22} \end{bmatrix}$ $X = \begin{bmatrix} x \\ y \end{bmatrix}$ and $C = \begin{bmatrix} r_1 \\ r_2 \end{bmatrix}$

We can now express the system written in matrix form as:

$$AX = C$$

If the inverse of A exists, we will rewrite the above matrix form as

$$X = A^{-1}C$$

and using this last line above, we can find the solution (x,y) to the given system.

Example 4. Solve the following system of equations.

$$x - y + z = 4$$
$$2x + y + 3z = 7$$
$$-x - 4y - z = 1$$

Solution: We will use the given equations in matrix form to solve this system. Let

$$A = \begin{bmatrix} 1 & -1 & 1 \\ 2 & 1 & 3 \\ -1 & -4 & -1 \end{bmatrix} \qquad X = \begin{bmatrix} x \\ y \\ z \end{bmatrix} \qquad C = \begin{bmatrix} 4 \\ 7 \\ 1 \end{bmatrix}$$

If we can find the inverse of matrix A, we can use our matrix equation:

$$X = A^{-1}C.$$

Use the method described at the beginning of this section and we find the inverse matrix A^{-1}. We calculate:

$$A^{-1} = \frac{1}{5} \begin{bmatrix} 11 & -5 & -4 \\ -1 & 0 & -1 \\ -7 & 5 & 0 \end{bmatrix}$$

Then, using $\quad X = A^{-1}C \quad$ we see:

$$\begin{bmatrix} x \\ y \\ z \end{bmatrix} = \frac{1}{5} \begin{bmatrix} 11 & -5 & -4 \\ -1 & 0 & -1 \\ -7 & 5 & 3 \end{bmatrix} \begin{bmatrix} 4 \\ 7 \\ 1 \end{bmatrix} = \begin{bmatrix} 1 \\ -1 \\ 2 \end{bmatrix}$$

We multiply the two matrices on the right side above and find the solution to the system.

The solution to the given system in this example is $(\, 1, -1, 2)$

Check:

	$x - y + z = 4$	
Given	$2x + y + 3z = 7$	Substitute the solution values into each.
	$-x - 4y - z = 1$	

$x - y + z =$	$(1) - (-1) + (2) =$	$1 + 1 + 2 = 4$	True
$2x + y + 3z =$	$2(1) + (-1) + 3(2) =$	$2 - 1 + 6 = 7$	True
$-x - 4y - z =$	$-(1) - 4(-1) - (2) =$	$-1 + 4 - 2 = 1$	True

The solution makes each equation a true statement and checks.

Example 3 can be solved using a graphing calculator. See Chapter 6, Example 51.

Section 5.5 Exercises

Find the inverse of each of the following matrices if the inverse exists.

1. $\begin{bmatrix} 1 & -1 \\ 2 & 0 \end{bmatrix}$

2. $\begin{bmatrix} -1 & -2 \\ 3 & 4 \end{bmatrix}$

3. $\begin{bmatrix} 3 & -1 \\ -5 & 2 \end{bmatrix}$

4. $\begin{bmatrix} 2 & -1 \\ 4 & 1 \end{bmatrix}$

5. $\begin{bmatrix} 1 & 2 \\ 3 & 4 \end{bmatrix}$

6. $\begin{bmatrix} 5 & 10 \\ -3 & -6 \end{bmatrix}$

7. $\begin{bmatrix} 1 & 2 \\ 3/2 & 3 \end{bmatrix}$

8. $\begin{bmatrix} 2 & 4 \\ 1 & 0 \end{bmatrix}$

9. $\begin{bmatrix} 1 & -1 & 1 \\ 2 & 1 & 0 \\ 1 & 0 & 1 \end{bmatrix}$

10. $\begin{bmatrix} 1 & 3 & 0 \\ 1 & 5 & 3 \\ 0 & 0 & 1 \end{bmatrix}$

11. $\begin{bmatrix} 2 & 2 & 2 \\ 4 & 5 & 0 \\ 0 & -1 & 3 \end{bmatrix}$

12. $\begin{bmatrix} -1 & 1 & -2 \\ 2 & 0 & 4 \\ 3 & 1 & 5 \end{bmatrix}$

13. $\begin{bmatrix} -2 & -7/2 & 2 \\ 1 & 1/2 & 0 \\ 1 & 2 & -1 \end{bmatrix}$

14. $\begin{bmatrix} 1 & 0 & 1/2 \\ 2 & 3 & 1 \\ 4 & 0 & 2 \end{bmatrix}$

15. $\begin{bmatrix} 2 & 0 & 1 \\ 1 & 2 & 2 \\ 4 & 0 & 2 \end{bmatrix}$

Solve the following systems using matrix inverses.

16. $\begin{aligned} 2x + y &= 5 \\ 3x - y &= 5 \end{aligned}$

17. $\begin{aligned} 2x + 3y &= 3 \\ 4x - y &= 13 \end{aligned}$

Section 5.6   Determinants

Every <u>square matrix</u> A is associated with a real number called the <u>determinant</u> of A.

The Determinant of a 2 x 2 matrix

The determinant of a 2 x 2 matrix A:

If $\qquad A = \begin{bmatrix} a_{11} & a_{12} \\ a_{21} & a_{22} \end{bmatrix},$

Then the **determinant** is defined as:

$$\delta(A) = \begin{vmatrix} a_{11} & a_{12} \\ a_{21} & a_{22} \end{vmatrix} = a_{11}a_{22} - a_{21}a_{12}.$$

Notice that the matrix symbol is not used with the determinant. Vertical lines are used to symbolize the determinant.

We will look at an example of finding the value of the determinant of a given matrix using the above definition.

Example 1.   If matrix $B = \begin{bmatrix} -2 & 4 \\ 6 & 8 \end{bmatrix},$

find $\delta(B)$, the determinant of matrix B.

Solution: Use the definition above to find the value of the determinant of the given 2 x 2 matrix.

From the definition $\quad \delta(B) = a_{11}a_{22} - a_{21}a_{12},$ and using the elements of the matrix

$$\delta(B) = -2(8) - 6(4) = -40$$

$$\delta(B) = -40.$$

Example 1 can be solved using a graphing calculator. See Chapter 6, Example 52.

The definition of a determinant can be extended to a 3 X 3 matrix as well.

Minors and Cofactors

Definition of Minors and Cofactors:

If $A = (a_{ij})$ is a square matrix of order n with n greater than 1, then:

1. The <u>minor M_{ij} of the element a_{ij}</u> is the determinant of the matrix of order $n-1$ obtained by deleting row i and column j from the given matrix.

2. The of <u>cofactor A_{ij} the element a_{ij}</u> is $A_{ij} = (-1)^{i+j} M_{ij}$

The above definition of a minor says that to find the minor of any element we delete the row and column in which the element appears and find the determinant of the resulting square matrix.

The cofactor is the minor with the appropriate sign attached.

Example 2:   Examples of minors and cofactors.

Matrix	Minor	Cofactor
$\begin{bmatrix} a_{11} & a_{12} & a_{13} \\ a_{21} & a_{22} & a_{23} \\ a_{31} & a_{32} & a_{33} \end{bmatrix}$	$M_{11} = \begin{vmatrix} a_{22} & a_{23} \\ a_{32} & a_{33} \end{vmatrix}$ $= a_{22}a_{33} - a_{32}a_{23}$	$A_{11} = (-1)^{1+1} M_{11} = M_{11}$
$\begin{bmatrix} a_{11} & a_{12} & a_{13} \\ a_{21} & a_{22} & a_{23} \\ a_{31} & a_{32} & a_{33} \end{bmatrix}$	$M_{12} = \begin{vmatrix} a_{21} & a_{23} \\ a_{31} & a_{33} \end{vmatrix}$ $= a_{21}a_{33} - a_{31}a_{23}$	$A_{12} = (-1)^{1+2} M_{12} = -M_{12}$
$\begin{bmatrix} a_{11} & a_{12} & a_{13} \\ a_{21} & a_{22} & a_{23} \\ a_{31} & a_{32} & a_{33} \end{bmatrix}$	$M_{23} = \begin{vmatrix} a_{11} & a_{12} \\ a_{31} & a_{32} \end{vmatrix}$ $= a_{11}a_{32} - a_{31}a_{12}$	$A_{23} = (-1)^{2+3} M_{23} = -M_{23}$

There are six other minors for the given 3 x 3 matrix that can be obtained in a similar manner.

To remember the sign associated with each cofactor, look at the following chart.

$$\begin{bmatrix} + & - & + & - & \ldots \\ - & + & - & + & \ldots \\ + & - & + & - & \ldots \\ - & + & - & + & \ldots \\ . & . & . & . & \\ . & . & . & . & \\ . & . & . & . & \end{bmatrix}$$

Example 3. Given matrix A

$$A = \begin{bmatrix} 1 & -2 & 3 \\ 4 & 2 & 5 \\ 2 & -7 & 0 \end{bmatrix} \quad \text{find minors } M_{11}, \ M_{21}, \ M_{22}, \text{ and cofactors } A_{11}, \ A_{21}, \ A_{22}.$$

Solution : Delete the appropriate rows and columns of A

$$M_{11} = \begin{vmatrix} 2 & 5 \\ -7 & 0 \end{vmatrix} = (2)(0) - (-7)(5) = 35$$

$$M_{21} = \begin{vmatrix} -2 & 3 \\ -7 & 0 \end{vmatrix} = (-2)(0) - (-7)(3) = 21$$

$$M_{22} = \begin{vmatrix} 1 & 3 \\ 2 & 0 \end{vmatrix} = (1)(0) - (2)(3) = -6$$

$$A_{11} = (-1)^{1+1} M_{11} = (1)(35) = 35$$

$$A_{21} = (-1)^{2+1} M_{21} = (-1)(21) = -21$$

$$A_{22} = (-1)^{2+2} M_{22} = (1)(-6) = -6$$

Determinant of a Square Matrix of Order 3

The determinant $\delta(A)$ of a square matrix of order 3:

$$\delta(A) = \begin{vmatrix} a_{11} & a_{12} & a_{13} \\ a_{21} & a_{22} & a_{23} \\ a_{31} & a_{32} & a_{33} \end{vmatrix} = a_{11}A_{11} + a_{12}A_{12} + a_{13}A_{13}$$

where a represents an element and A represents that element's cofactor.

Note that cofactors $A_{11} = (-1)^{1+1} M_{11} = M_{11}$, $A_{12} = (-1)^{1+2} M_{12} = -M_{12}$, and $A_{13} = (-1)^{1+3} M_{13} = M_{13}$.

Finding the Determinant of a Square Matrix of Order 3

To find the determinant $\delta(A)$ of a square matrix of order 3:
1. Use the elements of row 1.
2. Find the minor of each element in row 1.
3. Add the necessary signs.
4. Then the determinant for the matrix becomes:

$$\delta(A) = a_{11} M_{11} - a_{12} M_{12} + a_{13} M_{13}.$$

Example 4. Given matrix A. Find the determinant of A.

$$A = \begin{bmatrix} -1 & 3 & 2 \\ 1 & 4 & 0 \\ 3 & -2 & 5 \end{bmatrix}$$

Solution: We will use the definition: $\delta(A) = a_{11} M_{11} - a_{12} M_{12} + a_{13} M_{13}$

$$\delta(A) = -1 \begin{vmatrix} 4 & 0 \\ -2 & 5 \end{vmatrix} - 3 \begin{vmatrix} 1 & 0 \\ 3 & 5 \end{vmatrix} + 2 \begin{vmatrix} 1 & 4 \\ 3 & -2 \end{vmatrix}$$

$$= -1(4*5 - (-2*0)) - 3(1*5 - 3*0) + 2(1*(-2) - 3*4)$$

$$= -1(20) - 3(5) + 2(-14) = -20 - 15 - 28 = -63$$

Example 4 can be solved using a graphing calculator. See Chapter 6, Example 53.

Cramer's Rule

We have already learned how to solve systems of linear equations using the elimination method. **We can also use determinants to solve a system of linear equations**.

Given a general system of two linear equations in two variables:

$$a_1 x + b_1 y = c_1$$
$$a_2 x + b_2 y = c_2$$

To eliminate y and solve for x, we multiply both sides of equation (1) above by b_2 and multiply equation (2) above by $-b_1$ and then add the two new equations:

$$
\begin{aligned}
a_1 b_2 x + b_1 b_2 y &= c_1 b_2 \\
-a_2 b_1 x - b_1 b_2 y &= -c_2 b_1 \\
\hline
(a_1 b_2 - a_2 b_1)x \quad &= c_1 b_2 - c_2 b_1
\end{aligned}
$$

Solve for x:

$$x = \frac{c_1 b_2 - c_2 b_1}{a_1 b_2 - a_2 b_1}$$

To eliminate x and solve for y, multiply both sides of equation (1) by $-a_2$ and multiply equation (2) by a_1, and then add the two new equations.

$$
\begin{aligned}
-a_1 a_2 x - a_2 b_1 y &= -a_2 c_1 \\
a_1 a_2 x + a_1 b_2 y &= \quad a_1 c_2 \\
\hline
(a_1 b_2 - a_2 b_1)y &= a_1 c_2 - a_2 c_1
\end{aligned}
$$

Solve for y:

$$y = \frac{a_1 c_2 - a_2 c_1}{a_1 b_2 - a_2 b_1}$$

Both numerators and the common denominator of these fractional values for x and y can be written as determinants since

$$c_1 b_2 - c_2 b_1 = \begin{vmatrix} c_1 & b_1 \\ c_2 & b_2 \end{vmatrix} ; \qquad a_1 c_2 - a_2 c_1 = \begin{vmatrix} a_1 & c_1 \\ a_2 & c_2 \end{vmatrix} ; \qquad \text{and} \qquad a_1 b_2 - a_2 b_1 = \begin{vmatrix} a_1 & b_1 \\ a_2 & b_2 \end{vmatrix}$$

Cramer's Rule is the result.

Cramer's Rule for a 2 x 2 System

Cramer's Rule for 2 x 2 Systems:

Given the system: $\quad \begin{aligned} a_1 x + b_1 y &= c_1 \\ a_2 x + b_2 y &= c_2 \end{aligned}$

With $a_1 b_2 - a_2 b_1 \neq 0,$

$$x = \frac{\begin{vmatrix} c_1 & b_1 \\ c_2 & b_2 \end{vmatrix}}{\begin{vmatrix} a_1 & b_1 \\ a_2 & b_2 \end{vmatrix}} \qquad \text{and} \qquad y = \frac{\begin{vmatrix} a_1 & c_1 \\ a_2 & c_2 \end{vmatrix}}{\begin{vmatrix} a_1 & b_1 \\ a_2 & b_2 \end{vmatrix}}$$

A shorthand way of writing these two solutions is shown.

$$\begin{vmatrix} a_1 & b_1 \\ a_2 & b_2 \end{vmatrix} = D \qquad \begin{vmatrix} c_1 & b_1 \\ c_2 & b_2 \end{vmatrix} = D_x \qquad \begin{vmatrix} a_1 & c_1 \\ a_2 & c_2 \end{vmatrix} = D_y$$

Then Cramer's Rule can be written as:

$$x = \frac{D_x}{D} \qquad \text{and} \qquad y = \frac{D_y}{D} \qquad \text{where } D \neq 0$$

We will study example 5 to better understand the use of Cramer's Rule.

Example 5. Solve the following system using Cramer's Rule.

$$4x + 6y = 1$$
$$3x + 5y = -2$$

Solution: Using Cramer's Rule, we will solve for D, D_x, and D_y.

$$D = \begin{vmatrix} 4 & 6 \\ 3 & 5 \end{vmatrix} = 4*5 - 3*6 = 20 - 18 = 2$$

$$D_x = \begin{vmatrix} 1 & 6 \\ -2 & 5 \end{vmatrix} = 1*5 - (-2)*6 = 5 + 12 = 17$$

$$D_y = \begin{vmatrix} 4 & 1 \\ 3 & -2 \end{vmatrix} = 4*(-2) - 3*1 = -8 - 3 = -11$$

Using Cramer's rule we can solve for x and y :

$$x = \frac{D_x}{D} = \frac{17}{2} \qquad\qquad y = \frac{D_y}{D} = \frac{-11}{2}$$

The solution set to the given system is: $\left(\dfrac{17}{2}, -\dfrac{11}{2} \right)$.

Check: Test the solution values into the given system.

$$\begin{array}{l} 4x + 6y = 1 \\ 3x + 5y = -2 \end{array} \quad \text{using } x = \frac{17}{2}, \quad y = -\frac{11}{2}.$$

Equation 1:

$$4\left(\frac{17}{2}\right) + 6\left(-\frac{11}{2}\right) = \frac{68}{2} - \frac{66}{2} = \frac{2}{2} = 1 \qquad\qquad \text{True}$$

Equation 2:

$$3\left(\frac{17}{2}\right) + 5\left(-\frac{11}{2}\right) = \frac{51}{2} - \frac{55}{2} = -\frac{4}{2} - 2 \qquad\qquad \text{True}$$

Cramer's Rule can be generalized to include larger systems of equations.

Cramer's Rule for a 3 x 3 System

Cramer's Rule for 3 x 3 Systems:

Given the system:
$$a_1 x + b_1 y + c_1 z = d_1$$
$$a_2 x + b_2 y + c_2 z = d_2$$
$$a_3 x + b_3 y + c_3 z = d_3$$

With

$$D_x = \begin{vmatrix} d_1 & b_1 & c_1 \\ d_2 & b_2 & c_2 \\ d_3 & b_3 & c_3 \end{vmatrix} \qquad D_y = \begin{vmatrix} a_1 & d_1 & c_1 \\ a_2 & d_2 & c_2 \\ a_3 & d_3 & c_3 \end{vmatrix}$$

$$D_z = \begin{vmatrix} a_1 & b_1 & d_1 \\ a_2 & b_2 & d_2 \\ a_3 & b_3 & d_3 \end{vmatrix} \qquad D = \begin{vmatrix} a_1 & b_1 & c_1 \\ a_2 & b_2 & c_2 \\ a_3 & b_3 & c_3 \end{vmatrix}$$

Then the solution to the system would be defined as:

$$x = \frac{D_x}{D} \qquad y = \frac{D_y}{D} \qquad \text{and} \quad z = \frac{D_z}{D}$$

Example 6. Solve the following system using Cramer's Rule.

$$2x - y + 4z = -2$$
$$3x + 2y - z = -3$$
$$x + 4y + 2z = 17$$

Solution: Use Cramer's Rule for a 3 x 3 system. Begin by evaluating the needed determinants.

Find $D, D_x, D_y, and D_z$

$$D = \begin{vmatrix} 2 & -1 & 4 \\ 3 & 2 & -1 \\ 1 & 4 & 2 \end{vmatrix}$$

$$= 2(2*2 - 4*(-1)) - (-1)(3*2 - 1*(-1)) + 4(3*4 - 1*2) = 63$$

$$D_x = \begin{vmatrix} -2 & -1 & 4 \\ -3 & 2 & -1 \\ 17 & 4 & 2 \end{vmatrix}$$

$$= -2(2*2 - 4(-1)) + 1((-3)2 - 17(-1)) + 4((-3)4 - 17*2) = -189$$

Using the same process, we can find D_y and D_z.

$$D_y = \begin{vmatrix} 2 & -2 & 4 \\ 3 & -3 & -1 \\ 1 & 17 & 2 \end{vmatrix} = 252$$

$$D_z = \begin{vmatrix} 2 & -1 & -2 \\ 3 & 2 & -3 \\ 1 & 4 & 17 \end{vmatrix} = 126$$

Use Cramer's Rule, and solve for the three variables.

$$x = \frac{D_x}{D} = \frac{-189}{63} = -3$$

$$y = \frac{D_y}{D} = \frac{252}{63} = 4$$

$$z = \frac{D_z}{D} = \frac{126}{63} = 2$$

The solution to the given system is: $(-3, 4, 2)$.

Check: To check we will substitute our solution values into the given system of equations.

$$2x - y + 4z = -2$$

Given $3x + 2y - z = -3$ Check each equation.

$$x + 4y + 2z = 17$$

$2x - y + 4z =$	$2(-3) - (4) + 4(2) =$	$-6 - 4 + 8 \;\; = -2$ **True**
$3x + 2y - z =$	$3(-3) + 2(4) - (2) =$	$-9 + 8 - 2 \;\; = -3$ **True**
$x + 4y + 2z =$	$(-3) + 4(4) + 2(2) =$	$-3 + 16 + 4 = 17$ **True**

The solution to the given system is correct because the values make each equation a true statement.

Section 5.6 Exercises:

Find the value of each given determinant.

1. $\begin{vmatrix} -3 & \sqrt{6} \\ -\sqrt{6} & 2 \end{vmatrix}$

2. $\begin{vmatrix} \sqrt{2} & -1 \\ 5 & 2 \end{vmatrix}$

3. $\begin{vmatrix} x^2 & 3 \\ x & x^2 \end{vmatrix}$

4. $\begin{vmatrix} t^3 & -1 \\ t^2 & 2 \end{vmatrix}$

5. $\begin{vmatrix} -3 & -2 & 4 \\ 2 & -1 & 2 \\ -1 & 2 & 2 \end{vmatrix}$

6. $\begin{vmatrix} p & -2 & 0 \\ 1 & p & 1 \\ 3 & p & 2 \end{vmatrix}$

7. $\begin{vmatrix} s & 5 & -1 \\ 2 & s & -1 \\ 3 & 2 & -2 \end{vmatrix}$

8. $\begin{vmatrix} y^2 & y & -1 \\ y & 1 & -1 \\ 1 & 2 & 2 \end{vmatrix}$

Answer the following questions using the given matrix B.

$$B = \begin{bmatrix} 6 & -2 & 3 \\ 2 & 1 & 0 \\ 1 & -1 & 2 \end{bmatrix}$$

9. Find $M_{12}, M_{23},$ and M_{31}.

10. Find $M_{22}, M_{33},$ and M_{11}.

11. Find $B_{12}, B_{23},$ and B_{31}.

12. Find $B_{22}, B_{33},$ and B_{11}.

13. Find the determinant of B.

Solve each given system using Cramer's Rule.

14. $\begin{aligned} 2x - 3y &= 4 \\ x + 2y &= 6 \end{aligned}$

15. $\begin{aligned} 4x - 3y &= -3 \\ 7x + 2y &= 6 \end{aligned}$

16. $\begin{aligned} 4x + 2y &= 8 \\ -5x - 3y &= -12 \end{aligned}$

17. $\begin{aligned} 3x + 4y &= 2 \\ 5x - 7y &= -2 \end{aligned}$

18. $\begin{aligned} 3x - 5y &= 2 \\ 7x + 2y &= 9 \end{aligned}$

19. $\begin{aligned} x + y - z &= -2 \\ 2x - y + z &= -5 \\ x - 2y + 3z &= 4 \end{aligned}$

20. $\begin{aligned} x + 2y &= 10 \\ 3x + 4z &= 7 \\ -y - z &= 1 \end{aligned}$

Chapter 5 Summary

<u>Solving Systems of linear equations</u>:
1. Graph both equations and find the point of intersection.
2. Use the Substitution Method.
3. Use the Addition Method.

<u>Substitution Method</u>:
1. Solve one of the equations for one of the variables.
2. Substitute this solution into the other equation and thus get an equation in only one variable.
3. Find the solution to this new equation found in step 2.
4, Substitute the solution found in step 3 back into one of the original equations to find the value of the other variable.
5. Check the solution in both of the given equations.

<u>Addition Method</u>:
1. Multiply both sides of each equation by suitable numbers, so that when the equations are added, one of the variables is eliminated.
2. Add the two new equations.
3. The result of the addition is a new equation in only one variable.
4. Solve this single variable equation.
5. Substitute the solution back into one of the original equations to find the value of the second variable.
6. Check the solutions in both of the given equations.

<u>To Solve a System with Three Variables</u>:
1. Eliminate the same variable from each of two pairs of equations.
2. Then using the resulting equations, eliminate another variable.
3. The result of step 2 will be an equation with only one variable.
4. Solve this equation for the value of the variable.
5. Substitute this value in one of the equations found in step 1.
6. Solve for a second variable.
7. Substitute both of the values of the variables back into one of the original equations to find the value of the third variable.
8. It is helpful to number the equations as you go.

Steps for graphing an inequality with two variables:

1. Graph the line that would result if the inequality sign were changed to an = sign.
2. The line will divide the graph into 2 half-planes. One of these is the solution set.
3. To determine which half-plane (the one above or below the line) is the solution, pick a test point and see if this test point satisfies the given inequality.
4. If the test point satisfies the given inequality, shade the half-plane that includes the point.
5. If the test point does not satisfy the given inequality, shade the other side of the line.
6. Make the line a solid line if the inequality symbol is either $\geq$ or $\leq$.
7. Make the line a dotted line if the inequality symbol is either > or < .

Row operations on Matrices:

1. Any two rows can be interchanged.
2. All of the elements of a row can be multiplied by the same nonzero constant.
3. One row can be multiplied by a nonzero constant and then added to another row.

Row-Echelon Form of a Matrix:

A matrix is in row-echelon form if:

1. Unless the row has all 0's, the first nonzero element in the row is a 1.
2. For any 2 successive rows, the leading 1 in the upper row is to the left of the leading 1 in the lower row.
3. All of the rows that contain only zeros are at the bottom of the matrix.

To find the inverse of a square matrix:

1. Make a matrix that is a combination of the given matrix followed by an identity matrix of the same order.
2. Use elementary row operations to change the new matrix so that the identity matrix portion appears as the first matrix of the combination.
3. The second section of the combined matrix is the inverse.

Matrix Solution of Systems of Equations

For a system of n equations, write in Matrix Form:

$$AX = B$$

If the matrix has an inverse, then

$$X = A^{-1}B$$

Determinant

The determinant of a 2×2 matrix A

$$A = \begin{bmatrix} a_{11} & a_{12} \\ a_{21} & a_{22} \end{bmatrix},$$

is defined as

$$\delta(A) = \begin{vmatrix} a_{11} & a_{12} \\ a_{21} & a_{22} \end{vmatrix} = a_{11}a_{22} - a_{21}a_{12}$$

The determinant $\delta(A)$ of a square matrix of order 3:

$$\delta(A) = \begin{vmatrix} a_{11} & a_{12} & a_{13} \\ a_{21} & a_{22} & a_{23} \\ a_{31} & a_{32} & a_{33} \end{vmatrix} = a_{11}A_{11} + a_{12}A_{12} + a_{13}A_{13}$$

Cramer's Rule for 2×2 Systems:

Given the system:

$$a_1 x + b_1 y = c_1$$
$$a_2 x + b_2 y = c_2$$

With $a_1 b_2 - a_2 b_1 \neq 0$,

$$x = \frac{\begin{vmatrix} c_1 & b_1 \\ c_2 & b_2 \end{vmatrix}}{\begin{vmatrix} a_1 & b_1 \\ a_2 & b_2 \end{vmatrix}} \qquad \text{and} \qquad y = \frac{\begin{vmatrix} a_1 & c_1 \\ a_2 & c_2 \end{vmatrix}}{\begin{vmatrix} a_1 & b_1 \\ a_2 & b_2 \end{vmatrix}}$$

A shorthand way of writing these solutions is shown.

$$\begin{vmatrix} a_1 & b_1 \\ a_2 & b_2 \end{vmatrix} = D \qquad \begin{vmatrix} c_1 & b_1 \\ c_2 & b_2 \end{vmatrix} = D_x \qquad \begin{vmatrix} a_1 & c_1 \\ a_2 & c_2 \end{vmatrix} = D_y$$

Using this shorthand, we can find the variable values as:

$$x = \frac{D_x}{D} \qquad \text{and} \qquad y = \frac{D_y}{D} \qquad \text{where } D \neq 0$$

Cramer's Rule for 3 x 3 Systems:

Given the system:
$$a_1 x + b_1 y + c_1 z = d_1$$
$$a_2 x + b_2 y + c_2 z = d_2$$
$$a_3 x + b_3 y + c_3 z = d_3$$

With

$$D_x = \begin{vmatrix} d_1 & b_1 & c_1 \\ d_2 & b_2 & c_2 \\ d_3 & b_3 & c_3 \end{vmatrix} \qquad D_y = \begin{vmatrix} a_1 & d_1 & c_1 \\ a_2 & d_2 & c_2 \\ a_3 & d_3 & c_3 \end{vmatrix}$$

$$D_z = \begin{vmatrix} a_1 & b_1 & d_1 \\ a_2 & b_2 & d_2 \\ a_3 & b_3 & d_3 \end{vmatrix} \qquad D = \begin{vmatrix} a_1 & b_1 & c_1 \\ a_2 & b_2 & c_2 \\ a_3 & b_3 & c_3 \end{vmatrix}$$

$$x = \frac{D_x}{D} \qquad y = \frac{D_y}{D} \qquad \text{and} \quad z = \frac{D_z}{D}$$

Chapter 5 Review

Graph the following system of inequalities.

1. $2x - 3y < 5$
   $x + 2y > 3$

2. $x \geq y$
   $x + y \leq 0$

Solve each given system.

3. $x - 3y = -1$
   $2x + 2y = 6$

4. $2x + 3y = -1$
   $x - 2y = -4$

5. $4x + 2y - 2z = 4$
   $3x + 9y + 6z = 3$
   $2x + 2y + 2z = 4$

6. $2x + y + z = 9$
   $-x - y + z = 1$
   $6x - 2y + 2z = 18$

Write an equivalent matrix equation. Solve the system of equations using the inverse of the coefficient matrix.

7. $4x + 6y = 14$
   $2x - y = 3$

8. $2x + 3y - 4z = 6$
   $3x - y + 2z = 1$
   $-x + 4y - 3z = 5$

Find the value of each given determinant.

9. $\begin{vmatrix} 7 & -2 \\ 3 & -2 \end{vmatrix}$

10. $\begin{vmatrix} 1 & -2 & 0 \\ 2 & 1 & 4 \\ 3 & 3 & 1 \end{vmatrix}$

11. $\begin{vmatrix} -2 & 3 & 1 \\ 3 & -1 & 4 \\ -1 & 1 & 5 \end{vmatrix}$

Solve each system using Cramer's Rule.

12. $2x + 3y = 1$
    $x - 4y = -1$

13. $2x - 4y = 0$
    $5x - 6y = 4$

14. $3x - y + 2z = 4$
    $4x + 6y - 3z = 7$
    $5x - 4z + 3y = 4$

15. $5x - y + 3z = 8$
    $3x + 7y - 5z = 20$
    $4x - 3y + 7z = 2$

16. $x + 2y = 7$
    $4x - 3y = 1$

17. $5x - 3y = -1$
    $4x + 7y = 2$

CHAPTER 6
SOLUTIONS USING GRAPHING CALCULATOR

Example 1:
   If $f(x) = 2x^2 - 2x + 4$ find each of the following:
   a. $f(-2)$
   b. $f(0)$

Enter the equation into $Y_1 =$ and then either use the **TABLE** feature in the **ASK** mode or use the **VALUE** feature found in the **CALC** menu.
With either of these methods, we find that $f(-2) = 16$ and $f(0) = 4$.

Example 2:
Linear Regression Problem: Find the line of best fit that approximates the following data on world record times for the women's 100 meter dash.

Year	Time in Seconds
1952	11.4
1960	11.3
1972	11.07
1984	10.76

Enter the data: we will enter the years in L1, times in L2 using the **TABLE** feature.

1. Select **STAT**, then **Edit**, and the lists are visible on the home screen.
Clear all Y assignments and lists.
A list can be cleared by placing the cursor on the list name and pressing:

   CLEAR   and   ▼

2. Use the following: **STAT**   1
   1952   ENTER   1960   ENTER
   1972   ENTER   1984   ENTER
   ▲ 4times   ►
   11.4   ENTER   11.3   ENTER
   11.07 ENTER   10.76 ENTER

3. Find the best regression line:
   STAT ► **CALC** 4

4. Screen will show: LinReg($ax+b$)   Y$_1$

        ...

        LinReg

        y=$ax+b$

        $a=-0.0201190476$

        $b=50.70666667$

From this screen, we see that the regression line has the approximate equation
$y = -0.02x + 50.71$.

Example 3:
Relative Maxima and Minima Problem:

Use a graphing calculator to determine any relative maxima or minima of the function:
$$f(x) = 0.2x^3 - 0.8x^2 - 0.2x + 4$$

Solution:

First, graph the function: Set $Y_1 = 0.2x^3 - 0.8x^2 - 0.2x + 4$.

Adjust the window until a nice curve is seen. ($-10, 10, 1, -10, 10, 1. 1$)

Use the MAXIMUM and MINIMUM keys found in the CALC menu to find each relative maximum and minimum. Move the cursor to the left bound, right bound and guess value at each maximum and minimum.

The relative <u>maximum value</u> of the function is the y-value at the maximum point and is approximately 4.012 when the x-value is -0.119

The relative minimum value is 1.558 with an x-value of 2.786

Look at the graph: it is rising from the left and stops rising at the relative maximum.

From this point the graph decreases until it reaches the relative minimum, and then it begins to rise again.

<u>The function is increasing on the intervals</u> (use the x-values to represent intervals<u>:</u>

       ($-\infty, -0.119$) and ($1.558, \infty$),

<u>and decreasing on the interval</u>:

       ($-0.119, 1.558$).

Example 4:

Given $f(x) = 3x - 4$ and $g(x) = x^2 - 2x + 6$.

We found $(f \circ g)(5) = 59$ and

$$(g \circ f)(5) = 105.$$

Check these results using a graphing calculator.

1. On the equation screen we will enter: $Y_1 = 3x - 4$ for *f(x)* and
$$Y_2 = x^2 - 2x + 6 \text{ for } g(x).$$

2. On the home screen use the **VARS** function, then select **Y-VARS** to write $Y_1(Y_2(5))$ and $Y_2(Y_1(5))$.

The results are 59 and 105.

Example 5:

Determine if $x^2 + y^2 = 9$ is symmetric to the *x*-axis, the *y*-axis and the origin.

Graph this equation in two parts. Begin by solving the original equation for *y*. Enter the two solutions as:

Set $Y_1 = \sqrt{9 - x^2}$

Set $Y_2 = -\sqrt{9 - x^2}$

The graph is a circle with center at the origin and a radius of 3. Adjust the *y*-values in the Window to see a circle. Looking at the graph we see:

1. If the graph were folded on the *x*-axis, the parts of the graph above and below the axis are the same. Thus, there is symmetry on the *x*-axis.

2. If the graph were folded on the *y*-axis, the parts of the graph to the left and right of the axis are the same. Thus, there is symmetry on the *y*-axis.

3. If the graph is rotated 180°, the resulting graph is the same as the original graph. Thus, there is symmetry around the origin.

331

Example 6:

Test $y = x^2 + 4$ for symmetry to the x-axis, the y-axis and the origin.

Use a graphing calculator to graph the equation:

$Y_1 = x^2 + 4$

Look at what happens when folding the graph to determine symmetry. If the graph were folded along the x-axis, the parts on either side of the axis do not coincide. The equation is **not symmetric with respect to the x-axis**.

If the graph were folded along the y-axis, the parts on the left and right of the axis would coincide so the graph **is symmetric with respect to the y-axis**.

If the graph is rotated $180°$, the resulting graph is not the same as the original graph. Thus, there is **no symmetry around the origin**.

Example 7:

Are the given functions even, odd, or neither?

a. $f(x) = 2x^5 - x^3 + 4x$ b. $f(x) = 4x^4 + x^2$

a.   Graph setting $Y_1 = 2x^5 - x^3 + 4x$. Adjust the window to see the graph.

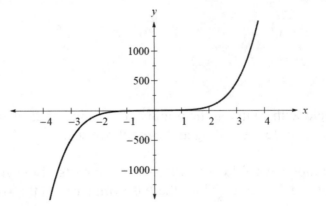

When looking at the graph, it appears that the function is symmetric with respect to the origin. Thus, **the function is odd**.

b. $f(x) = 4x^4 + x^2$

Set $Y_1 = 4x^4 + x^2$ and graph.   Adjust the Window as needed.

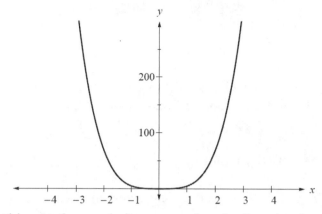

When looking at the graph, it appears that the function is symmetric with respect to the y-axis. Thus, **the function is even**.

Example 8.
For each , describe how the graph can be obtained from one of the basic graphs of x^2, x^3, and $|x|$

    a. $h(x) = x^2 - 4$ b. $h(x) = (x-3)^2$

    c $h(x) = |x| + 2$ d. $h(x) = |x-2|$

    e. $h(x) = x^3 + 1$ f. $h(x) = (x-3)^3$

Solution:

For each of these exercises graph the basic function and then the translated function and compare the two graphs.

    a. For $h(x) = x^2 - 4$,

        Set $Y_1 = x^2$ and   Set $Y_2 = x^2 - 4$. Then graph.
        Two graphs are drawn. The first is the basic graph and the second is the
        translated graph. The translation is: **down 4 units.**

    b. $h(x) = (x-3)^2$:   Use $Y_1 = x^2$ and $Y_2 = (x-3)^2$: **right 3 units.**

    c. $h(x) = |x| + 2$:   Use $Y_1 = |x|$ and $Y_2 = |x| + 2$: **up 2 units.**
             Absolute value function is found in **MATH, NUM** screen.

    d. $h(x) = |x-2|$:   Use $Y_1 = |x|$ and $Y_2 = |x-2|$: **right 2 units.**
             Absolute value function is found in **MATH, NUM** screen.

    e. $h(x) = x^3 + 1$:   Use $Y_1 = x^3$ and $Y_2 = x^3 + 1$: **up 1 unit.**

    f. $h(x) = (x-3)^3$ Use $Y_1 = x^3$ and $Y_2 = (x-3)^3$: **right 3 units.**

Example 9.

Solve: $4x - 3 = 2$.

Solution:
Use a graphing calculator to graph each side of this equation and then use the
INTERSECT feature on the **CALC** menu to find the solution.

1. Graph by setting

$$Y_1 = 4x - 3 \quad \text{and} \quad Y_2 = 2.$$

2. Use the **INTERSECT** on **CALC** screen to find where the two graphs intersect.   .

 The x-value of the intersection point is the solution to the equation.
We find this value to be 1.25.

If the solution is a rational number, we can change the answer to fraction form instead of
decimal form by using the **FRAC▶** on the **MATH** screen. (Enter 1.25 **FRAC▶**)
      The solution is the fraction 5/4.

Example 10:

Solve: $2(4 - 2x) = 5 - 3(x + 1)$

Solution: Use the **INTERSECT** feature on the **CALC** menu on a graphing calculator to
find the solution of the equation.

Set $Y_1 = 2(4 - 2x)$ and $Y_2 = 5 - 3(x + 1)$.

Use the **INTERSECT** in the **CALC** menu to find where the two graphs intersect.
Adjust the Window to see the intersection point if necessary. The x-value
of the intersection point is the solution to the equation. We find this value to be 6.

Example 11:

Find the zero of $f(x) = 6x - 3$.

Solution: Use the **ZERO** feature from the **CALC** menu to find the zero of

$$f(x) = 6x - 3$$

Set $Y_1 = 6x - 3$ and then graph.

Next, select the **CALC** menu and then choose **ZERO**.

We must enter a left and right bound and the guess choice on the x-intercept to get the result.

$$x = .5 \quad y = 0 \quad \text{and the point } (.5, 0) \text{ is the intercept}$$

The **zero is the x-coordinate of the x-intercept** and is 0.5.

Example 12:
  Add the given complex numbers and then simplify the result:

  a. $(7 + 4i) + (9 + 5i)$:

  Set the calculator to "$a + bi$" MODE, and then enter the complex numbers using the i key.
  $(7 + 4i) + (9 + 5i)$.   The i key is often located above the period key.

  The result is $16 + 9i$.

Example 13:
  Multiply and simplify the following complex numbers:

  a. $(1 - 3i)(1 + 2i)$ \qquad\qquad b. $(4 - 2i)^2$

Solution:

  Set the calculator to $a + bi$ **MODE**. Enter the problem as:

  a. $(1 - 3i)(1 + 2i)$ \qquad the result is: $7 - i$.

  b. $(4 - 2i)^2$ \qquad the result is: $12 - 16i$.

Example 14:

  Express in the form $a + bi$, where a and b are real numbers:

  $$\frac{2 - i}{3 - 4i}$$

Solution:

Set the calculator to $a+bi$ MODE, and then enter the problem as:

$$(2-i)/(3-4i)$$

The result is $0.4+0.2i$ or in fraction form is $\dfrac{2}{5}+\dfrac{1}{5}i$.

Example 15.

Solve: $x^2-3x+2=0$.

Solution:

The solutions of the equation $x^2-3x+2=0$ are the zeros of the function $f(x)=x^2-3x+2$.

Solutions are also the first coordinates of the x-intercepts of the graph of $f(x)=x^2-3x+2$.

Set $Y_1=x^2-3x+2$. Graph.

Look carefully and you will see two x-intercepts. Use the **ZERO** option in the **CALCULATE** menu. The x-value of one zero is 1 which is one of the solutions. The x-value of the other zero is 2 which is the other solution.

Solutions are: 1, 2.

Example 16.

Solve: $x^2-4x+1=0$.

Solution:

Set $Y_1=x^2-4x+1$ and graph the equation. There are two intercepts.

Use the **ZERO** feature in the **CALC** menu.

Use left bound, right bound and guess options to find each zero.

The x-values of the zeros are the solutions, and

$x=0.2679$ and 3.7321.

Example 17.

Solve $\dfrac{1}{2} - \dfrac{x-2}{3} = \dfrac{1}{6}$.

Solution:

Set Y_1 equal to the left side of the equation, and

Y_2 equal to the right side of the equation.
Graph.

Select the CALC option and choose INTERSECT.

The *x-coordinate* of the point of intersection of the two graphs is the solution to the equation.

The solution is: 3.

Example 18.

For the equation, $\dfrac{1}{x} + \dfrac{1}{x-3} = \dfrac{x-2}{x-3}$,   check the solutions of 3 and 1.

Solution:

Set Y_1 equal to the left side of the equation $Y_1 = 1/x + 1/(x-3)$, and

Y_2 equal to the right side of the equation $Y_2 = (x-2)/(x-3)$.

Use the **TABLE** method:

Look at the table values.
If $x = 1$, then $Y_1 = 0.5$ and $Y_2 = 0.5$.

If $x = 3$, then $Y_1 = $ ERROR and $Y_2 = $ ERROR

Thus $x = 1$ is a solution but $x = 3$ is not.

Example 19.

Solve $|x+1| + 4 = 7$

Solution: We will use $Y_1 = |x + 1| + 4$ by using the **ABS** function found in **MATH** then **NUM.**

> Set $Y_1 = \mathbf{abs}(x + 1) + 4.$
> Set $Y_2 = 7$
> and GRAPH.

Use the **CALC** menu and select the **INTERSECT** option.

Find the x- coordinates of the points of intersection.

The solutions are $x = 2$ and $x = -4$.

Example 20.
> Solve: $2x - 4 < 6 - 3x$

Solution: Set $Y_1 = 2x - 4$

$$Y_2 = 6 - 3x$$

Then use the **GRAPH** key.

The graph shows that for x values where $x < 2$, the graph of Y_1 lies below the graph of Y_2.

Therefore, on the interval $(-\infty, 2)$ we see from the graphs that $Y_1 < Y_2$.

Example 21.
> Find the zeros of $f(x) = x^3 - 2x^2 - 4x + 8$ and describe the graph at the location of these zeros.

Solution: Set $Y_1 = x^3 - 2x^2 - 4x + 8$.

Then use the GRAPH key to see the graph.

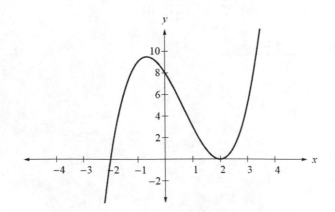

The graph shows that zeros occur at the x-values of -2 and 2.

Notice that the graph at the zero of -2 crosses the axis, and thus this zero of -2 has an odd multiplicity.

At the zero of 2 the graph is tangent to the axis (touches the axis but does not cross it), and thus this zero has an even multiplicity.

Example 22.

   Given $f(x) = 0.5x^3 - 0.9x^2 - 0.8x + 1$. Find the zeros of $f(x)$.

Solution: Set $Y_1 = 0.5x^3 - 0.9x^2 - 0.8x + 1$.

Graph the function and use the **ZERO** feature found in **CALC** to find the zeros of the function:

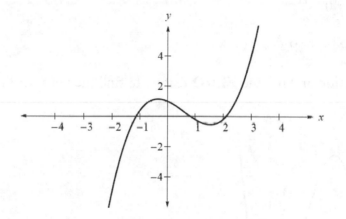

Select the **CALC** menu and select the **ZERO** feature. For each zero, use left bound, right bound, and guess options to find the zero.

The three zeros seen on the graph are:

   $x = -1.140,\ 0.831,\ \text{and}\ 2.105$.

Example 23.

Given $f(x) = 3x^4 - 5x^3 - 2x^2 + x - 4$, find $f(6)$.

Solution:

Set $Y_1 = 3x^4 - 5x^3 - 2x^2 + x - 4$ and go to the home screen.

Use the **VARS** menu to locate the **Y-Vars** option.

Select **Function**, then select Y_1 and then Y_1 will appear on the home screen.

Enter (6) and the home screen will show: $Y_1(6)$

Press **ENTER**. The answer will be on the home screen:

The result is $x = 2738$.

Example 24.

Given $f(x) = 6x^3 + 19x^2 + 2x - 3$. Find the factors of $f(x)$ and solve the equation $f(x) = 0$.

Solution: Set $Y_1 = 6x^3 + 19x^2 + 2x - 3$

We will graph the function and use the **ZERO** feature to find the zeros of the function:

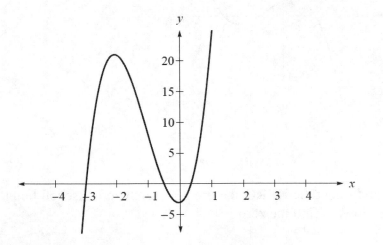

Adjust the window as necessary to see the graph.
Select the **CALC** menu and use the **ZERO** option.

The three zeros seen on the graph are:
-3, $-1/2$, $1/3$.

The factors are: $(x+3)(x+1/2)(x-3)$.

340

Example 25.

Given $f(x) = 2x^5 - 2x^4 - 8x^3 + 8x^2 - 24x + 24$

    a.   Find the rational zeros and then the other zeros; thus solve $f(x) = 0$.

    b.   Factor $f(x)$ into linear factors.

Solution:

    a.   Because the degree of $f(x)$ is 5, there are at most 5 distinct zeros. Using the Rational Zeros theorem, any rational zero of f must be of the form p/q,

        p is any factor of 24   and q is any factor of 2.

The possibilities are:

Possibilities for p	$\pm 1, \pm 3, \pm 4, \pm 6, \pm 8 \pm 12, \pm 24$
Possibilities for q	$\pm 1, \pm 2$

Possibilities for p/q :

$1, -1, 3, -3, 4, -4, 6, -6, 8, -8, 12, -12, 24, -24$ $1/2, -1/2, 3/2, -3/2$

Rather than using synthetic division to check each of these possibilities, we can graph the function:

    Set $Y_1 = 2x^5 - 2x^4 - 8x^3 + 8x^2 - 24x + 24$
Graph:

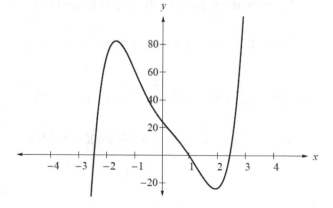

On a graph we can see only real zeros.
Look for zeros that appear to be near any of the possible rational zeros.

We see that $-5/2$, 1 and $5/2$ are <u>possibilities</u>:

Use synthetic division to check these possibilities:

$$\underline{1}\,\big|\quad\begin{array}{cccccc} 2 & -2 & -8 & 8 & -24 & 24 \\ & 2 & 0 & -8 & 0 & -24 \\ \hline 2 & 0 & -8 & 0 & -24 & 0 \end{array}$$

Since the remainder is zero, $x-1$ is a factor. Then:

$$f(x) = (x-1)(2x^4 - 8x^2 - 24)$$

$$f(x) = (x-1)*2*(x^4 - 4x^2 - 12)$$

$$f(x) = (x-1)*2*(x^2 - 6)(x^2 + 2)$$

Now set the factors equal to zero and solve.

$$x - 1 = 0 \qquad x^2 - 6 = 0 \qquad x^2 + 2 = 0$$

$$x = 1 \qquad\quad x^2 = 6 \qquad\quad x^2 = -2$$

$$x = 1 \qquad\quad x = \pm\sqrt{6} \qquad x = \pm\sqrt{2}i$$

There is only one rational zero which is 1.

The other zeros are irrational or imaginary.

b. The factorization into linear factors is:

$$f(x) = 2(x-1)(x+\sqrt{6})(x-\sqrt{6})(x+\sqrt{2}i)(x-\sqrt{2}i)$$

Example 26.

Given: $f(x) = \dfrac{1}{x-4}$

Find the domain and draw the graph.

Solution:

Set $Y_1 = \dfrac{1}{x-4}$. Graph.

The calculator will show the graph, and the domain can be seen.

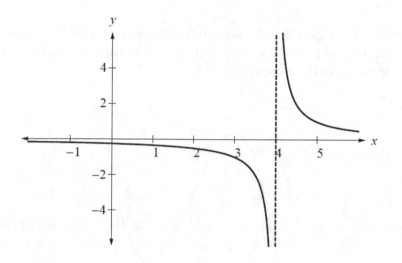

The dotted vertical line seen in the graph is a vertical asymptote, and the graph does not cross that line. Some calculators show this vertical line and others do not.

The domain cannot include the value $x = 4$ because of the vertical asymptote there:

Domain: $(-\infty, 4) \cup (4, \infty)$.

Using **DOT** Mode, the vertical asymptote is not seen, and the graph is easier to read.

Example 27.

Solve: $x^3 - 4x > 0$

Solution:

We first find the zeros of the function $f(x) = x^3 - 4x$:

Set $Y_1 = x^3 - 4x$

Then find the zeros using **ZERO** within the **CALC** menu.

The zeros are $-2, 0, 2$.

Option 1. The intervals using these zeros are:

$$(-\infty,-2), \qquad (-2,0), \qquad (0,2), \qquad \text{and} \quad (2,\infty).$$

We can use the **TABLE** feature in the **ASK** mode to find the sign within each interval.

Option 2. We determine the sign of $f(x)$ in each interval by looking at the graph of the function to see if the y-values of the graph are positive or negative in each interval.

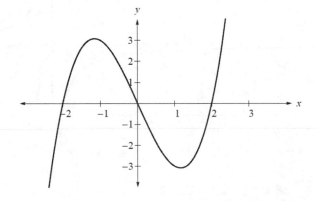

The graph is positive in two intervals. Thus the solution is:

$$(-2,0)\cup(2,\infty).$$

Example 28.

Solve: $2x^4 - 3x^3 - 5x^2 \le -x - 1$

Solution:

First, use addition to transform the right side of the inequality to zero.

Set $Y_1 = 2x^4 - 3x^3 - 5x^2 + x + 1 = 0.$

Graph the function and use the **ZERO** option in the **CALC** menu to find the zeros.

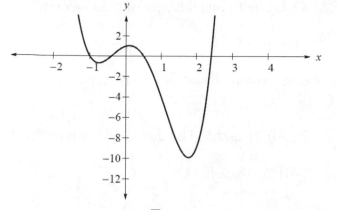

The zeros are: -1, $-.414\, or\, (1-\sqrt{2})$, $1/2$, $2.414\, or\, 1+\sqrt{2}$

These zeros define the intervals which need to be tested.

Looking at the graph we see the graph is below the x-axis (negative) in two intervals:

The solution is: $(-1,1-\sqrt{2})\cup(1/2,1+\sqrt{2})$

Example 29.

Solve $\dfrac{x-2}{x+2}\geq\dfrac{x+3}{x-1}$

Solution: Transform the right side of the inequality to zero using addition.

$$\frac{x-2}{x+2}-\frac{x+3}{x-1}\geq 0.$$

Set $Y_1=\dfrac{x-2}{x+2}-\dfrac{x+3}{x-1}$ and Graph.

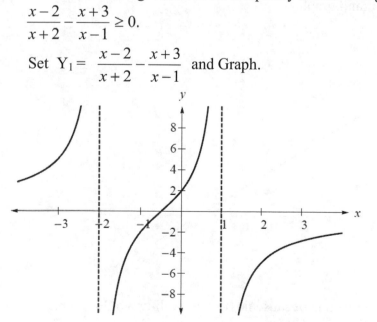

We see one zero (x-intercept).

Use the **ZERO** in the **CALC** feature to find this zero of the function.

The zero is $\quad x = -0.5$

By looking at the denominators, we find that the domain cannot contain the values of -2 and 1.

The critical values are: -2, -0.5, and 1. Use these to determine intervals:

$$(-\infty, -2), (-2, -0.5), (-0.5, 1), (1, \infty).$$

The graph shows where the inequality is positive and where it is negative. Notice that -0.5 should be included in the critical values since the inequality symbol is $\geq$ and it is also a zero. We are looking for positive values.

The solution set is the union of two of the intervals: $\quad (-\infty, -2) \cup [-1/2, 1)$.

Example 30.
Which of the following are one-to-one functions?

a. $f(x) = 6 - 2x$ b. $f(x) = x^2 + 3$

c. $f(x) = x^3 - 3x$

Solution: Graph each function and use the horizontal line test.

a. Set $Y_1 = 6 - 2x$ and graph.

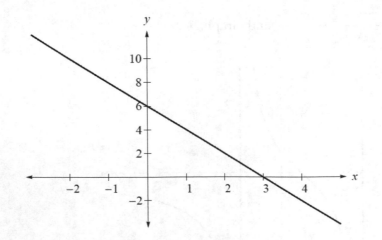

The function is one-to-one because no horizontal line would intersect the graph more than once.

b. Set $Y_1 = x^2 + 3$ and graph.

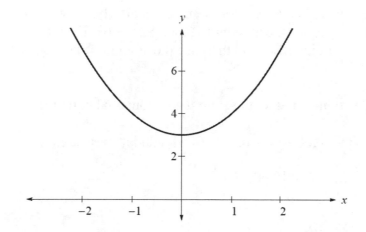

The function is not one-to-one since there would be many horizontal lines that intersect the graph more than once.

c. Set $Y_1 = x^3 - 3x$ and graph.

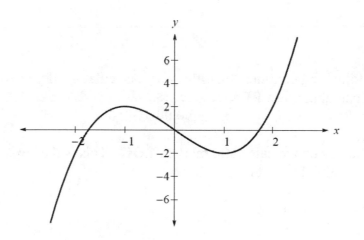

The function is not one-to-one since there are many horizontal lines that intersect the graph more than once.

<u>Example 31.</u> Use the formula:

$$A = P\left(1 + \frac{r}{n}\right)^{nt}$$

347

Where if P dollars is deposited into an account paying a rate of interest r compounded n times per year, then after t years the account will contain A.

If $10,000 is deposited at 10% interest, compounded quarterly, how many years must the money be deposited in order for the amount to reach $25,000? Define a function of time with the given money , and interest , and then use the amount of money in the account to solve for t.

Solution: Use the given information to set up the exponential equation:

$$A = 25{,}000 \quad P = 10{,}000 \quad r = 0.1 \quad n = 4 \text{ and let } x \text{ represent t}$$

$$25{,}000 = 10{,}000\left(1 + \frac{0.10}{4}\right)^{4t}$$

Let $Y_1 = 25{,}000$

Let $Y_2 = 10{,}000(1.025)^{4x}$

Graph both equations and use **INTERSECT** in the **CALC** menu to estimate the first coordinate of the point of intersection which is the x-value at that point.

For window use x-min $= 0$, x-max $= 10$, y-min $= 0$ and y-max $= 30000$.

The result is 9.277 years.

Example 32.
Find the following common logarithms on a calculator. If you are using a graphing calculator, use **REAL** mode.
a. log 45781   b. log 0.00003456   c. $\log(-2)$

Solution: Find the key on the calculator marked **LOG**. This is the key for the common logarithm. Use the **LOG** key with the numbers.

a. $\log 45781 = 4.66069$

b. $\log 0.00003456 = -4.48732$

c. $\log(-2)$ does not exist

These answers can be checked for correctness by raising 10 to the answers found and see that this indeed does equal the original number.

$$10^{4.66069} = 45781.49811$$

The slight difference from the original number 45781 is due to the rounding feature within the calculator.

Example 33.

With a calculator find each of the following natural logarithms.

a. $\ln 45781$ b. $\ln 0.00003456$ c. $\ln(-2)$

. d. $\ln 1$ e. $\ln 0$

Solution: Find the key on the calculator marked **LN**. This is the key for the natural logarithm. Use the **LN** key with the given numbers. Use the **REAL** Mode.

a. $\ln 45781 = 10.73162$

b. $\ln 0.00003456 = -10.27281$

c. $\ln(-2) = \text{does not exist}$

d. $\ln 1 = 0$

e. $\ln 0 = \text{does not exist}$

These answers can be checked for correctness by raising e to the answers found and see that this indeed does equal the original number.

Example 34. Graph $f(x) = \log_6 x$.

Solution: First change the base to base 10.
$$y = \log_6 x = \frac{\log x}{\log 6}$$

Set $Y_1 = \dfrac{\log x}{\log 6}$ and then graph.

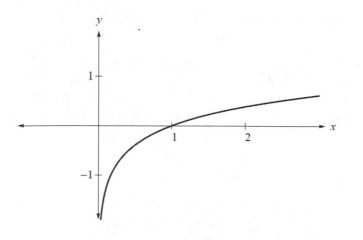

<u>**Example 35.**</u>

Solve: $\ln x - \ln(x+1) = 3\ln 4$

Solution: The solution of the equation $\ln x - \ln(x+1) = 3\ln 4$ is the zero of the function. Write the equation as a function:
$$f(x) = \ln x - \ln(x+1) - 3\ln 4$$

Set $Y_1 = \ln x - \ln(x+1) - 3\ln 4$

The solutions will be the first coordinate of any x-intercepts in the graph.

The graph is:

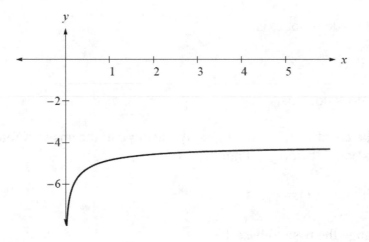

There is no x-intercept. The answer is: **no solution.**

<u>**Example 36**</u>

Solve: $\log_2(x+7) + \log_2 x = 3$

Solution: We must use the change of base formula to graph the equation.

Set $Y_1 = \dfrac{\log(x+7)}{\log 2} + \dfrac{\log x}{\log 2}$ Set $Y_2 = 3$

Graph the equations and use the **INTERSECT** in **CALC** to find the solution.

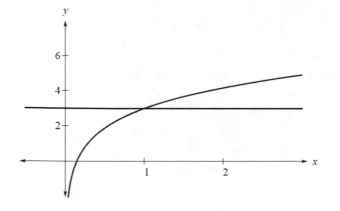

The solution is $x = 1$.

Example 37.

Solve: $\log_4 x = -1$

Solution: Use the change-of-base formula and graph the equations.

Set $Y_1 = \dfrac{\log x}{\log 4}$ Set $Y_2 = -1$

Graph and use **INTERSECT** in **CALC** to find the solution. The first coordinate of the point of intersection is the solution:

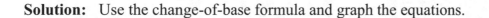

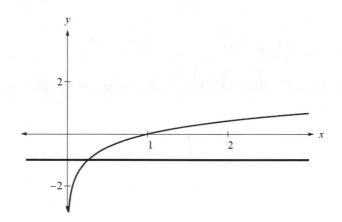

The solution is 0.25 and so $x = 1/4$.

Example 38.

Solve: $\log_3(x+3) + \log_3(x+5) = 1$

Solution: Use the change-of-base formula and graph the equations.

Set $Y_1 = \dfrac{\log(x+3)}{\log 3} + \dfrac{\log(x+5)}{\log 3}$ Set $Y_2 = 1$

Graph and use **INTERSECT** in **CALC** to find the solution. The first coordinate of the point of intersection is the solution.

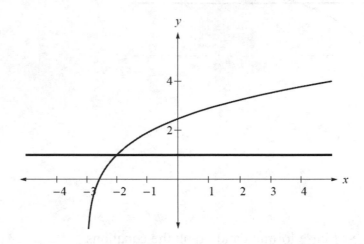

The solution is $x = -2$.

Example 39.

      Solve: $2^{4x-11} = 32$

Solution:

      Set $Y_1 = 2^{4x-11}$ using $2\wedge(4x-11)$ Let $Y_2 = 32$

Graph and use **INTERSECT** in **CALC** to find the first coordinate of the point of intersection.

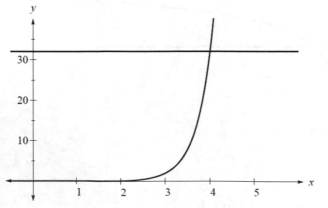

The solution is $x = 4$.

<u>Example 40.</u>

Solve: $3^x = 22$

Solution:

Set $Y_1 = 3^x$ Set $Y_2 = 22$

Graph and use **INTERSECT** in **CALC** to find the first coordinate of the point of intersection.

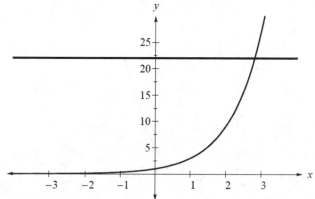

The solution is approximately 2.81359.

<u>Example 41.</u>

Solve: $2 = e^{0.4t}$

Solution:

Set $Y_1 = e^{0.4x}$ using $e^{\wedge}(0.4x)$ Set $Y_2 = 2$

Graph and use **INTERSECT** in the **CALC** Menu to find the first coordinate of the point of intersection.

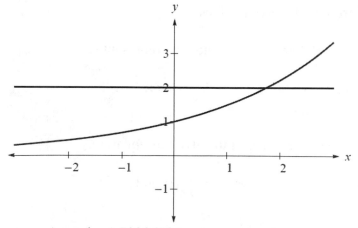

The solution is approximately 1.73286795.

Example 42.

Solve $e^x + e^{-x} - 8 = 0$.

Solution: We will graph the equation and find the **ZERO** in the **CALC** menu.

Set $Y_1 = e^x + e^{-x} - 8$

Graph, and then find the zeros.

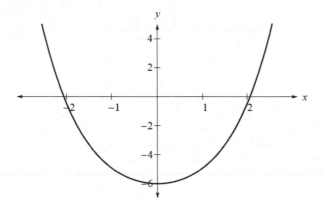

The zeros are approximately: -2.0634 and 2.0634.

Example 43.

Suppose $10,000 is invested at an interest rate of r, compounded continuously, and grows to $14,190.68 in 5 years. Find the interest rate.

Solution: Use the continuously compounded interest formula

$$A = Pe^{rt}$$

Substitute into the formula the given values

$A = 14,190.68$ $P = 10,000$ $t = 5$ and let x represent r.

$$14,190.68 = 10,000\, e^{5r}   \text{or} 1.419068 = e^{5r}$$

Use **INTERSECT** in the **CALC** menu to solve this equation.

Set $Y_1 = e^{5x}$ and   Set $Y_2 = 1.419068$

Graph. The first coordinate of the point of intersection will be the value of the variable.

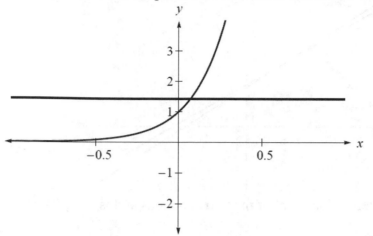

The intersection point $x = 0.07000006 \qquad y = 14190.68$.

The interest rate is the x-value and is 0.07 which is 7%.

Example 44.
Solve the given system of equations:

$$3x + 4y = 5$$
$$2x + 3y = 4$$

Solution: Before we can enter either equation into the calculator, we must solve each equation for y.

$$\begin{array}{c} 3x + 4y = 5 \\ 2x + 3y = 4 \end{array} \quad \text{becomes} \quad \begin{array}{c} y = 1/4(-3x + 5) \\ y = 1/3(-2x + 4) \end{array}$$

Set $Y_1 = 1/4(-3x + 5)$ and Set $Y_2 = 1/3(-2x + 4)$.

Graph the two equations and use **INTERSECT** in the **CALC** menu.

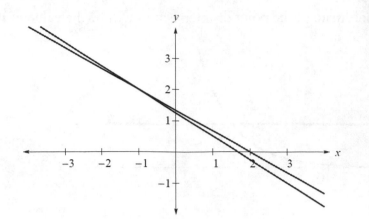

The solution is the intersection point of the two equations and is $(-1, 2)$.

By looking at the graph, we could not determine the exact value of the solution. Because we are able to use the **INTERSECT** Mode, we did find the solution.

Example 45.

John wants to invest $30,000. With part of his money he buys shares in a mutual fund, paying 9% per year. He invests the rest of the money in municipal bonds paying 10% per year. After the first year he earns interest of $2820. How much is invested at each rate?

Solution: Write a system of equations to solve this problem.

Let

x = the amount of money invested at 9%

y = the amount of money invested at 10%

Write the first equation about the total money invested.

$$x + y = 30000$$

The second equation calculates the interest earned in 1 year.

$$0.09x + 0.10y = 2820$$

Our system is:
$$x + y = 30000$$
$$0.09x + 0.10y = 2820$$

Solve each of these equations for y:

$$y = 30000 - x$$
$$y = 1/9(282000 - 9x)$$

356

Set $Y_1 = 30000 - x$ and Set $Y_2 = 1/9(282000 - 9x)$

Graph the two equations and use **INTERSECT** in the **CALC** menu.

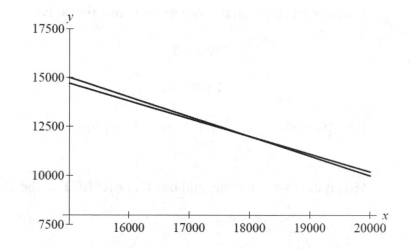

Using a calculator we can locate the point of intersection:

(18000, 12000)

$18,000 is invested at 9% and $12,000 is invested at 10%.

Example 46.

Six hundred tickets were sold for a school play. The price of tickets for adults was $3.00 and for children was $1.00. If the sale of tickets resulted in a total of $1400, how many tickets of each kind were sold?

Solution: We will write a system of equations to solve this problem.

Let: x = the number of adult tickets sold

y = the number of child tickets sold

Write one equation about the total number of tickets sold.

$x + y = 600$

Write a second equation about money.

$3.00x + 1.00y = 1400$

357

Our system is:

$$x + y = 600$$
$$3x + 1y = 1400$$

Before we can graph the system, we must first solve each equation for y:

$$y = 600 - x$$

$$y = 1400 - 3x$$

Set $Y_1 = 600 - x$ and Set $Y_2 = 1400 - 3x$

Graph the two equations and use **INTERSECT** in the **CALC** menu.

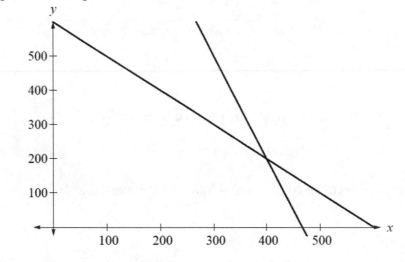

Finding the point of intersection, we get the solution: (400, 200).

400 adult tickets and 200 child tickets were sold.

Example 47.

Graph: $2x + y \leq 6$

Solution: To graph this inequality on a graphing calculator, we first must transform the inequality so that it zero is on the right side. Next change the symbol to equal and solve for y.

$$y = -2x + 6 \quad \text{(solve for } y\text{)}$$

358

Set $Y_1 = -2x + 6$.

Select the "shade below" for the graph style.

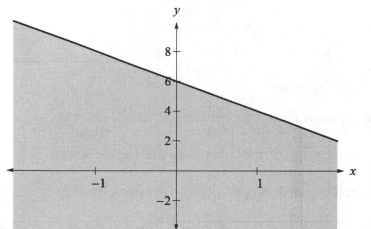

Example 48. Graph:
$$x + 2y \leq 6$$
$$x - y \geq 3$$

Solution: Convert each inequality to an equation.

$$x + 2y = 6 \qquad \text{and} \qquad x - y = 3$$

Solve each equation for y.

$$y = \frac{6 - x}{2} \qquad \text{and} \qquad y = x - 3$$

$$\text{Set} \quad Y_1 = \frac{6 - x}{2} \qquad \text{and} \qquad Y_2 = x - 3$$

Use different shading patterns on a graphing calculator to graph the system of inequalities. The solution set is the region shaded using both patterns.

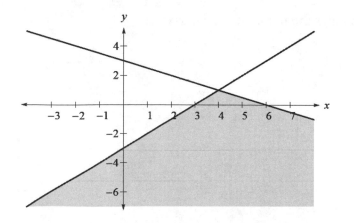

Example 49.
Find the product of the two given matrices:

$$A = \begin{bmatrix} 1 & 3 & -4 \\ 4 & 0 & -2 \end{bmatrix} \quad \text{and} \quad B = \begin{bmatrix} 5 & -4 & 2 & 0 \\ -1 & 6 & 3 & 1 \\ 7 & 0 & 5 & 8 \end{bmatrix}$$

Solution: To multiply matrices on a graphing calculator, first we enter each matrix.

Use the **MATRIX** mode to enter the matrix dimensions and each element.

After the matrices are entered, use matrix operations on the home screen:

use the **MATRIX** mode to enter the first matrix name on the home screen and then enter the second matrix name:

$$[A][B] \quad \text{and then } \textbf{ENTER}$$

The solution to the matrix multiplication will appear on the screen.

$$AB = \begin{bmatrix} -26 & 14 & -9 & -29 \\ 6 & -16 & -2 & -16 \end{bmatrix}$$

Example 50. Find the inverse of the matrix A.

$$A = \begin{bmatrix} 2 & 4 \\ 1 & 5 \end{bmatrix}$$

Solution: Enter the given matrix and then take the inverse.

First, using **MATRIX** Mode, enter the given matrix as 2 X 2 matrix A.

Return to the home screen and enter the name of the matrix:

$$[A]$$

Then use the reciprocal key:

$$[A]^{-1} \quad \text{and } \textbf{ENTER.}$$

The computer screen shows the solution matrix.

$$A^{-1} = \begin{bmatrix} 5/6 & -2/3 \\ -1/6 & 1/3 \end{bmatrix}$$

Example 51.

Solve the following system of equations:

$$x - y + z = 4$$
$$2x + y + 3z = 7$$
$$-x - 4y - z = 1$$

Solution:

We will write the system in matrix form and then use the fact that:

$$X = A^{-1}C$$

Matrix A is the coefficients of the equations of the system and matrix C is the coefficients of the solutions to the given system.

Use MATRIX mode to enter the two matrices.

$$A = \begin{bmatrix} 1 & -1 & 1 \\ 2 & 1 & 3 \\ -1 & -4 & -1 \end{bmatrix} \quad \text{and} \quad C = \begin{bmatrix} 4 \\ 7 \\ 1 \end{bmatrix}$$

On the home screen enter the matrix names and the inverse key for A:

$$[A]^{-1}[C] \quad \text{and then} \quad \textbf{ENTER}$$

The result is the matrix showing the solution: $(1, -1, 2)$.

Thus, $x = 1$, $y = -1$, and $z = 2$.

Example 52. If $B = \begin{bmatrix} -2 & 4 \\ 6 & 8 \end{bmatrix}$ find $\delta(B)$ which is the determinant of matrix B.

Solution: Begin by entering the matrix B in the calculator using **MATRIX**.

Then use the **MATRIX** and **MATH** menu and select : det(

Enter the name of the matrix and select the **ENTER** key.

$$\det\left([B]\right) = -40 \, .$$

Example 53.

Given matrix A. Find the determinant of A.

$$A = \begin{bmatrix} -1 & 3 & 2 \\ 1 & 4 & 0 \\ 3 & -2 & 5 \end{bmatrix}$$

Solution: Begin by entering the matrix into the calculator using **MATRIX**.

Then use the MATRIX MATH menu and select : det(

Enter the name of the matrix and select the Enter key.

$$\det\left([A]\right) = 63 \, .$$

Index

CHAPTER 1

Section 1.1

1. Yes, because no input value points to different output values.

3. Yes, because no input value points to different output values.

5. Yes, because no input value points to different output values.

7. Yes, because no input value points to different output values.

9. Yes, because no input value points to different output values.

11. Yes, because no input value points to different output values.

13. $f(1)$: Locate the point on the graph that has 1 for the x coordinate, $(1, -2)$. $f(1) = -2$.
    $f(3)$: Locate the point on the graph that has 3 for the x coordinate, $(3, 2)$. $f(3) = 2$.
    $f(4)$: Locate the point on the graph that has 4 for the x coordinate, $(4, 6)$.
    $f(4) = 6$.

15. $t(-2)$: Locate the point on the graph that has -2 for the x coordinate, $(-2, 0)$.
    $t(-2) = 0$.
    $t(0)$: Locate the point on the graph that has 0 for the x coordinate, $(0, 2)$. $t(0) = 2$.
    $t(1)$: Locate the point on the graph that has 1 for the x coordinate, $(1, 3)$. $t(1) = 3$.

17. (a) $f(0) = 0^2 + 3(0) = 0$;
    (b) $f(-1) = (-1)^2 + 3(-1) = -2$;
    (c) $f(5) = 5^2 + 3(5) = 40$;
    (d) $f(3m) = (3m)^2 + 3(3m) = 9m^2 + 9m$.

19. (a) $s(-2) = \dfrac{-2+2}{-2-1} = \dfrac{0}{-3} = 0$;
    (b) $s(0) = \dfrac{0+2}{0-1} = \dfrac{2}{-1} = -2$;
    (c) $s(1) = \dfrac{1+2}{1-1} = \dfrac{3}{0}$, undefined;
    (d) $s(\frac{1}{3}) = \dfrac{1/3+2}{1/3-1} = \dfrac{7/3}{-2/3} = \dfrac{7}{3} \bullet (-\dfrac{3}{2}) = -\dfrac{7}{2}$.

21. (a) $h(-2) = |-2| + 2 = 2 + 2 = 4$;
    (b) $h(-3) = |-3| + 2 = 3 + 2 = 5$;
    (c) $h(p) = |p| + 2$;
    (d) $h(0) = |0| + 2 = 0 + 2 = 2$.

23. (a) $d(2) = 2(2)^2 + 3(2) - 4 = 8 + 6 - 4 = 10$;
    (b) $d(-1) = 2(-1)^2 + 3(-1) - 4 = 2 - 3 - 4 = -5$;
    (c) $d(2m) = 2(2m)^2 + 3(2m) - 4 = 8m^2 + 6m - 4$;
    (d) $d(0) = 2(0)^2 + 3(0) - 4 = -4$.

25. All real numbers

27. All real numbers

29. $x^2 \neq 0 \Rightarrow x \neq 0$

31. All real numbers

33. All real numbers

35. $x + 2 \geq 0 \Rightarrow x \geq -2$; ALSO,
    $2x \neq 0$. Domain: $[-2, 0) \cup (0, \infty)$.

37. x^2 will never be negative, so domain is all real numbers.

Section 1.2

1. horizontal line: $m = 0$.

3. vertical line: no slope.

5. Start at an obvious point on the line, $(0, 0)$ and count rise/run to the next point. $\dfrac{2}{-2} = -1$

7. $\dfrac{2-1}{-3-4} = \dfrac{1}{-7} = -\dfrac{1}{7}$

9. $\dfrac{-9-(-1)}{-5-(-2)} = \dfrac{-8}{-3} = \dfrac{8}{3}$

11. $\dfrac{(-7/8)-(-1/8)}{(2/3)-(1/3)} = \dfrac{(-6/8)}{(1/3)} = -\dfrac{6}{8} \bullet \dfrac{3}{1} = -\dfrac{18}{8} = -\dfrac{9}{4}$

13. $\dfrac{6-6}{3-2} = \dfrac{0}{1} = 0$

15. $\dfrac{1-(-3)}{-1-(-2)} = \dfrac{4}{1} = 4$

17. $\dfrac{4-(-4)}{-9-(-9)} = \dfrac{8}{0}$, undefined $\Rightarrow$ no slope

19. $\dfrac{1.3-0}{3.7-4.5} = \dfrac{1.3}{-0.8} = -1.625$

21. $m = \dfrac{3}{2}$

23. This is a vertical line $\rightarrow$ no slope.

25. $2y = 4x + 6 \Rightarrow y = 2x + 3; \quad m = 2$

27. $m = -\dfrac{1}{3}$

29. This is a horizontal line $\rightarrow m = 0$

31. $\dfrac{1}{2}y = -x + 3 \Rightarrow 2(\dfrac{1}{2}y) = 2(-x+3) \Rightarrow y = -2x + 6;$
    $m = -2$

Section 1.3

1. $m = \dfrac{2}{5}; (0, -5)$

3. horizontal line $\rightarrow m = 0; (0, \dfrac{3}{4})$

5. $y = -\dfrac{1}{2}x + 7 \rightarrow m = -\dfrac{1}{2}; (0, 7)$

7. $3y = -2x + 12 \Rightarrow y = -\dfrac{2}{3}x + 4 \rightarrow m = -\dfrac{2}{3}; (0, 4)$

9. horizontal line $\rightarrow m = 0; \ (0, 3)$

11. $5y = -4x + 12 \Rightarrow y = -\dfrac{4}{5}x + \dfrac{12}{5} \rightarrow m = -\dfrac{4}{5}; (0, \dfrac{12}{5})$

Solutions for problems 13 – 19 omitted.

21. $y = 4x + 3$

23. $y = -3x + 4$

25. $y = -3.5x - 2$

27. $y - 3 = -\dfrac{2}{3}(x-4) \Rightarrow y = -\dfrac{2}{3}x + \dfrac{8}{3} + 3 \Rightarrow y = -\dfrac{2}{3}x + \dfrac{17}{3}$

29. $y - 3 = -3(x+2) \Rightarrow y = -3x - 6 + 3 \Rightarrow y = -3x - 3$

31. $m = \dfrac{5-3}{2-(-1)} = \dfrac{2}{3}$; *use either pt.:*

$$y - 3 = \dfrac{2}{3}(x - (-1))$$

$$y = \dfrac{2}{3}x + \dfrac{2}{3} + 3$$

$$y = \dfrac{2}{3}x + \dfrac{11}{3}$$

33. $m = \dfrac{4-1}{-1-6} = \dfrac{3}{-7}$; *use either pt.:*

$$y - 1 = -\dfrac{3}{7}(x - 6)$$

$$y = -\dfrac{3}{7}x + \dfrac{18}{7} + 1$$

$$y = -\dfrac{3}{7}x + \dfrac{25}{7}$$

35. $m = \dfrac{3-5}{2-0} = \dfrac{-2}{2} = -1$; *use either pt.:*

$$y - 5 = -1(x - 0) \Rightarrow y = -x + 5$$

37. horizontal: $y = -2$; vertical: $x = 0$

39. horizontal: $y = 2$; vertical: $x = 1$

41. $m_1 = \dfrac{2}{3}, \quad m_2 = -\dfrac{2}{3} \Rightarrow$ neither

43. $m_1 = -\dfrac{1}{4}, \quad m_2 = -4 \Rightarrow$ neither

45. $m_1 = 4; \ y = 2 - \dfrac{1}{4}x \rightarrow m_2 = -\dfrac{1}{4}$

    perpendicular

47. $m = 2$: parallel line is:

$$y - 4 = 2(x + 1)$$

$$y = 2x + 2 + 4$$

$$y = 2x + 6$$

perpendicular line is:

$$y - 4 = -\dfrac{1}{2}(x + 1)$$

$$y = -\dfrac{1}{2}x - \dfrac{1}{2} + 4$$

$$y = -\dfrac{1}{2}x + \dfrac{7}{2}$$

49. $y = -2x + 6 \rightarrow m = -2$:

parallel line is:

$$y + 1 = -2(x + 3)$$

$$y = -2x - 6 - 1$$

$$y = -2x - 7$$

perpendicular line is:

$$y + 1 = \dfrac{1}{2}(x + 3)$$

$$y = \dfrac{1}{2}x + \dfrac{3}{2} - 1$$

$$y = \dfrac{1}{2}x + \dfrac{1}{2}$$

51. $x = -1$ is a vertical line so it has no slope, m is undefined. Parallel line is $x = 3$; perpendicular line is $y = -2$.

53. True: vertical and horizontal lines are perpendicular.

55. False: both lines are vertical.

Section 1.4

1. parabola: increasing $(0, \infty)$;
   decreasing $(-\infty, 0)$; minimum $(0, 0)$

3. parabola: increasing $(0, \infty)$;
   decreasing $(-\infty, 0)$; minimum $(0, -3)$

5. horizontal line: constant $(-\infty, \infty)$

7. line: increasing $(-\infty, \infty)$

9. graph is V-shape: increasing $(0, \infty)$;
   decreasing $(-\infty, 0)$; minimum $(0, 2)$

11. $100 = 2L + 2W \Rightarrow 50 = L + W \Rightarrow W = 50 - L$

    Let $x = $ Length, so Width $= 50 - x$
    $Area = L \bullet W \Rightarrow A(x) = x(50 - x)$

13. The position of the airplane in relation to the ground and the airport is modeled by a right triangle. Label hypotenuse as d, the vertical height as 5000 and the horizontal length as h.
    Using the Pythagorean Theorem,
    $a^2 + b^2 = c^2$, we have
    $5000^2 + h^2 = d^2 \Rightarrow h = \sqrt{d^2 - 5000^2}$
    Therefore, $h(d) = \sqrt{d^2 - 5000^2}$

15. Use perimeter formula first to get an expression for L in terms of W:
    $P = 2L + 2W$
    $400 = 2L + 2W$
    $200 = L + W$
    $L = 200 - W$
    $A = L \bullet W \Rightarrow A(W) = (200 - W) \bullet W$

Section 1.5

1. $f(4) = 2(4)^2 = 32$
   $g(4) = 4(4) + 3 = 19$
   $(f + g)(4) = 32 + 19 = 51$

3. $f(-\frac{1}{2}) = 2(-\frac{1}{2})^2 = \frac{1}{2}$
   $g(-\frac{1}{2}) = 4(-\frac{1}{2}) + 3 = 1$
   $(fg)(-\frac{1}{2}) = \frac{1}{2}(1) = \frac{1}{2}$

5. $f(\sqrt{2}) = 2(\sqrt{2})^2 = 4$
   $g(\sqrt{2}) = 4\sqrt{2} + 3$
   $(\frac{f}{g})(\sqrt{2}) = \frac{4}{4\sqrt{2} + 3}$

7. $g(2) = 4(2) + 3 = 11$
   $(g + g)(2) = 11 + 11 = 22$

9. $f(-2) = 2(-2)^2 = 8$
   $g(-2) = 4(-2) + 3 = -5$
   $(\frac{f}{g})(-2) = -\frac{8}{5}$

11. $(f+g)(x) = 3x-2+4-2x = x+2$

$(f-g)(x) = (3x-2)-(4-2x)$
$= 3x-2-4+2x$
$= 5x-6$

$(fg)(x) = (3x-2)(4-2x)$
$= -6x^2+16x-8$

$(ff)(x) = (3x-2)(3x-2)$
$= 9x^2-12x+4$

$(\frac{f}{g})(x) = \frac{3x-2}{4-2x}$

$(gg)(x) = (4-2x)(4-2x)$
$= 16-16x+4x^2$

$(\frac{g}{f})(x) = \frac{4-2x}{3x-2}$

13. $(f+g)(x) = \sqrt{x+1}+x-2$

$(f-g)(x) = (\sqrt{x+1})-(x-2)$
$= \sqrt{x+1}-x+2$

$(fg)(x) = (\sqrt{x+1})(x-2)$
$= x\sqrt{x+1}-2\sqrt{x+1}$

$(ff)(x) = (\sqrt{x+1})(\sqrt{x+1}) = x+1$

$(\frac{f}{g})(x) = \frac{\sqrt{x+1}}{x-2}$

$(gg)(x) = (x-2)(x-2)$
$= x^2-4x+4$

$(\frac{g}{f})(x) = \frac{x-2}{\sqrt{x+1}}$

15. $(f+g)(x) = |x|+x-2$

$(f-g)(x) = |x|-(x-2) = |x|-x+2$

$(fg)(x) = |x|(x-2) = x|x|-2|x|$

$(ff)(x) = |x| \bullet |x| = |x^2|$

$(\frac{f}{g})(x) = \frac{|x|}{x-2}$

$(gg)(x) = (x-2)(x-2)$
$= x^2-4x+4$

$(\frac{g}{f})(x) = \frac{x-2}{|x|}$

17. $f(x+h) = 2(x+h)^2-1$
$= 2(x^2+2xh+h^2)-1$
$= 2x^2+4xh+2h^2-1$

$\frac{f(x+h)-f(x)}{h} = \frac{(2x^2+4xh+2h^2-1)-(2x^2-1)}{h}$

$= \frac{2x^2+4xh+2h^2-1-2x^2+1}{h}$

$= \frac{4xh+2h^2}{h}$

$= \frac{h(4x+2h)}{h}$

$= 4x+2h$

19. $f(x+h) = 3(x+h)^2+4(x+h)-5$
$= 3(x^2+2xh+h^2)+4x+4h-5$
$= 3x^2+6xh+3h^2+4x+4h-5$

$\frac{f(x+h)-f(x)}{h} = \frac{3x^2+6xh+3h^2+4x+4h-5-(3x^2+4x-5)}{h}$

$= \frac{3x^2+6xh+3h^2+4x+4h-5-3x^2-4x+5}{h}$

$= \frac{6xh+3h^2+4h}{h}$

$= \frac{h(6x+3h+4)}{h}$

$= 6x+3h+4$

21. $f(g(-2)) = f[(-2)^2-(-2)-6]$
$= f(4+2-6)$
$= f(0)$
$= 4(0)-1 = -1$

23. $f(g(0)) = f(0^2-0-6)$
$= f(-6)$
$= 4(-6)-1$
$= -24-1 = -25$

25. $f(g(x)) = f(x-2)$
$$= (x-2)+4$$
$$= x+2$$
Domain is all real numbers.
$g(f(x)) = g(x+4)$
$$= (x+4)-2$$
$$= x+2$$
Domain is all real numbers.

27. - 30. Answers are not unique.

27. $g(x) = (7-x); f(x) = x^3$

29. $g(x) = \sqrt{x} - 4; f(x) = x^2$

Section 1.6

1. – 3. are not included.

5. $f(x) = |x| = x,$ *for* $x > 0$;
$f(-x) = |-x| = x,$ *for* $x > 0$
Symmetric wrt $y - axis$.

7. Solve equation for y.
$$f(x) = \frac{1}{2}x + \frac{3}{2}$$
$$f(-x) = \frac{1}{2}(-x) + \frac{3}{2}$$
$$= -\frac{1}{2}x + \frac{3}{2}$$
$$-f(x) = -(\frac{1}{2}x + \frac{3}{2})$$
$$= -\frac{1}{2}x - \frac{3}{2}$$
No symmetry

9. Solve the equation for y.
$$f(x) = \frac{1}{3}x^2 - \frac{4}{3}$$
$$f(-x) = \frac{1}{3}(-x)^2 - \frac{4}{3}$$
$$= \frac{1}{3}x^2 - \frac{4}{3}$$
Symmetric wrt $y - axis$.

11. $f(x) = 4$ and $f(-x) = 4$
Symmetric wrt $y - axis$.

13. $f(x) = -2x^3$
$f(-x) = -2(-x)^3 = 2x^3$
$-f(x) = -(-2x^3) = 2x^3$
Symmetric wrt origin.

15. wrt $x - axis : (\frac{1}{2}, 0)$
wrt $y - axis : (-\frac{1}{2}, 0)$
wrt origin: $(-\frac{1}{2}, 0)$

17. wrt $x - axis : (2, -\frac{1}{3})$
wrt $y - axis : (-2, \frac{1}{3})$
wrt origin: $(-2, -\frac{1}{3})$

19. wrt $x - axis : (5, 4)$
wrt $y - axis : (-5, -4)$
wrt origin: $(-5, 4)$

21. $f(x) = 4x^3 + 3$
$f(-x) = 4(-x)^3 + 3$
$$= -4x^3 + 3$$
$-f(x) = -(4x^3 + 3)$
$$= -4x^3 - 3$$
Neither

23. $f(x) = x^6$

$f(-x) = (-x)^6 = x^6$

Even

25. $f(x) = \dfrac{1}{x}$

$f(-x) = \dfrac{1}{-x} = -\dfrac{1}{x}$

$-f(x) = -(\dfrac{1}{x}) = -\dfrac{1}{x}$

Odd

27. $f(x) = \sqrt{x+2}$

$f(-x) = \sqrt{-x+2}$

$-f(x) = -\sqrt{x+2}$

Neither

29. When the formula, x^2, is multiplied by -1, the graph is reflected across the $x-axis$.

31. When 2 is added to the x before the operation of squaring, the graph is shifted to the left 2 units.

33. When 3 multiplies the formula, x^2, the graph is stretched vertically by a factor of 3.

35. Subtracting 4 from x shifts the graph right 4 units. Subtracting 3 from the formula, $(\quad)^2$, shifts the graph down 3 units.

Review Chapter 1

1. No, 2 relates to 3 and to 7.
   Domain$\{2, 4, 6\}$; Range$\{3, 5, 7\}$

2. No, 2 relates to more than one unique value.
   Domain$\{2\}$; Range$\{4, 5, 6, 7\}$

3. Yes. Use vertical line test.

4. Yes. Use vertical line test.

5. Yes. Use vertical line test.

6. Using any real number for an input will result in a real number for the output. The domain is all real numbers.

7. $x \neq 0$ as division by 0 is not defined.
   Domain $(-\infty, 0) \cup (0, \infty)$

8. The denominator cannot have a value of 0.
   Find the values of x that make
   $x^2 - x - 6 = 0$.
   $(x-3)(x+2) = 0$
   $x - 3 = 0 \quad or \quad x + 2 = 0$
   $x = 3 \quad or \quad x = -2$
   Domain $\{x \neq 3, -2\}$
   $(-\infty, -2) \cup (-2, 3) \cup (3, \infty)$

9. Using any real number for an input will result in a real number for the output. The domain is all real numbers.

10. $f(2) = 2^2 - 2(2) + 1$
    $= 4 - 4 + 1 = 1$

11. $f(-2) = (-2)^2 - 2(-2) + 1$
    $= 4 + 4 + 1 = 9$

12. $f(y+2) = (y+2)^2 - 2(y+2) + 1$
$$= y^2 + 4y + 4 - 2y - 4 + 1$$
$$= y^2 + 2y + 1$$

13. $f(0) = 0^2 - 2(0) + 1 = 1$

14. $m = \dfrac{-1-(-3)}{4-2}$
$$m = \dfrac{2}{2} = 1$$

15. $m = \dfrac{3-3}{7-1}$
$$m = \dfrac{0}{6} = 0$$

16. $m = \dfrac{4-5}{2-2}$
$$= \dfrac{-1}{0}, \; undefined \Rightarrow no\ slope$$

17. $m = \dfrac{(5/8)-(2/3)}{(-1/8)-(1/3)}$
$$m = \dfrac{(15/24)-(16/24)}{(-3/24)-(8/24)}$$
$$m = \dfrac{(-1/24)}{(-11/24)}$$
$$m = \dfrac{-1}{24} \bullet \dfrac{24}{-11}$$
$$m = \dfrac{1}{11}$$

18. Solve the equation for y.
$$-2y = 3x + 9$$
$$y = \dfrac{3}{-2}x + \dfrac{9}{-2}$$
$$m = -\dfrac{3}{2}; \; y\text{-intercept } (0, -\dfrac{9}{2})$$

19. $y = -4x + 3$

20. $y - 4 = -\dfrac{1}{3}(x - 0)$
$$y = -\dfrac{1}{3}x + 4$$

21. $m = \dfrac{-1-(-3)}{-1-2} = -\dfrac{2}{3}$
Use either point.
$$y-(-1) = -\dfrac{2}{3}(x-(-1))$$
$$y+1 = -\dfrac{2}{3}(x+1)$$
$$y = -\dfrac{2}{3}x - \dfrac{2}{3} - 1$$
$$y = -\dfrac{2}{3}x - \dfrac{5}{3}$$

22. Solve both equations for y and compare the slopes.
$$-3y = -2x + 9$$
$$y = \dfrac{-2}{-3}x + \dfrac{9}{-3}$$
$$y = \dfrac{2}{3}x - 3; \quad m = \dfrac{2}{3}$$
$$4x - 12 = 6y$$
$$\dfrac{4}{6}x - \dfrac{12}{6} = y$$
$$y = \dfrac{2}{3}x - 2; \quad m = \dfrac{2}{3}$$
Slopes are equal so the lines are parallel.

23. Slope of both lines is 2 so the lines are parallel.

24. Slope of given line is 2; pt.(1,0):
$$y - 0 = 2(x - 1)$$
$$y = 2x - 2$$

25. Slope of the given line is 2. A line perpendicular has slope $-\dfrac{1}{2}$; pt $(2,-4)$:

$$y-(-4)=-\frac{1}{2}(x-2)$$

$$y+4=-\frac{1}{2}x+1$$

$$y=-\frac{1}{2}x-3$$

26. $y=7$ is a horizontal line so it has no slope. All horizontal lines will be parallel to it. Using the given point, $y=-2$.

27. $y=7$ has no slope. Perpendicular line through $(1,-2)$ is the vertical line $x=1$.

28. $f(2)=\sqrt{2+2}=2$

$$g(2)=2^2-2=2$$

$$(f+g)(2)=f(2)+g(2)$$

$$=2+2=4$$

29. $f(2)=\sqrt{2+2}=2$

$$g(2)=2^2-2=2$$

$$(f-g)(2)=f(2)-g(2)$$

$$=2-2=0$$

30. $f(1)=\sqrt{1+2}=\sqrt{3}$

$$(ff)(1)=f(1)\bullet f(1)$$

$$=\sqrt{3}\bullet\sqrt{3}=3$$

31. $f(g(x))=f(x-3)$

$$=(x-3)^2+(x-3)$$

$$=x^2-6x+9+x-3$$

$$=x^2-5x+6$$

$$g(f(x))=g(x^2+x)$$

$$=x^2+x-3$$

32. $x^2+2y^2=1$

symmetry wrt .x-axis?

$x^2+2(-y)^2=1$

$x^2+2y^2=1$, same as original, yes.

symmetry wrt y-axis?

$(-x)^2+2y^2=1$

$x^2+2y^2=1$, same as original, yes.

symmetry wrt origin?

$(-x)^2+2(-y)^2=1$

$x^2+2y^2=1$, same as original, yes.

33. Same steps and results as 32.

34. $x+2y=3$

symmetry wrt x-axis?

$x+2(-y)=3$

$x-2y=3$, not same as original, no.

symmetry wrt y-axis?

$(-x)+2y=3$

$-x+2y=3$, not same as original, no.

symmetry wrt origin?

$(-x)+2(-y)=3$

$-x-2y=3$, not same as original, no.

35. $y=x^2$

symmetry wrt x-axis?

$-y=x^2$, not same as original, no.

symmetry wrt y-axis?

$y=(-x)^2=x^2$, same as original, yes.

36. $y=-x^3$

symmetry wrt x-axis?

$-y=-x^3$, not same as original, no.

symmetry wrt y-axis?

$y=-(-x)^3=x^3$, not the same, no.

symmetry wrt origin?

$-y=-(-x)^3=x^3$

$-1(-y)=-1(x^3)$

$y=-x^3$, same as original, yes.

37. $y = x^4$

    Same steps and results as 35.

38. $y = |x| + 2$

    symmetry wrt x-axis?

    $-y = |x| + 2$, not same as original, no.

    symmetry wrt y-axis?

    $y = |-x| + 2$

    $y = |x| + 2$, same as original, yes.

    symmetry wrt origin?

    $-y = |-x| + 2$

    $-y = |x| + 2$, not same as original, no.

39. $y = |x + 2|$

    symmetry wrt x-axis?

    $-y = |x + 2|$, not same as original, no.

    symmetry wrt y-axis?

    $y = |-x + 2|$, not same as original, no.

    symmetry wrt origin?

    $-y = |-x + 2|$, not same, no.

40. Subtract 4 from the formula will shift the graph down:

    $y = x^2 - 4$

    Add 3 to the x before squaring will shift the graph left:

    $y = (x + 3)^2 - 4$

41. Add 2 to the formula will shift the graph up:

    $y = |x| + 2$

    Horizontal stretch factor of 3 is the result of dividing x by 3 before taking the absolute value:

    $y = \left|\dfrac{x}{3}\right| + 2$

CHAPTER 2
Section 2.1

1. $3x + 3 = 24$
   $3x + 3 - 3 = 24 - 3$
   $3x = 21$
   $(3x)/3 = 21/3$
   $x = 7$

3. $2x - 7 = 0$
   $2x - 7 + 7 = 0 + 7$
   $2x = 7$
   $(2x)/2 = 7/2$
   $x = 7/2$

5. $4 - p = 6$
   $4 - 4 - p = 6 - 4$
   $-p = 2$
   $(-1)(-p) = (-1)(2)$
   $p = -2$

7. $x + 2 = 2x - 5$
   $x - 2x + 2 - 2 = 2x - 2x - 5 - 2$
   $-x = -7$
   $(-1)(-x) = (-1)(-7)$
   $x = 7$

9. $5x + 4 = 3x + 10$
   $5x - 3x + 4 - 4 = 3x - 3x + 10 - 4$
   $2x = 6$
   $(2x)/2 = 6/2$
   $x = 3$

11. $5x + 4 - 2x = 2x - x + 14$
    $3x + 4 = x + 14$
    $3x - x + 4 - 4 = x - x + 14 - 4$
    $2x = 10$
    $(2x)/2 = 10/2$
    $x = 5$

13. $3(2t - 2) + 6 = 4(t - 2)$
    $6t - 6 + 6 = 4t - 8$
    $6t - 4t = 4t - 4t - 8$
    $2t = -8$
    $(2t)/2 = -8/2$
    $t = -4$

15. $f(x) = x + 3$
    $0 = x + 3$
    $-3 = x$

17. $f(x) = 5 - x$
    $0 = 5 - x$
    $x = 5$

19. $f(x) = 7 - 3x$
    $0 = 7 - 3x$
    $3x = 7$
    $(3x)/3 = 7/3$
    $x = 7/3$

21. $A = \frac{1}{2} bh$
    $2A = 2(1/2)bh$
    $2A = bh$
    $(2A)/b = (bh)/b$
    $(2A)/b = h$

23. $y = mx + b$
    $y - mx = mx - mx + b$
    $y - mx = b$

25. $P = 2L + 2W$
    $P - 2W = 2L + 2W - 2W$
    $P - 2W = 2L$
    $(P - 2W)/2 = (2L)/2$
    $(P - 2W)/2 = L$

27. $T = pcd + de$
$T = d(pc + e)$
$T/(pc + e) = [d(pc + e)]/(pc + e)$
$T/(pc + e) = d$

31. $m = n + nde$
$m = n(1 + de)$
$m/(1 + de) = [n(1 + de)]/(1 + de)$
$m/(1 + de) = n$

29. $2x + 3y = 6$
$2x + 3y - 3y = 6 - 3y$
$2x = 6 - 3y$
$(2x)/2 = (6 - 3y)/2$
$x = (6 - 3y)/2$

Section 2.2

1. $(4 + 3i) + (6 + 2i)$
$= 4 + 3i + 6 + 2i$
$= 4 + 6 + 3i + 2i$
$= 10 + 5i$

3. $(-3 - 2i) + (4 + 4i)$
$= -3 - 2i + 4 + 4i$
$= -3 + 4 - 2i + 4i$
$= 1 + 2i$

5. $(-4 - i) + (-2 - i)$
$= -4 - i - 2 - i$
$= -4 - 2 - i - i$
$= -6 - 2i$

7. $(3 - \sqrt{-16}) + (2 + \sqrt{-4})$
$= (3 - \sqrt{-1(16)}) + (2 + \sqrt{-1(4)})$
$= (3 - \sqrt{-1} \bullet \sqrt{16}) + (2 + \sqrt{-1} \bullet \sqrt{4})$
$= (3 - i4) + (2 + i2)$
$= 3 - 4i + 2 + 2i$
$= 3 + 2 - 4i + 2i$
$= 5 - 2i$

9. $(12 + 7i) - (6 - i)$
$= 12 + 7i - 6 + i$
$= 12 - 6 + 7i + i$
$= 6 + 8i$

11. $(-4 - 2i) - (-3 - i)$
$= -4 - 2i + 3 + i$
$= -4 + 3 - 2i + i$
$= -1 - i$

13. $2i(3 - 4i)$
$= 6i - 8i^2$
$= 6i - 8(-1)$
$= 6i + 8$
$= 8 + 6i$

15. $-4i(-6 + 2i)$
$= 24i - 8i^2$
$= 24i - 8(-1)$
$= 24i + 8$
$= 8 + 24i$

17. $(2 + 3i)(1 + 4i)$
$= 2(1) + 2(4i) + 3i(1) + 3i(4i)$
$= 2 + 8i + 3i + 12i^2$
$= 2 + 11i + 12(-1)$
$= 2 - 12 + 11i$
$= -10 + 11i$

19. $(3 - 4i)(2 - 6i)$
$= 3(2) + 3(-6i) - 4i(2) - 4i(-6i)$
$= 6 - 18i - 8i + 24i^2$
$= 6 - 26i + 24(-1)$
$= 6 - 24 - 26i$
$= -18 - 26i$

21. $(-2 - 3i)(-5 - i)$
$= -2(-5) - 2(-i) - 3i(-5) - 3i(-i)$
$= 10 + 2i + 15i + 3i^2$
$= 10 + 17i + 3(-1)$
$= 10 - 3 + 17i$
$= 7 + 17i$

23. $(4 - \sqrt{-9})(5 + \sqrt{-36})$
$= (4 - \sqrt{-1(9)})(5 + \sqrt{-1(36)})$
$= (4 - \sqrt{-1} \bullet \sqrt{9})(5 + \sqrt{-1} \bullet \sqrt{36})$
$= (4 - i3)(5 + i6)$
$= (4 - 3i)(5 + 6i)$
$= 4(5) + 4(6i) - 3i(5) - 3i(6i)$
$= 20 + 24i - 15i - 18i^2$
$= 20 + 9i - 18(-1)$
$= 20 + 18 + 9i$
$= 38 + 9i$

25. $(3+2i)^2 = (3+2i)(3+2i)$
$= 3(3) + 3(2i) + 2i(3) + 2i(2i)$
$= 9 + 6i + 6i + 4i^2$
$= 9 + 12i + 4(-1)$
$= 9 - 4 + 12i$
$= 5 + 12i$

27. $\dfrac{5-2i}{2+3i} = \dfrac{5-2i}{2+3i} \bullet \dfrac{2-3i}{2-3i}$
$= \dfrac{(5-2i)(2-3i)}{(2+3i)(2-3i)}$
$= \dfrac{10 - 15i - 4i + 6i^2}{4 - 6i + 6i - 9i^2}$
$= \dfrac{10 - 19i - 6}{4 + 9}$
$= \dfrac{4-19i}{13} = \dfrac{4}{13} - \dfrac{19}{13}i$

29. $\dfrac{1+i}{1-i} = \dfrac{1+i}{1-i} \bullet \dfrac{1+i}{1+i}$
$= \dfrac{(1+i)(1+i)}{(1-i)(1+i)}$
$= \dfrac{1+i+i+i^2}{1+i-i-i^2}$
$= \dfrac{1+2i-1}{1+1}$
$= \dfrac{2i}{2} = i$

31. i^{31} To simplify, divide the exponent by 4. The remainder is the exponent of the equivalent i term.
$31/4 = 7$ with remainder of 3.
Therefore, $i^{31} = i^3$
$= i^2 \bullet i$
$= -1 \bullet i$
$= -i$

33. i^{68} To simplify, divide the exponent by 4. The remainder is the exponent of the equivalent i term.
$68/4 = 17$ with 0 remainder.
Therefore, $i^{68} = i^0 = 1$

Section 2.3

1. $x^2 - x - 20 = 0$
   $(x-5)(x+4) = 0$
   $x-5 = 0, or, x+4 = 0$
   $x = 5, or, x = -4$

3. $2x^2 + x - 1 = 0$
   $(2x-1)(x+1) = 0$
   $2x-1 = 0, or, x+1 = 0$
   $x = \dfrac{1}{2}, or, x = -1$

5. $3x^2 - 12x = 0$
   $3x(x-4) = 0$
   $3x = 0, or, x-4 = 0$
   $x = 0, or, x = 4$

7. $5x^2 - 20 = 0$
   $5x^2 = 20$
   $x^2 = 4$
   $x = \pm\sqrt{4}$
   $x = \pm 2$

9. $4x^2 = 26$
   $x^2 = \dfrac{26}{4}$
   $x = \pm\sqrt{\dfrac{26}{4}}$
   $x = \pm\dfrac{\sqrt{26}}{\sqrt{4}}$
   $x = \pm\dfrac{\sqrt{26}}{2}$

11. $7x^2 + 14 = 0$
    $7x^2 = -14$
    $x^2 = -2$
    $x = \pm\sqrt{-2}$
    $x = \pm\sqrt{-1(2)}$
    $x = \pm\sqrt{-1} \bullet \sqrt{2}$
    $x = \pm i\sqrt{2}$

13. $5x^2 - 55 = 0$
    $5x^2 = 55$
    $x^2 = 11$
    $x = \pm\sqrt{11}$

15. $3x^2 - 6 = 0$
    $3x^2 = 6$
    $x^2 = 2$
    $x = \pm\sqrt{2}$

17. $3x^3 + 5x^2 - 2x = 0$
    $x(3x^2 + 5x - 2) = 0$
    $x(3x-1)(x+2) = 0$
    $x = 0, or, 3x-1 = 0, or, x+2 = 0$
    $x = 0, or, x = \dfrac{1}{3}, or, x = -2$

19. $x^2 + 4x = 5$
    $x^2 + 4x + 4 = 5 + 4$
    $(x+2)(x+2) = 9$
    $(x+2)^2 = 9$
    $x+2 = \pm\sqrt{9}$
    $x = -2 \pm 3$
    $x = -2+3 = 1 \ or \ x = -2-3 = -5$

21. $x^2 + 6x + 8 = 0$

$x^2 + 6x = -8$

$x^2 + 6x + 9 = -8 + 9$

$(x+3)(x+3) = 1$

$(x+3)^2 = 1$

$x + 3 = \pm\sqrt{1}$

$x = -3 \pm 1$

$x = -3 + 1 = -2$ OR

$x = -3 - 1 = -4$

23. $x^2 - 7x = 18$

$x^2 - 7x - 18 = 0$

$x = \dfrac{-(-7) \pm \sqrt{(-7)^2 - 4(1)(-18)}}{2(1)}$

$x = \dfrac{7 \pm \sqrt{49 - 4(-18)}}{2}$

$x = \dfrac{7 \pm \sqrt{49 + 72}}{2}$

$x = \dfrac{7 \pm \sqrt{121}}{2}$

$x = \dfrac{7 \pm 11}{2}$

$x = \dfrac{7 + 11}{2} = \dfrac{18}{2} = 9$ OR

$x = \dfrac{7 - 11}{2} = \dfrac{-4}{2} = -2$

25. $x^2 + 3x - 1 = 0$

$x = \dfrac{-3 \pm \sqrt{3^2 - 4(1)(-1)}}{2(1)}$

$x = \dfrac{-3 \pm \sqrt{9 + 4}}{2}$

$x = \dfrac{-3 \pm \sqrt{13}}{2}$

$x = \dfrac{-3 + \sqrt{13}}{2}$ OR

$x = \dfrac{-3 - \sqrt{13}}{2}$

27. $3x^2 = 6x + 7$

$3x^2 - 6x - 7 = 0$

$b^2 - 4ac = (-6)^2 - 4(3)(-7)$

$= 36 - 12(-7)$

$= 36 + 84 = 120$

The discriminant is positive but not a perfect square $\Rightarrow$ 2 irrational solutions.

29. $x^2 - 25 = 0$

$b^2 - 4ac = 0^2 - 4(1)(-25)$

$b^2 - 4ac = 100$

The discriminant is positive and a perfect square $\Rightarrow$ 2 rational solutions.

31. $x - 3\sqrt{x} - 4 = 0$

$x - 3x^{\frac{1}{2}} - 4 = 0$

Quadratic in $x^{\frac{1}{2}}$ so let $u = x^{\frac{1}{2}}$

which gives $u^2 = x$.

$u^2 - 3u - 4 = 0$

$(u - 4)(u + 1) = 0$

$u - 4 = 0, or, u + 1 = 0$

$u = 4, or, u = -1$

$x^{\frac{1}{2}} = 4, or, x^{\frac{1}{2}} = -1$

$(x^{\frac{1}{2}})^2 = 4^2 \rightarrow x = 16$ OR

$(x^{\frac{1}{2}})^2 = (-1)^2 \rightarrow x = 1$

When an equation is squared, it may create extraneous solutions, so all solutions must be checked.

$x = 16$ is a solution.

$x = 1$ is not a solution.

Section 2.4

1. $f(x) = x^2 - 4x - 12$

   a) vertex: $-\dfrac{b}{2a} = -\dfrac{-4}{2(1)} = 2$

   $$f(-\dfrac{b}{2a}) = f(2) = 2^2 - 4(2) - 12$$
   $$= 4 - 8 - 12 = -16$$

   vertex $(2, -16)$;

   b) axis of symmetry: $x = 2$;

   c) Coefficient of x^2 is positive so parabola opens up $\Rightarrow$ vertex is minimum.
   Minimum is -16.

3. $f(x) = x^2 - 8x + 12$

   a) vertex: $-\dfrac{b}{2a} = -\dfrac{-8}{2(1)} = 4$

   $$f(-\dfrac{b}{2a}) = f(4)$$
   $$= 4^2 - 8(4) + 12$$
   $$= 16 - 32 + 12 = -4$$

   vertex $(4, -4)$;

   b) axis of symmetry: $x = 4$;

   c) Coefficient of x^2 is positive so parabola opens up $\Rightarrow$ vertex is minimum.
   Minimum is -4.

5. $f(x) = 3x^2 + 9x + 12$

   a) vertex: $-\dfrac{b}{2a} = -\dfrac{9}{2(3)} = -\dfrac{3}{2}$;

   $$f(-\dfrac{b}{2a}) = f(-\dfrac{3}{2})$$
   $$= 3(-\dfrac{3}{2})^2 + 9(-\dfrac{3}{2}) + 12$$
   $$= 3(\dfrac{9}{4}) - \dfrac{27}{2} + 12$$
   $$= \dfrac{27}{4} - \dfrac{54}{4} + \dfrac{48}{4}$$
   $$= \dfrac{21}{4}$$

   vertex $(-\dfrac{3}{2}, \dfrac{21}{4})$;

   b) axis of symmetry: $x = -\dfrac{3}{2}$;

   c) Coefficient of x^2 is positive so parabola opens up $\Rightarrow$ vertex is minimum.
   Minimum is $\dfrac{21}{4}$.

7. $f(x) = -x^2 - 4x$

   a) vertex: $-\dfrac{b}{2a} = -\dfrac{-4}{2(-1)} = -2$

   $$f(-\dfrac{b}{2a}) = f(-4)$$
   $$= -(-2)^2 - 4(-2)$$
   $$= -4 + 8 = 4$$

   vertex $(-2, 4)$;

   b) axis of symmetry: $x = -2$;

   c) Coefficient of x^2 is negative so parabola opens down $\Rightarrow$ vertex is maximum.
   Maximum is 4.

9. $f(x) = -3x^2 - 2x + 1$

a) $-\dfrac{b}{2a} = -\dfrac{-2}{2(-3)} = \dfrac{2}{-6} = -\dfrac{1}{3}$

$f(-\dfrac{b}{2a}) = f(-\dfrac{1}{3})$

$\qquad = -3(-\dfrac{1}{3})^2 - 2(-\dfrac{1}{3}) + 1$

$\qquad = -3(\dfrac{1}{9}) + \dfrac{2}{3} + \dfrac{3}{3}$

$\qquad = -\dfrac{1}{3} + \dfrac{5}{3}$

$\qquad = \dfrac{4}{3}$

vertex: $(-\dfrac{1}{3}, \dfrac{4}{3})$;

b) axis of symmetry: $x = -\dfrac{1}{3}$;

c) Coefficient of x^2 is negative so parabola opens down $\Rightarrow$ vertex is maximum.

Maximum is $\dfrac{4}{3}$.

11. $f(x) = 2x^2 - 4x + 5$

a) $-\dfrac{b}{2a} = -\dfrac{-4}{2(2)} = 1$

$f(-\dfrac{b}{2a}) = f(1)$

$\qquad = 2(1)^2 - 4(1) + 5$

$\qquad = 3$

vertex: $(1, 3)$;

b) axis of symmetry: $x = 1$;

c) Coefficient of x^2 is positive so parabola opens up $\Rightarrow$ vertex is minimum. Minimum is 3.

13. $f(x) = x^2 - 7x + 6$

a) $-\dfrac{b}{2a} = -\dfrac{-7}{2(1)} = \dfrac{7}{2}$

$f(-\dfrac{b}{2a}) = f(\dfrac{7}{2})$

$\qquad = (\dfrac{7}{2})^2 - 7(\dfrac{7}{2}) + 6$

$\qquad = \dfrac{49}{4} - \dfrac{49}{2} + 6$

$\qquad = \dfrac{49}{4} - \dfrac{98}{4} + \dfrac{24}{4}$

$\qquad = -\dfrac{25}{4}$

vertex: $(\dfrac{7}{2}, -\dfrac{25}{4})$;

b) Coefficient of x^2 is positive so parabola opens up $\Rightarrow$ vertex is min.

Minimum is $-\dfrac{25}{4}$;

c) range: $[-\dfrac{25}{4}, \infty)$;

d) decreasing: $(-\infty, \dfrac{7}{2})$; increasing: $(\dfrac{7}{2}, \infty)$

15. $g(x) = -2x^2 + 6x - 5$

a) $-\dfrac{b}{2a} = -\dfrac{6}{2(-2)} = \dfrac{3}{2}$

$f(-\dfrac{b}{2a}) = f(\dfrac{3}{2})$

$= -2(\dfrac{3}{2})^2 + 6(\dfrac{3}{2}) - 5$

$= -2(\dfrac{9}{4}) + 9 - 5$

$= -\dfrac{9}{2} + 4$

$= -\dfrac{1}{2}$

vertex: $(\dfrac{3}{2}, -\dfrac{1}{2})$;

b) Coefficient of x^2 is negative so parabola opens down $\Rightarrow$ vertex is max.

Maximum is $-\dfrac{1}{2}$.

c) range: $(-\infty, -\dfrac{1}{2}]$;

d) increasing: $(-\infty, \dfrac{3}{2})$; decreasing: $(\dfrac{3}{2}, \infty)$

17. $s(t) = -16t^2 + 30t + 4$

The coefficient of t^2 is negative so the vertex is a maximum. 1st coordinate of vertex is time, 2nd coordinate is height.

$t = -\dfrac{b}{2a} = -\dfrac{30}{2(-16)} = \dfrac{15}{16} = 0.9375$ sec.

$s(-\dfrac{b}{2a}) = s(\dfrac{15}{16}) = 18.0625$ ft.

Section 2.5

When solving rational equations, always check the answers to make sure no denominator has a value of 0.

1. $\dfrac{1}{4} + \dfrac{1}{6} = \dfrac{1}{y}$

$\dfrac{12y}{1}(\dfrac{1}{4}) + \dfrac{12y}{1}(\dfrac{1}{6}) = \dfrac{12y}{1}(\dfrac{1}{y})$

$3y + 2y = 12$

$5y = 12$

$y = \dfrac{12}{5}$

Check answer.

3. $\dfrac{1}{x} + \dfrac{1}{2} = \dfrac{3}{4}$

$\dfrac{4x}{1}(\dfrac{1}{x}) + \dfrac{4x}{1}(\dfrac{1}{2}) = \dfrac{4x}{1}(\dfrac{3}{4})$

$4 + 2x = 3x$

$4 = x$

Check answer.

5. $\dfrac{1}{t} + \dfrac{1}{5} = \dfrac{t-1}{5t} + \dfrac{3}{10}$

$\dfrac{10t}{1}(\dfrac{1}{t}) + \dfrac{10t}{1}(\dfrac{1}{5}) = \dfrac{10t}{1}(\dfrac{t-1}{5t}) + \dfrac{10t}{1}(\dfrac{3}{10})$

$10 + 2t = 2(t-1) + 3t$

$10 + 2t = 2t - 2 + 3t$

$12 = 3t$

$4 = t$

Check answer.

7. $\dfrac{x}{2} = \dfrac{5}{x+3}$

$x(x+3) = 2(5)$

$x^2 + 3x = 10$

$x^2 + 3x - 10 = 0$

$(x+5)(x-2) = 0$

$x+5 = 0 \quad or \quad x-2 = 0$

$x = -5 \quad or \quad x = 2$

Check answers.

9. $\dfrac{x-1}{x^2-4} + \dfrac{1}{x-2} = \dfrac{x+4}{x+2}$

$\dfrac{x-1}{(x+2)(x-2)} + \dfrac{1}{x-2} = \dfrac{x+4}{x+2}$

$\dfrac{(x+2)(x-2)}{1}\left(\dfrac{x-1}{(x+2)(x-2)}\right) + \dfrac{(x+2)(x-2)}{1}\left(\dfrac{1}{x-2}\right) =$

$\dfrac{(x+2)(x-2)}{1}\left(\dfrac{x+4}{x+2}\right)$

$x-1+x+2 = (x-2)(x+4)$

$2x+1 = x^2 + 2x - 8$

$9 = x^2$

$x = \pm\sqrt{9}$

$x = \pm 3$

Check answers.

11. $\dfrac{1}{x-1} + \dfrac{2}{x} = \dfrac{x}{x-1}$

$\dfrac{x(x-1)}{1}\left(\dfrac{1}{x-1}\right) + \dfrac{x(x-1)}{1}\left(\dfrac{2}{x}\right) = \dfrac{x(x-1)}{1}\left(\dfrac{x}{x-1}\right)$

$x + 2(x-1) = x(x)$

$x + 2x - 2 = x^2$

$0 = x^2 - 3x + 2$

$0 = (x-2)(x-1)$

$0 = x-2 \quad or \quad 0 = x-1$

$x = 2 \quad or \quad x = 1$

Check answers. *x cannot equal* 1.

Solution is $x = 2$.

13. $\dfrac{5}{x+2} - \dfrac{x-1}{x-3} = -\dfrac{2}{x-3}$

$\dfrac{(x+2)(x-3)}{1}\left(\dfrac{5}{x+2}\right) - \dfrac{(x+2)(x-3)}{1}\left(\dfrac{x-1}{x-3}\right) =$

$\dfrac{(x+2)(x-3)}{1}\left(\dfrac{-2}{x-3}\right)$

$5(x-3) - (x+2)(x-1) = -2(x+2)$

$5x - 15 - (x^2 + x - 2) = -2x - 4$

$5x - 15 - x^2 - x + 2 = -2x - 4$

$4x - x^2 - 13 = -2x - 4$

$0 = x^2 - 6x + 9$

$0 = (x-3)(x-3)$

$x = 3$

Check answer. *x cannot equal* 3.

No solution

15. $\dfrac{1}{x} = \dfrac{1}{x^3}$

$1(x^3) = x(1)$

$x^3 = x$

$x^3 - x = 0$

$x(x^2 - 1) = 0$

$x(x+1)(x-1) = 0$

$x = 0 \quad or \quad x+1 = 0 \quad x-1 = 0$

$x = 0 \quad or \quad x = -1 \quad or \quad x = 1$

Check answers. *x cannot equal* 0. $x = \pm 1$

When solving radical equations, always check answers.

17. $\sqrt{3x-1} = -5$

$(\sqrt{3x-1})^2 = (-5)^2$

$3x - 1 = 25$

$3x = 26$

$x = \dfrac{26}{3}$

Check answers.

$\sqrt{3\left(\dfrac{26}{3}\right) - 1} = -5$

$\sqrt{26 - 1} = -5$

$\sqrt{25} = -5$

$5 = -5 \quad not \ true$

No solution

19. $\sqrt{x} = x$

$(\sqrt{x})^2 = x^2$

$x = x^2$

$0 = x^2 - x$

$0 = x(x-1)$

$0 = x$ $\quad or \quad$ $0 = x-1$

$x = 0$ $\quad or \quad$ $x = 1$

Check answers.

21. $y + 1 = \sqrt{2y + 10}$

$(y+1)^2 = (\sqrt{2y+10})^2$

$y^2 + 2y + 1 = 2y + 10$

$y^2 = 9$

$y = \pm\sqrt{9} = \pm 3$

Check answers. *y cannot equal* -3.

Solution is $y = 3$

23. $|x| = 4$

$x = 4$ $\quad or \quad$ $x = -4$

25. $|x+3| = 6$

$x+3 = 6$ $\quad or \quad$ $x+3 = -6$

$x = 3$ $\quad or \quad$ $x = -9$

27. $|x-3| = 7$

$x-3 = 7$ $\quad or \quad$ $x-3 = -7$

$x = 10$ $\quad or \quad$ $x = -4$

29. $|x+2| + 4 = 6$

$|x+2| = 2$

$x+2 = 2$ $\quad or \quad$ $x+2 = -2$

$x = 0$ $\quad or \quad$ $x = -4$

Section 2.6

1. $x + 5 < 4x - 10$

$-3x < -15$

$\dfrac{-3x}{-3} > \dfrac{-15}{-3}$

$x > 5$

3. $4x - 4 - 2x \geq 2 - 4x + 10$

$2x - 4 \geq -4x + 12$

$6x \geq 16$

$x \geq \dfrac{8}{3}$

5. $-\dfrac{1}{3}x \leq \dfrac{5}{4} + \dfrac{5}{6}x$

$12(-\dfrac{1}{3}x) \leq 12(\dfrac{5}{4}) + 12(\dfrac{5}{6}x)$

$-4x \leq 15 + 10x$

$-14x \leq 15$

$\dfrac{-14x}{-14} \geq \dfrac{15}{-14}$

$x \geq -\dfrac{15}{14}$

7. $-4 \leq x + 1 < 5$

$-5 \leq x < 4$

$[-5, 4)$

9. $-2 \leq x - 3 < 4$

$1 \leq x < 7$

$[1, 7)$

11. $-4 \leq -2x < 8$

$\dfrac{-4}{-2} \geq \dfrac{-2x}{-2} > \dfrac{8}{-2}$

$2 \geq x > -4$

$-4 < x \leq 2$ $\qquad I.N.\,(-4, 2]$

13. $2x < 10$ $\quad or \quad$ $x + 4 > 16$

$x < 5$ $\quad or \quad$ $x > 12$

$(-\infty, 5) \cup (12, \infty)$

15. $x+10 \le \dfrac{1}{3}$ or $x-20 \ge \dfrac{1}{2}$

$x \le \dfrac{1}{3}-10$ or $x \ge \dfrac{1}{2}+20$

$x \le -\dfrac{29}{3}$ or $x \ge \dfrac{41}{2}$

$(-\infty, -\dfrac{29}{3}] \cup [\dfrac{41}{2}, \infty)$

17. $|x| < 6$

$-6 < x < 6$ $I.N. (-6, 6)$

19. $|x+3| < 6$

$-6 < x+3 < 6$

$-9 < x < 3$ $I.N. (-9, 3)$

21. $|x+7| \ge 9$

$x+7 \ge 9$ or $x+7 \le -9$

$x \ge 2$ or $x \le -16$

$(-\infty, -16] \cup [2, \infty)$

23. $\left|x-\dfrac{1}{4}\right| < 6$

$-6 < x-\dfrac{1}{4} < 6$

$-6+\dfrac{1}{4} < x < 6+\dfrac{1}{4}$

$-\dfrac{23}{4} < x < \dfrac{25}{4}$

$(-\dfrac{23}{4}, \dfrac{25}{4})$

25. $|2x+4| \le 10$

$-10 \le 2x+4 \le 10$

$-14 \le 2x \le 6$

$-7 \le x \le 3$ $I.N. [-7, 3]$

27. $\left|x+\dfrac{4}{3}\right| \le \dfrac{8}{3}$

$-\dfrac{8}{3} \le x+\dfrac{4}{3} \le \dfrac{8}{3}$

$-\dfrac{12}{3} \le x \le \dfrac{4}{3}$

$-4 \le x \le \dfrac{4}{3}$ $I.N. [-4, \dfrac{4}{3}]$

29. $\left|\dfrac{2x-2}{3}\right| > 8$

$\dfrac{2x-2}{3} > 8$ or $\dfrac{2x-2}{3} < -8$

$2x-2 > 24$ or $2x-2 < -24$

$2x > 26$ or $2x < -22$

$x > 13$ or $x < -11$

$(-\infty, -11) \cup (13, \infty)$

Review Chapter 2

1. $5x-4=1$

$5x=5 \Rightarrow x=1$

2. $2x-5=5x+7$

$-3x=12$

$x=-4$

3. $4(x-2)=2(x+3)$

$4x-8=2x+6$

$2x=14$

$x=7$

4. $(2x-1)(3x+2)=0$

$\quad 2x-1=0 \quad or \quad 3x+2=0$

$\quad\quad x=\dfrac{1}{2} \quad or \quad x=-\dfrac{2}{3}$

5. $x^2+x-6=0$

$\quad (x+3)(x-2)=0$

$\quad x+3=0 \quad or \quad x-2=0$

$\quad\quad x=-3 \quad or \quad x=2$

6. $3x^2=8-2x$

$\quad 3x^2+2x-8=0$

$\quad (3x-4)(x+2)=0$

$\quad 3x-4=0 \quad or \quad x=-2$

$\quad\quad x=\dfrac{4}{3} \quad or \quad x=-2$

7. $4x^2=20$

$\quad\quad x^2=5$

$\quad\quad x=\pm\sqrt{5}$

8. $x^2-6=0$

$\quad\quad x^2=6$

$\quad\quad x=\pm\sqrt{6}$

9. $f(x)=6x-24$

$\quad 0=6x-24$

$\quad 24=6x \implies x=4$

10. $f(x)=x-5$

$\quad 0=x-5 \implies x=5$

11. $f(x)=3-9x$

$\quad 0=3-9x$

$\quad 9x=3 \implies x=\dfrac{1}{3}$

12. $f(x)=x^2+2x+1$

$\quad 0=x^2+2x+1$

$\quad 0=(x+1)(x+1)$

$\quad\quad x=-1$

13. $f(x)=x^2-2x-24$

$\quad 0=x^2-2x-24$

$\quad 0=(x-6)(x+4)$

$\quad x-6=0 \quad or \quad x+4=0$

$\quad\quad x=6 \quad or \quad x=-4$

14. $f(x)=2x^2+5x-3$

$\quad 0=2x^2+5x-3$

$\quad 0=(2x-1)(x+3)$

$\quad 2x-1=0 \quad or \quad x+3=0$

$\quad\quad x=\dfrac{1}{2} \quad or \quad x=-3$

15. $\dfrac{4}{x+2}+\dfrac{2}{x-1}=0$

$\quad \dfrac{(x+2)(x-1)}{1}(\dfrac{4}{x+2})+\dfrac{(x+2)(x-1)}{1}(\dfrac{2}{x-1})=$

$\quad\quad\quad\quad\quad\quad\quad\quad (x+2)(x-1)(0)$

$\quad 4(x-1)+2(x+2)=0$

$\quad 4x-4+2x+4=0$

$\quad 6x=0 \implies x=0$

Check answer for rational equations.

16. $\dfrac{3}{x}+\dfrac{2}{x+1}=0$

$\quad \dfrac{x(x+1)}{1}(\dfrac{3}{x})+\dfrac{x(x+1)}{1}(\dfrac{2}{x+1})=x(x+1)(0)$

$\quad 3(x+1)+2x=0$

$\quad 3x+3+2x=0$

$\quad 5x+3=0$

$\quad\quad x=-\dfrac{3}{5}$

Check answer for rational equations.

17. $\sqrt{3x+2}=\sqrt{5x+1}$

$\quad (\sqrt{3x+2})^2=(\sqrt{5x+1})^2$

$\quad 3x+2=5x+1$

$\quad -2x=-1$

$\quad\quad x=\dfrac{1}{2}$

Check answers for radical equations.

18. $-1 = \sqrt{x-4} - \sqrt{x-1}$

$\sqrt{x-1} - 1 = \sqrt{x-4}$

$(\sqrt{x-1} - 1)^2 = (\sqrt{x-4})^2$

$x - 1 - 2\sqrt{x-1} + 1 = x - 4$

$4 = 2\sqrt{x-1}$

$4^2 = (2\sqrt{x-1})^2$

$16 = 4(x-1)$

$16 = 4x - 4$

$20 = 4x \implies x = 5$

Check answers for radical equations.

19. $|x-3| = 4$

$x - 3 = 4 \quad or \quad x - 3 = -4$

$x = 7 \quad or \quad x = -1$

20. $|2x+3| = 15$

$2x + 3 = 15 \quad or \quad 2x + 3 = -15$

$2x = 12 \quad or \quad 2x = -18$

$x = 6 \quad or \quad x = -9$

21. $-4 \le 2x + 1 \le 5$

$-5 \le 2x \le 4$

$-\dfrac{5}{2} \le x \le 2$

$[-\dfrac{5}{2}, 2]$

22. $-1 < 2x - 3 \le 7$

$2 < 2x \le 10$

$1 < x \le 5$

$(1, 5]$

23. $3x < -6 \quad or \quad x + 2 > 5$

$x < -2 \quad or \quad x > 3$

$(-\infty, -2) \cup (3, \infty)$

24. $4x + 2 \le 6 \quad or \quad 2x \ge 10$

$4x \le 4 \quad or \quad x \ge 5$

$x \le 1 \quad or \quad x \ge 5$

$(-\infty, 1] \cup [5, \infty)$

25. $|4x - 1| < 3$

$-3 < 4x - 1 < 3$

$-2 < 4x < 4$

$-\dfrac{1}{2} < x < 1 \qquad I.N. \, (-\dfrac{1}{2}, 1)$

26. $|x + 5| \ge 3$

$x + 5 \ge 3 \quad or \quad x + 5 \le -3$

$x \ge -2 \quad or \quad x \le -8$

$(-\infty, -8] \cup [-2, \infty)$

27. $V = lwh$

$\dfrac{V}{lw} = \dfrac{lwh}{lw}$

$\dfrac{V}{lw} = h$

28. $v = \sqrt{3gp}$

$v^2 = (\sqrt{3gp})^2$

$v^2 = 3gp$

$\dfrac{v^2}{3p} = \dfrac{3gp}{3p}$

$\dfrac{v^2}{3p} = g$

29. $-\sqrt{-20} = -\sqrt{-1(20)}$

$= -\sqrt{-1} \bullet \sqrt{20}$

$= -i\sqrt{4(5)}$

$= -i\sqrt{4} \bullet \sqrt{5}$

$= -2i\sqrt{5}$

30. $\sqrt{-6} \bullet \sqrt{-12} = \sqrt{-1(6)} \bullet \sqrt{-1(12)}$

$= \sqrt{-1} \bullet \sqrt{6} \bullet \sqrt{-1} \bullet \sqrt{12}$

$= i \bullet \sqrt{6} \bullet i \bullet \sqrt{12}$

$= i^2 \sqrt{6(12)}$

$= -1\sqrt{72}$

$= -\sqrt{36(2)}$

$= -6\sqrt{2}$

31. $\dfrac{\sqrt{-36}}{-\sqrt{-64}} = \dfrac{\sqrt{-1(36)}}{-\sqrt{-1(64)}}$

$= \dfrac{\sqrt{-1}\bullet\sqrt{36}}{-\sqrt{-1}\bullet\sqrt{64}}$

$= \dfrac{i6}{-i8}$

$= -\dfrac{3}{4}$

32. $\sqrt{-48}\bullet\sqrt{-12} = \sqrt{-1(48)}\bullet\sqrt{-1(12)}$

$= \sqrt{-1}\bullet\sqrt{48}\bullet\sqrt{-1}\bullet\sqrt{12}$

$= i\sqrt{16(3)}\bullet i\sqrt{4(3)}$

$= 4i\sqrt{3}\bullet 2i\sqrt{3}$

$= 8i^2\sqrt{9}$

$= 8(-1)(3)$

$= -24$

33. $(4+2i)(5+i) = 20+14i+2i^2$

$= 20+14i+2(-1)$

$= 18+14i$

34. $(4-2i)-2(-3i) = 4-2i+6i$

$= 4+4i$

35. $\dfrac{2-3i}{1-2i} = \dfrac{(2-3i)(1+2i)}{(1-2i)(1+2i)}$

$= \dfrac{2+4i-3i-6i^2}{1+2i-2i-4i^2}$

$= \dfrac{2+i-6(-1)}{1-4(-1)}$

$= \dfrac{8+i}{5}$

$= \dfrac{8}{5}+\dfrac{1}{5}i$

36. $\dfrac{3-i}{3+i} = \dfrac{3-i}{3+i}\bullet\dfrac{3-i}{3-i}$

$= \dfrac{9-3i-3i+i^2}{9-3i+3i-i^2}$

$= \dfrac{9-6i+(-1)}{9-(-1)}$

$= \dfrac{8-6i}{10} = \dfrac{4}{5}-\dfrac{3}{5}i$

37. $x = \dfrac{-(-10)\pm\sqrt{(-10)^2-4(3)(-8)}}{2(3)}$

$x = \dfrac{10\pm\sqrt{100+96}}{6}$

$x = \dfrac{10\pm\sqrt{196}}{6}$

$x = \dfrac{10\pm 14}{6}$

$x = \dfrac{10+14}{6}$ or $x = \dfrac{10-14}{6}$

$x = 4$ or $x = -\dfrac{2}{3}$

38. $y = \dfrac{-(-4)\pm\sqrt{(-4)^2-4(1)(10)}}{2(1)}$

$y = \dfrac{4\pm\sqrt{16-40}}{2}$

$y = \dfrac{4\pm\sqrt{-24}}{2}$

$y = \dfrac{4\pm\sqrt{-1(4)(6)}}{2}$

$y = \dfrac{4\pm\sqrt{-1}\bullet\sqrt{4}\bullet\sqrt{6}}{2}$

$y = \dfrac{4\pm 2i\sqrt{6}}{2}$

$y = \dfrac{4}{2}\pm\dfrac{2i\sqrt{6}}{2}$

$y = 2\pm i\sqrt{6}$

39. $x^2 - 3x - 18 = 0$

$$x = \frac{-(-3) \pm \sqrt{(-3)^2 - 4(1)(-18)}}{2(1)}$$

$$x = \frac{3 \pm \sqrt{9 + 72}}{2}$$

$$x = \frac{3 \pm \sqrt{81}}{2}$$

$$x = \frac{3 + 9}{2} \quad or \quad x = \frac{3 - 9}{2}$$

$$x = 6 \quad or \quad x = -3$$

40. Equation is quadratic in x^2 so let
$u = x^2$. *Therefore*, $u^2 = x^4$.

$$x^4 - 3x^2 + 2 = 0$$
$$u^2 - 3u + 2 = 0$$
$$(u - 2)(u - 1) = 0$$
$$u = 2 \quad or \quad u = 1$$
$$x^2 = 2 \quad or \quad x^2 = 1$$
$$x = \pm\sqrt{2} \quad or \quad x = \pm 1$$

CHAPTER 3

Section 3.1

1. Exponent of 4: quartic
    Leading term: $3x^4$
    Leading coefficient: 3
    Degree: 4

3. Exponent of 1: linear
    Leading term: $0.3x$
    Leading coefficient: 0.3
    Degree: 1

5. Exponent of 2: quadratic
    Leading term: $134x^2$
    Leading coefficient: 134
    Degree: 2

7. Exponent of 3: cubic
    Leading term: $-3x^3$
    Leading coefficient: -3
    Degree: 3

9. No x: constant
    Leading term: -5
    Leading coefficient: -5
    Degree: 0

11. Degree of function is odd. Negative leading
    term $\rightarrow$ reflects over x-axis.
    Graph goes from $+\infty$ to $-\infty$.

13. Degree of function is even. Negative leading
    term $\rightarrow$ reflects over x-axis.
    Graph goes from $-\infty$ to $-\infty$.

15. Degree of function is odd. Graph goes from
    $-\infty$ to $+\infty$.

17. $f(x) = (x-3)^2(x-4)$
    $0 = (x-3)^2(x-4)$
    $x-3 = 0 \quad or \quad x-4 = 0$
    $\quad x = 3 \quad or \quad x = 4$
    3 is a zero with multiplicity of 2 and
    4 is a zero with multiplicity of 1.

19. $h(x) = -3(x-2)^3(x+2)$
    $\quad 0 = -3(x-2)^3(x+2)$
    $\quad x-2 = 0 \quad or \quad x+2 = 0$
    $\quad x = 2 \quad or \quad x = -2$
    2 is a zero with multiplicity of 3 and
    -2 is a zero with multiplicity of 1.

21. $f(x) = -2(x-1)^2(x+5)^3 x^4$
    $\quad 0 = -2(x-1)^2(x+5)^3 x^4$
    $\quad x-1 = 0 \quad or \quad x+5 = 0 \quad or \quad x = 0$
    $\quad x = 1 \quad or \quad x = -5 \quad or \quad x = 0$
    1 is a zero with multiplicity of 2, -5 is
    a zero with multiplicity of 3 and 0 is a
    zero with multiplicity of 4.

Section 3.2

1. Degree of $6 \Rightarrow$ maximum number of:
    a) real zeros is 6;
    b) x-intercepts is 6;
    c) turning points is 6-1 = 5.

3. Degree of $3 \Rightarrow$ maximum number of:
    a) real zeros is 3;
    b) x-intercepts is 3;
    c) turning points is 3-1 = 2.

5. Degree of $5 \Rightarrow$ maximum number of:
    a) real zeros is 5;
    b) x-intercepts is 5;
    c) turning points is 5-1 = 4.

7. Degree is even, leading coeff. is > 0:
    a) graph goes from ∞ to ∞;
    b) y-intercept is -6.

9. Degree is odd, leading coeff. is > 0:
   a) graph goes from $-\infty$ to $+\infty$;
   b) y-intercept is -2.

11. Degree is odd, leading coeff. is > 0:
   a) graph goes from $-\infty$ to $+\infty$;
   b) y-intercept is 4.

13 and 15 are not included.

17. $f(-2) = (-2)^3 + 5(-2)^2 - 6(-2) - 11$
    $\quad = -8 + 20 + 12 - 11 = 13$
    $f(1) = 1^3 + 5(1) - 6(1) - 11$
    $\quad = -11$
    There is a sign change so there is a zero between -2 and 1.

19. $f(-3) = 3(-3)^2 - (-3) - 7$
    $\quad = 27 + 3 - 7 = 23$
    $f(0) = 3(0)^2 - 0 - 7$
    $\quad = -7$
    There is a sign change so there is a zero between -3 and 0.

Section 3.3

1.
$$
\begin{array}{r}
4x+14 \\
x-3\overline{)4x^2+2x+42} \\
\end{array}
$$
$\qquad -(4x^2 - 12x)$
$\qquad\qquad 14x + 42$
$\qquad\qquad -(14x - 42)$
$\qquad\qquad\qquad 84$

R=84, $x-3$ is not a factor.

3.
$$
\begin{array}{r}
x^2 + 3x + 3 \\
x-1\overline{)x^3 + 2x^2 + 0x - 3} \\
\end{array}
$$
$\qquad -(x^3 - x^2)$
$\qquad\qquad 3x^2 + 0x$
$\qquad\qquad -(3x^2 - 3x)$
$\qquad\qquad\qquad 3x - 3$
$\qquad\qquad\qquad -(3x - 3)$
$\qquad\qquad\qquad\qquad 0$

R=0; $x-1$ is a factor.

5.
$$
\begin{array}{r}
4x^2 - 2x - 1 \\
x+2\overline{)4x^3 + 6x^2 - 5x - 2} \\
\end{array}
$$
$\qquad -(4x^3 + 8x^2)$
$\qquad\qquad -2x^2 - 5x$
$\qquad\qquad -(-2x^2 - 4x)$
$\qquad\qquad\qquad -x - 2$
$\qquad\qquad\qquad -(-x - 2)$
$\qquad\qquad\qquad\qquad 0$

R=0; $x+2$ is a factor.

7.
$$
\begin{array}{r}
x^2 - 2x + 4 \\
x+2\overline{)x^3 + 0x^2 + 0x - 27} \\
\end{array}
$$
$\qquad -(x^3 + 2x^2)$
$\qquad\qquad -2x^2 + 0x$
$\qquad\qquad -(-2x^2 - 4x)$
$\qquad\qquad\qquad 4x - 27$
$\qquad\qquad\qquad -(4x + 8)$
$\qquad\qquad\qquad\qquad -35$

$Q(x) = x^2 - 2x + 4; \quad R(x) = -35$

9.
$$2x^2+x-3$$
$$x-2\overline{)2x^3-3x^2-5x+4}$$
$$\underline{-(2x^3-4x^2)}$$
$$x^2-5x$$
$$\underline{-(x^2-2x)}$$
$$-3x+4$$
$$\underline{-(-3x+6)}$$
$$-2$$
$$Q(x)=2x^2+x-3; \quad R(x)=-2$$

11.
$$\underline{12|} \quad 1 \quad\quad 2 \quad -120$$
$$\quad\quad\quad 12 \quad 168$$
$$\overline{\quad\quad 1 \quad 14 \quad\quad 48}$$
R=48; 12 is not a zero.

13.
$$\underline{4} \quad 2 \quad -6 \quad -9 \quad 4$$
$$\quad\quad\quad 8 \quad\quad 8 \quad -4$$
$$\overline{\quad 2 \quad\quad 2 \quad -1 \quad\quad 0}$$
R=0; 4 is a zero.

15.
$$\underline{4} \quad 1 \quad 0 \quad\quad 0 \quad -64$$
$$\quad\quad\quad 4 \quad 16 \quad\quad 64$$
$$\overline{\quad 1 \quad 4 \quad 16 \quad\quad 0}$$
Quotient = $x^2+4x+16$; R=0

17.
$$\underline{2} \quad 1 \quad 2 \quad 1 \quad -5$$
$$\quad\quad\quad 2 \quad 8 \quad 18$$
$$\overline{\quad 1 \quad 4 \quad 9 \quad\quad 13}$$
Quotient = x^2+4x+9; R=13

19.
$$\underline{-2} \quad 2 \quad 1 \quad -10 \quad 0 \quad -2$$
$$\quad\quad\quad\quad -4 \quad\quad 6 \quad 8 \quad -16$$
$$\overline{\quad 2 \quad -3 \quad -4 \quad 8 \quad -18}$$
$R=-18 \Rightarrow f(-2)=-18$

21. Start using small values in synthetic division until the remainder is 0.
$$\underline{2} \quad 1 \quad 1 \quad -4 \quad -4$$
$$\quad\quad\quad\quad 2 \quad\quad 6 \quad\quad 4$$
$$\overline{\quad 1 \quad 3 \quad\quad 2 \quad\quad 0}$$
$R=0 \Rightarrow x-2$ is a factor. The quotient,
x^2+3x+2, is also a factor.
$$f(x)=x^3+x^2-4x-4$$
$$f(x)=(x-2)(x^2+3x+2)$$
$$0=(x-2)(x+2)(x+1)$$
$$x-2=0 \quad or \quad x+2=0 \quad or \quad x+1=0$$
$$x=2 \quad or \quad x=-2 \quad or \quad x=-1$$

Section 3.4

1.
$$(x-(-1))(x-3)(x-5)$$
$$=(x+1)(x^2-8x+15)$$
$$=x^3-8x^2+15x+x^2-8x+15$$
$$=x^3-7x^2+7x+15$$

3.
$$(x-4)(x-i)(x-(-i))$$
$$=(x-4)(x-i)(x+i)$$
$$=(x-4)(x^2-i^2)$$
$$=(x-4)(x^2-(-1))$$
$$=(x-4)(x^2+1)$$
$$=x^3+x-4x^2-4$$
$$=x^3-4x^2+x-4$$

5. $(x-(-4))(x-(1+\sqrt{2}))(x-(1-\sqrt{2}))$
$= (x+4)(x-1-\sqrt{2})(x-1+\sqrt{2})$
$= (x+4)(x^2-x+x\sqrt{2}-x+1-\sqrt{2}-x\sqrt{2}+\sqrt{2}-2)$
$= (x+4)(x^2-2x-1)$
$= x^3-2x^2-x+4x^2-8x-4$
$= x^3+2x^2-9x-4$

7. $(x-0)(x-3)(x-(-2))$
$= x(x-3)(x+2)$
$= x(x^2-x-6)$
$= x^3-x^2-6x$

9. $(x-(-2))^3(x-0)(x-2)$
$= x(x+2)^3(x-2)$
$= x(x+2)(x+2)(x+2)(x-2)$
$= x(x+2)(x+2)(x^2-4)$
$= x(x+2)(x^3-4x+2x^2-8)$
$= x(x^4-4x^2+2x^3-8x+2x^3-8x+4x^2-16)$
$= x(x^4+4x^3-16x-16)$
$= x^5+4x^4-16x^2-16x$

11. By the Conjugate Zeros Theorem, if $\sqrt{3}$ is a zero, then $-\sqrt{3}$ is also a zero.

13. By the Conjugate Zeros Theorem, if $2i$ is a zero, then $-2i$ is also a zero.

15. By the Conjugate Zeros Theorem, if $\sqrt{3}$ and $-2i$ are zeros, then $-\sqrt{3}$ and $2i$ are also zeros.

17. By the Conjugate Zeros Theorem, if $2+i$ is a zero, then $2-i$ is also a zero.
$(x-3)(x-(2+i))(x-(2-i))$
$= (x-3)(x-2-i)(x-2+i)$
$= (x-3)(x^2-2x+xi-2x+4-2i-xi+2i-i^2)$
$= (x-3)(x^2-4x+4-(-1))$
$= (x-3)(x^2-4x+5)$
$= x^3-4x^2+5x-3x^2+12x-15$
$= x^3-7x^2+17x-15$

19. By the Conjugate Zeros Theorem, if $\sqrt{2}$ and $-3i$ are zeros, then $-\sqrt{2}$ and $3i$ are also zeros.
$(x-\sqrt{2})(x+\sqrt{2})(x-3i)(x+3i)$
$= (x^2-2)(x^2-9i^2)$
$= (x^2-2)(x^2-9(-1))$
$= (x^2-2)(x^2+9)$
$= x^4+9x^2-2x^2-18$
$= x^4+7x^2-18$

21. $a_0=2,\ a_n=4$
Possible rational zeros:
$\dfrac{2}{4} \quad \Rightarrow \quad \dfrac{\pm 1,\pm 2}{\pm 1,\pm 2,\pm 4}$

$\Rightarrow \pm 1, \pm\dfrac{1}{2}, \pm\dfrac{1}{4}, \pm 2$

23. $a_0 = -4, \quad a_n = 1$

Possible rational zeros:

$\dfrac{-4}{1} \quad \Rightarrow \quad \dfrac{\pm 1, \pm 2, \pm 4}{\pm 1}$

$\Rightarrow \quad \pm 1, \pm 2, \pm 4$

Test these possible zeros using synthetic division to find a 0 remainder.

$$
\begin{array}{r|rrrr}
4 & 1 & -8 & 17 & -4 \\
  &   & 4 & -16 & 4 \\
\hline
  & 1 & -4 & 1 & 0
\end{array}
$$

$f(x) = (x-4)(x^2 - 4x + 1)$

$0 = (x-4)(x^2 - 4x + 1)$

$x - 4 = 0 \quad or \quad x^2 - 4x + 1 = 0$

$x = 4 \quad or \quad x = \dfrac{-(-4) \pm \sqrt{(-4)^2 - 4(1)(1)}}{2(1)}$

$x = \dfrac{4 \pm \sqrt{16-4}}{2}$

$x = \dfrac{4 \pm \sqrt{12}}{2}$

$x = \dfrac{4 \pm 2\sqrt{3}}{2}$

$x = 4 \quad or \quad x = 2 \pm \sqrt{3}$

25. Determine all possible rational zeros and test using synthetic division. A remainder of 0 indicates a factor.

$$
\begin{array}{r|rrrrr}
4 & 1 & 2 & -13 & -38 & -24 \\
  &   & 4 & 24 & 44 & 24 \\
\hline
  & 1 & 6 & 11 & 6 & 0
\end{array}
$$

$f(x) = (x-4)(x^3 + 6x^2 + 11x + 6)$

Repeat the above process for the 3rd degree factor.

$$
\begin{array}{r|rrrr}
-1 & 1 & 6 & 11 & 6 \\
   &   & -1 & -5 & -6 \\
\hline
   & 1 & 5 & 6 & 0
\end{array}
$$

$f(x) = (x-4)(x-(-1))(x^2 + 5x + 6)$

$f(x) = (x-4)(x+1)(x+3)(x+2)$

$0 = (x-4)(x+1)(x+3)(x+2)$

Zeros: $x = 4, -1, -3, -2$

Section 3.5

1. VA: $x - 4 = 0 \quad \Rightarrow \quad x = 4$

HA: degree of numerator, 0, is less than degree of denominator, 1. $\Rightarrow \quad y = 0$

3. VA: $x - 2 = 0 \quad \Rightarrow \quad x = 2$

HA: degree of numerator and denominator is the same $\Rightarrow \quad y = \dfrac{1}{1} = 1$

5. VA: $5x - 3 = 0 \quad \Rightarrow \quad x = \dfrac{3}{5}$

HA: degree of numerator and denominator is the same $\Rightarrow \quad y = \dfrac{4}{5}$

7. VA: $x^2 - 4 = 0 \quad \Rightarrow \quad x = \pm 2$

HA: degree of numerator, 0, is less than degree of denominator, 2 $\Rightarrow \quad y = 0$

9. VA: $x+1=0 \Rightarrow x=-1$

OA: degree of numerator, 2, is one more than degree of denominator, 1.

$$\begin{array}{r} x-1 \\ x+1\overline{)x^2+0x+3} \\ \underline{-(x^2+x)} \\ -x+3 \\ \underline{-(-x-1)} \\ 4 \end{array}$$

OA: $y=x-1$

11. VA: $(x-2)(3x-1)=0$

$\quad x-2=0 \qquad 3x-1=0$

$\quad x=2 \qquad\quad x=\dfrac{1}{3}$

11. Continued:

HA: $f(x)=\dfrac{x^2+2x-3}{3x^2-7x+2}$

Degree of numerator and denominator is the same $\Rightarrow \quad y=\dfrac{1}{3}$

13. VA: There is no value of x that will make the denominator equal to 0 so there is no VA.

HA: degree of numerator and denominator is the same $\Rightarrow \quad y=\dfrac{2}{1}=2$

15 – 19 are not included.

21. $f(x)=\dfrac{any\ number}{(x+3)(x-2)}$

Section 3.6

All of these problems can be solved using a graphing calculator. See Chapter 6, Examples 27, 28 and 29.

1. $0=x^2+3x-18$

$\quad 0=(x+6)(x-3)$

$\quad x+6=0 \quad or \quad x-3=0$

$\quad x=-6 \quad or \quad x=3$

3. See Example 1 in textbook.

$\quad x^2+3x-18\ge0$

$\quad (x+6)(x-3)\ge0$

Zeros, -6 and 3, divide the axis into intervals: $(-\infty,-6),(-6,3),(3,\infty)$.

INTERVAL	TEST VALUE	SIGN
$(-\infty,-6)$	$f(-7)=22$	positive*
$(-6,3)$	$f(0)=-18$	negative
$(3,\infty)$	$f(4)=10$	positive*

$(-\infty,-6]\cup[3,\infty)$

5. Referring to the table in #3, $(-6,3)$

7. See Example 1 in textbook.

Zeros, -1 and 2, divide the axis into intervals: $(-\infty,-1),(-1,2),(2,\infty)$.

INTERVAL	TEST VALUE	SIGN
$(-\infty,-1)$	$f(-2)=4$	positive*
$(-1,2)$	$f(0)=-2$	negative
$(2,\infty)$	$f(3)=4$	positive*

$(-\infty,-1)\cup(2,\infty)$

9. $(x-4)(x+3)>0$

Zeros, 4 and -3, divide the axis into intervals: $(-\infty,-3),(-3,4),(4,\infty)$.

INTERVAL	TEST VALUE	SIGN
$(-\infty,-3)$	$f(-4)=8$	positive*
$(-3,4)$	$f(0)=-12$	negative
$(4,\infty)$	$f(5)=8$	positive*

$(-\infty,-3)\cup(4,\infty)$

11. $x^2 - 36 > 0$

$(x+6)(x-6) > 0$

Zeros, 6 and -6, divide the axis into

intervals: $(-\infty, -6), (-6, 6), (6, \infty)$.

INTERVAL	TEST VALUE	SIGN
$(-\infty, -6)$	$f(-7) = 23$	positive*
$(-6, 6)$	$f(0) = -26$	negative
$(6, \infty)$	$f(7) = 23$	positive*

$(-\infty, -6) \cup (6, \infty)$

13. $x^2 + 6x + 8 < 0$

$(x+4)(x+2) < 0$

Zeros, -4 and -2, divide the axis into

intervals: $(-\infty, -4), (-4, -2), (-2, \infty)$.

INTERVAL	TEST VALUE	SIGN
$(-\infty, -4)$	$f(-5) = 3$	positive
$(-4, -2)$	$f(-3) = -1$	negative*
$(-2, \infty)$	$f(0) = 8$	positive

$(-4, -2)$

15. See Example 2 in textbook.

$x(x^2 - 5) \le 0$

$x(x + \sqrt{5})(x - \sqrt{5}) \le 0$

Zeros, $0, -\sqrt{5}, \sqrt{5}$, divide the axis into

intervals: $(-\infty, -\sqrt{5}), (-\sqrt{5}, 0), (0, \sqrt{5})$.

INTERVAL	TESTVALUE	SIGN
$(-\infty, -\sqrt{5})$	$f(-3) = -12$	negative *
$(-\sqrt{5}, 0)$	$f(-1) = 4$	positive
$(0, \sqrt{5})$	$f(1) = -4$	negative *

$(-\infty, -\sqrt{5}] \cup [0, \sqrt{5}]$

17. The critical values, 3 and -6, divide the

axis into intervals: $(-\infty, -6), (-6, 3), (3, \infty)$.

INTERVAL	TESTVALUE	SIGN
$(-\infty, -6)$	$f(-7) = 10$	positive
$(-6, 3)$	$f(0) = -\dfrac{1}{2}$	negative *
$(3, \infty)$	$f(4) = \dfrac{1}{10}$	positive

$(-6, 3]$

-6 is not included as it would make the

denominator equal to 0. 3 is included as it

would make the fraction equal to 0.

19. See Example 3 in textbook.

$\dfrac{4}{x+1} - \dfrac{2}{x+3} < 0, \quad x \ne -1 \ or -3$

$\dfrac{4(x+3) - 2(x+1)}{(x+1)(x+3)} < 0$

$\dfrac{4x + 12 - 2x - 2}{(x+1)(x+3)} < 0$

$\dfrac{2x + 10}{(x+1)(x+3)} < 0$

$\dfrac{2(x+5)}{(x+1)(x+3)} < 0$

The critical values, $-5, -1, -3$, divide the

axis into intervals:

$(-\infty, -5), (-5, -3), (-3, -1), (-1, \infty)$

INTERVAL	TESTVALUE	SIGN
$(-\infty, -5)$	$f(-6) = -0.1\overline{3}$	negative *
$(-5, -3)$	$f(-4) = 0.\overline{6}$	positive
$(-3, -1)$	$f(-2) = -6$	negative*
$(-1, \infty)$	$f(0) = 3.\overline{3}$	positive

$(-\infty, -5) \cup (-3, -1)$

Review Chapter 3

1. $0 = x^2 - 4$

   $x^2 = 4$

   $x = \pm 2$, zeros

   Graph is a parabola that opens up. Graph shows one relative minimum at $(0, -4)$. No maximum. Domain: every real number used as an input value for the function gives a real number as an output, so the domain is every real number, $(-\infty, \infty)$. The range extends up from the minimum, -4, with no limit, $[-4, \infty)$.

2. $0 = x^3 \implies x = 0$, zero

   Looking at the graph, there is no highest or lowest point, no max or min.
   Domain: every real number used as an input value for the function gives a real number as an output, so the domain is every real number, $(-\infty, \infty)$. Range: $(-\infty, \infty)$.

3. $0 = (x - 1)^2$

   $0 = x - 1 \implies x = 1$, zero

   Graph shows one relative minimum at $(1,0)$; no maximum. Domain: every real number used as an input value for the function gives a real number as an output, so the domain is every real number, $(-\infty, \infty)$. The range extends up from the minimum, 0, with no limit, $[0, \infty)$.

4. Standard form: $f(x) = -7x^3 + 5x + 2$

   Exponent 3 → cubic

   Leading term: $-7x^3$

   Leading coefficient: -7

   Degree: 3

5. Standard form: $f(x) = -37x^4 + 3x$

   Exponent 4 → quartic

   Leading term: $-37x^4$

   Leading coefficient: -37

   Degree: 4

6. Exponent 1 → linear

   Leading term: $17x$

   Leading coefficient: 17

   Degree: 1

7. No variable → constant

   Leading term: 4

   Leading coefficient: 4

   Degree: 0

8. Standard form: $f(x) = 3x^2 + 2x - 12$

   Exponent 2 → quadratic

   Leading term: $3x^2$

   Leading coefficient: 3

   Degree: 2

9. degree is odd, lead coefficient is positive

   $\implies$ as $x \to -\infty, f(x) \to -\infty$

   and as $x \to +\infty, f(x) \to +\infty$.

10. degree is even, lead coefficient is negative

    $\implies$ as $x \to -\infty, f(x) \to -\infty$

    and as $x \to +\infty, f(x) \to -\infty$.

11. $0 = (x - 2)^3 (x)(x + 2)^2$

    $x - 2 = 0 \implies x = 2$, multiplicity of 3;

    $x = 0$, multiplicity of 1;

    $x + 2 = 0 \implies x = -2$, multiplicity of 2.

12. $0 = x^4 - 10x^2 + 9$

    $0 = (x^2 - 9)(x^2 - 1)$

    $0 = (x + 3)(x - 3)(x + 1)(x - 1)$

    $x + 3 = 0 \implies x = -3$, multiplicity of 1;

    $x - 3 = 0 \implies x = 3$, multiplicity of 1;

    $x + 1 = 0 \implies x = -1$, multiplicity of 1;

    $x - 1 = 0 \implies x = 1$, multiplicity of 1.

13. $0 = x^3 + 3x^2 - 25x - 75$

    $0 = x^2(x+3) - 25(x+3)$

    $0 = (x+3)(x^2-25)$

    $0 = (x+3)(x+5)(x-5)$

    $x+3=0 \Rightarrow x=-3$, multiplicity of 1;

    $x+5=0 \Rightarrow x=-5$, multiplicity of 1;

    $x-5=0 \Rightarrow x=5$, multiplicity of 1.

14. $f(-2) = 4(-2)^2 - 8(-2) - 3$

    $= 16 + 16 - 3$

    $= 29$

    $f(0) = 4(0)^2 - 8(0) - 3$

    $= -3$

Because $f(-2)$ and $f(0)$ have different signs, this indicates there is a zero between -2 and 0.

15. $f(2) = 2(2)^3 - 6$

    $= 2(8) - 6$

    $= 10$

    $f(3) = 2(3)^3 - 6$

    $= 2(27) - 6$

    $= 48$

Both $f(2)$ and $f(3)$ are positive. The Intermediate Value Theorem does not allow us to determine if there is a real zero between 2 and 3.

16.

3	1	3	−12	4
		3	18	18
	1	6	6	22

Quotient: $x^2 + 6x + 6$; R = 22

17.

2	1	0	0	0	−16
		2	4	8	16
	1	2	4	8	0

Quotient: $x^3 + 2x^2 + 4x + 8$; R = 0

18.

1	1	−3	−6	8
		1	−2	−8
	1	−2	−8	0

R = 0; 1 is a zero.

−2	1	−3	−6	8
		−2	10	−8
	1	−5	4	0

R = 0; -2 is a zero.

19.

$-\sqrt{2}$	4	0	−8
		$-4\sqrt{2}$	8
	4	$-4\sqrt{2}$	0

R = 0; $-\sqrt{2}$ is a zero.

3	4	0	−8
		12	36
	4	12	28

R = 28; 3 is not a zero.

20. $f(x) = (x^2+9)(x^2-4)$

    $f(x) = (x^2+9)(x+2)(x-2)$

    $0 = (x^2+9)(x+2)(x-2)$

    $x^2+9=0$ or $x+2=0$ or $x-2=0$

    $x^2=-9$ or $x=-2$ or $x=2$

    $x = \pm\sqrt{-9}$

    $x = \pm 3i$ or $x = \pm 2$

21. $f(x) = x^3 + x + 3x^2 + 3$

    $f(x) = x(x^2+1) + 3(x^2+1)$

    $f(x) = (x^2+1)(x+3)$

    $0 = (x^2+1)(x+3)$

    $x^2+1=0$ or $x+3=0$

    $x^2=-1$ or $x=-3$

    $x = \pm\sqrt{-1}$

    $x = \pm i$ or $x = -3$

22. By the Conjugate Zeros Theorem, if $\sqrt{5}$ is a zero, then $-\sqrt{5}$ is also a zero.

$(x-\sqrt{5})(x+\sqrt{5})$

$= x^2 - 5$

23. By the Conjugate Zeros Theorem, if i is a zero, then $-i$ is also a zero.

$(x-(-2))(x-i)(x-(-i))$

$= (x+2)(x-i)(x+i)$

$= (x+2)(x^2 - i^2)$

$= (x+2)(x^2 - (-1))$

$= (x+2)(x^2 + 1)$

$= x^3 + 2x^2 + x + 2$

24. $(x+5)(x-5) < 0$

Zeros, $-5 \text{ and } 5$, divide the axis into intervals: $(-\infty, -5), (-5, 5), (5, \infty)$.

INTERVAL	TESTVALUE	SIGN
$(-\infty, -5)$	$f(-6) = 11$	positive
$(-5, 5)$	$f(0) = -25$	negative*
$(5, \infty)$	$f(6) = 11$	positive

$(-5, 5)$; Endpoints. are not included because of $<$ symbol.

25. $x^2 - 6x + 9 > 0$

$(x-3)(x-3) > 0$

Zero, 3, with multiplicity of 2 divides the axis into intervals: $(-\infty, 3), (3, +\infty)$.

INTERVAL	TESTVALUE	SIGN
$(-\infty, 3)$	$f(0) = 9$	positive*
$(3, +\infty)$	$f(4) = 1$	positive*

$(-\infty, 3) \cup (3, +\infty)$; 3 is not included because of $>$ symbol.

26. $\dfrac{x-3}{x+1} < 0, \; x \neq -1$

Critical values, 3 and -1, divide the axis into intervals: $(-\infty, -1), (-1, 3), (3, +\infty)$.

INTERVAL	TESTVALUE	SIGN
$(-\infty, -1)$	$f(-2) = 5$	positive
$(-1, 3)$	$f(0) = -3$	negative*
$(3, +\infty)$	$f(4) = \dfrac{1}{5}$	positive

$(-1, 3)$; 3 is not included because of $<$ symbol.

CHAPTER 4

Section 4.1

1. Interchange the ordered pairs:
   $\{(4, 5), (3, -2), (7, 4)\}$

3. Interchange the x and y:
   $x = 3y + 2$

5. Interchange the x and y:
   $x = 2y^2 - 1y$

7. Interchange the x and y:
   $y = x^2 + 7x$

9. and 11. are not included.

13. $f(x) = 4x - 3$. Assume that $f(a) = f(b)$
   and determine if $a = b$.
   $f(a) = 4a - 3 \quad and \quad f(b) = 4b - 3$
   $$\begin{aligned} f(a) &= f(b) \\ 4a - 3 &= 4b - 3 \\ 4a &= 4b \\ a &= b \end{aligned}$$

15. Use any pair of opposites for input values
   and show they equal the same output value.
   $f(1) = 1^2 + 2 = 3$ and
   $f(-1) = (-1)^2 + 2 = 3$.

17. Not one-to-one

19. Not one-to-one

21. Graph is a parabola so there is a horizontal
   line that will intersect it twice. Not one-to-one.

23. The horizontal line test indicates the
   function is one-to-one.
   $$f(x) = \frac{1}{x}$$
   $$y = \frac{1}{x}$$
   $$x = \frac{1}{y}$$
   $$xy = 1$$
   $$y = \frac{1}{x}$$
   $$f^{-1}(x) = \frac{1}{x}$$

25. The horizontal line test indicates the
   function is one-to-one.
   $$f(x) = 4x - 2$$
   $$y = 4x - 2$$
   $$x = 4y - 2$$
   $$4y = x + 2$$
   $$y = \frac{x + 2}{4}$$
   $$f^{-1}(x) = \frac{x + 2}{4}$$

Section 4.2

1. $f(x) = 2^x - 2$ is a shift down of 2 units for $f(x) = 2^x$ because every y-coordinate has 2 subtracted. Pt$(0, 1)$ shifted down to $(0, -1)$; Pt$(1, 2)$ shifted down to $(1, 0)$. Graph e.

3. $f(x) = e^x + 1$ is a shift up 1 unit for $f(x) = e^x$ because every y-coordinate has 1 added. Pt$(0, 1)$ shifted up to $(0, 2)$. Graph a.

5. $f(x) = 3^{-x} - 1$ is a shift down 1 unit and reflection across y-axis for $f(x) = 3^x$ because every y-coordinate has 1 subtracted and every x-coordinate is multiplied by -1. Pt$(0, 1)$ shifted to $(0, 0)$; Pt$(1, 3)$ shifted to $(-1, 2)$. Graph c.

7.-23. Check graphs with a graphing calculator.

9. reflection across y-axis

11. reflection across x-axis

13. shift down 2

15. shift right 1

17. shift down 1

19. shift down 2

21. shift right 2

23. reflection across y-axis

Section 4.3

1.-7. Refer to Example 7 in textbook. Make a table choosing values for y and calculating x. Check graphs with a graphing calculator.

9. $\log_2 32 = x$

$2^x = 32$
$2^x = 2^5$
$x = 5$

11. $\log_6 36 = x$

$6^x = 36$
$6^x = 6^2$
$x = 2$

13. $\log 1 = x$ (no base given means base 10)

$10^x = 1$
$10^x = 10^0$
$x = 0$

15. $\log 0.01 = x$ (no base given means base 10)

$10^x = 0.01$
$10^x = \dfrac{1}{100}$
$10^x = \dfrac{1}{10^2}$
$10^x = 10^{-2}$
$x = -2$

17. $\ln 0 = x$ (ln has base e)

Undefined. By definition, the number you take the 'logarithm of' must be > 0.

19. $\ln e = x$ (ln has base e)

$e^x = e^1$
$x = 1$

21. $\log 100 = x$

$10^x = 100$

$10^x = 10^2$

$x = 2$

23. $\log_4 4^3 = x$

$4^x = 4^3$

$x = 3$

25. $\log_4 \sqrt[3]{4} = x$

$\log_4 4^{\frac{1}{3}} = x$

$4^x = 4^{\frac{1}{3}}$

$x = \dfrac{1}{3}$

27. $\ln e^{\frac{1}{2}} = x$ (ln has base e)

$e^x = e^{\frac{1}{2}}$

$x = \dfrac{1}{2}$

29. $10^4 = 10000$

$\log_{10} 10000 = 4$

$\log 10000 = 4$

31. $m^t = 4$

$\log_m 4 = t$

33. $\log 8 = 0.9031$

$10^{0.9031} = 8$

35. $\log_a R = p$

$a^p = R$

37. $\log_3 24 = \dfrac{\log 24}{\log 3}$

39. Decibels $= 10(\log \dfrac{I}{I_0})$

Calculator is needed.

a) Decibels $= 10(\log \dfrac{115\,I_0}{I_0})$

$= 10(\log 115)$

$= 20.6070$

b) Decibels $= 10(\log \dfrac{1200000000\,I_0}{I_0})$

$= 10(\log 1200000000)$

$= 90.7918$

c) Decibels $= 10(\log \dfrac{895000000000\,I_0}{I_0})$

$= 10(\log 895000000000)$

$= 119.5182$

d) Decibels $= 10(\log \dfrac{109000000000000\,I_0}{I_0})$

$= 10(\log 109000000000000)$

$= 140.3743$

Section 4.4

1. – 11. Apply Properties of Logarithms.

13. $\log_7 5rs^3t^6$

$= \log_7 5 + \log_7 r + \log_7 s^3 + \log_7 t^6$

$= \log_7 5 + \log_7 r + 3\log_7 s + 6\log_7 t$

15. $\log_b (\dfrac{x^8}{y^5 z^3})^{\frac{1}{2}}$

$= \log_b \dfrac{x^4}{y^{\frac{5}{2}} z^{\frac{3}{2}}}$

$= \log_b x^4 - (\log_b y^{\frac{5}{2}} z^{\frac{3}{2}})$

$= \log_b x^4 - (\log_b y^{\frac{5}{2}} + \log_b z^{\frac{3}{2}})$

$= \log_b x^4 - \log_b y^{\frac{5}{2}} - \log_b z^{\frac{3}{2}}$

$= 4\log_b x - \dfrac{5}{2}\log_b y - \dfrac{3}{2}\log_b z$

17. $\log_b (30 \cdot 4) = \log_b 120$

19. $\log_b x^{\frac{1}{2}} + \log_b w^3 - \log_b q^5$

$= \log_b (x^{\frac{1}{2}} w^3) - \log_b q^5$

$= \log_b \dfrac{x^{\frac{1}{2}} w^3}{q^5}$ or $\log_b \dfrac{\sqrt{x}(w^3)}{q^5}$

21. $\log_b 14 = \log_b (2 \cdot 7)$

$= \log_b 2 + \log_b 7$

$= 0.3010 + 0.8451$

$= 1.1461$

23. $\log_b \dfrac{2}{7} = \log_b 2 - \log_b 7$

$= 0.3010 - 0.8451$

$= -0.5441$

Section 4.5

1. $4^x = 64$

$4^x = 4^3$

$x = 3$

3. $3^x = 28$

$\log 3^x = \log 28$

$x\log 3 = \log 28$

$x = \dfrac{\log 28}{\log 3}$

5. $81 = 3^{4x} \bullet 9^{2x}$

$3^4 = 3^{4x} \bullet (3^2)^{2x}$

$3^4 = 3^{4x} \bullet 3^{4x}$

$3^4 = 3^{8x}$

$4 = 8x$

$\dfrac{1}{2} = x$

7. $2^{3x-1} = \dfrac{1}{2}$

$2^{3x-1} = 2^{-1}$

$3x - 1 = -1$

$3x = 0$

$x = 0$

9. $e^{-0.4t} = 0.06$

$\ln e^{-0.4t} = \ln 0.06$

$-0.4t \ln e = \ln 0.06$

$-0.4t(1) = \ln 0.06$

$t = -\dfrac{\ln 0.06}{0.4}$

11. $(5.3)^x = 52$

$\ln(5.3)^x = \ln 52$

$x \ln 5.3 = \ln 52$

$x = \dfrac{\ln 52}{\ln 5.3}$

13. $\log_4 x = 9$

$4^9 = x$

$x = 262144$

15. $\ln x = 2$ (ln is base e)

$e^2 = x$

17. $\log(x(x-3)) = 1$

$10^1 = x(x-3)$

$10 = x^2 - 3x$

$0 = x^2 - 3x - 10$

$0 = (x-5)(x+2)$

$x = 5 \quad or \quad x = -2$

$\log(-2)$ is not defined.

$x = 5$ is the only solution.

19. $2\ln(x+3) - \ln(x+1) = 3\ln 2$

$\ln(x+3)^2 - \ln(x+1) = \ln 2^3$

$\ln \dfrac{(x+3)^2}{(x+1)} = \ln 8$

$\dfrac{(x+3)^2}{(x+1)} = 8$

$(x+3)^2 = 8(x+1)$

$x^2 + 6x + 9 = 8x + 8$

$x^2 - 2x + 1 = 0$

$(x-1)(x-1) = 0$

$x = 1$

21. $\ln(x+2) = \ln e^{\ln 2} - \ln x$

$\ln(x+2) = \ln 2 - \ln x$

$\ln(x+2) = \ln \dfrac{2}{x}$

$x + 2 = \dfrac{2}{x}$

$x(x+2) = 2$

$x^2 + 2x = 2$

$x^2 + 2x - 2 = 0$

$x = \dfrac{-2 \pm \sqrt{2^2 - 4(-2)}}{2}$

$x = \dfrac{-2 \pm \sqrt{12}}{2}$

$x = \dfrac{-2 \pm 2\sqrt{3}}{2}$

$x = -1 \pm \sqrt{3}$, but $-1 - \sqrt{3} < 0$

$x = -1 + \sqrt{3}$

23. $\log_8(x-5) = \dfrac{2}{3}$

$8^{\frac{2}{3}} = x - 5$

$(\sqrt[3]{8})^2 = x - 5$

$2^2 = x - 5$

$9 = x$

Section 4.6

1. 1980 population, P_0: 231,000,000
   Rate of growth: 1.03% = 0.0103
   Time: 2025-1980 = 45
   $$P = P_0 e^{rt}$$
   $$P = 231,000,000(e)^{0.0103(45)}$$
   $$P = 367.204 \text{ million}$$

3. $N(t) = N_0 e^{-0.15t}$
   $N_0 = 25,000,000$
   $t = 10 \text{ yrs.}$
   $$N(10) = 25(e)^{-0.15(10)}$$
   $$= 5.578 \text{ million}$$

5. Refer to Example 2
   $y = 2000(e)^{-0.5t}$ where 2000 is the initial amount. Half the initial amount is 1000.
   $$1000 = 2000(e)^{-0.5t}$$
   $$\frac{1}{2} = e^{-0.5t}$$
   $$\ln(\frac{1}{2}) = \ln e^{-0.5t}$$
   $$\ln(\frac{1}{2}) = -0.5t$$
   $$\frac{\ln(\frac{1}{2})}{-0.5} = t$$
   $$t = 1.386 \text{ days}$$

7. $y = y_0 e^{0.5t}$
   $$4(200) = 200(e)^{0.5t}$$
   $$4 = e^{0.5t}$$
   $$\ln 4 = \ln e^{0.5t}$$
   $$\ln 4 = 0.5t$$
   $$t = \frac{\ln 4}{0.5}$$
   $$t = 2.773 \text{ months}$$

9. Ratio C14 to C12 is $\frac{1}{5}$.
   $$\frac{R}{r} = e^{\frac{t \cdot \ln 2}{5600}}$$
   $$\frac{1}{5} = e^{\frac{t \cdot \ln 2}{5600}}$$
   $$\ln(\frac{1}{5}) = \ln e^{\frac{t \cdot \ln 2}{5600}}$$
   $$\ln(\frac{1}{5}) = \frac{t \cdot \ln 2}{5600}$$
   $$5600 \ln(\frac{1}{5}) = t \cdot \ln 2$$
   $$t = \frac{5600 \ln(\frac{1}{5})}{\ln 2}$$
   $$t = -13002.797$$
   The age of the object is 13002.8 yrs.

11. $$\frac{R}{r} = e^{\frac{t \cdot \ln 2}{5600}}$$
   $$\ln(\frac{R}{r}) = \ln e^{\frac{t \cdot \ln 2}{5600}}$$
   $$\ln(\frac{R}{r}) = \frac{t \cdot \ln 2}{5600}(\ln e)$$
   $$5600 \ln(\frac{R}{r}) = t \cdot \ln 2$$
   $$t = \frac{5600 \ln(\frac{R}{r})}{\ln 2}$$

13. $A = Pe^{rt}$
   $P = 40,000; \ r = 0.04; \ A = 2P = 80,000$
   $$80,000 = 40,000(e)^{0.04t}$$
   $$2 = e^{0.04t}$$
   $$\ln 2 = \ln e^{0.04t}$$
   $$\ln 2 = 0.04t(\ln e)$$
   $$\frac{\ln 2}{0.04} = t = 17.3 \text{ yrs.}$$

15. $A = Pe^{rt}$

$\dfrac{A}{P} = e^{rt}$

$\ln(\dfrac{A}{P}) = \ln e^{rt}$

$\ln(\dfrac{A}{P}) = rt(\ln e)$

$\ln(\dfrac{A}{P}) = rt$

$t = \dfrac{\ln(\dfrac{A}{P})}{r} = \dfrac{1}{r}(\ln\dfrac{A}{P})$

Review Chapter 4

1. Interchange x and y coordinates in each ordered pair.

2. Interchange x and y in the equation.

3. Interchange x and y in the equation.

4. The horizontal line test proves this is a one-to-one function.

5. There is a horizontal line that crosses the graph more than once, therefore, this is not a one-to-one function.

6. The horizontal line test proves this is a one-to-one function.

7. $f(x) = 4 - 3x$

$y = 4 - 3x$

$x = 4 - 3y$

$3y = 4 - x$

$y = \dfrac{4 - x}{3}$

$f^{-1}(x) = \dfrac{4 - x}{3}$

8. $f(x) = \sqrt[3]{x - 2}$

$y = \sqrt[3]{x - 2}$

$x = \sqrt[3]{y - 2}$

$x^3 = y - 2$

$y = x^3 + 2$

$f^{-1}(x) = x^3 + 2$

9. $f(x) = e^x$

$y = e^x$

$x = e^y$

$\ln x = \ln e^y$

$\ln x = y(\ln e)$

$y = \ln x$

$f^{-1}(x) = \ln x$

10. $f(x) = \log x$

$y = \log x$

$x = \log y$

$10^x = y$

$f^{-1}(x) = 10^x$

11. Use calculator, graph $\dfrac{\log x}{\log 2}$. (c)

12. Adding 2 to the x shifts the graph of $\log_3 x$ left 2 units. Use calculator, graph $\dfrac{\log(x+2)}{\log 3}$. (d)

13. Create a table of values, pick a number for x and calculate the corresponding y. Plot the points and check with calculator. (e)

14. Adding 2 to the formula shifts the graph of 4^x up 2 units. (b)

15. Subtracting 3 from the formula shifts the graph of e^x down 3 units. (a)

16. $x = \log_8 64$

$8^x = 64$

$8^x = 8^2$

$x = 2$

17. $x = \log 1000$

$10^x = 1000$

$10^x = 10^3$

$x = 3$

18. $x = \ln e^2$

$x = 2\ln e$

$x = 2$

19. $x = \log 10^3$

$x = 3\log 10$

$x = 3$

20. $\log_3 x = 2$

$3^2 = x$

21. Use definition of logarithm: $b^N = M$

22. Use definition of logarithm: $\log_5(\dfrac{1}{25}) = -2$

23. Use definition of logarithm: $\ln 40 = x$.

24. $\log_4 10 = \dfrac{\log 10}{\log 4} = \dfrac{1}{\log 4}$

25. $\log \dfrac{x^2 y^4}{z^5} = \log(x^2 y^4) - \log z^5$

$= \log x^2 + \log y^4 - \log z^5$

$= 2\log x + 4\log y - 5\log z$

26. $3^4 = x$

$x = 81$

27. $4^{x-1} = 8^x$

$\log 4^{x-1} = \log 8^x$

$(x-1)\log 4 = x\log 8$

$x\log 4 - \log 4 = x\log 8$

$x\log 4 - x\log 8 = \log 4$

$x(\log 4 - \log 8) = \log 4$

$x\log(\dfrac{4}{8}) = \log 4$

$x = \dfrac{\log 4}{\log(\dfrac{1}{2})}$

Using calculator $x = -2$

28. $\log_x 32 = 5$

$x^5 = 32$

$(x^5)^{\frac{1}{5}} = 32^{\frac{1}{5}}$

$x = \sqrt[5]{32} = 2$

29. $\log_2 x(x-6) = 4$

$2^4 = x^2 - 6x$

$0 = x^2 - 6x - 16$

$0 = (x-8)(x+2)$

$x = 8 \quad or \quad x = -2$

$\log_2(-2)$ is not defined.

$x = 8$

30. $\log x^2 = \log x$

$x^2 = x$

$x^2 - x = 0$

$x(x-1) = 0$

$x = 0 \quad or \quad x = 1$

$\log 0$ is not defined.

$x = 1$

CHAPTER 5

Section 5.1

1.-5. Use a graphing calculator.
See Chapter 6, Example 44.

7. Eq 1: $x + y = 5$
   Eq 2: $2x - y = 4$
   From Eq.1: $x = 5 - y$
   Substitute into Eq.2:
   $2(5 - y) - y = 4$
   $10 - 2y - y = 4$
   $-3y = -6$
   $y = 2$
   Substitute into either Eq.
   Eq 1: $x + 2 = 5$
   $x = 3$

9. Eq 1: $y + 2x = 6$
   Eq 2: $4x - y = 6$
   From Eq. 1: $y = 6 - 2x$
   Substitute into Eq. 2:
   $4x - (6 - 2x) = 6$
   $4x - 6 + 2x = 6$
   $6x = 12$ so $x = 2$
   Substitute into either Eq.
   Eq 1: $y + 2(2) = 6$
   $y = 2$

11. Eq 1: $2x - 4y = -4$
    Eq 2: $3x + 2y = 10$
    From Eq. 1: $2x = 4y - 4$
    $x = 2y - 2$
    Substitute into Eq. 2:
    $3(2y - 2) + 2y = 10$
    $6y - 6 + 2y = 10$
    $8y = 16$ so $y = 2$
    Substitute into either Eq.
    Eq 1: $2x - 4(2) = -4$
    $2x = 4$ so $x = 2$

13. Eq 1: $x + 3y = 5$
    Eq 2: $x - 3y = -1$
    $\overline{2x = 4}$ so $x = 2$
    Substitute into either Eq.
    Eq 1: $2 + 3y = 5$
    $y = 1$

15. Eq 1: $(3x + 4y = 6) \bullet 3$
    Eq 2: $(4x - 3y = 8) \bullet 4$
    Eq 1: $9x + 12y = 18$
    Eq 2: $16x - 12y = 32$
    $\overline{25x = 50}$ so $x = 2$
    Substitute into either Eq.
    Eq 1: $3(2) + 4y = 6$
    $4y = 0$ so $y = 0$

17. Eq 1: $(2x - 3y = 10) \bullet 2$
    Eq 2: $-4x + 6y = 15$
    Eq 1: $\underline{4x - 6y = 20}$
    $0 = 35$ *not true*
    No solution

19. Eq 1: $(0.5x - 0.4y = 1) \bullet 10$
    Eq 2: $(0.3x + 0.2y = 0.6) \bullet 10$
    Eq 1: $5x - 4y = 10$
    [Eq 2: $(3x + 2y = 6) \bullet 2$]
    Eq 2: $6x + 4y = 12$
    $\overline{11x = 22}$ so $x = 2$
    Substitute into either Eq.
    Eq 1: $0.5(2) - 0.4y = 1$
    $-0.4y = 0$ so $y = 0$

21. $a = adult\ tickets$ and $c = child\ tickets$

Eq 1: $(a+c=15{,}000) \bullet (-30)$

Eq 2: $40a+30c = 510{,}000$

Eq 1: $\underline{-30a-30c=-450{,}000}$

$10a \quad\quad = 60{,}000 \quad so \quad a=6000$

Substitute into either Eq.

$6000+c=15000 \quad so \quad c=9000$

23. Solution $x=20\%=0.2$

Solution $y=2\%=0.02$

Eq 1: $x+y=25$

Eq 2: $0.2x+0.02y=25(0.056)$

[Eq 1: $(x+y=25) \bullet (-0.02)$]

Eq 1: $\underline{-0.02x-0.02y=-0.5}$

$0.18x \quad\quad = 0.9$

$x=5$

From Eq 1: $5+y=25 \quad so \quad y=20$

Section 5.2

1.
$x+2y-3z=1:A$
$2x-y-z=-3:B$
$3x+3y+2z=16:C$

$-2(A):-2x-4y+6z=-2$

$B:\ \underline{2x-y-z=-3}$

$-5y+5z=-5$

$-y+z=-1:D$

$-3(A):-3x-6y+9z=-3$

$C:\ \underline{3x+3y+2z=16}$

$-3y+11z=13:E$

$-3(D):\ 3y-3z=3$

$E:\ \underline{-3y+11z=13}$

$8z=16 \quad so \quad z=2$

Substitute in $D:-y+2=-1 \quad so \quad y=3$

Substitute y, z into any original equation.

$A:x+2(3)-3(2)=1 \quad so \quad x=1$

3.
$3x+y-z=2:A$
$-2x-2y+3z=-11:B$
$x+3y-2z=11:C$

$2(C):\ 2x+6y-4z=22$

$B:\underline{-2x-2y+3z=-11}$

$4y-z=11:D$

$-3(C):-3x-9y+6z=-33$

$A:\ \underline{3x+y-z=2}$

$-8y+5z=-31:E$

$2(D):\ 8y-2z=22$

$E:\underline{-8y+5z=-31}$

$3z=-9 \quad so \quad z=-3$

Substitute in $D:4y-(-3)=11$

$4y=8 \quad so \quad y=2$

Substitute y,z into any original equation.

$A:3x+2-(-3)=2$

$3x=-3 \quad so \quad x=-1$

5. $2x - y + 2z = 7 : A$
   $x + 2y - z = -9 : B$
   $3x - 4y + 2z = 8 : C$

   $-2(B): -2x - 4y + 2z = 18$
   $\underline{A: \quad 2x - y + 2z = 7}$
   $\qquad -5y + 4z = 25 : D$

   $-3(B): -3x - 6y + 3z = 27$
   $\underline{C: \quad 3x - 4y + 2z = 8}$
   $\qquad -10y + 5z = 35 : E$

   $-2(D): 10y - 8z = -50$
   $\underline{E: -10y + 5z = 35}$
   $\qquad -3z = -15 \quad so \quad z = 5$
   $D: -5y + 4(5) = 25$
   $\qquad -5y = 5 \quad so \quad y = -1$
   $A: 2x - (-1) + 2(5) = 7$
   $\qquad 2x + 11 = 7$
   $\qquad 2x = -4 \quad so \quad x = -2$

7. $3x + 5y + 4z = 1 : A$
   $x + 4y - z = 5 : B$
   $2x - 3y + 4z = -2 : C$

   $4(B): 4x + 16y - 4z = 20$
   $\underline{C: 2x - 3y + 4z = -2}$
   $\qquad 6x + 13y \quad = 18 : D$

   $4(B): 4x + 16y - 4z = 20$
   $\underline{A: 3x + 5y + 4z = 1}$
   $\qquad 7x + 21y \quad = 21$
   $\qquad x + 3y \quad = 3 : E$

   $-6(E): -6x - 18y = -18$
   $\underline{D: \quad 6x + 13y = \quad 18}$
   $\qquad -5y = 0 \quad so \quad y = 0$
   $D: 6x + 13(0) = 18 \quad so \quad x = 3$
   $A: 3(3) + 5(0) + 4z = 1$
   $\qquad 9 + 4z = 1$
   $\qquad 4z = -8 \quad so \quad z = -2$

9. $2x + 2y + 3z = 3 : A$
   $x + 3y + z = 0 : B$
   $4x + 6y - 4z = -5 : C$

   $-2(B): -2x - 6y - 2z = 0$
   $\underline{A: \quad 2x + 2y + 3z = 3}$
   $\qquad -4y + z = 3 : D$

   $-4(B): -4x - 12y - 4z = 0$
   $\underline{C: \quad 4x + 6y - 4z = -5}$
   $\qquad -6y - 8z = -5 : E$

   $8(D): -32y + 8z = 24$
   $\underline{E: -6y - 8z = -5}$
   $\qquad -38y = 19 \quad so \quad y = -\dfrac{1}{2}$

   $D: \quad -4(-\dfrac{1}{2}) + z = 3$
   $\qquad 2 + z = 3 \quad so \quad z = 1$
   $A: 2x + 2(-\dfrac{1}{2}) + 3(1) = 3$
   $\qquad 2x - 1 + 3 = 3$
   $\qquad 2x = 1 \quad so \quad x = \dfrac{1}{2}$

11. $x + 2y + 3z = 5 : A$
    $2x + z = 3 : B$
    $3y - 2z = 11 : C$

    $-2(A): -2x - 4y - 6z = -10$
    $\underline{B: \quad 2x + \quad z = \quad 3}$
    $\qquad -4y - 5z = -7 : D$

    $-5(C): -15y + 10z = -55$
    $\underline{2(D): \quad -8y - 10z = -14}$
    $\qquad -23y = -69 \quad so \quad y = 3$
    $C: 3(3) - 2z = 11$
    $\qquad -2z = 2 \quad so \quad z = -1$
    $B: 2x + (-1) = 3$
    $\qquad 2x = 4 \quad so \quad x = 2$

13. $2x + 4y - z = 3 : A$
$3x - 5y = -19 : B$
$4y - 10z = 18 : C$

$-1(C): \quad -4y + 10z = -18$
$\underline{A : 2x + 4y - z = 3}$
$2x + 9z = -15 : D$

$5(A) : 10x + 20y - 5z = 15$
$\underline{4(B) : 12x - 20y = -76}$
$22x - 5z = -61 : E$

$-11(D) : -22x - 99z = 165$
$\underline{E : 22x - 5z = -61}$
$-104z = 104 \quad so \quad z = -1$

$C : 4y - 10(-1) = 18$
$4y = 8 \quad so \quad y = 2$
$A : 2x + 4(2) - (-1) = 3$
$2x + 9 = 3$
$2x = -6 \quad so \quad x = -3$

15. $x =$ bonds at 4%
$y =$ stocks at 5%
$z =$ hedge fund at 7%
$x + y + z = 50{,}000 : A$
$0.04x + 0.05y + 0.07z = 2220 : B$
$x = 2y \quad so \quad x - 2y = 0 : C$

$-1(C) : -x + 2y = 0$
$\underline{A : x + y + z = 50{,}000}$
$3y + z = 50{,}000 : D$

$-4(A) : -4x - 4y - 4z = -200{,}000$
$\underline{100(B) : 4x + 5y + 7z = 222000}$
$y + 3z = 22{,}000 : E$

$-3(D) : -9y - 3z = -150{,}000$
$\underline{E : y + 3z = 22{,}000}$
$-8y = -128{,}000 \quad so \quad y = 16{,}000$

$C : x - 2(16{,}000) = 0 \quad so \quad x = 32{,}000$
$A : 32{,}000 + 16{,}000 + z = 50{,}000$
$z = 2{,}000$

Section 5.3

All solutions are graphs with a shaded region.
See Chapter 6, Examples 47 and 48.
Use a graphing calculator to draw the graph of
the related equation.
Use a test point to determine the shaded region.
Use solid line for $\geq, \leq$, use dotted line for $>, <$.

Section 5.4

Key to the notation:
"Number • (Row#) gives new entries for Row#"
Example: $2(R3) \to R3$

1. $\begin{bmatrix} 2 & -1 & | & 4 \\ 1 & 3 & | & 4 \end{bmatrix}$

3. $\begin{bmatrix} 1 & 4 & -2 & | & 5 \\ 1 & 0 & 3 & | & 7 \\ 0 & 2 & 1 & | & 4 \end{bmatrix}$

5. $\begin{bmatrix} 2 & 3 & | & 7 \\ 4 & -2 & | & 6 \end{bmatrix}$

$\frac{1}{2}(R1) \to R1$

$\begin{bmatrix} 1 & \frac{3}{2} & | & \frac{7}{2} \\ 4 & -2 & | & 6 \end{bmatrix}$

$-4(R1) \to R2$

$\begin{bmatrix} 1 & \frac{3}{2} & | & \frac{7}{2} \\ 0 & -8 & | & -8 \end{bmatrix}$

$-\frac{1}{8}(R2) \to R2$

$\begin{bmatrix} 1 & \frac{3}{2} & | & \frac{7}{2} \\ 0 & 1 & | & 1 \end{bmatrix}$

$-\frac{3}{2}(R2) + R1 \to R1$

$\begin{bmatrix} 1 & 0 & | & 2 \\ 0 & 1 & | & 1 \end{bmatrix}$
$x = 2, \quad y = 1$

7. $\begin{bmatrix} 3 & 4 & | & 4 \\ 4 & -2 & | & -2 \end{bmatrix}$

Switch R1 and R2
$\begin{bmatrix} 4 & -2 & | & -2 \\ 3 & 4 & | & 4 \end{bmatrix}$

$\frac{1}{4}(R1) \to R1$

$\begin{bmatrix} 1 & -\frac{1}{2} & | & -\frac{1}{2} \\ 3 & 4 & | & 4 \end{bmatrix}$

$-3(R1) + R2 \to R2$

$\begin{bmatrix} 1 & -\frac{1}{2} & | & -\frac{1}{2} \\ 0 & \frac{11}{2} & | & \frac{11}{2} \end{bmatrix}$

$\frac{2}{11}(R2) \to R2$

$\begin{bmatrix} 1 & -\frac{1}{2} & | & -\frac{1}{2} \\ 0 & 1 & | & 1 \end{bmatrix}$

$\frac{1}{2}(R2) + R1 \to R1$

$\begin{bmatrix} 1 & 0 & | & 0 \\ 0 & 1 & | & 1 \end{bmatrix}$
$x = 0, \quad y = 1$

9. $\begin{bmatrix} 3 & -4 & | & 5 \\ 1 & 5 & | & 8 \end{bmatrix}$

Switch R1 and R2

$\begin{bmatrix} 1 & 5 & | & 8 \\ 3 & -4 & | & 5 \end{bmatrix}$

$-3(R1) + R2 \rightarrow R2$

$\begin{bmatrix} 1 & 5 & | & 8 \\ 0 & -19 & | & -19 \end{bmatrix}$

$-\dfrac{1}{19}(R2) \rightarrow R2$

$\begin{bmatrix} 1 & 5 & | & 8 \\ 0 & 1 & | & 1 \end{bmatrix}$

$-5(R2) + R1 \rightarrow R1$

$\begin{bmatrix} 1 & 0 & | & 3 \\ 0 & 1 & | & 1 \end{bmatrix}$

$x = 3, \quad y = 1$

11. $\begin{bmatrix} 3 & 2 & -1 & | & 4 \\ 4 & -1 & 2 & | & 5 \\ 2 & -1 & -1 & | & 0 \end{bmatrix}$

$\dfrac{1}{3}(R1) \rightarrow R1$

$\begin{bmatrix} 1 & \dfrac{2}{3} & -\dfrac{1}{3} & | & \dfrac{4}{3} \\ 4 & -1 & 2 & | & 5 \\ 2 & -1 & -1 & | & 0 \end{bmatrix}$

$-4(R1) + R2 \rightarrow R2$
$-2(R1) + R3 \rightarrow R3$

$\begin{bmatrix} 1 & \dfrac{2}{3} & -\dfrac{1}{3} & | & \dfrac{4}{3} \\ 0 & -\dfrac{11}{3} & \dfrac{10}{3} & | & -\dfrac{1}{3} \\ 0 & -\dfrac{7}{3} & -\dfrac{1}{3} & | & -\dfrac{8}{3} \end{bmatrix}$

11. Continued:

$-\dfrac{3}{11}(R2) \rightarrow R2$

$\begin{bmatrix} 1 & \dfrac{2}{3} & -\dfrac{1}{3} & | & \dfrac{4}{3} \\ 0 & 1 & -\dfrac{10}{11} & | & \dfrac{1}{11} \\ 0 & -\dfrac{7}{3} & -\dfrac{1}{3} & | & -\dfrac{8}{3} \end{bmatrix}$

$-\dfrac{2}{3}(R2) + R1 \rightarrow R1$

$\dfrac{7}{3}(R2) + R3 \rightarrow R3$

$\begin{bmatrix} 1 & 0 & \dfrac{3}{11} & | & \dfrac{14}{11} \\ 0 & 1 & -\dfrac{10}{11} & | & \dfrac{1}{11} \\ 0 & 0 & -\dfrac{27}{11} & | & -\dfrac{27}{11} \end{bmatrix}$

$-\dfrac{11}{27}(R3) \rightarrow R3$

$\begin{bmatrix} 1 & 0 & \dfrac{3}{11} & | & \dfrac{14}{11} \\ 0 & 1 & -\dfrac{10}{11} & | & \dfrac{1}{11} \\ 0 & 0 & 1 & | & 1 \end{bmatrix}$

$-\dfrac{3}{11}(R3) + R1 \rightarrow R1$

$\dfrac{10}{11}(R3) + R2 \rightarrow R2$

$\begin{bmatrix} 1 & 0 & 0 & | & 1 \\ 0 & 1 & 0 & | & 1 \\ 0 & 0 & 1 & | & 1 \end{bmatrix}$

$x = 1, \quad y = 1, \quad z = 1$

13. $\begin{bmatrix} 2 & 4 & -2 & | & 8 \\ 3 & 2 & 1 & | & 0 \\ 1 & 3 & -3 & | & 8 \end{bmatrix}$

Switch R1 and R3

$\begin{bmatrix} 1 & 3 & -3 & | & 8 \\ 3 & 2 & 1 & | & 0 \\ 2 & 4 & -2 & | & 8 \end{bmatrix}$

$-3(R1) + R2 \rightarrow R2$
$-2(R1) + R3 \rightarrow R3$

$\begin{bmatrix} 1 & 3 & -3 & | & 8 \\ 0 & -7 & 10 & | & -24 \\ 0 & -2 & 4 & | & -8 \end{bmatrix}$

$-\dfrac{1}{7}(R2) \rightarrow R2$

$\begin{bmatrix} 1 & 3 & -3 & | & 8 \\ 0 & 1 & -\dfrac{10}{7} & | & \dfrac{24}{7} \\ 0 & -2 & 4 & | & -8 \end{bmatrix}$

$-3(R2) + R1 \rightarrow R1$
$2(R2) + R3 \rightarrow R3$

$\begin{bmatrix} 1 & 0 & \dfrac{9}{7} & | & -\dfrac{16}{7} \\ 0 & 1 & -\dfrac{10}{7} & | & \dfrac{24}{7} \\ 0 & 0 & \dfrac{8}{7} & | & -\dfrac{8}{7} \end{bmatrix}$

$\dfrac{7}{8}(R3) \rightarrow R3$

$\begin{bmatrix} 1 & 0 & \dfrac{9}{7} & | & -\dfrac{16}{7} \\ 0 & 1 & -\dfrac{10}{7} & | & \dfrac{24}{7} \\ 0 & 0 & 1 & | & -1 \end{bmatrix}$

13. Continued:

$-\dfrac{9}{7}(R3) + R1 \rightarrow R1$

$\dfrac{10}{7}(R3) + R2 \rightarrow R2$

$\begin{bmatrix} 1 & 0 & 0 & | & -1 \\ 0 & 1 & 0 & | & 2 \\ 0 & 0 & 1 & | & -1 \end{bmatrix}$

$x = -1, \quad y = 2, \quad z = -1$

15. $\begin{bmatrix} 2 & -1 & 5 & | & 6 \\ 1 & 2 & -4 & | & 4 \\ 3 & -1 & 2 & | & 5 \end{bmatrix}$

Switch R1 and R2

$\begin{bmatrix} 1 & 2 & -4 & | & 4 \\ 2 & -1 & 5 & | & 6 \\ 3 & -1 & 2 & | & 5 \end{bmatrix}$

$-2(R1) + R2 \rightarrow R2$
$-3(R1) + R3 \rightarrow R3$

$\begin{bmatrix} 1 & 2 & -4 & | & 4 \\ 0 & -5 & 13 & | & -2 \\ 0 & -7 & 14 & | & -7 \end{bmatrix}$

$-\dfrac{1}{5}(R2) \rightarrow R2$

$\begin{bmatrix} 1 & 2 & -4 & | & 4 \\ 0 & 1 & -\dfrac{13}{5} & | & \dfrac{2}{5} \\ 0 & -7 & 14 & | & -7 \end{bmatrix}$

$-2(R2) + R1 \rightarrow R1$
$7(R2) + R3 \rightarrow R3$

$\begin{bmatrix} 1 & 0 & \dfrac{6}{5} & | & \dfrac{16}{5} \\ 0 & 1 & -\dfrac{13}{5} & | & \dfrac{2}{5} \\ 0 & 0 & -\dfrac{21}{5} & | & -\dfrac{21}{5} \end{bmatrix}$

15. Continued:

$-\dfrac{5}{21}(R3) \to R3$

$$\begin{bmatrix} 1 & 0 & \dfrac{6}{5} & \bigm| & \dfrac{16}{5} \\ 0 & 1 & -\dfrac{13}{5} & \bigm| & \dfrac{2}{5} \\ 0 & 0 & 1 & \bigm| & 1 \end{bmatrix}$$

$-\dfrac{6}{5}(R3) + R1 \to R1$

$\dfrac{13}{5}(R3) + R2 \to R2$

$$\begin{bmatrix} 1 & 0 & 0 & \bigm| & 2 \\ 0 & 1 & 0 & \bigm| & 3 \\ 0 & 0 & 1 & \bigm| & 1 \end{bmatrix}$$

$x = 2, \quad y = 3, \quad z = 1$

17. $\begin{bmatrix} 2 & 1 & -1 & \bigm| & 5 \\ 1 & 3 & -1 & \bigm| & 6 \\ 3 & -2 & -1 & \bigm| & 2 \end{bmatrix}$

Switch R1 and R2

$$\begin{bmatrix} 1 & 3 & -1 & \bigm| & 6 \\ 2 & 1 & -1 & \bigm| & 5 \\ 3 & -2 & -1 & \bigm| & 2 \end{bmatrix}$$

$-2(R1) + R2 \to R2$

$-3(R1) + R3 \to R3$

$$\begin{bmatrix} 1 & 3 & -1 & \bigm| & 6 \\ 0 & -5 & 1 & \bigm| & -7 \\ 0 & -11 & 2 & \bigm| & -16 \end{bmatrix}$$

$-\dfrac{1}{5}(R2) \to R2$

$$\begin{bmatrix} 1 & 3 & -1 & \bigm| & 6 \\ 0 & 1 & -\dfrac{1}{5} & \bigm| & \dfrac{7}{5} \\ 0 & -11 & 2 & \bigm| & -16 \end{bmatrix}$$

17. Continued:

$-3(R2) + R1 \to R1$

$11(R2) + R3 \to R3$

$$\begin{bmatrix} 1 & 0 & -\dfrac{2}{5} & \bigm| & \dfrac{9}{5} \\ 0 & 1 & -\dfrac{1}{5} & \bigm| & \dfrac{7}{5} \\ 0 & 0 & -\dfrac{1}{5} & \bigm| & -\dfrac{3}{5} \end{bmatrix}$$

$-5(R3) \to R3$

$$\begin{bmatrix} 1 & 0 & -\dfrac{2}{5} & \bigm| & \dfrac{9}{5} \\ 0 & 1 & -\dfrac{1}{5} & \bigm| & \dfrac{7}{5} \\ 0 & 0 & 1 & \bigm| & 3 \end{bmatrix}$$

$\dfrac{2}{5}(R3) + R1 \to R1$

$\dfrac{1}{5}(R3) + R2 \to R2$

$$\begin{bmatrix} 1 & 0 & 0 & \bigm| & 3 \\ 0 & 1 & 0 & \bigm| & 2 \\ 0 & 0 & 1 & \bigm| & 3 \end{bmatrix}$$

$x = 3, \quad y = 2, \quad z = 3$

Section 5.5

1. $\begin{bmatrix} 1 & -1 & | & 1 & 0 \\ 2 & 0 & | & 0 & 1 \end{bmatrix}$

$-2(R1) + R2 \rightarrow R2$

$\begin{bmatrix} 1 & -1 & | & 1 & 0 \\ 0 & 2 & | & -2 & 1 \end{bmatrix}$

$\dfrac{1}{2}(R2) \rightarrow R2$

$\begin{bmatrix} 1 & -1 & | & 1 & 0 \\ 0 & 1 & | & -1 & \frac{1}{2} \end{bmatrix}$

$R1 + R2 \rightarrow R1$

$\begin{bmatrix} 1 & 0 & | & 0 & \frac{1}{2} \\ 0 & 1 & | & -1 & \frac{1}{2} \end{bmatrix}$

Inverse is $\begin{bmatrix} 0 & \frac{1}{2} \\ -1 & \frac{1}{2} \end{bmatrix}$

The inverse can be found using a graphing calculator. See Chapter 6, Example 50.

3. $\begin{bmatrix} 3 & -1 & | & 1 & 0 \\ -5 & 2 & | & 0 & 1 \end{bmatrix}$

$\dfrac{1}{3}(R1) \rightarrow R1$

$\begin{bmatrix} 1 & -\frac{1}{3} & | & \frac{1}{3} & 0 \\ -5 & 2 & | & 0 & 1 \end{bmatrix}$

$5(R1) + R2 \rightarrow R2$

$\begin{bmatrix} 1 & -\frac{1}{3} & | & \frac{1}{3} & 0 \\ 0 & \frac{1}{3} & | & \frac{5}{3} & 1 \end{bmatrix}$

$R1 + R2 \rightarrow R1$

$\begin{bmatrix} 1 & 0 & | & 2 & 1 \\ 0 & \frac{1}{3} & | & \frac{5}{3} & 1 \end{bmatrix}$

$3(R2) \rightarrow R2$

$\begin{bmatrix} 1 & 0 & | & 2 & 1 \\ 0 & 1 & | & 5 & 3 \end{bmatrix}$

Inverse is $\begin{bmatrix} 2 & 1 \\ 5 & 3 \end{bmatrix}$

The inverse can be found using a graphing calculator. See Chapter 6, Example 50.

5. $\begin{bmatrix} 1 & 2 & | & 1 & 0 \\ 3 & 4 & | & 0 & 1 \end{bmatrix}$

$-3(R1) + R2 \to R2$

$\begin{bmatrix} 1 & 2 & | & 1 & 0 \\ 0 & -2 & | & -3 & 1 \end{bmatrix}$

$R1 + R2 \to R1$

$\begin{bmatrix} 1 & 0 & | & -2 & 1 \\ 0 & -2 & | & -3 & 1 \end{bmatrix}$

$-\dfrac{1}{2}(R2) \to R2$

$\begin{bmatrix} 1 & 0 & | & -2 & 1 \\ 0 & 1 & | & \dfrac{3}{2} & -\dfrac{1}{2} \end{bmatrix}$

The inverse is $\begin{bmatrix} -2 & 1 \\ \dfrac{3}{2} & -\dfrac{1}{2} \end{bmatrix}$

The inverse can be found using a graphing calculator. See Chapter 6, Example 50.

7. $\begin{bmatrix} 1 & 2 & | & 1 & 0 \\ \dfrac{3}{2} & 3 & | & 0 & 1 \end{bmatrix}$

$-\dfrac{3}{2}(R1) + R2 \to R2$

$\begin{bmatrix} 1 & 2 & | & 1 & 0 \\ 0 & 0 & | & -\dfrac{3}{2} & 1 \end{bmatrix}$

When any row of either matrix has all 0's, no inverse exists.
This result can be found using a graphing calculator. See Chapter 6, Example 50.

9. – 15. Use a graphing calculator as demonstrated in Chapter 6, Example 50.

17. See Chapter 6, Example 51. Using a calculator, let A be the coefficient matrix and B the constant matrix.

$A = \begin{bmatrix} 2 & 3 \\ 4 & -1 \end{bmatrix}$ and $B = \begin{bmatrix} 3 \\ 13 \end{bmatrix}$

On the Home screen, key in $[A]^{-1}[B]$ then enter. The displayed matrix will be the solution: $\begin{bmatrix} 3 \\ -1 \end{bmatrix}$ which shows that

$x = 3, \quad y = -1$.

Section 5.6

1. $-3(2) - (-\sqrt{6})(\sqrt{6})$
   $= -6 - (-6)$
   $= -6 + 6$
   $= 0$

3. $x^2(x^2) - x(3)$
   $= x^4 - 3x$

5. $-3\begin{vmatrix} -1 & 2 \\ 2 & 2 \end{vmatrix} - (-2)\begin{vmatrix} 2 & 2 \\ -1 & 2 \end{vmatrix} + 4\begin{vmatrix} 2 & -1 \\ -1 & 2 \end{vmatrix}$

   $= -3(-1 \bullet 2 - 2 \bullet 2) + 2(2 \bullet 2 - (-1) \bullet 2) + 4(2 \bullet 2 - (-1)(-1))$
   $= -3(-2 - 4) + 2(4 + 2) + 4(4 - 1)$
   $= -3(-6) + 2(6) + 4(3)$
   $= 42$

7. $s\begin{vmatrix} s & -1 \\ 2 & -2 \end{vmatrix} - 5\begin{vmatrix} 2 & -1 \\ 3 & -2 \end{vmatrix} + (-1)\begin{vmatrix} 2 & s \\ 3 & 2 \end{vmatrix}$

$= s(-2s - (-1 \bullet 2)) - 5(-2 \bullet 2 - 3(-1)) - 1(2 \bullet 2 - 3s)$

$= s(-2s + 2) - 5(-4 + 3) - 1(4 - 3s)$

$= -2s^2 + 2s + 5 - 4 + 3s$

$= -2s^2 + 5s + 1$

9. $M_{12} = \begin{vmatrix} 2 & 0 \\ 1 & 2 \end{vmatrix}$

$\qquad = 2(2) - 1(0)$

$\qquad = 4$

$M_{23} = \begin{vmatrix} 6 & -2 \\ 1 & -1 \end{vmatrix}$

$\qquad = 6(-1) - 1(-2)$

$\qquad = -6 + 2$

$\qquad = -4$

$M_{31} = \begin{vmatrix} -2 & 3 \\ 1 & 0 \end{vmatrix}$

$\qquad = -2(0) - 1(3)$

$\qquad = -3$

11. $B_{12} = (-1)^{1+2} M_{12}$

$\qquad = (-1)^3 \begin{vmatrix} 2 & 0 \\ 1 & 2 \end{vmatrix}$

$\qquad = -1(2 \bullet 2 - 1 \bullet 0)$

$\qquad = -1(4 - 0)$

$\qquad = -4$

$B_{23} = (-1)^{2+3} M_{23}$

$\qquad = (-1)^5 \begin{vmatrix} 6 & -2 \\ 1 & -1 \end{vmatrix}$

$\qquad = -1(6 \bullet (-1) - 1 \bullet (-2))$

$\qquad = -1(-6 + 2)$

$\qquad = 4$

$B_{31} = (-1)^{3+1} M_{31}$

$\qquad = (-1)^4 \begin{vmatrix} -2 & 3 \\ 1 & 0 \end{vmatrix}$

$\qquad = 1(-2 \bullet 0 - 1 \bullet 3)$

$\qquad = -3$

13. $\delta(B) = 6\begin{vmatrix} 1 & 0 \\ -1 & 2 \end{vmatrix} - (-2)\begin{vmatrix} 2 & 0 \\ 1 & 2 \end{vmatrix} + 3\begin{vmatrix} 2 & 1 \\ 1 & -1 \end{vmatrix}$

$= 6(1 \bullet 2 - (-1) \bullet 0) + 2(2 \bullet 2 - 1 \bullet 0) + 3(2 \bullet (-1) - 1 \bullet 1)$

$= 6(2 - 0) + 2(4 - 0) + 3(-2 - 1)$

$= 12 + 8 - 9$

$= 11$

15. $a_1 = 4,\ b_1 = -3,\ c_1 = -3$

$a_2 = 7,\ b_2 = 2,\ c_2 = 6$

$x = \dfrac{\begin{vmatrix} -3 & -3 \\ 6 & 2 \end{vmatrix}}{\begin{vmatrix} 4 & -3 \\ 7 & 2 \end{vmatrix}} = \dfrac{-6 - (-18)}{8 - (-21)} = \dfrac{12}{29}$

$y = \dfrac{\begin{vmatrix} 4 & -3 \\ 7 & 6 \end{vmatrix}}{\begin{vmatrix} 4 & -3 \\ 7 & 2 \end{vmatrix}} = \dfrac{24 - (-21)}{8 - (-21)} = \dfrac{45}{29}$

To solve using a graphing calculator, see Chapter 6, Example 51.

Let $A = \begin{bmatrix} 4 & -3 \\ 7 & 2 \end{bmatrix}$ and $B = \begin{bmatrix} -3 \\ 6 \end{bmatrix}$

The solution is $[A]^{-1}[B] = \begin{bmatrix} 12/29 \\ 45/29 \end{bmatrix}$

17. $a_1 = 3$, $b_1 = 4$, $c_1 = 2$

$a_2 = 5$, $b_2 = -7$, $c_2 = -2$

$$x = \frac{\begin{vmatrix} 2 & 4 \\ -2 & -7 \end{vmatrix}}{\begin{vmatrix} 3 & 4 \\ 5 & -7 \end{vmatrix}} = \frac{-14 - (-8)}{-21 - 20} = \frac{-6}{-41} = \frac{6}{41}$$

$$y = \frac{\begin{vmatrix} 3 & 2 \\ 5 & -2 \end{vmatrix}}{\begin{vmatrix} 3 & 4 \\ 5 & -7 \end{vmatrix}} = \frac{-6 - 10}{-21 - 20} = \frac{16}{41}$$

To solve using a graphing calculator, see Chapter 6, Example 51.

Let $A = \begin{bmatrix} 3 & 4 \\ 5 & -7 \end{bmatrix}$ and $B = \begin{bmatrix} 2 \\ -2 \end{bmatrix}$

The solution is $[A]^{-1}[B] = \begin{bmatrix} \dfrac{6}{41} \\ \dfrac{16}{41} \end{bmatrix}$

19. Use a calculator to find the determinants as shown in Chapter 6, Example 53.

$a_1 = 1$, $b_1 = 1$, $c_1 = -1$, $d_1 = -2$

$a_2 = 2$, $b_2 = -1$, $c_2 = 1$, $d_2 = -5$

$a_3 = 1$, $b_3 = -2$, $c_3 = 3$, $d_3 = 4$

$$D = \begin{vmatrix} 1 & 1 & -1 \\ 2 & -1 & 1 \\ 1 & -2 & 3 \end{vmatrix} = -3$$

$$D_x = \begin{vmatrix} -2 & 1 & -1 \\ -5 & -1 & 1 \\ 4 & -2 & 3 \end{vmatrix} = 7$$

$$D_y = \begin{vmatrix} 1 & -2 & -1 \\ 2 & -5 & 1 \\ 1 & 4 & 3 \end{vmatrix} = -22$$

$$D_z = \begin{vmatrix} 1 & 1 & -2 \\ 2 & -1 & -5 \\ 1 & -2 & 4 \end{vmatrix} = -21$$

$$x = \frac{D_x}{D} = \frac{7}{-3} = -\frac{7}{3}$$

$$y = \frac{D_y}{D} = \frac{-22}{-3} = \frac{22}{3}$$

$$z = \frac{D_z}{D} = \frac{-21}{-3} = 7$$

Review Chapter 5

1. & 2. Change the inequalities to equal signs. Graph each line using a dotted line for > or < and a solid line for $\geq or \leq$. Choose a test point to identify the solution region for each inequality. The intersection of the two shaded regions is the solution to the system. See Chapter 6, Example 48.

3. Eq 1: $\qquad x - 3y = -1$
   Eq 2: $\qquad 2x + 2y = 6$
   $-2(Eq\ 1): -2x + 6y = 2$
   _____
   Eq 3: $\qquad\qquad 8y = 8$ so $y = 1$
   Substitute into either equation:
   Eq 1: $x - 3(1) = -1$ so $x = 2$

4. Eq 1: $\qquad 2x + 3y = -1$
   Eq 2: $\qquad x - 2y = -4$
   $-2(Eq\ 2): -2x + 4y = 8$
   _____
   Add Eq 1 and new Eq 2:
   Eq 3: $\qquad\qquad 7y = 7$ so $y = 1$
   Substitute into either equation:
   Eq 2: $x - 2(1) = -4$ so $x = -2$

5. Using a graphing calculator, solve by multiplying the inverse of the coefficient matrix times the constant matrix.

   Let $A = \begin{bmatrix} 4 & 2 & -2 \\ 3 & 9 & 6 \\ 2 & 2 & 2 \end{bmatrix}$ and $B = \begin{bmatrix} 4 \\ 3 \\ 4 \end{bmatrix}$

   $[A]^{-1}[B] = \begin{bmatrix} 2 \\ -1 \\ 1 \end{bmatrix}$

   $x = 2, \quad y = -1, \quad z = 1$
   See Chapter 6, Example 51.

6. Using a graphing calculator, solve by multiplying the inverse of the coefficient matrix times the constant matrix.

   Let $A = \begin{bmatrix} 2 & 1 & 1 \\ -1 & -1 & 1 \\ 6 & -2 & 2 \end{bmatrix}$ and $B = \begin{bmatrix} 9 \\ 1 \\ 18 \end{bmatrix}$

   $[A]^{-1}[B] = \begin{bmatrix} 2 \\ 1 \\ 4 \end{bmatrix}$

   $x = 2, \quad y = 1, \quad z = 4$
   See Chapter 6, Example 51.

7. Let $A = \begin{bmatrix} 4 & 6 \\ 2 & -1 \end{bmatrix}$ and $B = \begin{bmatrix} 14 \\ 3 \end{bmatrix}$

   $[A]^{-1}[B] = \begin{bmatrix} 2 \\ 1 \end{bmatrix}$

   $x = 2, \quad y = 1$
   See Chapter 6, Example 51

8. Let $A = \begin{bmatrix} 2 & 3 & -4 \\ 3 & -1 & 2 \\ -1 & 4 & -3 \end{bmatrix}$ and $B = \begin{bmatrix} 6 \\ 1 \\ 5 \end{bmatrix}$

   $[A]^{-1}[B] = \begin{bmatrix} 9/11 \\ 16/11 \\ 0 \end{bmatrix}$

   $x = \dfrac{9}{11}, \quad y = \dfrac{16}{11}, \quad z = 0$
   See Chapter 6, Example 51.

9. determinant $= 7(-2) - 3(-2)$
   $\qquad\qquad\quad = -14 + 6$
   $\qquad\qquad\quad = -8$

10. $\delta[A] = a_{11}M_{11} - a_{12}M_{12} + a_{13}M_{13}$

$$= 1\begin{vmatrix} 1 & 4 \\ 3 & 1 \end{vmatrix} - (-2)\begin{vmatrix} 2 & 4 \\ 3 & 1 \end{vmatrix} + 0\begin{vmatrix} 2 & 1 \\ 3 & 3 \end{vmatrix}$$

$$= 1(1-12) + 2(2-12) + 0$$

$$= -11 - 20$$

$$= -31$$

For calculator solution, see Chapter 6, Example 53.

11. $\delta[A] = -2\begin{vmatrix} -1 & 4 \\ 1 & 5 \end{vmatrix} - 3\begin{vmatrix} 3 & 4 \\ -1 & 5 \end{vmatrix} + 1\begin{vmatrix} 3 & -1 \\ -1 & 1 \end{vmatrix}$

$$= -2(-5-4) - 3(15+4) + 1(3-1)$$

$$= 18 - 57 + 2$$

$$= -37$$

For calculator solution, see Chapter 6, Example 53.

12. $a_1 = 2, \quad b_1 = 3, \quad c_1 = 1$

   $a_2 = 1, \quad b_2 = -4, \quad c_2 = -1$

$$x = \dfrac{\begin{vmatrix} 1 & 3 \\ -1 & -4 \end{vmatrix}}{\begin{vmatrix} 2 & 3 \\ 1 & -4 \end{vmatrix}} = \dfrac{-4+3}{-8-3} = \dfrac{-1}{-11} = \dfrac{1}{11}$$

$$y = \dfrac{\begin{vmatrix} 2 & 1 \\ 1 & -1 \end{vmatrix}}{\begin{vmatrix} 2 & 3 \\ 1 & -4 \end{vmatrix}} = \dfrac{-2-1}{-8-3} = \dfrac{-3}{-11} = \dfrac{3}{11}$$

13. $a_1 = 2, \quad b_1 = -4, \quad c_1 = 0$

   $a_2 = 5, \quad b_2 = -6, \quad c_2 = 4$

$$x = \dfrac{\begin{vmatrix} 0 & -4 \\ 4 & -6 \end{vmatrix}}{\begin{vmatrix} 2 & -4 \\ 5 & -6 \end{vmatrix}} = \dfrac{0+16}{-12+20} = 2$$

$$y = \dfrac{\begin{vmatrix} 2 & 0 \\ 5 & 4 \end{vmatrix}}{\begin{vmatrix} 2 & -4 \\ 5 & -6 \end{vmatrix}} = \dfrac{8-0}{-12+20} = 1$$

14. Use a calculator to find the determinants as shown in Chapter 6, Example 53.

   $a_1 = 3, \quad b_1 = -1, \quad c_1 = 2, \quad d_1 = 4$

   $a_2 = 4, \quad b_2 = 6, \quad c_2 = -3, \quad d_2 = 7$

   $a_3 = 5, \quad b_3 = -4, \quad c_3 = 3, \quad d_3 = 4$

$$D = \begin{vmatrix} 3 & -1 & 2 \\ 4 & 6 & -3 \\ 5 & -4 & 3 \end{vmatrix} = -47$$

$$D_x = \begin{vmatrix} 4 & -1 & 2 \\ 7 & 6 & -3 \\ 4 & -4 & 3 \end{vmatrix} = -47$$

$$D_y = \begin{vmatrix} 3 & 4 & 2 \\ 4 & 7 & -3 \\ 5 & 4 & 3 \end{vmatrix} = -47$$

$$D_z = \begin{vmatrix} 3 & -1 & 4 \\ 4 & 6 & 7 \\ 5 & -4 & 4 \end{vmatrix} = -47$$

$$x = \dfrac{D_x}{D} = \dfrac{-47}{-47} = 1$$

$$y = \dfrac{D_y}{D} = \dfrac{-47}{-47} = 1$$

$$z = \dfrac{D_z}{D} = \dfrac{-47}{-47} = 1$$

15. Use a calculator to find the determinants as shown in Chapter 6, Example 53.

$a_1 = 5, \ b_1 = -1, \ c_1 = 3, \ d_1 = 8$

$a_2 = 3, \ b_2 = 7, \ c_2 = -5, \ d_2 = 20$

$a_3 = 4, \ b_3 = -3, \ c_3 = 7, \ d_3 = 2$

$$D = \begin{vmatrix} 5 & -1 & 3 \\ 3 & 7 & -5 \\ 4 & -3 & 7 \end{vmatrix} = 100$$

$$D_x = \begin{vmatrix} 8 & -1 & 3 \\ 20 & 7 & -5 \\ 2 & -3 & 7 \end{vmatrix} = 200$$

$$D_y = \begin{vmatrix} 5 & 8 & 3 \\ 3 & 20 & -5 \\ 4 & 2 & 7 \end{vmatrix} = 200$$

$$D_z = \begin{vmatrix} 5 & -1 & 8 \\ 3 & 7 & 20 \\ 4 & -3 & 2 \end{vmatrix} = 0$$

$$x = \frac{D_x}{D} = \frac{200}{100} = 2$$

$$y = \frac{D_y}{D} = \frac{200}{100} = 2$$

$$z = \frac{D_z}{D} = \frac{0}{100} = 0$$

16. $a_1 = 1, \quad b_1 = 2, \quad c_1 = 7$

$a_2 = 4, \quad b_2 = -3, \quad c_2 = 1$

$$x = \frac{\begin{vmatrix} 7 & 2 \\ 1 & -3 \end{vmatrix}}{\begin{vmatrix} 1 & 2 \\ 4 & -3 \end{vmatrix}} = \frac{-21 - 2}{-3 - 8} = \frac{-23}{-11} = \frac{23}{11}$$

$$y = \frac{\begin{vmatrix} 1 & 7 \\ 4 & 1 \end{vmatrix}}{\begin{vmatrix} 1 & 2 \\ 4 & -3 \end{vmatrix}} = \frac{1 - 28}{-3 - 8} = \frac{-27}{-11} = \frac{27}{11}$$

17. $a_1 = 5, \quad b_1 = -3, \quad c_1 = -1$

$a_2 = 4, \quad b_2 = 7, \quad c_2 = 2$

$$x = \frac{\begin{vmatrix} -1 & -3 \\ 2 & 7 \end{vmatrix}}{\begin{vmatrix} 5 & -3 \\ 4 & 7 \end{vmatrix}} = \frac{-7 + 6}{35 + 12} = \frac{-1}{47}$$

$$y = \frac{\begin{vmatrix} 5 & -1 \\ 4 & 2 \end{vmatrix}}{\begin{vmatrix} 5 & -3 \\ 4 & 7 \end{vmatrix}} = \frac{10 + 4}{35 + 12} = \frac{14}{47}$$